Engineers and inventors

General Editor
David Abbott PhD

PETER BEDRICK BOOKS
New York

First American edition published in 1986 by
Peter Bedrick Books
125 East 23 Street
New York, NY 10010

Copyright © 1985 David Abbott

93 92 91 90 89 88 87 86   1 2 3 4 5 6 7 8 9

Published by agreement with Muller, Blood & White Ltd., London

Library of Congress Cataloging-in-Publication Data
Main entry under title:

The Biographical dictionary of scientists. Engineers and inventors.

   Includes index.
   1. Engineers—Biography. 2. Inventors—Biography.
I. Abbott, David, 1937–   . II. Title: Engineers and
inventors.
TA139.B56   1986   620′.0092′2   [B]   85-20008
ISBN 0-87226-009-7

Manufactured in the United States of America
Distributed in the USA by Harper & Row
and in Canada by Book Center, Montreal

Printed on acid-free paper

Contents

Acknowledgements

Many people are involved in the creation of a major new series of reference books. The General Editor and the publishers are grateful to all of them and wish to thank particularly the contributing authors; Gareth Ashurst; Jim Bailey; Mary Basham; Alan Bishop; William Cooksey; David Cowey; Lloyd Lindo; Robert Matthews; Patricia Nash; Valerie Neal; Mary Sanders; Robert Smith and David Ward. Our thanks are also due to the contributing consultant: Keld Fenwick; to Bull Publishing Consultants Ltd, whose experience in the development of reference books has made a significant contribution to the series: John Clark; Wendy Allen, Martyn Page, Polly Powell and Sandy Shepherd; and to Mick Saunders for his artwork.

Historical
Introduction

The existence of modern Man is powerful evidence of his ability to invent. Were it not for the invention of simple tools made from sharp-edged stones some two million years ago, it is doubtful whether the relatively weak and slow Australopithecus would have survived for long. Such tools enabled early Man to fight off predators and to hunt for food.

As well as being surrounded by potentially hostile animals, early Man was at the mercy of the climate. It was the second of the major inventions of pre-history, a means of creating fire, that enabled him to survive the Ice Ages. Homo erectus (Peking Man) was using this to live through the second Ice Age some 400,000 years ago.

These two inventions served Man well for an extremely long time. Not until the formation of Jericho, the world's first walled town, c. 7000BC does another major invention reveal itself, in the development of pottery. Copper, and the alloy made from copper and tin called bronze, also appeared at around that time.

Behind the foundation of Jericho, were the beginnings of organized agriculture, and it was this that provided the stimulus for the development on increasingly sophisticated tools, such as the plough and the sickle.

That most famous, and significant, of inventions of the ancient world, the wheel, first appeared around 3000BC, in what is now southern Russia. These early wheels were solid, wooden and fixed to sleds which had previously been dragged across the ground. Although its first use was in transporting heavy loads, the wheel and axle combination later became a feature of milling devices, and irrigation systems. Sumerian and Assyrian engineers used wheel-driven water drawing devices in irrigation networks which are still in use today.

For several thousand years, these early inventions were enlarged and improved upon, without any major advances being made. By the time Archimedes (c.287-c.212BC) was investigating the principle of the lever and producing his famous helical screw, the scene of the most significant developments had shifted from the Middle East to Greece. The measurement of time in particular remained a continuing challenge, and by the second century BC, Ctesibius of Alexandria had developed the Egyptian clepsydra (water-clock) to give accuracy not surpassed until well into the Middle Ages.

Hero of Alexandria (c.AD60) was the last of the Greek technologists, his most famous invention being of the aeolipile, a primitive steam turbine that gave a hint, as early as the first century BC of the potency of steam as a power-source.

Roman and Chinese influences

Despite their astonishing ability in geometry, physics and mathematics, the Greeks were unable to make the advance which transformed architecture and civil engineering: the arch. The pre-Roman Etruscans used the semicircular arch as an architectural feature, but it was the Romans who put the arch to full use. Because of its ability to spread imposed stresses more evenly, the arch allowed greater spans in buildings than the Greeks' simple pillar-and-beam arrangements. Aqueducts comprising 6 metre-wide arches were possible as early as 142BC, as evidenced by the Pons Aemilius in Italy.

Combining the structural economy of the arch with the availability of good cement the Romans set up an infrastructure and communications network that gave them a standard of living hitherto unprecedented in history. It also enabled them to extend that standard, and maintain it by its armies, over a similarly unprecedented expanse of the world.

One major difficulty facing the Romans was the shortage of manpower. As a result of the lack of an efficient means of harnessing animals to ploughs and other implements, the Romans had to use the weaker human to provide the power. It was the Chinese who first produced an efficient animal harness, freeing the human from such drudgery, and enabling animals to be used in tandem to haul great loads. The harness did not reach the West, however, until the ninth century, well after the fall of the Roman Empire. China was the birthplace of a number of other major inventions: of paper from pulp (by Ts'ai Lun c.AD 100), of the magnetic compass and of gunpowder, c.500 and 850 respectively.

The development of Western technology

It was also around this time that north-western

Europe began its climb to ascendency in technology that it has held onto for centuries since. The poorer climate of this region, combined with the need to develop a new form of agriculture, was responsible for the emergence around the eighth century of the crop rotation methods still used today. The wind was put to use in both sea-going vessels and land-based mills. The region grew more populous and, by the eleventh century, northern Europeans were moving their influence into the Mediterranean and Middle East.

As the societies grew, becoming more complex, the need for metals for housing, tools, equipment and coinage increased concomitantly. This caused a renewed interest in the extraction and treatment of ores, which were also in increasing demand by rulers anxious to develop weapons capable of keeping their rivals at bay. Many of these rulers, notably in fifteenth-century Italy, employed engineers to come up with new systems for both defence and attack. Undoubtedly the most famous such engineer was Leonardo da Vinci (1452-1519), military engineer to the Duke of Milan. Among the thousands of pages of da Vinci's notes are to be found an astonishing number of prescient plans for modern-day inventions: tanks, submarines, helicopters and a whole range of firearms.

The Renaissance was ushered in by one of the most influential inventions in history: the development of the movable type printing press by Johannes Gutenberg (c. 1397-1468) of Mainz, Germany. The Gutenberg Bible, the first book to be printed using this process, appeared in 1454. The Englishman William Caxton set up a press in England in 1476. As well as disseminating religous knowledge over a far wider scale, the invention enabled the speeding up of the transfer of technological advances from one country to another.

Steam power and the Industrial Revolution
The ever-increasing use of metals made mining the focus of much effort in the fifteenth century, one of the biggest problems being that of adequately draining the mines. Pumping water fast enough and in sufficient volume was also a problem facing those wanting to create more agricultural land from poorly-drained areas, and to supply towns with their needs. By the mid-seventeenth century, a number of patents had been granted to water pumps which used a new, remarkably versatile source of power: steam.

Thomas Savery (c. 1650-1715) demonstrated an engine for 'raising of water and occasioning motion to all sorts of mill works, by the impellant force of fire', to the Royal Society of London in 1699. He formed a partnership with Thomas Newcomen (1663-1729) and together used the power of steam, in the form of a beam piston engine, to maintain the mines of Staffordshire, Cornwall and Newcastle in workable condition.

Newcomen steam engines grew in popularity during the eighteenth century, and it was while repairing a model one used on the physics course at Glasgow University in 1763 that the young James Watt (1736-1819) saw how major improvements could be made, improvements that led to Watt's condenser engine completely replacing the earlier model by 1800.

Through its predominace as a manufacturing market, Britain was able to reap rich rewards but competition from overseas urged on the hunt for greater efficiency of production. Technologists were at the forefront of this effort, with John Kay's (1704-1780) invention of the flying shuttle for the production of textiles leading to James Hargreaves' (1720-1778) spinning Jenny. Arkwright's (1732-1792) spinning machine was the centrepiece of the first cotton factory of 1771, and semi-automated mass production as a technique was born. The Industrial Revolution, which is arguably still under way, had begun.

The end of the eighteenth century saw Richard Trevithick (1771-1833) experimenting with the use of steam to provide motive power for boats, road vehicles and locomotives on steel rails. Dogged by bad luck, his ideas did not achieve the success or acclaim they deserved, and the world had to wait longer than it should have for the full exploitation of steam in such applications. French engineers had more success initially, with Nicholas Joseph Cugnot (1725-1804) developing a three-wheeled steam-powered tractor, c.1770, capable of 6km/h (3.5mph). The Montgolfier brothers Joseph-Michael (1740-1810) and Jacques Etiènne (1745-1799) were responsible for the first sustaihed flight by man, aboard a hot-air balloon, in 1763.

By the time Trevithick left England for Peru, his high-pressure engine had shown that steam was amply capable of providing a mobile power source. He returned to find his place as the greatest engineer in the new technology usurped by others. Most famous of these was George Stephenson (1781-1848), whose steam locomotives were responsible for the setting up of the first practical passenger railway ever built, in 1825, between Stockton and Darlington.

Rapid communication, which remains a hall mark of an advanced technological society, became of increasing importance as the nineteenth century wore on, both in peace-time and in war. Thomas Telford (1757-1834) became famous for his canals and aqueduct building, enabling very large loads to be transported using little motive power. In France, the quality of the roads built by

Pierre Trésaguet (1716-1796) made the rapid strikes of Napolean's armies possible. By contrast, Britain's roads were in an appalling state through years of neglect and the operation of the Turnpike Trusts. The scientific approach to road construction devised by John McAdam (1756-1836) radically improved this aspect of Britain's infrastructure.

Steam power also found its way into oceangoing vessels. Robert Fulton (1765-1815) returned from Europe, where he had seen what steam engines were capable of, to set up the first regular steamship service, between New York and Albany, in 1807. Whether steam-powered ships were capable of a longer journey, in particular across the Atlantic Ocean, was a major debating point when Isambard Kingdom Brunel's (1806-1859) *Great Western* succeeded in sailing to New York without refuelling, in 1838. Brunel went on to design and launch the first iron ship (and the first to use a screw propellor, rather than paddle wheels) the *Great Britain*, and the colossal *Great Eastern*, whose steadiness and manoeuvrability was put to use in a key event in another field of technology altogether: the laying of the Atlantic telegraph cable in 1865.

Such very long distance communication was made possible by advances in understanding of electricity, and the translation of this into devices that could transmit and receive messages at the speed of light. The first successful system was brought out by Charles Wheatstone (1802-1875), in which electrical signals deflected magnetized needles indicating letters of the alphabet. The development of a communication system using a code of dots and dashes to represent the letters by Samuel Morse (1791-1872) proved so successful it is still in use today.

The outbreak of the Crimean War involving the British, French and Turkish against the Russians led Henry Bessemer (1813-1898) to develop the method for removing impurities, in particular carbon, from molten iron, thus enabling steel to be produced cheaply in the quantities required by both military and civilian engineers. The war also resulted in the development of the first wrought-iron breech-loading gun by William Armstrong (1847-1908).

The wars affecting the United States also assisted the development of weapons on that side of the Atlantic. The war against Mexico, which broke out in 1846, accelerated the revolution in small arms manufacture initiated by Samuel Colt (1814-1862), who had produced the first revolver in 1836. The Civil War of 1861-1865 prompted Richard Gatling (1818-1903) to develop the rapid fire-gun that bears his name.

The internal combustion engine
It was around the middle of the nineteenth century that attention began to shift from steam to gas and other combustible materials as a means of providing motive power. As early as 1833, an engine that ran on an inflammable mixture of gas and air had been described, and a number of the fundamental principles of the fuel-powered engine had been described by the time Jean Lenoir (1822-1900) began building engines using the system which operated smoothly in 1860. Together, Nikolaus Otto (1832-1891) and Eugen Langen managed by 1877 to solve the basic problems facing the development of the four-stroke internal combustion engine. This work led to the development of the modern motor car, and of powered flight. Gottlieb Daimler (1834-1900) was to join the pair as an engineer, leaving in 1883 to develop lighter, more efficient high-speed engines capable of driving cycles and boats, as well as automobiles.

Rudolph Diesel (1858-1913) experimented with internal combustion engines during the 1890s; by using the heat developed by compression of the fuel-air mixture, rather than a spark from an ignition system, to ignite the mixture, Diesel succeeded in producing an engine that could use cheaper fuels than the Otto cycle engines. However, the high pressures produced in the engines required the use of very heavy-gauge metal, with consequent weight-power ratio problems. Later advances in metallurgy enabled this disadvantage to be significantly reduced, with the result that the Diesel engine is still used in a wide range of vehicles today.

Work by the Americans, as well as the Germans, succeeded in bringing the power of the internal combustion engine to bear on the problem of powered flight. Early work on the flow of air over gliders by Otto Lilienthal (1848-1896) and others established a body of knowledge needed to supplement the work of earlier enthusiasts such as George Cayley (1773-1857), who had defined the basic aerodynamic forces acting on a wing as early as 1799.

Internal combustion engines, coupled to balloons to form airships, were in use by the turn of the century. The first flight of a heavier than air machine powered by a light, efficient internal combustion engine was constructed by the Wright brothers Orville (1871-1948) and Wilbur (1867-1912) on 17 December, 1903. As well as finding a suitable engine for such a machine, the Wrights had succeeded in solving the problem of controlling the aeroplane in all three axes.

Electricity as a source of power
Despite the success of the internal combustion en-

gine in powering a wide range of machines, the use of water and steam as power sources remained important in another major field of technology: the generation of electricity. Water had been used to drive turbines of increasing efficiency for many years when Charles Parsons (1854-1931) adapted the basic design of a water turbine to enable a jet of steam to impart its kinetic energy to a series of turbine blades which then rotate. By combining this rotation with the ability of a dynamo to convert rotary motion into electric power, the electric generator was born. The first ever turbine-powered·generating station was set up in 1888, using four Parsons turbines each developing 75kW (100hp). Direct use of the mechanical power developed by steam was made in Parson's 44.7 ton (44 tonne) Turbinia, whose turbine engine developed 1.5MW (2,000hp), enabling it to travel at 60km/h (37mph) in 1897.

Work by Joseph Swan (1828-1914) in England and Thomas Edison (1847-1931) in the United States finally resulted in the creation of a long-lasting light source powered by electricity - the filament lamp - around 1880.

While Germany and the United States were quick to use electrical power to bring about a revolution in their industrial processes, the availability of cheap labour and concentration on waning industries based on traditional raw material inhibited the adoption of electrical power in Britain. Concentration on telegraphic technology and the generation of electric illumination did have an indirect advantage, however. The invention of the two-electrode electric valve, the diode, by John Fleming (1849-1945) provided a new outlet for the vacuum bulb technology. Such developments as radio communication, radar, television and the computer all benefited from this.

Communication over long distances without the use of cables - 'wireless' communication - had been a practical possibility from the day when the electromagnetic wave physicist James Clerk Maxwell's (1831-1879) theory combining electrical and magnetic phenomena had been investigated by Heinrick Hertz (1857-1894) in 1888. Both transmitters and detectors of these radio waves were developed until Guglielmo Marconi (1874-1937) succeeded in transmitting messages over a few yards using electromagnetic waves in 1895. By 1901, he had succeeded in sending signals right across the Atlantic.

More sophisticated communication was made possible by Lee De Forest (1873-1961) and Reginald Fessenden (1866-1932), and their invention of the triode amplifier and amplitude modulation respectively. These advances enabled speech and sound to be transmitted over very long distances, and gave birth to modern communications.

Developments of the war years

World War I (1914-1918) saw the use of technology on an unprecedented scale. Although many of the advances then simply led to the deaths of hundreds of thousands of troops, many later found major applications in peacetime. An excellent example of this is provided by the development of the nitrogen fixation process to an industrial scale by Karl Bosch (1874-1940). This enabled the Germans to manufacture explosives such as TNT without relying on foreign imports of nitrogen-bearing materials, capable of being blockaded by the allies. In peacetime, the process allowed the cheap manufacture of fertilizers, equally vital to the survival of a country.

The war also had a profound effect on the aircraft industry. Starting the war as chiefly reconnaisance vehicles, the aircraft became directly involved in the fighting by the end, and mass production of tens of thousands became necessary. Governments spent money on research, accelerating advances in aerodynamics and power systems enormously. Civil aviation, begun by the Germans before the war, benefited, initially using modified military aircraft; the famous Imperial Airways started up in 1924.

As with the automobile, engineers started to look at new power sources for the aircraft. The use of gas turbines was put forward in 1926, a suggestion turned into reality by Frank Whittle (1907-) in 1930. By combining a gas turbine with a centrifugal compressor, he created the jet engine.

The inter-war years saw considerable advances in rocket technology: an area of engineering that was to enable Man to leave the planet of his birth. The Chinese had used solid-fuelled rockets in battles as early as 1232; their direct ancestors are still to be seen strapped to the central booster of the Space Shuttle of the 1980s. It was Konstantin Tsiolkovskii (1857-1935) who pointed out that liquid propellants had distinct advantages of power and controllability over solid fuels. The American astronautics pioneer Robert Goddard (1882-1949) succeeded in launching the first liquid-fuelled rocket in 1926. Just 35 years later, Soviet engineers used a liquid-filled booster to send the first man into earth orbit. Eight years after that Man had set foot on another celestial body for the first time.

By the 1920s, a number of devices born in research laboratories had become established as massively popular forms of entertainment. The work of George Eastman (1854-1932), Thomas Edison (1847-1931) and others brought photography and sound-and-motion 'movie' pictures to millions. A working system of television was devised by John Baird and shown in 1925, while the modern electronic system later adopted as standard for television was demonstrated by Vladimir Zworykin (1889-   ) in 1929. The British Broadcasting Corporations's forebear, the British Broadcasting Company, was formed in 1922, transmitting radio programmes to the public on a national scale.

In 1936, experimental television broadcasts were made by the BBC from Alexandra Palace near London.

The growth in the use of electrical power put greater emphasis on ways of generating it cheaply. The United States in particular built many large storage dams, producing electricity by hydroelectic turbine technology. By 1920 some 40 per cent of America's electricity was generated by this means. But developments in particle physics during these years were beginning to show that the fundamental constituents of matter would be capable of providing another, far more concentrated, form of energy: atomic power. By 1939, and the outbreak of World War II, a number of physicists had begun to appreciate the possibilities offered by 'chain reactions' involving the fission of unstable chemical elements such as uranium.

The war itself again proved to be a sharp stimulus for the refinement of old ideas and the development of new ones. Radar, devised by Robert Watson-Watt (1892-   ) in 1935, was developed into a national defence system against aircraft that were growing ever faster and more deadly. More sophisticated weapons and ever more complex message encoding systems resulted in the development of early electronic computers. These were needed to rapidly sift through data and perform arithmetical operations upon it, and also carry out numerical integrations which were particularly useful in the precise calculation of the trajectories for artillery shells. The pioneering work on mechanical computing machines by Charles Babbage (1792-1871) in the early 1800s was transformed by the introduction of electronic devices by Vannevar Bush (1890-1974) and others during the war years.

The inter-war ideas of jet and rocket propulsion were used in the development of fighter aircraft and missiles such as the 'V' (vergeltung) 1 and 2, powered by ram-jet and liquid fuel respectively. Most devastating of all was the use of the chain reaction of atomic energy in an uncontrolled explosive device against the Japanese in 1945. Although the use of the atomic bomb finally ended World War II, the world still lives under the threat of their use, in still more deadly form, to this day. The use of the first atomic bombs has tended to overshadow another event in the development of atomic power that took place during the war. This was the setting up of the first controlled atomic chain reaction in 1942 by a team of scientists at the University of Chicago, which paved the way for the peaceful use of atomic power to generate electricity.

The Age of the Microchip

While the demand for yet more electric power grew among industrial nations mass-producing cars, ships and aircraft, ways of reducing the complexity and power consumption of electronic devices such as computers, radios and televisions were being sought. Most crucial of these was the invention of the transistor, by researchers at Bell Laboratories in America, in 1948. These tiny semiconductor-based devices could achieve the rectification and amplification of the thermionic valves of the pre-war years at a fraction of the power consumption. The use of such devices in still smaller form allowed the miniaturization of electronic devices to continue to the stage where the computing power of a whole room of electric devices and thousands of valves can now be contained on a $5mm^2$ slice of silicon, 1mm thick.

Computing power packed into smaller volumes has been the driving force of many areas of technology over the last 40 years. It made possible the era of manned space flight, where keeping the mass of all components to a minimum is vital. Telecommunication satellites, such as *Telstar*, (which in 1962 transmitted the first live television pictures across the Atlantic), weather satellites and planetary probes were all made possible as a result of the semiconductor breakthrough. New materials capable of withstanding the hostile environment of space were also produced, many of which found uses back on Earth.

An ancient desire of Man to be rid of drudgery and physical labour is also becoming increasingly close to realization as a result of such devices. Robots are now finding their way into more mass-production industries, such as car manufacturing. The use of robots today is the result of advances in the two fields of mechanization and control over the last 200 years. Oliver Evans (1755-1819) and Joseph Jacquard (1752-1834) had devised automatic textile production systems by the turn of the eighteenth century. Jacquard's use of punched cards by which the looms for weaving could be programmed has proved particularly prescient. Control methods such as feedback (which had been employed by Watt in his centrifugal steam governor), and servo mechanisms were also crucial to the development of the modern robots. By combining these ideas with the new electronic technology, the first industrial robots made their appearance in the United States in 1961, where they were tended die-casting equipment.

Despite the proven ability of these robots to carry out welding, spraying and other manual tasks, there are still areas where humans remain the best solution; visual inspection of products is an example. The reason for this is that despite the apparent simplicity of such tasks, the computing power necessary to enable a robot to inspect and work on products is enormous. Not until still more powerful computers have been successfully coupled to the robot will it reach its full potential.

What computing power is available today has proved invaluable, nonetheless. Computer-aided design and manufacture has enabled new ideas in fields from architecture to aircraft manufacture to be tried out, tested and produced far more quickly and cheaply. The influence of the computer is felt in everyday life, from the diagnosis of disease by the CAT scanner invented by Godfrey Hounsfield (1919-   ) to the production of bank statements.

Power sources for the future

Even if, between them, the robot and the computer free us from manual labour, power will still be needed in vast quantities to process the raw material from which goods are produced. There is still, therefore, considerable interest in finding ways of generating cheap power. Using nuclear fission has proved only a partial answer to the question of what will replace the burning of hydrocarbons such as coal to generate electricity. Public concern about both its inherent safety and the toxic waste produced has cast a shadow over the long-term future of fission-generated electricity.

Engineers and physicists in Europe, the United States, the Soviet Union and Japan are currently studying the process of these doubts. Using hydrogen and its isotopes derived from sea-water, they hope to be able to mimic the reactions that have kept the Sun burning for thousands of millions of years. The engineering difficulties presented by trying to keep a plasma stable at a temperature of 100 million degrees are immense, but the use of the Russian tokamak magnetic control system appears to be a possible solution.

Others are turning to less exotic sources of energy, such as the wind, solar energy and tides, to find better ways of exploiting them and generating cheap, clean power.

Western developed nations appear to be facing perhaps the inevitable problem stemming from rapid technological advance: coming to terms with freedom from labour. It may be said that, having released us from drudgery, engineers will increasingly be called upon to give us new forms of entertainment, and new systems of health care for the sickly. In theory at least, automation should allow us to enjoy the same standard of living without having to work for it. Whether or not such a system fulfils the basic needs of Man remains to be seen.

That western society now finds itself presented with such a problem is a measure of the speed with which technological change has taken place over the last two centuries. While the earliest inventions had been forced by a desire to meet basic needs, modern technology now enables the people of developed nations to live long, healthy lives in complete comfort and general contentment.

For the majority of the world's people, such a lifestyle remains a dream; millions remain caught in a battle with the elements simply to stay alive. Many third world countries lack even adequate water supplies and communication systems. Facts like these clearly show that there remains plenty of scope for the use of innovation and invention by the engineer of tomorrow.

A

Appert, Nicolas (*c.1750-1841*), was a French confectioner and inventor who originated the modern process of thermal sterilization of food in sealed containers; he has become known as the father of canning.

Appert was born *c.*1750 in France, at Chalons-sur-Marne, just east of Paris. He was self-educated and, as the son of an innkeeper, at an early age learned methods of brewing and pickling. He served his apprenticeship as a chef and confectioner at the Palais Royal Hotel in Châlons and was later employed by the Duke and Duchess of Deux-Ponts. By 1780 he had settled in Paris where he became widely known as a confectioner. The feeding of Napoleon's armies and the Navy was becoming a problem and new methods of preventing food decay were needed urgently. In 1795, the French Directory offered a prize for a practical method of preserving food, which encouraged Appert to begin a 14-year period of experimentation. In 1804, with the financial backing of De la Reyniere, he opened the world's first canning factory - the House of Appert - in Massy, south of Paris. By 1809 he had succeeded in preserving certain foods in glass bottles that had been immersed in boiling water. After his methods had been favourably tested and approved by the French Navy and the Consulting Bureau of Arts and Manufacturers, he was awarded the prize of 12,000 francs on 30 January 1810. One of the conditions of the award was that he should write and publish a detailed description of the processes he used. In 1811 he published *The Art of Preserving all kinds of Animal and Vegetable Substances for Several Years*. The following year he was presented with a gold medal by the Society for the Encouragement of National Industry, and ten years later was given the title 'Benefactor of Humanity'. The fall of Napoleon, however, marked the end of his financial success, and his factories were destroyed by enemy action. He died in poverty in Massy on 3 June 1841. The cannery he founded continued to operate until 1933.

At the time Appert began his investigations into the preservation of perishable foods, chemistry was in its infancy and bacteriology was unknown. The only reference Appert had to similar work was to that of Lazzaro Spallanzani (1729-1799) in 1765, on the preservation of food by heat sterilization. Appert's final successful results were

produced, therefore, by trial and error - with a little insight. He based his methods on the heating of food to temperatures above $100^{\circ}C$ ($212^{\circ}F$), using an autoclave (which he perfected) and then sealing the food container to prevent putrefaction. Initially, he used glass jars and bottles stoppered with corks and re-inforced with wire and sealing wax, but in 1822 he changed to cylindrical tin-plated steel cans. He experimented with about 70 foods until he achieved his objective.

In addition to his work on food preservation, Appert was also responsible for the invention of the bouillon cube and he devised a method of extracting gelatin from bones without using acid; he also popularized the use of cylindrical containers for preserved foods. Appert's work was the foundation for the development of the modern canning industry although he himself could give no scientific explanation for the effectiveness of his methods. It was not until about 1860 that the biological causes of food decay became known as a result of the research begun by Louis Pasteur

Arkwright, Richard (*1732-1792*), was a prominent English pioneer in Britain's Industrial Revolution (1733-*c.*1840). His spinning machinery, which replaced and increased the speed and efficiency of handspinning, transformed the textile industry.

Born in Preston, Lancashire, England on 23 December 1732, Arkwright was the youngest of 7 surviving children of poor parents. He had little formal education but was taught to read by an uncle and educated himself until quite late in life.

Arkwright first worked as a barber-wigmaker using his own process for preparing and dyeing wigs. When the wig trade declined he turned his attention to engineering, and especially to the textile industry which was then being industrialized following John Kay's invention of the Flying Shuttle (1733), the introduction of a carding machine (1760) and of James Hargreaves' spinning jenny (1767, patented 1770). The jenny partly did away with old fashioned handwheel spinning, but only for spinning the weft. The roving process was still performed by hand, since the Jenny did not have sufficient strength for the warp, the longitudinal threads.

In 1767, Arkwright, probably unaware of Hargreaves' work, began to develop a machine which could spin by rollers. With this, Arkwright applied a new principle rather than simply mechanizing handwheel methods. His spinning frame consisted of four pairs of rollers acting by tooth and pinion. The top roller was covered with leather, to enable it to take hold of the cotton material. The lower was fluted longitudinally to let the cotton pass through it. One pair of rollers revolved more quickly than its corresponding pair, and so the rove was drawn to the requisite fineness for twisting. This was accomplished by spindles, or flyers, placed in front of each set of rollers.

Arkwright's spinning frame was patented in 1769. He set up a small factory at Nottingham, followed two years later by another at Cromford, Derbyshire. His partners there included Jedediah Strutt and Samuel Need, owners of a patent for the manufacture of ribbed stockings. At Cromford, the machines were run by water power, and the spinning frame therefore became known as the 'water' frame: it was later renamed 'throstle' with the advent of steam power in 1785.

The stockings woven on the spinning frame, from yarn of hard, firm texture and smooth consistency, were superior to those woven from handspun cotton. Other manufacturers who had declined to use the yarn were later to regret their decision. In 1773 Arkwright produced the first cloth made entirely from cotton, when he used thread as warp for the manufacture of calico: previously, the warp was of linen, and only the weft was of cotton.

The new material attracted enthusiastic demand, especially after 1774, when a special Act of Parliament was passed exempting Arkwright's goods from the double duty imposed on cottons by an Act of 1736. (The 1736 Act had been designed to protect woollen manufacturers against the calico cottons of India, where the British East India Company was active in trade).

By 1775, Arkwright's factories, sited countrywide, were employing a sequence of machines to carry out all cotton manufacturing operations, from carding, drawing and roving to spinning. The prosperity of the cotton industry was thus assured, and Arkwright's inventions were later adapted, with equal success, for the woollen and worsted trades. With his comprehensive machinery, Arkwright was an improver and adapter rather than an inventor. To a great extent he incorporated the ideas of others, including fundamental and original ideas, which was why the comprehensive patent he took out in 1775 was later rescinded. This did not detract from Arkwright's achievement, however, and in 1786 his work was acknowledged by King George III with a knighthood. Further recognition followed in 1787, when Arkwright was made High Sheriff of Derbyshire.

Arkwright was the archetypal product of a new industrial age which enabled men of ingenuity and determination to rise to eminence from a state of poverty. Apart from his technical achievements, he was also notable for his organization of large-scale factory production and the division of labour between machines and work force. By 1782 Arkwright employed 5,000 workers and had a capital of £200,000. He died, rich and respected, at Cromford on 3 August 1792.

Armstrong, William George *(1810-1900)*, was the British engineer and inventor who revolutionized the manufacture of big guns in the mid-eighteenth century. He was also responsible for pioneering developments in hydraulic equipment.

Armstrong was born in Newcastle-upon-Tyne on 26 November 1810. He attended private schools in Newcastle and Whickham, and later completed his formal education at a grammar school in Bishop Auckland. Following this, he studied law in London. In 1833 he returned to Newcastle and was engaged in private practice as a solicitor. In his spare time he carried out numerous scientific experiments.

In 1839 he constructed an overshot waterwheel and soon afterwards he designed a hydraulic crane, which contained the germ of the ideas underlying all the hydraulic machinery for which he subsequently became famous. Abandoning his law practice in 1847, he founded an engineering works at Elswick to specialize in building hydraulic cranes. In 1850 he invented the hydraulic pressure accumulator and in 1854 he designed submarine mines for use in the Crimean War. A year later Armstrong designed a three-pounder gun with a barrel made of wrought iron wrapped round an inner steel tube. In 1859 he established the Elswick Ordnance Company for making the Armstrong gun for the British army. In the same year, he was appointed Chief Engineer of Rifled Ordnance at Woolwich, and received a knighthood. A government decision to revert to the production and use of muzzle-loading guns led to his resignation from Woolwich. He improved the design of his original gun and, by 1880, had completed the design of a 6-inch (150mm) breech-loading gun with a wire-wound cylinder. This design was adopted by the British government and was the prototype of all subsequent artillery.

In 1882 Armstrong established a new shipbuilding yard at Elswick for the construction of warships. Five years later he was raised to the peerage and created Baron Armstrong of Craigside. He also entered into partnership with Joseph Whitworth (1803-1887) to form the famous Armstrong-Whitworth company at Openshaw, Manchester.

Although Armstrong initially chose law as his career, he soon switched to engineering. Even before he had abandoned his law practice, he had constructed an overshoot water-wheel, having become engrossed with water-wheels as a source of power when, on a fishing holiday in Dentdale, he saw an overshoot water wheel and observed that only about a twentieth of the energy available was being utilized. His original invention of 1839 was improved upon by his production of a rotary water motor.

His invention of a hydro-electric machine, which generated electricity by steam escaping-through nozzles from an insulated boiler, originated in a report he read of a colliery engineman who noticed that he had received a sharp electric shock on exposing one hand to a jet of steam issuing from a boiler with which his other hand was in direct contact.

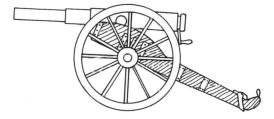

Armstrong's breech-loading gun of 1855, with a rifled barrel made of wrought iron, was not an immediate success but was later to revolutionize British artillery.

Armstrong's first hydraulic crane depended simply on the pressure of water acting directly on a piston in a cylinder. The resulting movement of the piston produced a corresponding movement through suitable gears. The first example was erected on the quay at Newcastle in 1846 - the pressure being obtained from the ordinary water mains of the town. The merits and advantages of this device soon became widely appreciated.

In 1850 a hydraulic installation was required for a new ferry station at New Holland on the Humber estuary. The absence of a water mains of any kind, coupled with the prohibitive cost of a special reservoir because of the character of the soil, made it necessary for Armstrong to invent a fresh piece of apparatus. This became known as the hydraulic accumulator. It consisted of a large cylinder containing a piston that could be loaded to any desired pressure - the water being pumped in below it by a steam engine or other prime mover. With various modifications, this device made possible the installation of hydraulic power in almost any situation. In particular it could be used on board ship, and its application to the manipula-

tion of heavy naval guns made it among the most important of Armstrong's inventions.

The Elswick works had originally been founded for the manufacture of this hydraulic machinery, but it was not long before it became the birthplace of a revolution in gun-making. Modern artillery dates from 1855 when Armstrong's first gun made its appearance. This weapon embodied all the essential features which distinguish the ordnance of today from the cannon of the Middle Ages.

There had been little change in heavy guns for 500 years. Their barrels were cast in bronze and they were loaded from the muzzle. Armstrong used the advances of the nineteenth century in metallurgy and chemistry, together with his own inventive genius. His gun was built up of rings of metal shrunk upon an inner steel barrel. It was loaded at the breech and it was rifled, and it threw not a round ball but an elongated shell. The British army adopted the Armstrong gun in 1859.

Britain had thus originated an armament superior to that possessed by any other nation at that time. But in 1863 defects in the breech mechanism caused a disagreement with the government over this decision, Armstrong resigned his Woolwich appointment and devoted his time to improving the original design. He succeeded and, after 17 years (in 1880), the government acknowledged his improvements and breech-loading guns was one of his earliest ideas. This was his use of steel wire. He perceived that to coil many turns of wire round an inner barrel was a logical extension of the large hooped method that had been used in the gun designed by him in 1855.

Auer, Carl *See* Von Welsbach, Freiherr

Ayrton, William Edward *(1847-1908)*, was a British physicist and electrical engineer who invented many of the prototypes of modern electrical measuring instruments. He also created in 1873 the world's first laboratory for teaching applied electricity in Tokyo.

Ayrton was born in London on 14 September 1847, the son of a barrister. He was educated at University College School from 1859 to 1864, when he entered University College, London. In 1867 he obtained an honours degree in mathematics and joined the Indian Telegraph Service. He was sent to Glasgow to study electricity under William Thomson (later Lord Kelvin) and, after practical study at the works of the Telegraph and Maintenance Company, he went to Bombay in 1868 as an assistant superintendent.

In 1872 he returned to England and was placed in charge of the Great Western telegraph factory under Thomson and Fleeming Jenkin. A year later he accepted the chair of Physics and Telegraphy at the new Imperial Engineering College in Tokyo - founded by the Japanese government and at that time the world's largest technical university. There he created the first laboratory in the world for teaching applied electricity.

In 1878 Ayrton returned to England and in 1879 he became Professor at the City and Guilds of the London Institute for the advancement of technical education. His first class consisted of one man and a boy. From 1881 to 1884 he acted as Professor of Applied Physics at the new Finsbury Technical College and became the first Professor of Physics and Electrical Engineering at the new Central Technical College - now the City and Guilds College, South Kensington. He held this post until he died in London on 8 November 1908.

In 1881 Ayrton and John Perry invented the surface-contact system for electric railways with its truly absolute block system of telegraphic signalling, which, together with Fleeming Jenkin, they applied to 'telpherage' (a system of overhead transport) and a line based on it system was installed at Glynde in Sussex. In that year (1882) they also brought out the first electric tricycle.

There followed a whole series of new, portable electrical measuring instruments including the ammeter (so-named by its inventors), an electric power meter, various forms of improved voltmeters, and an instrument used for measuring self and mutual induction. In this, great use was made of an ingeniously devised flat spiral spring which yields a relatively large rotation for a small axial elongation. These instruments served as the prototypes for the many electrical measuring instruments which came into use in countries all over the world as electical power became generally employed for domestic and industrial purposes. Ayrton's instruments gave the electrical engineer the means of measuring almost every electrical quantity he had to deal with, and his electric meter was the only one to be awarded prizes at the Paris Exhibition in 1899.

Besides his contribution to the advancement of the practical aspect of electrical engineering, Ayrton was also a great teacher of the subject. His system of teaching was adopted and extended throughout the profession. He published many scientific papers and a book entitled *Practical Electricity*.

His wife Bertha also achieved renown for her researches into the electric arc and she had the distinction of becoming the first woman member of the Institute of Electrical Engineers.

B

Babcock, George Herman *(1832-1893)*, was the American co-inventor of the first polychromatic printing press, but is chiefly remembered for the Babcock Wilcox steam boiler, devised with his partner, Stephen Wilcox.

Born at Unadilla Forks, near Otego, New York, on 1 June 1832, Babcock inherited his engineering and mechanical expertise from both sides of his family. When he was 12, the Babcock family moved to Westerly, Rhode Island.

Babcock first went to work with his father, Asher, in daguerrotype and job printing for newpapers. It was during this period, up to 1854, that Babcock and his father invented the polychromatic printing press. Father and son also invented a job printing press which is still manufactured today.

Moving to Brooklyn, New York in 1860, Babcock held many posts, first in the offices of a patents solicitor, then with the Mystic Iron Works and afterwards as chief draughtsman at the Hope Iron Works, Providence, Rhode Island.

At Providence, Babcock and Stephen Wilcox met again, and became involved in steam engineering. Together, they tackled the contemporary problems of steam boilers. Since their introduction in the 18th century, fire-tube boilers had been bedevilled by structural problems. Explosions, often fatal, were a constant danger when large quantities of water and steam were contained in boilers not built to withstand the strains imposed upon them. In the 19th century, the growing use of steam power and of engines operating at ever higher pressures increased the incidence of such disasters.

The water-tube boiler was developed as a safer replacement, and it was to the improvement of this early model that Babcock and Wilcox applied themselves. Their design for a sectionally-headed boiler was one of the earliest with automatic cut-off, being based on a safety water tube patented by Wilcox in 1856. This was the first engine to have front and rear water spaces connected by slanting tubes, the steam space being situated above. The Babcock-Wilcox boiler, patented in 1867, employed cast iron steam generating tubes placed in vertical rows over a grate. Steel or wrought iron tubes connected them with headers leading to the separating drum, where the water was separated from the steam and re-circulated.

The new boiler, considerably more powerful

than its predecessors, was able to withstand very high pressures and also ensured a high standard of protection against explosions. It was first manufactured at Providence, and then in New York, where the firm of Babcock and Wilcox was incorporated in 1881. The boilers were also built in New Jersey, at Elizabethport, and at a specially-designed plant at Bayonne.

Patent restrictions on the design of steam boilers made the Babcock-Wilcox model expensive, and it fell behind the competition when the patents expired and the cheap engines invaded the market. The high quality of the boiler, however, ensured its continuation and the design was still being used 70 years after its inception. The firm of Babcock and Wilcox still exists, and today manufactures modern high quality steam boilers.

Babcock actively promoted his company's product by lecturing at technical institutes and colleges, an activity for which his impressive presence and personality made him especially suitable. In 1887, Babcock was president of the American Society of Mechanical Engineers, and was also seen frequently at meetings of technical societies. A sincerely religious man, a member of the Seventh Day Baptists, Babcock took great personal interest in the welfare of his employees and in his public duties: these included the presidencies of the Board of Trustees of Alfred University and, at his home of Plainfield, New Jersey, of the Board Education and the Public Library.

Babcock was alert and energetic to the end of his life. By the age of 60, he had acquired a fair knowledge of the French language. He died on 16 December, 1893.

Baird, John Logie *(1888-1946)*, was a Scottish inventor who was the first person to televise an image, using mechanical (non-electronic) scanning. He also gave the first demonstration of colour television.

Baird was born in Helensburgh, Dunbartonshire on 13 August 1888. He was educated at Larchfield Academy and later took an engineering course at the Royal Technical College, Glasgow. He then studied at Glasgow University, but World War I interrupted his final year there. Rejected as physically unfit for military service, Baird became a superintendent engineer with the Clyde Valley Electrical Power Company. In 1918 he gave up engineering because of ill-health and set himself up in business, marketing successfully such diverse products as patent socks, confections and soap in Glasgow, London and the West Indies. Persistent ill health, leading to a complete physical and nervous breakdown in 1923, forced him to retire to Horsham in Sussex.

Many inventors had patented their ideas about television - the electrical transmission of images in motion simultaneously with accompanying sound - but only a few, including Baird, pursued a practical study of the problem based on the use of mechanical scanners. In 1907 Boris Rosing had proposed that, in a television system which used mirror-scanning in the camera, a cathode-ray tube with a fluorescent screen should be fitted into the receiver. In 1911 A.A Campbell Swinton had suggested that magnetically deflected cathode-ray tubes should be used both in the camera and the receiver.

On his retirement, Baird concentrated on solving the problems of television. Having little money, his first apparatus was crude and makeshift, set up on a washstand in his attic room. A tea-chest formed the base of his motor, a biscuit tin housed the projection lamp, and cheap cycle-lamp lenses were incorporated into the design. The whole contraption was held together by darning needles, pieces of string and scrap wood. Yet within a year he had succeeded in transmitting a flickering image of the outline of a Maltese cross over a distance of a few metres.

Baird took his makeshift apparatus to London where, in one of two attic rooms in Soho, he proceeded to improve it. In 1925 he achieved the transmission of an image of a recognizable human face and the following year, on 26 January, he gave the world's first demonstration of true television before an audience of about 50 scientists at the Royal Institution, London. Baird used a mechanical scanner which temporarily changed an image into a sequence of electronic signals that could then be reconstructed on a screen as a pattern of half-tones. The neon discharge lamp Baird used offered a simple means for the electrical modulation of light at the receiver. His first pictures were formed of only 30 line repeated approximately 10 times a second. The results were crude but it was the start of television as a practical technology.

By 1927, Baird had transmitted television over 700km (435 miles) of telephone line between London and Glasgow and soon after made the first television broadcast using radio, between London and the SS *Berengaria*, halfway across the Atlantic Ocean. He also made the first transatlantic television broadcast between Britain and the United States when signals transmitted from the Baird station in Coulson, Kent, were picked up by a receiver in Hartsdale, New York.

By 1928 Baird had succeeded in demonstrating colour television. The simplest way to reproduce a colour image is to produce the red, blue, and green primary images separately and then to superimpose them so that the eye merges the three images into one full-colour picture. Baird used three projection tubes arranged so that each threw a picture on to the same screen. By using only one amplifier chain and one cathode-ray tube which sequentially amplified the red, blue and green signals, he overcame the problem of over-registration of the three images and matched the three channels. He used two rotating discs - each with segments of red, green and blue light filters, rotating in synchronism before the camera tube and the receiver tube. Each primary-coloured filter remained over the tube face for the period of one field. Although partly successful, Baird's method had two major drawbacks. One was that the picture being transmitted consisted mainly of tones of one hue, say green, then the other two fields (red and blue) showed as black and each green field was succeeded by black ones, resulting in excessive flickering. The other was that the system required three times the bandwidth available.

Baird's black-and-white system was used by the BBC in an experimental television service in 1929. At first, the sound and vision were transmitted alternately, but by 1930 it was possible to broadcast them simultaneously. In 1936, when the public television service was started, his system was threatened by one promoted by Marconi-EMI. The following year the Baird system was dropped in favour of the Marconi electronic system, which gave a better definition.

Despite his bitter disappointment, Baird continued his experimental work in colour television. By 1939 he had demonstrated colour television using a cathode-ray tube which he had adapted as the most successful method for producing a well-defined and brilliant image. Baird's inventive and engineering abilities were widely recognized. In 1937, he became the first British subject to receive the Gold Medal of the International Faculty of Science. The same year, he was elected Fellow of the Royal Institute of Edinburgh, where a plaque was erected to commemorate his demonstration of true television in 1926. Baird also became an Honorary Fellow of the Royal Society of Edinburgh, Fellow of the Physical Society and Associate of the Royal Technical College.

He continued his research on stereoscopic and large screen television until his death, at Bexhill on Sea, Sussex, on 14 June 1946.

Baker, Benjamin *(1840-1907)*, was an English engineer most famous for his design of the Forth Bridge in Scotland.

Baker was born on 31 March 1840 at Keyford, Frome, Somerset. He attended the grammar school at Cheltenham until he was sixteen when he was apprenticed at Neath Abbey ironworks. In 1860 he left this firm and became

assistant to William Wilson who designed Victoria Station in London. Two years later he joined the staff of Sir John Fowler, (becoming his partner in 1875) and became particularly involved with the construction of the Metropolitan and District lines of the London Underground. This project demanded considerable ingenuity to overcome the many hazards caused by difficult soils, underground water and the ruins of Roman and other civilizations. Baker incorporated an ingenious energy conservation measure in the construction of the Central Line: he dipped the line between stations to reduce the need both for braking to a halt and for the increase in power required to accelerate away.

During the 1870s there was much interest in extending the Scottish East Coast Railway from Edinburgh to Dundee. This required the building of bridges across the Forth and Tay. The original Tay Bridge, which had been built by Sir Thomas Bouch of wrought iron lattice girders, collapsed under an express train during a storm on the night of 28 December 1879. This structure had been a considerable accomplishment, and indeed Bouch had built many successful bridges to similar designs. However it had been built without sufficient allowance for the force of the wind when the train was on the centre span. In addition, certain elements in its design were unsuitable, and inadequate supervision had blighted its construction. When the Tay disaster struck Bouch had already begun work on a bridge across the Forth.

It was only with great reluctance that the government authorities allowed an attempt to build a bridge across the Forth, but this time Baker was in charge. Baker's design had several features that made a repetition of the disaster unlikely. Mild steel, which was considerably stronger than the same weight of wrought iron, had become available through the new Siemens Open-Hearth process. This meant that the structure would be relatively light. Better estimates of the wind force which structures were required to withstand in storms were also available. Nevertheless, a rail bridge was a very difficult undertaking since the Forth was 6m (200ft) deep. A site allowing the use of the little island of Inchgarvie as a foundation for the central pier was chosen; the two main spans were then each of 521m (1,710ft). A cantilever structure, which supports the bridge platform by projecting girders, was used since a suspension bridge, in which the platform hangs from catenaries, was not considered sufficiently stable in high winds for a railway. Indeed Bouch's original design was for a stiffened suspension bridge, but this was abandoned after the Tay Bridge disaster.

The bridge was opened on 4 March 1890 by Edward VII when he was Prince of Wales. It has been in service ever since. For this achievement Baker was knighted by Queen Victoria.

Although the Forth Bridge made Baker famous, hehas many other projects, both in Britain and abroad, to his credit. He worked on the Hudson River tunnel and at the docks at Hull, and played a prominent part in engineering development work in Egypt - he was involved with the Aswan Dam which realized the dream of desert irrigation. A little while before he began work on the Forth Bridge, he designed the large wrought iron vessel in which Cleopatra's Needle, the obelisk on the Thames Embankment was brought to England. The Needle was lost at sea, but when found later it was safely preserved within the hull of Baker's ship.

In his later years, Baker built up a large practice and was held in great esteem as a successful engineer who respected the theory of engineering. Although he had only a little formal education in this, he expressed it with great practical ability and artistry. He was made a Fellow of the Royal Society in 1880. He died, a bachelor, on 19 May 1907.

Barnes Wallis   *See* Wallis, Barnes Neville

Bazalgette, Joseph William *(1819-1891)*, was the British civil engineer who designed the main drainage scheme for London and supervised its installation between 1859 and 1875. He was also mainly responsible for the London embankments, for new bridges over the river Thames, and for the Woolwich steam ferry.

Bazalgette was born at Enfield, Middlesex, on 28 March 1819. He was educated at private schools and at the age of 17 became a pupil of the civil engineer John Benjamin McNeil. For a short time he was employed on drainage and reclamation work in Northern Ireland. In 1842 he set up in business in Westminster as a consulting engineer - being chiefly engaged on railway work. In 1849 he joined the staff of the Metropolitan Commission of Sewers, a body which had been created in 1848 to replace the eight separate municipal bodies responsible for the drainage of London. In 1855, following two cholera epidemics in London, the Metropolitan Board of Works was created by Act of Parliament, and Bazalgette was appointed its chief engineer. In 1856 he presented his plans for a main drainage scheme for the entire metropolis, and the plans were put into operation two years later. By 1865 most of the work had been done, and the nearly completed system was officially opened by the Prince of Wales (later King Edward VII). The whole scheme was finally completed in 1875. It involved no less than 160km (100 miles) of large-diameter sewers and it was the first major civil engineering project to make extensive use of the new Portland cement - more than 70,000 tonnes (69,000 tons) were used. The system had its outfalls some 19km (12 miles) below London Bridge at Barking in Essex and Crossness in Kent, and it incorporated three large pumping stations. The scheme also involved a new Thames Embankment between Westminster and Blackfriar's Bridges - reclaiming altogether 16 hectares (38 acres) of mudback and converting it into parkland (now the Victoria Embankment Gardens) between the Hungerford Railway Bridge and Waterloo Bridge. In 1874 the Chelsea Embankment was laid over the new sewers just completed there, and in 1869 the Albert Embankment, opposite the Houses of Parliament, was built as a flood-control installation.

Bazalgette was also responsible for the alteration of many of London's old bridges made necessary by the Toll Bridges Act of 1887. He designed new bridges for Putney and Battersea and designed the installation for the steam ferry between North and South Woolwich. He also prepared plans for a bridge over the river near the Tower of London and for a tunnel under it at Blackwall, but died before these projects could be carried out.

His considerable achievements in civil engineering are commemorated by a mural monument incorporating a bronze bust which was erected in his memory on the Thames Embankment at the foot of Northumberland Avenue. He removed one of the main causes of epidemics from what was then the world's major city, contributed greatly to hygienic living conditions for people today who live closely associated in large numbers.

Bazalgette's contribution to the health and well-being of his fellow countrymen was recognized when he received a knighthood in 1874. He became President of the Institution of Civil Engineers in 1884, having first become a member in 1838. He died at his home in Wimbledon Park, London, on 15 March 1891.

Bell, Alexander Graham, *(1847-1922)* was the Scottish-born American scientist who invented the telephone. He became the first man to trasmit the human voice by electrical means and the telephone system he initiated is now known and used world-wide.

Bell was born in Edinburgh on 3 March 1847. Until the age of 11 he was taught at home by his mother. After graduating from the Edinburgh Royal High School at the age of 15, he went to London and lived with his grandfather, who was widely known as a speech tutor. From him Bell gained a knowledge of the mechanisms of speech and sound. In 1867, after a year of teaching and studying at Bath, he became an assistant to his father, who had originated the phonetic 'visible speech' system for teaching the deaf.

After the death of his second brother in 1870 the family moved to Brantford, Ontario, for health reasons. In April 1871, Bell started giving instruction in 'visible speech' to teachers of the deaf in and around Boston, Massachusetts, and by 1873 he was Professor of Vocal Physiology at Boston University, a post he held for four years.

Bell's interest in speech and sound began at a very early age. As a boy he had constructed an automaton - using rubber, cotton and a bellows - simulating the human organs of speech. He had even experimented with the throat of his pet Skye terrier, attemptingto turn co-operative growls into words.

In 1874 he was granted patents on a multiple or harmonic telegraph for sending two or more messages simultaneously over the same wire. Elisha Grey had already developed the telegraph and, at this time, several men had become aware of the possibility of transmitting the human voice by electrical means. Bell,with Thomas A. Watson as his assistant, had devised a transmitter for all the various voice frequencies by placing a magnetized reed in the centre of a circular diaphragm that was set to vibrate at the human voice. The vibrating reed induced varying electrical oscillations in a associated electromagnet. The same device, at the distant end of the circuit, functioned as a receiver.

The following year, Bell and Watson improved on this, and on 10 March 1876 Bell became the first person ever to transmit speech from one point to another by electrical means. The first message travelled only the distance from one room to the next, but two months later the first 'long distance' voice message travelled 13km (8 miles) from Paris to Brantford, Ontario; before the end of the year, this distance had been increased to 229km (143 miles). The patent for the telephone invented by Bell was granted in 1876. From then on, the telephone system spread rapidly across the country.

With the financial independence he had gained through the success of his telephone system Bell was able to set up a laboratory at Baddeck Day, on the Bras d'Or lakes of Cape Breton Island, Nova Scotia. Among the first fruits of his work here was the photophone, which used the photo-resistive properties of selenium crystals to apply the telephone principle to transmitting words in a beam of light. Bell thus achieved the first wire-less transmission of speech and from these principles evolved the photoelectric cell and other developments. Had coherent light (lasers) or optical fibres been available to him, Bell might have been able to develop the photo-phone into something useful. As it was, he seemed to recognize its potential instinctively for in in 1921, in an age of intercontinental radio, he declared that the photophone was his greatest invention. The spectrophone, for carrying out spectrum analysis by means of sound, followed.

Bell established the Volta Laboratory in Washington and patented the gramophone and wax recording cylinder which were commercially successful improvements on Thomas Edison's first phonograph and cylinders of metal foil. The laboratory also experimented with flat disc records, electroplating records and impressing permanent magnetic fields on records - the embryonic tape recorder. Bell's entire share of 200,000 dollars from the sale of some of his patents served to guarantee the perpetuation of the Volta Bureau which he had formed for all conceivable kinds of research into deafness.

In 1881, Bell developed two telephonic devices for locating metallic masses (usually bullets) in the human body. One, an induction balance method, was first tried out on President Garfield, who was assassinated in 1881, while the other, a probe, was widely used until the advent of X-rays. At the Baddeck Bay laboratory, he built hydrofoil speed boats and sea-water converting units. He made man-carrying kites employing the tetrahedral design for strength and lift.

Some idea of the true breadth of Bell's inventiveness can be gained by his lesser-known developments. These included an air-cooling system, a special strain of sheep (which he claimed produced twin or triplet lambs in more than half the births), the forerunner of the iron lung, and a sorting machine for punch-coded census cards.

In 1882 Bell became a citizen of the United States and moved to Washington DC. In 1888, he became a founder member of the National Geographic Society.

The commercial success of his many inventions made Bell a wealthy man. He was also the recipient of many awards. In 1876, he received the Gold Medal awarded by the judges at the Centennial Exhibition in Philadephia where his prototype telephone was first shown. In 1880 he received the Volta Prize in France and was made an officer of the French Legion of Honour. From 1898 to 1903 he was President of the National Geographic Society, and in 1898 he was appointed Regent of the Smithsonian Institution.

In 1917 a massive granite and bronze memorial was erected in Bell's honour at Brantford, Ontario. After his death on 2 August 1922 at his winter home at Baddeck Bay, a museum was built by the Canadian government at Baddeck as a permanent reminder of his achievements.

Bell, Patrick *(1799-1869)*, was the Scottish clergyman who invented one of the first successful reaping machines. It is probable that later commercially successful machines owed much to his pioneering work.

Bell was born in April, 1799, on a farm of which his father was a tenant in the parish of Auchterhouse, a few miles north-west of Dundee, Scotland. He studied for the ministry at St Andrew's University, and it was there in 1827 that he turned his attention to the construction of a machine which he (like many other inventors) thought would considerably reduce the labour of the grain harvest.

Harvesting equipment has progressed most since the beginning of the 19th century when Bell made his important contribution. Since then, methods have advanced from the use of the primitive sickle to the self-propelled combine-harvester. It is said that the grain-harvesters of Egypt in 3000 BC could have been used by most farm workers 4,800 years later without any additional training being needed.

It was the invention of the reaper that opened the way to the complete mechanization of the grain harvest, and many attempts were made from the end of the 18th century to cut corn by machine.

The way most of these machines performed has been lost to history and it was not until Bell's machine appeared that the record becomes clearer. He started trials in deep secrecy inside a barn on a crop which had been planted by hand, stalk by stalk. In 1828, he and his brother carried out night-time trials which were a success, leading them to exhibit the machine the following year. In the years to 1832 at least 20 machines were produced, 10 of them cutting 130 hectares (320 acres) in Britain and 10 going for export. Six reapers were exhibited at the Great Fair in New York in 1851. That year also saw the Great Exhibition in London, at which reapers by Hussey and McCormick were exhibited, both of them showing similarities to the Bell machines. This was the turning point for mechanical harvesting; mechanization gradually invaded farms and the sickle and scythe were virtually ousted by the 20th century.

Bell's reaper was pushed from behind by a pair of horses and the standing cereals were brought on to the reciprocating cutter bar by horizontally revolving rods similar to the reels seen on modern combine harvesters. The cut cereal fell on to an inclined rotating canvas cylinder and was sheaved and stooked by hand. One of Bell's machines was used on his brother's farm for many years until, in 1868, it was bought by the museum of the Patents Office where it was afterwards kept. He did not take out a patent and the design

was improved upon and reintroduced as the 'Beverly Reaper' in 1857.

In recognition of his sevices to agriculture, Bell was presented with £1,000 and a commemorative plate by the Highland Society, the money being raised mainly from the farmers of Scotland. He also received the honorary degree of LL.D from the University of St Andrews.

Although Bell did not achieve the fame of others such as McCormick, his work was of fundamental value and importance in the successful advancement of agricultural methods to the now well-established mechanized farming used today.

Bell died in 1869 in the parish of Carmylie, Arbroath, of which he had been ordained Minister in 1843.

Benz, Carl, *(1844-1929)*, was the German engineer who designed and built the first commercially successful motor car.

Benz was born in Karlsruhe, Germany, on 26 November 1844, the son of an engine driver, Johann Georg Benz, who died when Karl was two. He was educated at the gymnasium and polytechnic in his home town and began his career as an ordinary worker in a local machine shop when he was 21. Benz appears to have consciously shaped his career, moving from mechanical work on steam engines to design work with a more general engineering company in Mannheim, and then to a larger firm of engineers and ironfounders. In 1871 he returned to Mannheim, married Berta Ringer the following year, and opened a small engineering works in partnership with August Ritter..

After severe financial difficulties, Benz, now on his own, produced a two-stroke engine of his own design in 1878 and in 1883, after more financial difficulties, attracted enough support to found a new firm, Benz and Co. In 1885, he produced what is generally recognized to have been the first vehicle successfully propelled by an internal combustion engine.

The motor car he produced stemmed from over 150 years of experimental work by many engineers working in many different fields. Benz was the first person to bring together the many threads to produce and exploit a commercially viable road vehicle. The evolution of the modern motorcar really began when Joseph Cugnot built his steam-driven gun carriage in 1769. Many other steam-driven vehicles followed, including that of Trevithick (1802). Whether the Belgian, Lenoir, or the Austrian, Marcus, was the first to produce a carriage driven by an internal combustion engine is a matter for dispute. Lenoir's machine of 1862 was driven by one of his gas engines and is said to have moved at 5km/h (3mph). Marcus' machine is said to have run in 1868 and was certainly exhibited at the Vienna Exhibition in 1873. Neither, however, came to anything; Lenoir's had to carry about its own supply of town gas and was immensely heavy, while the Marcu engine had no clutch and was difficult to start.

In 1878 Benz produced his first two-stroke, 0.75kW (1hp) engine in the factory he had founded at Mannheim in 1872. The commerical success of this enabled him to found a new company, Benz and Co., and to experiment with the construction of motor vehicles as well as engines. As it happened, the timing was critical because Otto and Beau de Rochas had each independently developed four-stroke engines. As a result of litigation between the two inventors, the Otto cycle became available to Benz and he was thus able to build a suitable power unit for his three-wheeled Tri-car.

In the Spring of 1885, he produced what is generally regarded as the world's first vehicle successfully propelled by an internal combustion engine. It used an Otto cycle four-stroke engine which gave about 0.56kW (0.75hp) at 250rpm and achieved a speed of up to 5km/h (3mph) during a journey of 91m (100yd) on private ground adjoining the Mannheim workshop. Benz firmly believed that this vehicle would be a completely new system and not simply a carriage with a motor replacing the horse. The engine had a massive flywheel and was mounted horizontally in the rear, using electric ignition by coil and battery. The cooling system consisted simply of a cylinder jacket in which the water boiled away, being topped up as necessary. It had a carburettor of Benz's own design which vapourized the fuel over a hot spot.

By the autumn, the prototype Tri-car was covering 1km (c.1000yd) at 12km/h (7.5mph) and had become a familiar sight on the streets of the town. The production model Tri-car appeared in 1886-1887 and had a 1kW (1.5hp) single cylinder engine. The following year a Tri-car with an occasional extra seat and a 2hp twin cylinder engine appeared. Although the three-seat version was available for the Munich exhibition of 1888, Benz decided to exhibit a two-seater and won a gold medal for it.

Like most innovators, Benz had to contend with apathy and official hostility. There was also little demand for his Tri-cars at that time because of the public's general rejection of such 'monsters' and the severe restrictions placed on their use on public roads. British law, for instance, framed mainly with road-running steam engines in mind, required that all such vehicles have three drivers, be preceded by a man carrying a red flag and did not move faster than 6.4km/h (4mph). This kind of control did nothing to promote sales. However, there was sufficient financial interest shown in France to enable Benz to improve his vehicles still further.

Benz laid down his first four-wheeled prototype in 1891 and by 1895, he was building a range of four-wheeled vehicles that were light, strong, inexpensive and simple to operate. These automobiles had engines of 1-5.5kW (1.5-6hp) and ran at speeds of about 24km/h (15mph). Between 1897 and 1900 improved models appeared in increasing numbers - in particular, the Benz Velo 'Comfortable' of which over 4,000 were sold. At £135 each, they found a steady sale.

Benz and Co was now a thriving concern and, in 1899, it was turned into a limited company. Although Benz retired from the board at the time of the transformation, the company he founded grew to become world-famous for its production of high performance cars. Under the gifted Hans Nibel as chief designer, the firm produced very successful racing cars and luxury limousines. In 1926, the company merged with the other famous German firm of Daimler - a firm which had developed at the same time as Benz and Co., along very similar lines and from similar beginnings - to form the the world famous Daimler-Benz company.

Benz died on 4 April 1929, at Ladenburg.

Berthoud, Ferdinand, *(1727-1807)* was a Swiss clockmaker and a maker of scientific instruments. He improved the work of John Harrison, devoting 30 years' work to the perfection of the marine chronometer, giving it practically its modern form.

Son of Jean Berthoud, the architect and judiciary, Berthoud was born near Couvet. He was apprenticed to his brother, Jean-Henry, at the age of 14. In 1745 he went to Paris and in 1764 was appointed Horologer de la Marine. He made over 70 chronometers using a wide variety of mechanisms, and wrote ten volumes on the subject, many of them of considerable importance in his field.

In the early 18th century clockmakers devoted much effort to the construction of chronometers that could be used at sea. This was because if the navigator did not know the time at the zero meridian it was impossible for him to plot his precise position. Since the different astronomical methods of measuring longitude gave inadequate results, the solution seemed to lie in finding ways of making very accurate clocks whose workings would not be disturbed by the motion of the ship.

The English clockmaker John Harrison (1693-1776) was undoubtedly the first maker of a timepiece that could be used satisfactorily at sea. In 1735 he completed his first marine chronometer; this was tested at sea and gave results which were good enough for further financial help to be given to its maker but not good enough for the reward offered under an Act passed by the British Parliament in 1714.

Harrison's chronometer number 4 was completed in 1759 and was tested at sea. While this met the requirements of the Act, the responsible authorities in England, the Board of Longitude, still demanded numerous trials. Tested over long distances, his chronometer consistently showed variations, involving errors in the calculation of longitudes, that were less than the maximum of half a degree stipulated by the Board of Longitude. It was not until 1772, when Harrison was 80, and after long years of argument that he received the whole award of £20,000.

Harrison had already obtained remarkable results when Berthoud began his investigations, which were conducted mainly from 1760 to 1768. He was a skilled clockmaker by the time he began to devote himself to the problem of marine chronometers and his work was guided by wide experience as well as his outstanding practical ability.

The range of parts constructed by Berthoud is large but the complete clocks made for his experiments numbered only seven or eight. His clocks number 1 and 2 were made in 1760 and 1763 respectively. Though number 2 was noticeably smaller than the first, these two instruments were still rather bulky. Berthoud put two circular balance wheels oscillating in opposite directions into these designs, which connected to one another by means of a toothed wheel. Their axes rested on roller bearings. A bimetallic grid iron, already widely used by clockmakers since its invention by Harrison, compensated for variations in the length of the spiral.

The escapement was made more complicated in clock number 2, in which Berhoud introduced an equalizing remontoir to compensate for errors caused by variations in the driving force of the escapements. A spring barrel fitted with a fuse was initially chosen as the source of motive power, a system still used in modern marine chronometers. However, Berthoud temporarily abandoned this system soon afterwards. In his third watch, also made in 1763, Berthoud used a bimetallic strip for thermal compensation and a single balance wheel. Retaining the single balance wheel suspended by a wire and guided by rollers, he then returned to the gridiron method of compensation for the construction of his subsequent clocks. Numbers 6 and 8 (1767) of these ensured his success.

In this series the motive power was produced by weights placed on a vertical metal plate which descended the length of three brass columns. An escapement with ruby cylinders was used, all parts being relatively compact. The mechanism was above the gridiron, the two occupying the top part of the clock, which was enclosed in a long glass cylinder. The three brass columns guiding the descent of the weight took up almost the whole height of this cylinder. A horizontal dial covered the glass box.

Clocks 6 and 8 were tested at sea in 1768 and 1769 and showed variations in their working of the order of from 5 to 20 seconds a day.

We known of only five chronometers made by John Harrison, who did not reach his goal until his last years. Berthoud, on the other hand, was able to continue working for another 30 years after his initial success. Abandoning the roller suspension of the balance wheel, he adopted a pivot suspension. He came back to compensation by bimetallic strips, eliminating the cumbersome gridiron and used a balance wheel compensated by four small weights. Two of these weights were fixed and the two others were carried by a bimetallic strip which moved towards or away from the arbor according to variations in temperature. Berthoud also eventually returned to the spring drive. His nephew, Pierre-Louis Berthoud (1754-1813) succeeded him in his work as a marine clock maker and began to industrialize the construction of chronometers as an industry in France.

Bessemer, Henry *(1813-1898)*, was a British engineer and inventor of the Bessemer process for the manufacture of steel, first publicly announced at a meeting of the British Association in 1856. His process was the first cheap, large-scale method of making steel from pig-iron. Bessemer had many other inventions to his credit but none is comparable to that with which his name is linked and which earned him a fortune.

With the French Revolution, the French Huguenot Bessemer family moved to England and their son Henry was born at Charlton, near Hitchin in Hertfordshire, on 19 January 1813. He inherited much skill and enterprise from his father who was associated with the firm founded by William Caslon, one of the pioneers in the development of movable type for printing. His earliest years were spent in his father's workshop where he found every chance to develop his inclinations as an inventor. At the age of 17 he went to London where he put to use his knowledge of easily fusible metals and casting in the production of artwork. His work was noticed and he was invited to exhibit at the Royal Academy. In about 1838 Bessemer invented a typesetting machine and a little later he perfected a process for making imitation Utrecht velvet. In this his combined mechanical skill and artistic capacity proved useful, for he not only had to design all the machinery but he also had to engrave the embossing rolls.

In about 1840, encouraged by his great friend the printer Thomas de la Rue, Bessemer turned his attention to the manufacture of bronze powder and gold paint. At that time Germany had the monopoly in this industry, having learned its secrets from China and Japan. Bessemer's product was at least equal to that from Germany and one-eighth of the price. Between 1849 and 1853 he became interested in the process of sugar refining and obtained no less than 13 patents for machinery for this. He also invented a new method of making lead pencils. But it was the bronze powder and gold paint process, the secrets of which were kept in the Bessemer family for 40 years, that provided the capital needed to set up the small ironworks in St Pancras, London, where his experiments led to the invention of the Bessemer steelmaking process. This was his greatest achievement and at the time was of enormous industrial importance.

With the Crimean War of the early 1850s Bessemer turned his energies to the problems of high gas pressures in guns which were probably caused by early attempts at rifling. When he offered his services to the British military commanders they showed no interest, so Bessemer turned to the Britain's ally, France. The French military, which had used rifled weapons intermittently for years, expressed interest, and Napoleon III encouraged Bessemer to experiment further. With weapons that fire from rifled barrels, the projectile has to fit tightly or it is not set spinning by the helical grooves in the barrel. The tight fit leads to high pressures, and many early weapons exploded, killing the gun crew. Bessemer set out to find a form of iron strong enough to resist these pressures.

At that time steel was expensive and cast iron, although very hard, was extremely brittle. The carbon in cast iron could be laboriously removed to form practically pure wrought iron which was not brittle but ductile. Steel, with a carbon content between that of cast iron and wrought iron, was both hard and tough. But, to make steel, cast iron had to be converted into wrought iron and carbon had then to be added - a laborious and time-consuming process. Bessemer considered the contemporary method of converting cast iron to wrought iron. A carefully measured quantity of iron ore was added to cast iron and then heated to the molten stage, when the oxygen in the iron ore combined with the carbon in the the cast iron to form carbon monoxide (which was burned off), and leaving pure iron. Bessemer considered adding the oxygen directly as a blast of air,

although it seemed likely that the cold air would cool and therefore solidify the molten iron. When he tried the process, however, he found that the reverse was true: the blast of air burned off the carbon and other impurities and the heat generated served to keep the iron molten - indeed the temperature was raised. By stopping the process at the right time he found that he could produce steel without the intermediate wrought iron stage, and that its cost was reduced dramatically.

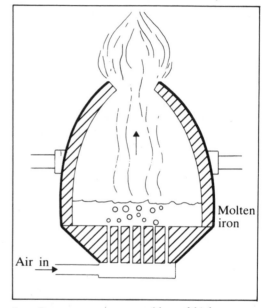

Molten iron

Air in

In a Bessemer converter, a blast of high-pressure air oxidizes impurities in molten iron and converts it to steel.

Ironmakers were enthusiastic when in 1856 Bessemer announced his discovery, and vast sums of money were invested in equipment for the new process. But instead of becoming a hero, Bessemer was derided, because the steel that was produced was of a very poor grade. In his original experiments Bessemer had used phosphorus-free ore, while the ironmakers had used ore containing phosphorous. Bessemer assured the ironmakers that good steel could be made if the appropriate ore was used, but they would not listen. In 1860 Bessemer erected his own steel works in Sheffield, importing phosphorous-free iron ore from Sweden. The high-grade steel he made was sold for a fraction of the current price; one report claims that he could undercut his rivals by £20 per ton. Ironmasters, feeling the sting of competition, applied for licences and the royalties made Bessemer a very rich man. He retired at the comparatively early age of 56 but continued inventing. One of his later schemes, was a stabilized saloon for an ocean-going ship, the theory being that sea-sick passengers would not feel the motion of the vessel. The scheme was not a success and Bessemer had his fingers severely burnt, losing around £34,000 in the venture.

The recognition Bessemer received for his steel-making process was however richly deserved for his method of making cheap steel benefitted the whole world. He was not allowed to accept the Legion of Honour offered to him by the French Emperor, but he received many other honours and became a Fellow of the Royal Society in 1879. He was knighted in the same year for services to the Inland Revenue 40 years before when, before he was 20, he played an important part in the construction of the first method for stamping deeds, a method which was adopted by the British government. He died at Denmark Hill, London, on 15 March 1898. No less than six towns in the United States were named after him.

Bickford, William *(1774-1834)*, was an English leather merchant who invented the miner's safety fuse. He made a major contribution to safety and productivity in the mines and quarries, and even after electric ignition was introduced in 1952 the majority of charges were set off using fuses not very different from the one patented by him in 1831.

Bickford was born in Devonshire, and having tried unsuccessfully to carry on a currier's business (dressing and colouring tanned leather) in Truro, he set up as a leather merchant in Tuckingmill near Camborne in Cornwall. He was deeply distressed by the high casualty rate and terrible injuries suffered by local tin miners, and set out to discover a safe means of igniting charges. His first attempt failed, but his second resulted in a reliable fuse.

Gunpowder had been used for blasting since the early 1600s. The powder was put into a brass ball or 'pulta', the outside being covered with cotton soaked in saltpetre and dipped in molten pitch and sulphur. The powder was fired from outside through a small hole drilled through the brass case. Once the pitch was lit, the pulta was pushed into a crack in the rock.

The first borehole blasts were carried out by Casper Weindl in a mine near Ober-Biberstollen, about 75 miles north of Budapest. In England, gunpowder was probably first used for blasting at the Ecton copper mine near the Derbyshire-Staffordshire border. The shot holes were filled with powder and then 'stemmed' or, as a contemporary account puts it: blocked 'by stones and rubbish ramm'd in (except a little place that is left for a Train) the powder by the help of that train being fir'd'. The method had spread to quarries by the early 1670s.

By the end of the 18th century an extremely popular type of fuse made of goose quills was being used. The quills were cut so that they could be inserted one into the other and then filled with powder. Such fuses could be ignited directly, that is without any delaying element such as the sulphur mannikin. However, the quills were often broken or pushed apart during stemming so that an irregular or even a damp column of powder was left to act as a very uncertain fuse. Quil fuses frequently apparently failed and then rekindled so that the miner, who went to inspect the apparently extinct fuse, was injured in the blast.

Bickford's safety fuse provided a dependable means for conveying flame to the charge so that the danger of such hang fires was virtually eliminated. Its timing (the time required for a given length to burn) was more accurate and consistent than that of its predecessors, and it had much better resistance to water and to general abuse. The burning section was protected by the stemming in each shot hole so that several holes could be fired at a time without the fusing of the last being destroyed by the blast from the first.

This and other techniques which the new fuse allowed increased not only safety, but also productivity, quickly making it popular among both miners and management. Many different types were subsequently made for volley firing, for use in flammable atmospheres and for other applications. Bickford went into partnership with Thomas Davey, a working miner and a Methodist class leader, to construct the machinery for fuse production.

The first method used a funnel which trickled black powder into the centre of 12 yarns as they were spun. The process was discontinuous, producing 20m (65ft) lengths of semifuse which were then 'countered' by twisting on a second set of yarns in the opposite direction to make a second 'rod' which would not unwind. The fuse was then covered with a layer of tar and resin. Later the process became continuous so that the length produced was limited only by interruptions in the process. This method, with refinements, is still in use today.

Bickford fell seriously ill in 1832 and took no further part in the exploitation of his invention. After his death in 1834 a fuse-making factory was built at Tuckingmill and continued in production until July 1961. Factories were later set up in Lancashire and also in America, France, Saxony, Austrial Hungary and Australia, the organization becoming one of the major units of Explosive Trades Limited, later to become Imperial Chemical Industries.

Bigelow, Erastus Brigham *(1814-1879)*, was the American inventor-industrialist who devised, among many such machines, the first power loom for weaving ingrain carpets and a loom for manufacturing Wilton and Brussels carpets.

Bigelow's beginnings at West Boylston, Massachusetts, where he was born on 2 April 1814, were so impoverished that he was forced to go out to work at the age of 10. Bigelow's father, a small farmer, also worked as a chairmaker and wheelwright. Until 1834, Bigelow did any work he could find - on neighbouring farms, playing the violin in the church orchestra or at local country dances, as a store clerk and as a stenography teacher - Nevertheless he hankered after a formal education. He had hopes of entering Harvard University as a medical student and afterwards, of a professorial or literary career.

Though these hopes never materialized, Bigelow's natural talent for mechanics and mathematics could not be suppressed. At the age of 8 he mastered arithmetic without the aid of a teacher. Bigelow produced his first loom for weaving coach lace to trim stagecoach upholstery in 1837, at the age of 23. This was followed by more looms for the manufacture of ginghams, silk brocatelle, counterpanes and other figured fabrics.

In about 1839 Bigelow met Alexander Wright, a Scots mechanic settled in America who had recently set up a small carpet weaving business with three looms and twenty workers. Wright had heard of Bigelow's mechanized coach-lace loom and encouraged Bigelow to look into the possibility of inventing a power loom for ingrain-type carpets. Wright discovered that, despite 40 years of experiment in Europe, no satisfactory machine with this capability had yet been devised.

Like his predecessors, Bigelow faced many complex problems: how to set needles for the mechanical interweaving of up to three piles at a time, how to provide accurate timing for the take-up beam of the fabric, how to create a firm and even selvage, how to contol the smooth surface with repeating patterns of uniform length so that they matched when seamed, and how to control the timing of several shuttle boxes.

The resultant loom had a long gestation and most of the cost was borne by the Clinton Company which Bigelow and his brother Horatio set up in 1843 to manufacture ginghams. In exchange, the company required exclusive rights to the machine which, after several modifications was at last ready for use, late in 1846. Bigelow's power loom proved capable of producing up to 16.5sq. metres (20sq.yds) a day of two-ply goods and 11.7sq. metres (14 sq.yds) of three-ply. It was a great improvement on his earlier machines, which could produce only the simplest of patterns, allowing patterns with large flowers and sweeping foliage, asymmetrically arranged, to be produced. There was some popular criticism about the 'unnaturalness of walking on flowers' and geometric patterns were suggested instead. However, patterns with large floriated scrolls of the type woven by Bigelow's machines were ideal for incorporating the serrations around the leaf and flower-edges which 'hid' the uneven joins of the interchange of coloured threads. Bigelow's power loom for weaving Brussels and Wilton carpets was developed between 1845 and 1851 and together with his other machines brought the Clinton Company great riches. The town of Clinton, Massachusetts, which had started humbly as a factory village, grew up around the Bigelow plant. Later, other Bigelow mills were established at Lowell, Massachusetts and Humphreysville, Connecticut. Bigelow's looms transformed the carpet industry in the United States which until then had been outpaced by Britain, where weaving skills were greater and labour less costly. In fact, in the mid-19th century, the United States imported more British carpeting - an average of 550,000 sq. metres (660,000 sq.yds) a year - than was produced by all American factories put together. Ironically, when imported into Britain, Bigelow's looms gave the British an advantage over their French rivals because of their cost-cutting and because carpets could now be made of virtually any colour, to virtually any pattern.

Bigelow, who died in Boston on 6 December 1879, helped found the Massachusetts Institute of Technology in 1861. Six volumes of his English patents, with the original drawings, are preserved by the Massachusetts Historical Society.

Birkeland, Christian *See* Eyde, Samuel

Booth, Herbert Cecil *(1871-1955)*, was an English mechanical and civil engineer best known for his invention of the vacuum cleaner in 1901.

Booth was born on 4 July 1871 in Gloucester, England, where he was educated at the college school and, later, the county school. He studied engineering at the City and Guilds Institute between 1889 and 1892.

In 1901, the same year in which he formed his own engineering consultancy, Booth conceived the principle of his vacuum cleaner after witnessing a somewhat self-defeating operation at St Pancras Station, London - the cleaning of a Midland Railway train carriage by means of compressed air which simply blew a great cloud of dust around, allowing it to settle elsewhere. Booth realized that a machine to suck in the dust and trap it so that it could be disposed of afterwards would circumvent this unhygienic problem. Booth demonstrated his idea to his companions at St Pancras by placing his handkerchief over his mouth and sucking in his breath. A ring of dust particles appeared where his mouth had been. There was also, of course, a use for Booth's invention in the cleaning of houses, which was then done with handbrushes or with simple sweepers which pushed dust into a box, or with feather dusters which just removed dirt from one place to another. Booth's cleaner replaced these methods of cleaning carpets, upholstery and surfaces with the air suction pump principle. In his machine, one end of the tube was connected to the pump, while the other, with nozzle attached, was pushed over the surface being cleaned. The cleaner incorporated an air filter to cleanse the air passing through and also served to collect the dust.

Because of the large size and high price of early vacuum cleaners and the fact that few houses had mains electricity, Booth initially offered cleaning services rather than machine sales. The large vacuum cleaner, powered by petrol or electric engine and mounted on a four wheeled horse carriage was parked in the street outside a house while large cleaning tubes were passed in through the windows. The machine was such a novelty that society hostesses held special parties at which guests watched operatives cleaning carpets or furniture. Transparent tubes were provided so that the dust could be seen departing down them. Booth's machines received a great popular boost when they were used to clean the blue pile carpets laid in Westminster Abbey for the coronation of King Edward VII in 1902.

Smaller, more compact indoors vacuum cleaners followed, but until the first electrically-powered model appeared in 1905, two people were required to operate them - one to work the pump by bellows or a plunger, the other to handle the cleaning tube. Booth formed his British Vacuum Cleaner Company in 1903, running it in parallel with his equally successful engineering consultancy. His work in the latter area had begun with a post as a draughtsman with Britain's premier marine engine company, Maudslay, Sons and Field. There, Booth worked on the design of engines for two Royal Navy battleships. At this time Booth's keen insight into technological problems and his original flair were noticed by W.B Bassett, one of Maudslay's directors. Bassett was interested in Great Wheels, and in 1894 he chose Booth to work first on the Wheel at Earl's Court, London and afterwards on similar structures in Blackpool and Vienna, and on the 61m (200ft) diameter Great Wheel in Paris.

Booth's design principles were, in essence the same as those governing the design of modern long span suspension bridges. Later in 1902, Booth directed the erection of the Connel Ferry Bridge over Loch Etive, Scotland.

From 1903 until his retirement in 1952, three years before his death at Croydon, Surrey on 14 January 1955, Booth remained chairman of the British Vacuum Cleaner Company. He took special interest in the industrial potential of his famous invention and personally pioneered the development of cleaning installations in large industrial establishments. Both here and in the domestic context - even though he regarded the home vacuum cleaner as something of a toy - Booth was most gratified by the fact that his machines allowed higher standards of hygiene and counteracted dust related diseases.

Bosch, Karl *(1874-1940)*, was a German chemist who developed the industrial synthesis of ammonia, leading to the cheap production of agricultural fertilizers and of explosives.

Bosch was born on 27 August 1874 in Cologne, the eldest son of an engineer. He showed an early aptitude for the sciences and, following a year gaining practical work experience as a metalworker, he went to the University of Leipzig, where he studied chemistry under the noted organic chemist Johannes Wislicenus; he took his doctorate in 1898.

The year after graduating Bosch took a job with the major German chemicals company, Badische Anilin & Sodafabrik (BASF) and by 1902 was working on methods of 'fixing' the nitrogen present in the Earth's atmosphere, a subject for which he was to become famous. At that time, the only major sources of nitrogen compounds essential for the production of fertilizers and explosives were in the natural deposits of nitrates in Chile, thousands of kilometres from industrial Europe. Industrial production of ammonia using the nitrogen in the air would end this dependency on foreign sources.

In 1908 Bosch learned of the work of his fellow-countryman Fritz Haber (1868-1934), who had also been considering the problem. Haber had studied ways of combining nitrogen with hydrogen to form ammonia under the influence of high pressure and metal catalysts. Bosch's employers seized on the work, with its promise of endless supplies of nitrogen compounds, and made him responsible for making Haber's process commercially viable.

He set up a team of chemists and engineers to study the processes Haber had succeeded in producing under laboratory conditions, and to scale them up. For example, the carbon-steel vessels used by Haber to combine to nitrogen and hydrogen was attacked by the hydrogen, causing failure under the high temperature and pressure conditions needed for the reaction to take place. Alloy steel replacements were brought in by Bosch and his team. To produce the required volumes of hydrogen, Bosch also introduced the water-gas shift reaction, where carbon monoxide is combined with steam to produce carbon dioxide and hydrogen. Different catalysts were also investigated.

By the time World War I broke out in 1914, Bosch had completed what was then the largest ever feat of chemical engineering, and the BASF ammonia plant at Oppau was producing 36,000 tonnes of the material in sulphate form using the Haber-Bosch process. Following the heavy demands for its product from the military, the plant was expanded, and another much larger factory was set up in Leuna. At the end of the war, Bosch acted as technical advisor to the German delegation at the armistice and peace conferences.

Following World War I, BASF continued to profit from the work of Bosch, remaining leaders in the technology during the 1920s. Despite further involvement in scientific work on the synthesis of methyl alcohol and of petrol from coal tar, Bosch himself became increasingly involved in adminstration. He was chairman of the vast industrial conglomerate IG Farbeninindustrie AG after its formation from the merger of BASF with other major German industrial concerns in 1925. By 1935, he was chairman of its supervisory board. Illness prevented his close involvement in the group in later years (which were darkened by the rise of the Nazis).

Bosch was also recognized for his work by the scientific community, which bestowed numerous honorary degrees on him including, in 1931, the Nobel Prize in Chemistry, jointly with his compatriot Friedrich Bergius for their work on high-pressure synthesis reactions.

An essentially withdrawn character, Bosch shunned public appearances, and published little. He died in Heidelberg on 26 April 1940.

Boulton, Matthew *(1728-1809)*, was a British manufacturer whose financial support and enthusiasm were of importance in the promotion of James Watt's steam engine.

Boulton was born on 3 September in Birmingham, and it was near there in 1762 that he built his Soho factory. He produced small metal articles such as buckles, buttons, gilt and silver wares, Sheffield plate and the like, having succeeded to his father's business of silver stamper three years earlier. The Soho factory was original in combining workshops of different trades with a warehouse and merchanting lines. Boulton wished to obtain not only the best workmen but the finest artistry for his products, and to this end sent out agents to procure him the best examples of art work not only in metal but also in pottery and other materials.

The growth of the factory led to an increased need for a motive power other than water which was poorly supplied at Soho. This resulted in a meeting with James Watt, who had just developed a steam engine which Boulton was convinced would prove the answer to his wants. In 1769, when Watt's partner became bankrupt, Boulton took his place. Six years later the two men became partners in a steam engine business, obtaining a 25-year extension of the patent. The inventiveness of Watt and the commercial enterprise of Boulton secured the steam engine's future, but not before Boulton had brought himself to the verge of bankruptcy through his support. Helped by the engineer William Murdoch, they established the steam engine by erecting pumps in machines to drain the Cornish tin mines. Boulton foresaw a great industrial demand for steam power and urged Watt to develop the double-action rotative engine patented in 1782 and the Watt engine (1788) to drive the lapping machines in his factory. The testing period of the steam engine was a long one and Boulton was more than 60 years old before it began to make a profitable return.

In 1786 Boulton applied steam power to coining machines, obtaining a patent in 1790. So successful was the process that as well as his home market Boulton supplied coins to foreign governments and to the East India Company. In 1797 he was commissioned to reform the copper currency of the realm. One result of this highly successful venture was to make the counterfeiting of coins much more difficult. Boulton also supplied machines for the Royal Mint near Tower Hill, London, and these continued in efficient operation until 1882.

In 1785 Boulton was made a Fellow of the Royal Society, but submitted no papers to it subsequently. A friendly and generous man, he was acquainted with all the leading scientists of his day. He died in Birmingham on 17 August 1809.

Bourdon, Eugène *(1808-1884)*, was a French instrument maker who developed the first compact and reliable high-pressure gauge.

Born in Paris on 8 April 1808, Bourdon was set to follow his father and become a merchant, but more practical inclinations led him to set up, at the age of 24, his own instrument and machine shop. By 1835 he had established himself at Faubourg du Temple in Paris, where he was to work for the next 37 years.

Bourdon was born into the age of steam, with the opening of George Stephenson's Liverpool to

Manchester Railway taking place in 1830. Bourdon's work reflected this: in the same year that his new instrument works opened in 1832, he presented a model steam engine (complete with glass cylinders) to the Société d'Encouragement pour l'Industrie National. He was to make more than 200 small steam engines at his works, chiefly from demonstration purposes.

Following Richard Trevethick's work with high-pressure steam engines around the turn of the previous century (Watt's earlier engines worked at atmospheric pressure), the problem of measuring high pressures in such engines became apparent. Watt had used a fairly imprecise device for showing the variation of pressure in his relatively low-pressure systems, but the major difficulty lay at the higher pressures. As one atmosphere pressure is equivalent to 76cm (30in) of mercury in U-tube manometer, there was clearly a problem of providing a compact, yet accurate pressure gauge.

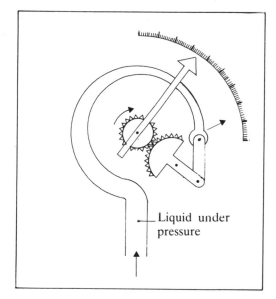

In a Bourdon gauge, liquid (or gas) under pressure flows into a tapering, curved tube closed at one end. The tube tends to straighten, causing movement of levers and gears which turn a pointer round a scale calibrated in pressure.

Bourdon's solution to the problem was simple and ingenious, and is described in the patent for this 'metallic manometer' of 18 June 1849. An ordinary bicycle pump can be used to demonstrate the principle. By pumping air into the rubber connection dangling at the end of the pump, the connector becomes horizontal. This is because the pressure in the tube exceeds that outside (which is

usually atmospheric), and the initially oval cross section of the tube becomes circular, causing the tube to straighten.

In the Bourdon gauge, a metal tube, sealed at one end, is subjected at the other to the pressure through a link to a quadrant rack, geared by a small pinion fixed to the back of a pointer. This moves across the calibrated scale. By using tubes of suitable thickness, a wide range of pressures can be measured using a variety of guages, from fractions of an atmosphere to as much as 8,000 atmospheres, in both liquids and gases. It remains the most widely used gauge for measuring so wide a range of fluid pressures.

Bourdon was, apparently, led to his invention by noticing the change that occurred in a lead cooling coil under internal pressure. Just 2 years after its invention, the Bourdon Gauge had become so renowned for its practicality and versatility that it won for its inventor the Legion of Honour.

By 1872, at the age of 64, Bourdon decided to pass over the management of his business to his sons. Nevertheless, he continued to experiment with instruments during the following 14 years, until his death on 29 September 1884 from a fall while testing a new form of anemometer.

Bramah, Joseph *(1748-1814)*, was one of the most outstanding British engineers of his day. He took out patents for 18 inventions, of which the hydraulic press was probably to be the most significant. Nevertheless, his training of a whole generation of engineers in the craft of precision engineering at the dawn of the Industrial Revolution was probably an even greater legacy to his country than any of his individual inventions.

Bramah was born Joe Brammer on 13 April 1749, in Stainborough, near Barnsley, Yorkshire. He began his employment by working on his father's farm but the age of 16 was made lame in an accident. He became apprenticed to a carpenter and cabinet maker, and on completing his apprenticeship made his way to London to set up his own business. A stream of inventions followed, one of the most useful being the flushing water closet he produced in 1778. When the patent was taken out he changed the spelling of his name to the more fashionable sounding Bramah. In 1784 he patented his most celebrated invention, the Bramah lock. Designed to foil thieves, a specimen of the lock was exhibited in a shop window in 1784 with a 200-guinea reward for anyone who could succeed in picking it. Bramah kept the money for the rest of his lifetime, 67 years passing before the lock was finally opened by a mechanic after 51 hours work. Such an effective lock could be produced only by high precision engineering and machine tools of the finest quality.

To assist him with his work Bramah took into his employ a young blacksmith named Henry Maudslay (the later friend and partner of Sir Mark Isambard Brunel), whose mechanical skill was at least equal to Bramah's. In 1795 Bramah produced the hydraulic press. This device makes use of Pascal's law: pressure exerted upon the smaller of two pistons results in a greater force on the larger one, both cylinders being connected and filled with liquid. For an important part of his press, the seal which ensured water-tightness between the plunger and the cylinder in which it worked, he was particularly indebted to Maudslay who, then only 19, produced the leather U-seal which expands under the fluid pressure.

The possibilities water offered as a means of propulsion were always in the forefront of Bramah's mind. In 1785 he suggested the locomotion of ships by means of screws; in 1790 and 1793 he constructed the hydraulic transmission of power. Among Bramah's other inventions were a machine for numbering bank notes, a beer pump, and machines for making paper and for the manufacture of aerated waters. He also produced a machine which made nibs for pens.

Bramah died in London on 9 December, 1814 and was buried in Paddington churchyard. His press laid the foundation for a whole technology, applications of which include the car-jack, presses for baling waste paper and metal, and the hydraulic braking system for cars and other vehicles which ensures that the brakes on all the wheels operate simultaneously and evenly. Massive girders could be jacked into place, providing a powerful tool for such bridge-builders as Robert Stephenson who used hydraulics to position the massive tubular spans of the bridges over the river Conway and the Menai Straits. Extrusion and forging presses still employ the principles for which Bramah laid the working foundations.

Brindley, James *(1716-1772)*, was a British engineer who, in spite of the most formidable handicaps, became a pioneer of canal building.

Brindley was born near Buxton, Derbyshire, in 1716. Apprenticed to a millwright at the age of 17, he appears to have been completely devoid of promise even at this humble pursuit until the erection of a paper mill with certain novel features brought out in him a remarkable mechanical sense. As a result he was put in charge of his master's shop.

On his master's death Brindley set up his own business at Leek, Staffordshire, where he was soon running a thriving business repairing old machinery and installing new machines. Wedg-

woods, then only a small pottery firm, employed him to construct flint mills. He completed the machinery for a silk mill at Congleton in Cheshire and had some limited success in improving the machinery then used to draw water from mines, although this problem was not effectively solved until the advent of the steam engine.

In 1759 Brindley was engaged by the Duke of Bridgwater to construct a canal to transport coal from the Duke's mines at Worsley to the textile manufacturing centre of Manchester. He persuaded the Duke to change his plan of using locks and rivers and approve instead a revolutionary scheme, including a subterranean channel extending from the barge basin at the head of the canal into the river, and the Barton Aqueduct -12m high (40ft) - carried the canal over the river Irwell. Brindley's mechanical skill enabled him to construct impervious banks by 'puddling' clay and the canal simultaneously acted as a mine drain, a feeder for the main canal at the summit level and a barge-carrying canal.

Brindley's achievement, remarkable enough for any man, is made still more noteworthy by his almost complete absence of any formal schooling. He was virtually illiterate, barely able to write his name. He made no calculations or drawings of the tasks he set himself but worked out everything in his head. He was, in a most extreme form, a natural engineer.

The success of the Worsley scheme established Brindley as the leading canal builder in England. His next commission was to construct the Bridgwater canal linking Manchester and Liverpool, after which came others, the most important being the Grand Union Canal which connected Manchester with the Potteries in the Midlands, Derby and Birmingham (completely transforming) the life of the Midlands - the population of the Potteries trebled between 1760 and 1785 the Oxford Canal, the old Birmingham and the Chesterfield Canals, the Staffordshire and Worcestershire Canals, and the Coventry Canal. All these were designed and with only one exception executed by Brindley. In all he constructed 584km (360 miles) of canals.

It is said of Brindley that when faced with an apparently intractable problem he would go home and think it over in his bed. This must not lead one to assume, however, that he took a phlegmatic attitude to his work. He died from his excessive and arduous labours on 27 September 1772, at Turnhurst, Staffordshire.

Brinell, Johann August *(1849-1925)*, was a Swedish metallurgist who developed what became known as the Brinell hardness test, a rapid non-destructive method of estimating metal hardness.

Brinell was born at Bringetofta and attended technical school at Boras. On leaving school he worked as a mechanical designer. In 1875 he was appointed chief engineer at the iron works at Lejofors, and it was there that he became interested in metallurgy. In 1882 he became chief engineer at the Fagersta iron works. While at Gagersta he studied the internal composition of steel during heating and cooling, and devised the hardness test which was put on trial at the Paris Exhibition of 1900. The test is based on the impression left by a small hardened steel ball after it is pushed into a metal with a given force. With minor innovations the test remains in use today. Brinell also carried out investigations into the abrasion resistance of selected materials. He died in Stockholm in 1925.

Based on the idea that a material's response to a load placed on one small point is related to its ability to deform permanently, the hardness test is performed by pressing a hardened steel ball (Brinell test) or a steel or diamond cone (Rockwell test) into the surface of the test piece. The hardness is inversely proportional to the depth of penetration of the ball or cone.

Brunel, Isambard Kingdom *(1806-1859)*, was the only son of Marc Isambard Brunel, and pursued a similar career, marked by hugely ambitious projects unparalleled in engineering history, becoming ever more ambitious as the years progressed.

Born in Portsmouth in 1806, at the age of 14 he was sent to France to the College of Caen in Normandy and later to the Henri Quatre school in Paris. Brunel was appointed resident engineer on his father's Thames Tunnel enterprise when only 19. This promising start was abruptly ended when he was seriously injured by a sudden flood of water into the tunnel. Whilst recuperating from this accident at Bristol, he entered a design competition, submitting four designs for a suspension bridge over the river Avon. The judge, Thomas Telford, rejected all of them in favour of his own. After many battles and a second contest, one of Brunel's designs was accepted. Work on the bridge began in 1833, but owing to lack of funds it was not completed until after its designer's death.

In 1833 Brunel was appointed to carry out improvements on the Bristol docks to enable heavily-loaded merchantmen to berth more easily. It was while working on this project that Brunel's interest in the potential of railways was fired. The famous Rainhill Trials, at which Stephenson's *Rocket* had triumphed, had been held four years previously.

Brunel completed a survey for constructing a railway from London to Bristol which was to be known (with a grandiloquence typical of Brunel)

as the Great Western Railway. This characteristic love of the outsize was again evident in Brunel's decision to adopt a broad gauge of 2.1m (7ft) for his locomotives, a choice which had the advantage of offering greater stability at high speeds. This size was in contrast to Stephenson's 'standard' of 1.44m (4ft 8.5in).

In all, Brunel was responsible for building more than 2,600km (1,600 miles) of the permanent railway of the west of England, the Midlands, and of South Wales. He also constructed two railway lines in Italy, acted as advisor on the construction of the Victoria line in Australia and on the East Bengal railway in India. The bridges which Brunel designed for his railways are also worthy of note. Maidenhead railway bridge had the flattest archheads of any bridge in the world when it was opened, and Brunel's use of a compressed-air caisson to install the pier foundations for the bridge helped considerably to win acceptance of the compressed air technique in underwater and underground constructions.

However, many of Brunel's viaducts were work-a-day timber structures which used cheap, readily-available materials and were designed so that renewal of members was quick and simple. They were only replaced when timber for repair rose to an uneconomic price. Of all the railway bridges Brunel produced, the last and the greatest was to be the Royal Albert, crossing the river Tamar at Saltash. It has two spans of 139m (455ft) and a central pier built on the rock, 24m (80ft) above the high water mark. The bridge was opened in 1859, the year of Brunel's death.

No sooner, it was said, had Brunel provided a new land link between Bristol and London through his Great Western Railway than he decided to extend the link to New York. The means of achieving his aim came in the shape of ships: the *Great Western*, launched in 1837, the *Great Britain* of 1843 and the *Great Eastern* of 1858. Each was the largest steamer in the world at the time of its launch.

Brunel's predilection for large vessels was not simply the outcome of his love for the outsize: there was sound engineering reasoning behind his designs. At the time, there was a strong body of scientific opinion which held that ships could never cross the Atlantic under steam alone because they could not carry enough coal for the journey. And building a larger ship was no remedy, it was argued, because doubling the size of the vessel doubled the drag forces it had to overcome, thus doubling the power needed and therefore the amount of coal required. Brunel was probably the only man of his time who could see the fallacy of this argument. This lay in the fact that the coal-carrying capacity of a ship is roughly proportional to the cube of the vessel's leading dimension, while the water resistance increases only as the square of this dimension. The voyage of the *Great Western* proved Brunel right: when she docked after her first transatlantic voyage she had 200 tonnes of coal left in her bunkers.

The *Great Western* 2,340 tonnes (2,300 tons) displacement, was a timber vessel driven by paddles. Her crossing of the Atlantic in the unprecedented time of 15 days brought, after initial wariness, the most enthusiastic acclaim and established a regular steamship between Britain and America.

Brunel's next ship, the *Great Britain* of 3,676 tonnes (3,618 tons) displacement, represented a great advance in the design of the steamship. She had an iron hull and was the first ship to cross the Atlantic powered by a propellor. The value of her revolutionary hull was made clear on her maiden voyage, when she was beached in Dundrum Bay on the Southern Coast of Ireland. She remained there for the best part of a year without suffering serious structural damage. As a passenger ship, the *Great Britain* was an unprecedented success, remaining in service for 30 years, sailing to San Francisco, journeying regularly to Australia and even serving as a troopship.

Then, in what was thought to be the final chapter of her life, the ship was badly damaged off Cape Horn in 1866, managing to struggle to the Falkland Islands only to be condemned. She lay, a hulk that refused to rot, in Sparrow cove until she was salvaged by the *Great Britain* project, set up in 1968. Through the efforts of the enthusiasts, who towed her to Montevideo and from there to Bristol, the *Great Britain* entered the dock where she was made on 19 July 1970, exactly 127 years-from the day she was floated out.

On January 31, 1858 Brunel witnessed the spectacular sideways launching of his last ship, the *Great Eastern,* which was to remain the largest ship in service until the end of the 19th century. Well over ten times the tonnage of his first ship, it was 211m (692ft) in length, had a displacement of 32,513 tonnes (32,000 tons), and was the first ship to be built with a double iron hull. She was driven by both paddles and a screw propellor.

Initially the *Great Eastern* was beset with problems. There was constant trouble with her engines and the day after she set out on a new commissioning trial Brunel, who was too ill to be on the vessel, was struck down with paralysis. Unable to delegate responsibility, the work and worry of his many other enterprises had finally broken his health. He died at his home in London on 15 September 1859, having heard that an explosion aboard the *Great Eastern* had apparently brought this most ambitious enterprise to nothing. Despite the damage this was not the end of his great ship. She was used successfully as a troop ship, and her greatest moment came in 1866 when, under the supervision of the great physicist Lord Kelvin, when she was used to lay down the first successful transatlantic cable.

Brunel was elected to the Royal Society in 1830, at the age of 24, and was made a member of most of the leading scientific societies in Britain and abroad. These honours, however, seem scant reward for such a giant in an age which bred such engineering giants. He was the last, and the greatest, of them all.

Brunel, Marc Isambard *(1769-1849),* was a French-born English inventor and engineer who is best remembered for his success in overcoming the age old problem of tunnelling in strata beneath water. His most notable achievement was the construction of the Thames Tunnel.

Born in Hacqueville in Normandy, Brunel served 6 years in the French navy, but left France in 1793, then at the peak of Revolutionary fervour, because of his royalist sympathies. His new home was the United States where he practised as an architect and civil engineer in New York, finally becoming the city's chief engineer. Here, besides surveying, canal engineering and constructing buildings, he advised on the improvement of the defences of the channel between Staten Island and Long Island, built an arsenal, and designed a cannon foundry.

While he was in America, Brunél developed an improved method for manufacturing ships' pulley blocks: at the time a 74-gun ship used 1,400 blocks, all of which had to be made by hand. Acting on the advice of a friend, Brunel sailed for England in 1799 and took the drawings of his invention to Henry Maudslay in London.

Maudslay, a pioneer of machine tools and a former pupil of Joseph Bramah, was impressed by Brunel's designs with the result that the 43 machines operated by 10 men produced blocks superior in quality and consistency to those which previously 100 men had made by hand. Historically it was a portent of what was soon to become a universal trend: specialist machine tools, each performing one of a series of operations and taking over almost all the many labours formerly performed by hand.

Brunel was a tireless and prolific inventor. Among the gadgets he devised were machines for sawing and bending timber, bootmaking, knitting stockings, printing, copying drawings and manufacturing nails.

In 1814 the first of a series of disasters overtook Brunel when fire badly damaged his sawmill at Battersea. The heavy loss this occasioned him brought to the surface the financial incompetence with which his partners were conducting his enterprises. Brunel soon found himself heavily in debt, a condition which worsened when in the following year the final defeat of Napoleon at Waterloo brought peace to Europe, the government accordingly ceasing to pay for a workshop producing army boots. In 1821 Brunel was imprisoned for several months for debt, being released only when friends eventually obtained from the government a grant of £5,000 for his discharge on the condition that he should remain in England.

In 1825 Brunel started work on his last and longest commission: the construction of a tunnel under the Thames to link Rotherhithe with Wapping. Brunel took out a patent on a revolutionary tunnelling shield in 1818, a move that hastened his subsequent appointment as engineer of the Thames Tunnel Company. Although the project ended in success it underwent many reverses, took 18 years to complete and shattered Brunel's health long before its completion.

At the time of the tunnel's construction, nothing so ambitious had been attempted before. The shield Brunel had designed covered the area to be excavated and consisted of 12 separate frames comprising altogether 36 cells in each of which a workman could be engaged at the workface independently of the others. The whole device obtained its propulsion from screw power which drove it forward in 114mm (4.5in) steps (the width of a brick) as the work progressed.

All too often, however, excavation had to stop. Five times water burst through the thin layer of earth beneath which the diggers worked, forcing a halt. Fortunately the shield always held, preventing total catastrophe. The long delays caused by these reverses put the scheme's finances under a severe strain. At one point, the whole operation came to a halt through lack of funds, the tunnel was bricked up and for 7 years no more work was done. When the operation was resumed, a much larger shield was introduced to cover the 120m (400ft) of the tunnel already constructed. The excavations took place only 4m (14ft) under the riverbed at its lowest point.

The Thames tunnel was opened in 1843, and was the first public sub-aqueous tunnel ever built. Of a horseshoe cross-section, its total length was 406m(1,506ft)and its width 11m(37ft) by height 7m(23ft).Brunel, elected to the Royal Society in 1814, was knighted in reward for his labours in 1814. The public flocked to go through the long awaited tunnel and in three and a half months more than a million people had passed through it. The first trains used the tunnel in 1865. It is now part of the London Underground system.

Bush, Vannevar *(1890-1974)*, was an American electrical engineer and scientist who developed several mechanical and mechanical-electrical analogue computers which were highly effective in the solution of differential equations. During World War II he was scientific advisor to President Roosevelt and was instrumental in the initiation of the atomic bomb project. Later he greatly influenced the development of post-war science and engineering in the United States, being instrumental in the setting-up and running of the Office of Scientific Research and Development and its successor, the Research and Development Board.

Bush was born in Everett, Massachusetts. His father had first been a sailor but later became a clergyman. During his childhood Vannevar developed an interest in practical things and constructed a radio receiver when they were almost unknown. He attended a local high school and then went on to Tufts College. He was forced to supplement the little money he had to support himself by washing dishes and giving private coaching in mathematics. In 1913 Bush received BSc and MSc degrees, the latter being for a thesis on a machine for plotting the profile of the land. He patented this device, which combined a gear mechanism mounted between two bicycle wheels which recorded the vertical distance the machine had risen while a paper was moved forward proportional to the distance travelled; a pen recorder drew the profile. After graduation he obtained a job as an engineer with the General Electric Company, but was made redundant shortly afterwards. This misfortune inspired him to read for a doctorate in engineering at the Massachusetts Institute of Technology (MIT). He proved himself so able at his task that he gained his degree in 1916 after only one year of study. From 1932 he held senior positions at MIT, including that of Dean of the Engineering School. He died of a stroke on 28 June 1974.

During World War I he worked on a magnetic device for detecting submarines. In 1919 he returned to MIT and was appointed associate professor of power transmission. In his research on the distribution of electricity, many problems arose which contained differential equations. Such equations, containing differential coefficients, can be difficult and time-consuming to solve in an explicit way, even if a solution is possible - an algebraic solution is of little use to a practising engineer who needs numbers with which to work. In about 1925 Bush began to construct what he called the Product Integraph. It contained a linkage to form the product of two algebraic functions and represent it mechanically. He also devised a watt-hour meter, a direct ancestor of the electricity meter now found in nearly all homes, which integrated the product of electric current and voltage. By similarly using current and voltage to represent equations, his 'calculus' machine was able to evaluate integrals involved in the solution of differential equations.

The Product Integraph, while suitable for solving the problems Bush had encountered, was limited to the solution of first order differential equations. A device capable of the solution of second order equations would be much more useful to electrical engineers, and to scientists generally. There was, however, a complication in coupling two watt-hour meters together. Bush found the solution by coupling one of the meters to a mechanical device known as a Kelvin Integrator, after the physicist Lord Kelvin. In this a small wheel of radius r rests on a disc a distance y from its centre. The disc is turned at a uniform rate x and the value for y is varied by moving the rotating dic and shaft along racks. The small wheel is connected to the output shaft, which gives a mechanical analogy of the integral $1/r \ y \ dx$

In 1931 Bush began work on an almost totally mechanical, and very much more ambitious machine known as the Differential Analyser. This machine had 6 integrators, 3 input tables and an output table, which showed the graphical solution of an equation. The Bush analyser was the model for developments in the mechanical world, and many similar machines were built. One, a large differential analyser at Manchester University was completed in 1935 and now an exhibit in the Science Museum, London.

Following the success of the Differential Analyser, Bush built several specific purpose analysers for solving problems related to electrical networks and for the evaluation of particular types of integrals. Then he built another large analyser, this time with many of the operations electrified, and a tape input that reduced the time taken for setting up a problem from days to minutes.

Bush's machines, and others that had been built in the United States, were used during World War II for military purposes, particularly the calculation of artillery range tables. The same military applications spawned the new machine, the digital electronic computer, which was to be the downfall of mechanical analogue devices.

One of Bush's other inventions was a cipher-breaking machine which played a large part in breaking Japanese codes. One of his less practical devices was a bird perch which dropped the birds the garden owner did not want to encourage. There were also many more patented and unpatented inventions to Bush's name.

C

Callendar, Hugh Longbourne *(1863-1930)*, was the British physicist and engineer who carried out fundamental investigations into the behaviour of steam. One of the results was the compilation of reliable steam tables that enabled engineers to design advanced steam machinery.

Callendar was born on 18 April 1863, at Hatherop, Gloucestershire. Callendar was educated at Marlborough where he was joint editor of the school magazine. At Marlborough he spent his spare time reading science although he was a classics scholar. He obtained first class honours degrees in classics (1884) and mathematics (1885) at Cambridge, then studied physics under Sir J.J Thomson. After becoming a fellow of Trinity College, Cambridge in 1886, with a substantial research grant, he started to study medicine, devised his own shorthand system then entered Lincoln's Inn to study law in 1889.

From 1888 to 1893 he was Professor of Physics at the Royal Holloway College, Egham. Thomson persuaded him to take up science in earnest, and in 1893 he accepted a professorship in physics at McGill College, Montreal. After 6 months there, he returned to marry Victoria Mary Stewart, whom he had met at Cambridge. They returned to Montreal together and in 1898 the family, which now included three children, left Montreal when Callendar was offered the Chair of Physics at University College, London.

In 1901 much larger chemistry and physics departments were built for the Royal College of Science in South Kensington and Callendar was appointed the new Professor of Physics, a chair which he held for 29 years. In 1905 he went to Spain to observe a total eclipse of the Sun for the Royal Society, using his own design of shielded coronal thermopile.

He moved his family to Ealing in 1906 and was elected President of the Royal Physical Society for the 1910-1911 term, having been treasurer for ten years. In 1912 he was President of Section A of the British Association.

During World War I Callender was a consultant to the Board of Inventions which received more than 100,000 'war-winning' ideas. In 1902 he published his great treatise, *'The properties of steam and thermodynamic theory of turbines'*, and was invited by Sir Charles Parsons to become a consultant.

In addition to his main research on steam, he

served as Director of Engine Research for the Air Ministry from 1924. Callendar died of pneumonia on 21 January 1930 in London; his wife survived him by 28 years.

Unlike most gases, steam used to power boilers, engines, turbines and other equipment does not follow easily-interpreted laws. Its behaviour must therefore be predicted by the use of tables or graphs. Steam tables had been produced in different countries from experimental results but the researches did not take into account the laws of thermodynamics, so the tables were unreliable. Callendar was the first to compile accurate tables, and these accelerated the development of turbines and other equipment dramatically.

While he was at Cambridge Callendar's main research was on the platinum resistance thermometer with which he obtained an accuracy of $0.1^{\circ}C$ ($14^{\circ}F$) in $1000^{\circ}C$ ($1832\,F$) - about 100 times better than previous results. It was not until 40 years later, in 1928, that the method was adopted as an international standard.

This work led to recording temperatures on a moving chart, a principle now fundamental to any branch of science or industry which requires a continuous record of temperatures.

Callendar's research topics were varied, most of them connected with thermodynamics. He carried out experiments on the flow of steam through nozzles, producing much information of great value to steam turbine designers. With the collaboration of Howard Turner Barnes in Montreal, he developed his method of continuous electric calorimetry used to measure the specific heat of liquids. He also worked on anti-knock additives for fuels.

Callendar was not only an experimental physicist but also a talented engineer and mechanic (he converted the Stanley steam car to run on compressed air). He gave engineers fundamental tool with which they advanced the state of engineering, leading to the highly efficient plant in operation in the early 1980s.

Carnegie, Andrew *(1835-1919)*, was a Scottish-born American industrialist whose willingness to adopt new methods of steel-making was instrumental in advancing both the techniques and commercial potential of the iron and steel industry.

Carnegie was born in Dunfermline into a poor weavers's family which, when he was 13 years old, emigrated to the United States. He was largely self-educated and began work as a telegraph messenger. After having held a variety of jobs and having saved some capital, he bought shares in a railroad company and land containing oil in Pennsylvania. These investments laid the foundation for his eventual huge fortune. After the American Civil War he became an iron manufacturer and built great iron and steel works in Pittsburgh. Apart from his fame as a steel-maker he is best known for his philanthropic activities, giving much of his fortune to the provision of libraries, a craft school, music centre and many other public amenities in the United States, Britain and Europe. Carnegie scorned the word 'philanthropist', calling himself, in his later years, 'a distributor of wealth for the improvement of mankind.'

The American iron industry received a great impetus from the Civil War. Until this time the country had no great steel industry, but the sudden demand for war materials, railway supplies and the like brought fortunes to the previously struggling ironmasters of Pittsburgh. Carnegie was 30 years old when the war ended and he had not yet begun his work in this field. It was not until 1873 that he concentrated on steel, having made a small fortune in oil and taken several trips to Europe selling railroad securities. His operations in bond selling, soil dealing and bridge-building were so successful that conservative Pittsburgh businessmen regarded him with a mixture of doubt and jealousy. Carnegie's European tours, however, had results of great consequence. He came into close touch with British steel makers - then the world's leaders - and became closely acquainted with the Bessemer process and he formed a friendship with Henry Bessemer (1813-1898), which was maintained until the latter's death.

Bessemer patented his process for the manufacture of steel in 1856, (based on the idea of blowing air through the molten steel to oxidize impurities) which the Carnegie Company adopted with great success. Then in 1867, William Siemens (1823-1883) invented the open-hearth process, after the French engineer Pierre Emile Martin had made the first open-hearth furnace. Always adventurous, and with tremendous foresight, Carnegie scrapped most of the equipment used in the old processes and invested heavily in the new one. Pittsburgh is situated conveniently near to abundant supplies of coal, iron ore and limestone and has become the leading iron and steel producing centre in the world.

Carnegie's success was the result of optimism, enthusiasm and courage. He was not a gambler; he detested the speculative side of Wall Street. He did make one gamble of titanic proportions however - and won. He wagered everything he possessed on the industrial future of the United States and its economic potential. He was probably the most daring man in American industry; his insistence on having the most up-to-date machines, his readiness to discard costly equipment as soon as something better appeared has become a tradition in the steel trade.

Cartwright, Edmund *(1743-1828)*, was a British clergyman who invented various kinds of textile machinery, the most significant of which was the power loom which helped initiate the Industrial Revolution.

Cartwright was born in Marnham, Nottinghamshire, and received his early education at Wakefield Grammar School. At the age of only 14 he went to University College, Oxford, and the regulations were changed to enable him to be awarded his BA earlier than usual (in 1764). In that same year he was elected a Fellow of Magdalen College, gaining his MA two years later. He recieved the perpetual curacy of Brampton near Wakefield, and became rector of Goadby Marwood, Leicestershire, in 1779. He was prebendary of Lincoln from 1786 until his death in 1828.

Cartwright was an innovator, always curious and on the look-out for new ways of doing things. At Goadby Marwood he made agricultural experiments on his glebe land, and while on holiday at Matlock he visited the spinning mills of Richard Arkwright (1732-1792) at nearby Cromford. Artkwright had watched cotton weavers working in their homes. They used cotton thread from the side of the loom (the weft), but he noticed that they wove it in and out of Irish linen threads stretching lengthwise. When he asked the reason for this, he was told that they could not spin cotton thread which was fine or strong enough to use for the warp. This motivated Arkwright to invent the spinning frame and, watching it working, Cartwright remarked that Artkwright would have to set his wits to work to invent a weaving-mill. Soon after returning home Cartwright himself set about this task, devoting all his spare time and money to experiment.

Cartwright had never seen the working of the hand-loom and the first machine he made was an inadequate substitute for it. However, he patented it in 1785 and move to Doncaster in the same year where his wife had inherited some property. There he continued to improve the simple water-driven machine, and visited Manchester to have it criticized by the local workmen; he also tried to enlist the help of the local manufacturers. Disappointed in this hope and having taken out two more patents for futher improvements in his loom, he set up a factory at Doncaster for weaving and spinning. His power-loom now worked well and became the parent of all those in use today. It contained an ingenious mechanism which substituted for the hands and feet of the ordinary hand-loom weaver. There was a beam on which the required number of warp-ends was wound side by side, in perfect order. A device called a let-off motion held the warp-ends in place and let them go forwards only as required. The ends were threaded through eyes (loops) in sets of cords or wires called healds, and there was an apparatus which raised some sets of healds and lowered others, thus making a tunnel, called a shed, between the lower and upper warp ends (The healds could be reversed so that the upper and lower layers of warp ends changed places.) The weft was carried to and fro through the shed by the shuttle. There was a device for pressing the weft up tightly against the already woven cloth, and another for keeeping the cloth taut and rolling it up as fast as it was woven.

For centuries Yorkshire had been a principal seat of woollen manufacture, and in 1789 at Doncaster Cartwright invented a wool-combing machine which contributed greatly to lessening the cost of manufacture. Even in the earlier stages of its development, one machine did the work of 20 hand-combers. Petitions against its use poured into the House of Commons from the wool-combers - some 50,000 in number - and a committee was appointed to inquire into the matter; nothing came of the wool-combers agitation.

Cartwright's Doncaster factory was enlarged when a steam engine was erected to power it, and in 1799 a Manchester firm contracted with Cartwright for the use of 400 of his power-looms and built a mill where some of these were powered by steam. The Manchester mill was burned to the ground, probably by workmen who feared to lose their jobs, and this catastrophe prevented other manufacturers from repeating the experiment. Cartwright's success at Doncaster was obstructed by opposition and by the costly character of his processes; in 1793, deeply in debt, he relinquished his works at Doncaster and gave up his property to his creditors. In 1807, however, 50 prominent Manchester firms petitioned the government to bestow a substantial recognition of the services rendered to the country by Cartwright's invention of the power-loom. Cartwright too petitioned the House of Commons, which in 1809 voted him £10,000.

Cayley, George *(1773-1857)*, was an English baronet who spent much of his life experimenting with flying machines, particularly kites and gliders. He eventually constructed a man-carryng glider, but never ventured into the realms of powered flight.

Cayley was born at Brompton, in Yorkshire, the son of wealthy parents. He received a good education and from an early age showed a keen observation and an enquiring mind. Throughout his life he could turn his attention to almost any problem with a degree of success. He is particularly associated with aeronautics and the teaching of engineering, and in later life he helped to found the Regent Street Polytechnic in London.

Cayley first began experimenting with flight after patiently observing how birds use their wings. He realized that they have two functions: the first is a sort of sculling action by the wing tips which provides thrust; the second is the actual lift, achieved by the shape of the wing, which we now refer to as an aerofoil. Air rushing faster over the curved surface of the upper wing creates low pressure and a sucking effect. As a result, the higher pressure on the under surface of the wing gives lift.

His first attempt at a flying invention was a kite fitted with a long stick, a moveable tail for some control, and a small weight at the front for balance. His idea was to create a design which would glide safely but with enough speed to give lift. Spurred on by the success of his first design, he wrote in his diary of how nice it was to see it in flight and 'it gave the idea that a larger instrument would be a better and safer conveyance down the Alps than even a sure-footed mule'.

In 1808, Cayley constructed a glider with a wing area of nearly 28sq. metres (300sq.ft), and was probably the first person to achieve flight with a machine heavier than air. During the next 45 years he worked on many aspects of flight, including helicopters, streamlining, parachutes and the idea of biplanes and triplanes. Eventually, in 1853, he built a triplane glider which carried his reluctant coachman 275m (900ft) across a small valley - the first recorded flight by a person in an aircraft. Although delighted with the results he had attained, he realized that control of flight could not be mastered until a lightweight engine was developed to give the thrust and lift required.

The developments from Cayley's experiments are plain for everyone to see in the modern world, with the use of the aeroplane as a common means of transport. The first successful sustained flight was made by du Temple's clockwork model in 1857 (the year Cayley died) and the first actual man-carrying powered flight was in 1874, but the plane did take off down a slope. It was another 16 years before a piloted plane managed a level-ground take-off, and this was Ader's *Eole*; it hopped about 50m (160ft). True success came with the Wright brothers and the key to their success was, as Cayley had predicted, a lightweight engine.

Churchward, George Jackson *(1857-1933)*, was the British locomotive engineer who contributed much to the Great Western Railway's pre-eminence in locomotive performance and design.

During two decades he produced a range of supremely functional and handsome locomotives, revolutionizing British locomotive practice with steam pressures of 1,551kN/sq. metres (225 psi) superheating, long-travel valves, tapered boilers and cylindrical smokeboxes. He applied his ideas on boiler development to his now almost legendary *Great Bear* of 1908, the longest and most powerful locomotive then built, and his theories on boiler design could still be developed even today.

Churchward was born into a farming comunity South Devon hamlet of Stoke Gabriel. He inherited no engineering tradition but at school was brilliant at mathematics and keenly interested in the nearby broad-gauge South Devon Railway, which he joined in 1873 as a locomotive apprentice at Newton Abbot. In 1876, when the South Devon was absorbed into the GWR, he transferred to the drawing office at Swindon Works. He was soon promoted to inspector of materials, then was appointed assistant manager of the carriage and wagon works (1882), becoming manager in 1885. In 1895 he was promoted to assistant locomotive works manager, and then a few months after to manager. One year later, still in this post, he was appointed assistant locomotive carriage and wagon superintendent to work closely with William Dean.

Churchward became chief mechanical engineer of the GWR in 1902 and introduced a locomotive standardization programme. By 1907 all the standard types had been built in prototype batches. Retiring in December 1921, to be succeeded by C.B Collett, he continued to visit Swindon Works almost daily, a custom which tragically led to his death. On the foggy morning of 19 December 1933 he was hit by one of his successor's locomotives, No 4085 *Berkeley Castle*, and died instantly.

When Churchward was appointed to work under Dean, the GWR had a varied collection of locomotives. At only 57, Dean was unhappily deteriorating mentally, but instead of compelling him to retire early the railway's directors brought in Churchward. He was assured that eventually he would take over from Dean, and was given covert approval to start planning the modernization of the entire locomotive fleet.

Churchward envisaged a locomotive stock of only a dozen classes to handle all traffic, and incorporating standardized boilers, wheels, motion, cylinders and tenders. He had already evolved four standard boiler types to suit all his locomotive classes. Greatly impressed with the flat-topped Belpaire fire-box, tapered boiler, long smokebox and combined cylinder casting and half smokebox saddle of US practice, he soon introduced these as standard features on his engines. He developed much longer valve travels with high piston speeds, higher steam pressures and increasing bearing surfaces to fit his concept of a basic two-cylinder engine with sufficient power and flexibility to meet all foreseeable traffic needs.

His first new locomotives, the Atbara class 4-4-0s, were refined into the hugely successful City class 4-4-0s of 1903. On 9 May 1904 one of these, *City of Truro* (now preserved in the GWR museum at Swindon) reached the then incredible speed of 164.63km/h (102.3mph) down Wellington Bank, Somerset, on a train of five mail vans - 148 tons loaded.

Churchward was impressed with the French Nord Railway's de Glehn 4-cylinder 4-4-2 compounds with 1565kN/sq. metres (227 psi) boiler pressure. He purchased one for trials in October 1903, at the same time building *Albion,* a 2-cylinder 4-6-0 with a 1551kN/sq. metres (225 psi) boiler, rebuilt a year later as a 4-4-2 and 4-6-0 wheel arrangements. Churchward built a further 19 locomotives similar to *Albion* - 13 as 4-4-2s and 6 as 4-6-0s. In 1906 he built a 4-cylinder simple expansion 4-4-2, *North Star,* later converted to a 4-6-0. The French cylinder arrangement was adopted and the tapered boiler worked at 1551kN/sq. metres (225 psi) (far higher than on any railway's locomotives in the UK). The 4-6-0 wheel layout was chosen because it gave twice the adhesion on gradients.

North Star was first of the famous Stars designed for non-stop long-distance running, and the subsequent production run, starting with *Dog Star* in 1907, represented a masterpiece of design with features adopted years later by other locomotive engineers. Between 1907 and 1927 Churchward's 4-6-0s reigned supreme over all other British express locomotives.

In 1908 he produced the giant 4-6-2 *Great Bear*, the first 'Pacific' built in this country and the only one until Gresley's *Great Northern* of 1922. Actually a 'Star' in its basic machinery but with an enormous boiler, it was 55 per cent more powerful and 30 per cent heavier than the 'Stars'. It was the longest and heaviest engine in the country but its performance was by no means exceptional and its weight restricted it to the London to Bristol main line. It served, however, as a potent prestige symbol and featured prominently in GWR publications for many years.

Churchward was not one of the great inventors, and he was almost alone in his close interest in overseas locomotive practice. He could, however, recognize good ideas which he could apply to his own special problems. He perfected his original concept of long-lap, long valve travel, which turned out to be one of the biggest step forwards in steam locomotive development.

Cierva, Juan de la *(1895-1936)*, was a Spanish aeronautical engineer who invented the rotating-wing aircraft known as the autogyro.

Cierva was born at Murcia in south-eastern Spain on 21 September 1895, the son of the Conservative politician, Juan de la Cierva y Penafiel (1864-1938). He was educated in Madrid at the engineering school called the Escuela Especial de Caminos, Canales y Puertos. During his six years there he also studied theoretical aerodynamics on his own, especially the work of Frederick Lanchester (1868-1946). Soon after leaving school he followed his father into politics and was elected to the Cortes, the Spanish parliament, in 1919 and 1922. He showed little enthusiasm for politics, however, for his real interest was the designing of flying machines.

In 1919 he entered a competition to design a military aircraft for the Spanish government. His plan was for a three-engined biplane bomber with an aerofoil section of his own design. When it was tested in May 1919 engine failure caused it to stall in mid-air, and the plane crashed. This accident led Cierva to turn away from fixed-wing flying machines and to search for a machine with a rotating-wing mechanism that would be less vulnerable to engine failure. His first three designs, which all had blades fixed to the motor shaft, were unsuccessful. His fourth design introduced freely-rotating wings. On 19 January 1923 the new gyroplane, to which Cierva gave the name Autogiro, was tested at Getafe, Spain, and it flew for 182 metres (200 yds).

The autogyro consisted of one nose-mounted engine driving a conventional propeller, a fuselage, and a large, freely-rotating rotor mounted horizontally above the fuselage. Allowing the blades of the motor to pivot on hinges, instead of being rigidly fixed to the shaft, largely solved the problem of uneven lift being generated by the advancing and retreating blades. In order to gain sufficient lift for the aurogyro to take off, rope was wound many times around the rotor shaft and then pulled by a gang of men to turn the rotor quickly.

After the initial success of 19 January three more test flights were quickly arranged and just two days later, on 21 January, the autogyro completed a 4km (2.5 mile) circuit in three-and-a-half minutes. The usefulness of the new machine to the police and maritime rescue services was immediately recognized and, after minor adjustments were made to eliminate teething troubles, full-scale production began in 1925 with the founding of the Cierva Autogyro Company in England. Cierva became technical director and on 18

September 1928 he flew one of the company's aircraft across the English Channel. He then flew one all the way to Spain; and in 1929 he demonstrated his new invention at the National Air Races held at Cleveland, Ohio. Cierva continued to exeriment and to test his own aircraft until he was killed in a crash at Croydon Aerodrome, just south of London, on 9 December 1936.

There is an essential difference between Cierva's machine and the modern helicopter. A helicopter has a powered rotor that rotates horizontally overhead, enabling the machine to rise vertically. As a result, it needs only a small space in which to take off and land. During flight, motion backwards and forwards is achieved by altering the inclination of the rotor blades. To stop the plane from rotating with the rotor, a small secondary rotor is is fitted to the tail; a helicopter can also hover. Cierva's autogyro, on the other hand, was designed in some respects like an ordinary aeroplane, with a propeller to pull it through the air. But instead of fixed wings on each side, it had a revolving rotor - a rotating wing - overhead to provide lift at slow forward speeds and allow it almost vertical descent, although it is not capable of vertical ascent nor the 3600 manoeuvrability of the helicopter. It was this difference that constituted the basis of his invention and which made the autogyro the prototype, and provided some of the performance features of the modern helicopter.

Cockerell, Christopher (Sydney) *(1910-   )*, is the British engineer who invented the hovercraft. This has led to the establishment of a new industry and has stimulated world-wide interest. He also made a major contribution to aircraft radio navigation and communications.

Educated at Gresham's school, Holt, and Peterhouse, Cambridge, where he read engineering, Cockerell graduated in 1931 and spent two years in Bedford with the engineering firm of W H Allen & Sons. He then returned to Cambridge for two years of research into wireless, which was his hobby.

He joined the Marconi Wireless Telegraph Co in 1935, working on VHF transmitters and direction finders, and during World War II, on navigational and communication equipment for bombers, and later, on radar. During this period he filed 36 patents, the most interesting of which are frequency division (1935), the linearization of a transmitter by feedback (1937), pulse differentiation (1938) and various navigational systems.

In 1950 Cockerell left Marconi's and started up a boat hire business on the Norfolk Broads, building boats and caravans. Trained as a de-

velopment engineer, he set himself the task of trying to make a boat go faster. First experiments were on the air lubrication of a hull and later on a 6.1m (20ft) launch.

He was appointed consultant (hovercraft) to the Ministry of Supply and has been director of and consultant to a number of firms working in the field. The winner of many awards and distinctions, Cockerell is a Fellow of the Royal Society. In the 1970s and 1980s he has interested himself in the generation of energy by wavepower and has been chairman of Wavepower Ltd since 1974, the year he was made an Honorary Fellow of Peterhouse.

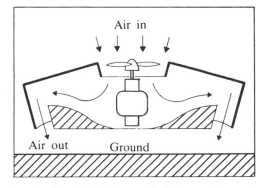

Cockerell's original hovercraft design made use of a peripheral jet of compressed air to achieve lift.

A number of engineers had earlier suggested the use of air lubrication for the reduction of drag. Indeed in the 1870s the British engineer, John Thorneycroft, built test models to check the drag on a ship's hull with a concave bottom in which air could be contained between the hull and the water.

Cockerell concluded after his first experiments with air lubrication that a major reduction in drag could be obtained only if the hull could be supported over the water by a really thick air cushion. This was because the fine structure of the upward pressure of the water, with the craft in motion over waves, varied so much that the pressure peaks broke through the layer of air. With a thin cushion, the best that could be attained was a 50 per cent reduction in skin friction drag.

The first concept of a hovercraft was a sidewalled craft with hinged doors to contain the air, capable of lifting over a wave. The next idea was a water curtain discharged inwards and downwards across the front and back of the craft. The third conception was to replace the water curtain by thin air jets across the bow and stern pointing towards the athwartships centreline of the craft.

The next step for a faster amphibious craft, was a peripheral downward and inward-facing thin jet all round the periphery of the craft. Calculations showed that the power could be provided if the cushion pressure was kept down to reasonable limits. The power requirement was confirmed by some primitive experiments using tin cans as a simple way of constructing an annular jet. This concept was tried out in the experimental SR N1 in 1959.

The first true hovercraft was a 762mm (2ft 6in) balsawood model weighing 127.6g (4.5oz) made in 1955 and powered by a model aircraft petrol engine. It could travel at 20.8km/h (13mph) over land or water. Cockerell's first hovercraft patent was filed on 12 December 1955 and in the following year he formed Hovercraft Ltd. He then began the thankless task of trying to interest manufacturers - shipbuilders said it was an aircraft and aircraft manufacturers said it was a ship.

Realizing that the hovercraft would have considerable military potential, Cockerell approached the Ministry of Supply, the Government's procurement agency for defence equipment. The air cushion vehicle was promptly classified 'secret' in 1956. This meant considerable delays but finally the secret leaked out, the project was declassified and the National Research Development corporation decided to back the idea in 1958. Saunders Roe Ltd, a manufacturer with flying-boat history (and therefore both aircraft and marine experience) built the SR N1 which crossed the English Channel with the inventor on deck.

In the waiting period (1957) Cockerell had come to the conclusion that the hovercraft could not go fast in a seaway without diving into it. He came up with the idea of flexible skirts which gave rise to much derision because nobody could believe that a piece of fabric could be made to support 100 tonnes with a mere $2,873N/m^2$ (60lb/ft^2) compared with, say, $206,843N/m^2$ (30lb/in^2) for a motor car tyre.

Manufacturers and operators in many parts of the world became interested and craft were made in the United States, Japan, Sweden and France while in Britain other companies also began to manufacture. The SR N4 maintained commercial cross-Channel car ferry services in the severest weather conditions and the AP 1-88, the world's first diesel-powered hovercraft, went into service in early 1983.

Apart from passenger and car ferry applications, craft have been used for seismic surveys over shallow water or desert and in search and rescue operations. Military uses include troop carrying during amphibious assaults and as logistic support craft. Future military uses include mine counter-measure work, anti-submarine work, aircraft carrying and missile launching.

Air cushion trains have potential speeds of 480km/h (300mph) and the cost of track for these would be much less than that for conventional trains. However, because the air cushion requires considerable energy to maintain it, opinion has swung towards magnetic levitation for advanced tracked transport.

The technology has been applied to load lifters for heavy industrial plant when crossing bridges that were not stressed for the axle loading involved if normal wheeled transport was to be used. In hospitals, airbeds for supporting burned patients use the hovercraft principle; the hover-mower is one of the most common applications; hovercraft transport heavy loads in Arctic regions; there are few fields where the hovercraft principle is not showing ever-widening applications.

Cockerill, Wilham *(1759-1832)*, was a British engineer who is generally regarded as the founder of the European textile machinery industry.

Cockerill was born in Lancashire, and throughout his childhood showed a remarkable talent for anything mechanical. Being brought up in a district greatly involved in the production of cloth, he naturally found an outlet for his particular genius constructing machinery for that use.

His working career began with the building of 'roving billies' and 'flying shuttles', but in 1794 he decided to seek his fortune elsewhere and chose Russia as the most likely place. He found employment in St Petersburg and, under the patronage of Catherine II, enjoyed a fair measure of success for as long as she ruled. On her death, however, her successor, the madman Paul, imprisoned Cockerill for failing to complete a contract within the given time.

Eventually he escaped to Sweden and there tried to arouse an interest in a textile industry. The Swedes rejected his ideas, and so in 1799 he migrated to Belgium, where he established a flourishing business at Verviers as a manufacturer of textile machinery. In 1802 he was joined in partnership by a James Holden, but their association was short-lived and in 1807 Cockerill transferred his interests to Liège. There, together with his three sons William, Charles and John - who also shared his enthusiasm for constructing machines - he built up a highly successful business making carding machines, spinning frames and looms for the French woollen industry.

After retiring from the firm in 1814 he went to live at the home of his son Charles, at Aix-la-Chapelle (Aachen), and remained there until his death in 1832.

The invention of John Kay's flying shuttle in 1733 had helped to speed up the process of weaving in the English textile industry, but not until the latter half of the 1700s were other significant mechanical designs introduced to streamline the production further. Cockerill's childhood saw the coming of James Hargreaves's 'spinning jenny' in 1770, which enabled spinners to spin several threads at once; Richard Arkwright's water frame, which brought water power to the spinning machines; and the invention of a rotary carding machine to make the possibility of mass production a reality. By the time Cockerill left for Russia in 1794 he had mastered all the techniques of manufacturing the new machines.

Basing his designs on the English machines, Cockerill was able to build up a reputation for first-class workmanship and attention to detail. When, after his previous disappointments, he eventually founded his business in Liège he found a ready market in France. In fact, it was during the era of Napoleon that Cockerill achieved his greatest esteem and his efforts were to a large extent reponsible for breaking the monopoly England had previously held over the continental market.

Colt, Samuel *(1814-1862)*, was the American inventor of what was probably the most successful family of revolving pistols of his time, which revolutionized military tactics.

Born on 19 July 1814, at Hartford, Connecticut, Colt had made up his mind as a boy to become an inventor but his early inventions (which included an abortive four-barrel rifle) were somewhat unreliable. One of his discoveries was that it was possible to fire gunpowder using an electric current. He applied this principle to an explosive mine, but after a disasterous public demonstration (which covered all the spectators with mud), he was sent off to Amherst Academy. Unfortunately, as a result of a fire caused by another of his experiments, he was asked to leave there as well. He then became apprenticed as a seaman.

During a journey to India in 1830, aboard the brig Corlo, Colt made some observations that were to change his life. In watching the helmsman and the wheel he operated, Colt noticed that whichever way the wheel turned, each of its spokes always lined up with a clutch that locked it into position. Colt conceived the idea that the mechanism of the helmsman's wheel could be applied to a firearm.

Grasping the opportunity presented by this, he left the sea at the age of 18 to raise money for a professionally-built prototype. Ever resourceful, he travelled America as 'Dr Coult', giving demonstrations of nitrous oxide (laughing gas) to willing audiences in a series of adventures worthy of Huckleberry Finn.

By 1835, Colt had perfected his revolver, which emulated the helmsman's wheel with its rotating breech which turned, locked and unlocked by cocking the hammer. That year, Colt took out patents in Britain and France and, in 1836, in his native United States. On 5 March 1836 Colt set up a company in Paterson, New Jersey, the Patent Arms Manufacturing Company, where he produced the Colt Paterson, a five-shot revolver with folding trigger and a number of different rifles and shotguns based on the same revolving principle. These models were revolutionary in a market still dominated by the cumbersome 'pepperbox' type of revolver, with their revolving barrels. In the resulting conflict of ideas, in and amid apathy among firearms buyers stemming from the price and unreliability of the early models, Colt's company failed in 1842.

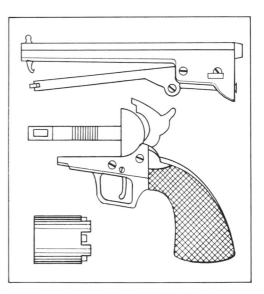

Colt's revolvers, such as this 1851 'Navy', were manufactured to high tolerances using parts that were interchangeable, so that spare parts bought anywhere were guaranteed to fit.

Colt temporarily turned his attention to inventing electrically discharged submarine mines and running a telegraph business. Events, however, soon restored him to his original course when, in 1846, the Mexican-American War broke out. Colt Paterson revolvers had come into the possession of the Texas Rangers, who persuaded the government to order Colt revolvers for use in the War. Colt had to be tracked down first, but was of course delighted with an order to make 1,000 pistols for the army. Having no factory of his own, Colt contracted the work out to Eli Whitney at Whitneyville, Connecticut, and before long the US Army was receiving supplies of the new revolver. Captain Walker, who had succeeded in tracing Colt, contributed his own ideas to the .44 calibre revolver, which became known as the Colt Walker 'Dragoon'. The pioneers then starting to open up the American West adopted the Colt with alacrity, since it was superior to the one- or double-shot pistol against hostile Indians and wild life.

Colt used the profits from his early sales to buy land at Hartford, where in 1847 he rented premises and in 1854 built a large factory. Colt's Hartford company is still in existence; the factory burnt down in 1864, but was later rebuilt. Colt could now increase the types of firearms he produced, and by 1855 he had the largest private armoury in the world. One of Colt's new weapons was the .31 caliber Pocket Model first produced in 1848, and in 1851 he produced his famous percussion revolver, the .36 calibre Colt Navy. The Rootes .28 and the Army followed in 1860, and the Police Model in 1862.

By this time, the American Civil War had begun. Colt, whose pre-war sympathies were with the secessionist Confederate South, changed allegiance to the Unionist North once fighting started in 1860 and supplied thousands of guns to the United States government.

While his patents (which he defended vigorously) lasted, Colt had a virtual monopoly of the firearms market. In time, however, his rivals found ways around the restrictions of the patent laws, and eventually the patents simply expired.

In the teeth of bitter opposition from established British arms manufacturers, Colt set up a factory in Pimlico, London, in 1852. He also decided to show his revolver at the Great Exhibition of the same year. Orders to equip the British armed forces, including those fighting in the Crimea, followed, with customers being supplied by a variety of models produced in both Hartford and London. The Pimlico factory closed down in 1856, but Colt retained an agency in London until 1913.

By the time of his death at Hartford, on 10 January 1862, Colt could leave behind a vast and efficient company, and a considerable personal fortune. He had succeeded in marketing a well-conceived product whose success stemmed from the mass production of interchangeable parts which needed little hand finishing in assembly. As a result, he made a major contribution to both the development of repeating firearms and to the process of mass production by machine tools.

Corliss, George Henry *(1817-1888)*, was an American engineer and inventor of many improvements to steam engines, particularly the Corliss valve for controlling the flow of steam to and through the cylinder(s).

Little is known about the early life of Corliss except that he was born on 2 June 1817 in Easton, New York. By the time he was in his late twenties he had moved to Providence, Rhode Island (1844), where he became interested in steam engines, concerning himself particularly with attempts to improve their performance.

He took out the first of his many patents in 1849, for the Corliss valve. In 1856 he founded the Corliss Engine Company which was to become one of the largest steam engine manufacturers in the United States and, incidentally, helped to make Providence a major tool and machinery centre. His company designed and built the largest steam engine then in existence to power all the exhibits in the Machinery Hall at the 1876 Philadelphia Centenial Exposition. With a weight of 630 tonnes and a 9 metre flywheel, the engine was not surprisingly billed as the 'Eighth Wonder of the World'.

In the 1840s the most advanced valves then in use suffered from several disadvantages inherent to their design. Most regulated steam flow by sliding a plate over the port into the piston chamber in such a way that while steam entered one end of the chamber it was exhausted from the other. Unequal wear on the sliding parts caused them to lose their steam-tight fit; they were also heavy to operate and, with the steam entering and exhausting through the same passage, they suffered considerable heat loss.

An essential feature of the Corliss valve was the separate inlet and exhaust port at each end of the cylinder (giving a total of four valve units per engine in twin cylinder engines). This saved heat loss and also cut down the 'dead' space at the ends of the chamber using older valves where the ports were located along the side of the chamber. Of equal significance to this was Corliss's realization that for maximum efficiency the valves must open and close as quickly as possible. This he achieved by a spring-loaded action.

Like any good invention the basic principle of the valve was very simple. On the first stroke, one inlet valve opened, allowing steam under pressure to enter that end of the cylinder and force the piston to move to where an exhaust valve was open. On the next stroke these two valves closed, and the other inlet and exhaust valves opened again allowing steam to enter the cylinder and force the piston to move back in the other direction. Because of its compact size, the reduced wear on moving parts, and heat saved by having separate steam inlet and outlet paths, this valve greatly improved the efficiency of large steam engines. The success of Corliss's design is best shown by the fact that it continued in use for as long as large steam engines were manufactured, long after its inventor's death on 2 February 1888.

Cousteau, Jacques-Yves *(1910-   )*, is the French diver who invented the aqualung and pioneered many of the diving techniques used today.

Cousteau was born on 11 June 1910 at Saint André in the Gironde. He became a gunner in the French navy shortly before the outbreak of World War II, and worked in Marseille for Naval Intelligence during the Nazi Occupation. His interest in diving came in 1936 when he borrowed a pair of goggles and peered beneath the surface of the Mediterranean. He was instantly captivated by what he saw. Throughout the occupation he and his colleagues Frederick Dumas, Phillipe Taillez and Emile Gagnan experimented with diving techniques in comparative peace.

Cousteau initially experimented with available naval equipment. Le Prieur had invented the compressed air cylinder in 1933 that released a continuous flow of air through the face mask. This system restricted the diver to very short periods of time beneath the surface. Cousteau designed an oxygen rebreathing apparatus that would give him longer dives, but after two near-fatal accidents he abandoned his ideas. He also tested the Fernez equipment, which fed compressed air to the diver from the surface, and again was nearly killed in the process.

The turning point came in 1942, when Cousteau met Emile Gagnan, an expert on industrial gas equipment. Gagnan had designed an experimental demand valve for feeding gas to car engines. Together, Gagnan and Cousteau developed a self-contained compressed air 'lung', the aqualung. In June 1943 Cousteau made his first dive with it, achieving a depth of 18m (60ft).

In 1945, Cousteau founded the French Navy's Undersea Research Group. Much of its early diving work involved locating and defusing the mines left behind by the Germans. He fitted out and commanded the Group's research ship, the *Elie Monnier*, on many oceanographic expeditions.

In 1951 he set out in the research ship *Calypso* on a four-year voyage of exploration beneath the oceans the world. He went on to make a series of films about his many voyages aboard the ship, becoming a popular television personality as a result.

The aqualung has changed very little since Cousteau's original design. A free-swimming, air-

breathing diver can now descend to depths of over 60m (200ft) and carry out work. Greater depths require extreme care and sophisticated gas mixtures to avoid danger.

Without Cousteau's contribution to the science of diving, the massive underwater tasks performed offshore for the oil industry and others would have been vastly more difficult. The foundations he laid for modern divers are being built upon constantly, allowing more difficult tasks to be carried out in ever more adverse condtions.

Cort, Henry *(1740-1800)*, was a British inventor who devised a method of producing high-quality iron using a reverberating furnace.

Cort was born in Lancaster, and at the age of 25 he left his home town to seek his fortune in London. He became an agent for the Navy and was responsible for purchasing their guns. At this time (1765) all the best metal suitable for arms manufacture was imported from abroad, mainly from Russia, Sweden and North America. Cort, realizing the potential, experimented to find a method of making this high grade metal in England, and in 1775 he set up his own forge at Fontley, near Farnham.

By 1784 he was in a position to apply for a patent on his process of 'puddling and rolling', which allowed bar-iron to be produced on a large scale and of a high quality. The process came at a particularly fortunate time for England's iron production, for with the advent of the Napoleonic Wars, pig-iron requirements rose from 40,000 tonnes in 1780 to 400,000 tonnes by 1820. But he was somewhat unwise in his choice of financial backer. He chose Samuel Jellicoe, a naval paymaster, who without Cort's knowledge obtained the money from public funds. When Jellicoe was found out he committed suicide and Cort, having handed over the rights to his patent as security for the capital, was left bankrupt. His patent was confiscated by the Admiralty and he was forced to watch the iron-masters of England grow wealthy on his hard work. He and his large family were reduced to living off a pension of £200 a year, which the state eventually granted him.

The skill of iron smelting has been known for centuries. Using a blast furnace fired by charcoal, the process remained unchanged until the early 1700s, when several people attempted to better the traditional ways. Three main factors limited production. The first was the choice of fuel. Using charcoal meant that the iron works, of necessity, were sited near forests. The second was the source of power to work the bellows and the forge-hammer. A water wheel was a natural solution, but its efficiency depended upon the amount of water available and as a result production was often seasonal. The fluctuation of water supply also influenced the third factor, transport, which relied heavily on the rivers.

Coal answered the first problem, the steam engine was the solution for the power, and canals took over from natural waterways. Coal however, although cheaper, still produced a poor quality iron and it was not until Abraham Darby used coal, converted to coke, at his Coalbrookdale works (and combined it with the right type of ore) that a pig-iron was made that could be forged into bar-iron. Even so, the quality tended to be unreliable.

Cort experimented and found a solution in his 'puddling and rolling' process, which removed the impurities by stirring the pig-iron on the bed of a reverberatory furnace. (This is a furnace with a low roof, so that the flames in passing to the chimney are reflected down on to the hearth, where the ore to be smelted can be heated without its coming into direct contact with the fuel.) The 'puddler' turned and stirred the mass until it was converted into a malleable iron by the decarburizing action of air circulating through the furnace. The iron was then run off, cooled and rolled into bars with the aid of grooved rollers.

The significance of Cort's work was such that at last England did not have to rely on imported iron and could become self-sufficient. His method of manufacture combined previously separate actions into one process, producing high-class metal relatively cheaply and quickly, allowing iron production to increase to meet the growing needs of the industrial age.

Cotton, William *(1786-1866)*, was a British inventor, financier and philanthropist who greatly publicized the work of an earlier hydrographer and inventor, Joseph Huddart. He is probably best known, however, for inventing a knitting machine which made possible significant advances in the production of hosiery.

Cotton was born in Leyton, Essex. On leaving school at the age of 15, he entered a counting-house as a clerk and all subsequent progress was as a result of self-education. In 1807 he was admitted to a partner in the firm of Huddart & Co. in Limehouse, London. This business had been founded a few years earlier to promote the manufacture - on a large scale - of an ingenious cordage-making machine designed by Joseph Huddart. The attention of Huddart was drawn to this field when, in the course of travelling for the East India Company, he saw a ship's cable snap. He thereupon worked on a method 'for the equal distribution of the strains upon the yarn'. When put on the market, his machine was to bring him an appreciable fortune.

Cotton did well in Huddart's firm and was eventually entrusted with its general management. He disposed of Huddart's machinery to the government in 1838. In the same year he wrote a memoir of Huddart with an account of his inventions, which was privately printed in 1855. In recognition of this publication he received a silver medal from the Institution of Civil Engineers.

In 1821 Cotton was elected a Director of the Bank of England, a position he continued to hold until a few months before his death. He held the Governershipof the Bank of England over the years 1843 to 1846. A lasting memorial of his tenancy of this high office came about through his invention of the 'governor' and automatic weighing machine for sovereigns. It weighed these coins at a rate of 23 per minute, discharging the full and underweight specimens into separate compartments.

Although Cotton prospered in business, it is nevertheless as a philanthropist that he is chiefly remembered, notably for the building of schools, churches and lodging houses in the East End of London. After his death he was commemorated by a painted window in St Paul's Cathedral, raised by public subscription.

It was not until 1864 that Cotton secured a patent for the knitting machine to be used in hosiery, the principal invention for which he is remembered. The machine he produced was remarkable for its adaptability: it had a straight-bar frame which automatically made fully-fashioned stockings knitted flat and sewn up the back.

Subsequent improvements to Cotton's original machine have largely been directed at either increasing the capacity of the machine or producing fabric of even finer gauge. Increased capacity can be attained only by the use of larger and faster models, and finer gauge work requires finer needles and sinkers. A modern machine making fully fashioned silk or nylon hose may have as many as 40 needles to 2.5cm (1in) and may produce 32 stockings at once. The reliability of such machines obviously depends on the accuracy with which they are made, and in this respect the hosiery industry owes much to improvements in engineering techniques. Towards the end of the nineteenth century the making of hosiery machines became an important industry in Germany and the United States, and in time the types used in these countries became also widely used in Britain.

Crompton, Rookes Evelyn Bell *(1845-1940)*, was a British engineer who became famous as a pioneer of the dynamo, electric lighting and road transport. During his long lifetime he also contributed to the development of various standards, both electrical and mechanical, including the British

Association standards for small screw threads. In his later years, through experiment and design, he contributed to the design of the military tank.

Crompton was born near Thirsk in Yorkshire on 31 May 1845. His early days were spent in nearby Ripon. When he was eleven he accompanied his parents to Gibralter on HMS *Dragon*, which was commanded by his mother's cousin. He then sailed on to the Crimea as a cadet on the same ship, and visited his brother during the siege of Sebastopol. When he returned to school in the autumn of 1856 - still only 12 years old - he was one of the youngest decorated members of the Royal Navy, with the Crimea Medal and the Sebastopol Clasp.

In 1858, after two years at Elstree, he entered Harrow School. During his holidays he built first a model steam-driven road locomotive, and then a full-size one called *BlueBell*. On leaving school in 1864 he went to India as an army officer. During his service there he continued to develop his road vehicles and transferred out of his regiment so that he could concentrate his efforts on the development of steam locomotives for road haulage. The results were successful both in India and at home, but they were in many ways ahead of their time. The poor quality of roads, the cheapness of other forms of transport and the developing railway system were to eclipse his pioneering work in this area.

On his return from service he became involved with the Stanton Iron Works in Derbyshire, which was owned by a branch of his family. He redesigned the works and brought some dynamos from France to power his electric lighting system. This innovation spread to other firms. At first he acted as a supplier of the lighting sets, and then as a manufacturer through his firm of Crompton and Co. Electrical Engineers. These were the early days of electricity generation and Crompton found an area ready for exploitation. He developed and manufactured generating systems for lighting town halls, railway stations and small residential areas. Direct current electricity of about 400 volts was generated and used with large storage batteries to allow the systems to operate smoothly within a range of demands. Later the supply of electricity became a highly profitable and fast growing area, particularly with the coming of Swan's incandescent filament lamp, and Crompton's Kensington Court Electric Light Co. Ltd. was formed. He believed strongly in his direct current system with batteries, and there was much competition between him and his younger contemporary Ferranti, with his rival alternating current system. As time went on Ferranti's method proved the better for large distribution networks, but Crompton's machines fared very well within their limitations.

During the Boer War, Crompton served in South Africa as commandant of the Electrical Engineers Royal Engineers Volunteer Corps, which was later to become the Royal Corps of Electrical and Mechanical Engineers (REME). At the beginning of the present century he returned to road transport, and contributed considerably to the principles of automobile engineering and the maintenance and design of roads which would withstand the new demands put upon them. He was a founder member of what is now the Royal Automobile Club.

His firm, which had manufactured all kinds of electrical machinery and instruments, became, after a merger in 1927, Crompton Parkinson Ltd. He continued as a director. In his later years he was internationally respected as an expert electrical engineer and a foremost authority on storage batteries. He used his influence to achieve standardization in industry generally, and was involved in the founding of the National Physical Laboratory and what is now the British Standards Institution. Heavy industry had the Whitworth Standard for screw threads, but there was no such standard for the small screws used in instruments. Crompton was a prime mover in the formation of the British Association committee which eventually developed the well known BA Standards.

During World War I he was an adviser on the design and production of military tanks, having been appointed by Winston Churchill (who was then First Lord of the Admiralty). Crompton carried out much research of his own but the final vehicle embodied the work of several designers.

Many honours were awarded to him, including honourary membership and medals of the engineering Institutions. He was elected a Fellow of the Royal Society in 1933. Crompton died at Azerley Chase, Yorkshire, on 15 February 1940, aged 94 years.

Crompton, Samuel *(1753-1827)*, was a British inventor whose machine for spinning fine cotton yarn - the spinning mule - revolutionized the industrial production of high-quality cotton textiles.

Crompton was born 3 December 1753 on a small farm at Firwood near Bolton, Lancashire. His parents were poor and from an early age he was expected to work alongside them on their piece of land. When he was six years old his father died, and his mother was forced to rely heavily upon the cottage industry of spinning and weaving to support the family. Samuel had to help with this too, and he grew up familiar with all the associated problems. These experiences were to influence him for the rest of his life.

At the age of 21, with years of home spinning

and weaving behind him, he resolved to try to design a better method for spinning the yarn than James Hargreaves' spinning jenny (patented in 1770). The jenny's yarn tended to break frequently and produced a coarse cloth which was commercially suitable only for the working-class market.

It took Crompton five years of hard work and all his money to develop a machine that span a yarn so fine and continuously that it revolutionized the cotton industry. The machine became known as a local wonder, and people flocked to Crompton's house to catch a glimpse of his spinning mule. Unfortunately, because he had used all his savings, he had no means of patenting the design and he lived in fear of someone stealing his idea. Eventually, he was persuaded to reveal his invention to a group of Bolton's manufacturers, who promised to pay him a generous subscription in return. This never materialized other than the initial payment of £67 6s 6d (£67.32).

Aggrieved at his treatment by the Bolton manufacturers, he tried to set up his own company, but having 'sold' his new machine, he was soon outpaced by the other manufacturers (with better resources) and forced to sell up. By 1812 the boost given to the cotton industry by the introduction of Crompton's mule was at last recognized, and a sum of approximately £500 was raised by subscription. A national award was also sought, and this time £5,000 was offered, but Crompton was far from satisfied and returned home to Bolton from London, a broken man.

Once again he tried to enter business, this time as a partner in a cotton firm. Ultimately this too failed, and he was forced to turn to the generosity of friends for an annuity. He died on 26 June 1827 at Bolton, a saddened man.

Crompton's new invention, which contributed so much to the wealth of the textile industry, was called the mule because, just like the animal of that name, it was a hybrid. His machine used the best from the spinning jenny and from Richard Arkwright's water frame of 1768. The strong, even yarn it produced was so fine that it could be used to weave delicate fabrics such as muslin which became particularly fashionable among the middle and upper classes, creating a new market for the British cotton trade. As a direct result of the better and faster method for spinning, which took the job out of the home and into the factories, coupled with the increase of raw cotton available from America, the cotton trade entered a Golden Age. The introduction of the power loom in the early 1800s further mechanized production and made the system of using home weavers practically obsolete. The Industrial Revolution had begun in the textile industry.

Cugnot, Nicolas Joseph *(1725-1804)*, was a French soldier and engineer who was the first to make a self-propelled road vehicle (in 1769). His three-wheeled machine was designed for towing guns: the front wheel was driven by a two-cylinder steam engine, and it could carry four people at a walking pace. As such it was the first automobile.

Cugnot was born at Void, Meuse. As a young man he joined the French army and served for a time in Germany and Belgium, inventing a new kind of rifle used by French troops under Marshal du Saxe, who encouraged him to work on a steam-propelled gun-carriage. After serving in the Seven Years War, Cugnot returned to Paris in 1763 as a military instructor. He also devoted his time to writing military treatises and exploring a number of inventions he had conceived during his campaigning, obtaining official help from the Duc de Choiseul, then Minister of War. His major invention was a steam-propelled tractor for hauling artillery. He built two models, the first appearing in 1769 and the second in 1770. By that time he had also constructed a truck, now preserved in the Conservatoire des Arts et Métiers, Paris. The truck ran at a speed of 3-5km/h (2-3mph) before a large crowd of official spectators, and Cugnot was commissioned to make a larger one. The fall of the Duc de Choiseul led to the project being shelved and the truck was not tested further. Granted a pension in 1779 from the Ministry of War, Cugnot migrated to Brussels. The pension stopped at the outbreak of the French Revolution. In 1798 Napoleon asked the Institut de France to enquire into Cugnot's machine, but nothing came of this.

In 1698 the English inventor Thomas Savery (c.1650-1715) had invented a steam engine designed for pumping water out of mines. This was the first practical use of the steam engine, but the engine itself was inefficient and wasted a lot of steam. In 1690 the French physicist Denis Papin (1647-c.1712) designed a superior engine, employing high-pressure steam expansively without condensation. Cugnot improved on this, making an engine driven by the movements of two piston rods working from two cylinders (which, like the boiler, were made of copper); it carried no reserves of water or fuel. Although it proved the viability of steam-powered traction, the problems of water supply and pressure maintenance severely handicapped the vehicle.

Cugnot's vehicle was a huge, heavy tricycle and his model of 1769 was said to have run for 20 minutes while carrying 4 people, and to have recuperated sufficient steam pressure to move again after standing for 20 minutes. Cugnot was an artillery officer and the more-or-less steam-tight pistons of his engine were made possible by

Cugnot's steam tricycle tractor of 1769, designed to pull heavy guns, was the first self-propelled road vehicle.

the invention of a drill that accurately machined cannon bores. The first post-Cugnot steam carriage appears to have been that built in Amiens in 1790, although followers of Cugnot were soon on the road in other countries, notably in Britain. Steam buses were running in Paris about 1800. Oliver Evans (1755-1819) of Philadelphia ran an amphibious steam dredger through the streets of that city in 1805. English exponents of the new form of propulsion became active, and by the 1830s the manufacture and use of steam road carriages had approached the status of an industry. James Watt's foreman William Murdock (1754-1839) ran a model steam carriage on the roads of Cornwall in 1784, and Robert Fourness showed a working three-cylinder tractor in 1788. Richard Trevithick (1771-1833) developed Murdock's ideas and at least one of his carriages with driving wheels 4.8m (10ft) in diameter ran in London.

Between 27 February and 22 June 1831, steam coaches ran about 6,500km (4,000 miles) on the regular Gloucester-Cheltenham service, carrying some 3,000 passengers. Thus many passengers had been carried by steam carriage before railways which were to cause their demise, had accepted their first paying passenger. The decline did not mean that all effort in this field would be abandoned, and much attention was given to the steam tractor as a prime mover. Beginning in about 1868, Britain was the scene of a vogue for light, steam-powered personal carriages; if the popularity of these vehicles had not been hindered by legislation, it would certainly have resulted in the appearance of widespread enthusiasm for motoring in the 1860s rather than in the 1890s. Steam tractors, or traction engines, were also used in agriculture and on the roads. It is thus possible to argue that the line from Cugnot's first lumbering vehicle runs unbroken to the twentieth-century steam automobiles which were made as late as 1926.

D

Daimler, Gottlieb Willhelm *(1834-1900)*, was the German engineer who designed internal combustion engines of relatively advanced performance for automobiles, developing the motorcar possibly more than Carl Benz, (who had run a car at an earlier date).

Born at Schorndorf near Stuggart on 17 March 1834, Daimler's technical education began in 1848 when he became a gunsmith's apprentice. Following a period at technical school in Stuttgart and factory experience in a Strasbourg engineering works, he completed his formal training as a mechanical engineer at the Stuttgart Polytechnic in 1859. He returned to Grafenstadt to do practical work for a while and then, sponsored by a leading Stuttgart benefactor, travelled to England where he worked for Joseph Whitworth. He then moved to France, where he many have seen Lenoir's newly developed gas engine.

Daimler spent the next ten years in heavy engineering. He joined Bruderhaus Maschinen-Fabrik in Reutlingen as manager in 1863, and there met William Maybach, with whom he was to be closely involved for the rest of his life.

Daimler's work on the internal combusition engine began in earnest in 1872 when he teamed up with Dr Nikolaus August Otto, (later to become famous for the Otto cycle) and Peter Langen, at the Gasmotoren-Fabrik Deutz where Daimler was technical director. One of Daimler's first moves was to sign up Maybach as chief designer. Daimler was to work with Otto and Langen for the next ten years, studying gas engines (which resulted in Otto's historic patent of 1876) and perhaps also petrol engines.

Differences of opinion led to Daimler leaving the firm in 1881. After making a brief trip to Russia to study oil, he returned to Germany and bought a house in Cannstatt, a suburb of Stuttgart. It was in the summer-house of this building that Daimler's first engines were built.

When he started work with Maybach, gas engines were being operated at 150 to 250rpm. Daimler's first working petrol-fuelled unit, built in 1883, was an air-cooled, single cylinder engine with a large cast iron flywheel running at 900rpm. With four times the number of power strokes per unit time, his engine had a very much greater output for a given size and weight. In itself, the use of petrol was not new: in 1870 Julius Hock in Vienna had built an engine working on Lenoir's principle. A piston drew in half a cylinder-full of mixture, which was fired when the piston was half way down the cylinder. Without compression, the power produced was very low and the fuel consumption massive.

The genius of Daimler and Maybach lay in the combining of four of the elements essential the modern car engine: the four-stroke Otto cycle, the vaporization of the fuel with a device similar to a carburettor, low weight and high speeds. Lenoir had used electric ignition, but this proved unreliable; Daimler and Maybach used an igniter tube that was light, worked well and operated independently of engine speed.

Daimler's second engine, which ran later the same year, was a 0.4kW (0.5hp) vertical unit. It was fitted to a cycle in November 1885, (possibly even earlier) creating the world's first motor cycle. Daimler was apparently not impressed with the possibilities of motorized two-wheelers and went on to try his engine as the power source for a boat.

In 1889 Daimler produced two cars, and obtained a licence to Panhard and Levassor in Paris to sell them. The first was a light four-wheeler with a tubular frame and a vertical, single-cylinder, water-cooled engine in the rear. It also featured a novel four-speed gear transmission to the rear wheels, and engine cooling water circulated through the frame, which acted as a radiator. The second car of 1889 had a belt drive and a vee-twin engine.

The two cars are important in that they show that Daimler had revised his earlier opinion that motorcars would be straight conversions of horse-drawn carriages. (Benz, on the other hand, had conceived his vehicle for motor-drive from the outset; nevertheless, Daimler's models were in many ways more advanced than the contemporary Benz models).

In 1886, Daimler approached Sarazin, a representative of Otto and Langen at the Deutz works, eager to increase sales of his engines overseas. Sarazin persuaded Panhard and Levassor to manufacture Daimler engines under licence, but died before they went into production. The firm succeeded in entering the motor industry with the Daimler licence, following the marriage of Levassor to Sarazin's widow in 1890.

The Daimler Motoren Gesellschaft was also founded in 1890, but Daimler and Maybach both retired the following year to concentrate on technical and commercial development work, only to rejoin in 1895.

A Daimler-powered car won the 1894 Paris to Rouen race, the first international motor contest, organized to promote the concept of motoring. Six years after this great success, on 6 March 1900,

Daimler died from heart disease, and was buried in Cannstatt.

Dancer, John Benjamin *(1812-1887)*, was a British optician and instrument maker who applied his knowledge of physics to various inventions, particularly the development of microphotography.

Dancer was born in London on the 8 October 1812. Both his father and grandfather were manufacturers of 'Optical, Philosophical and Nautical Instruments'. In 1818 the family moved to Liverpool where his father, Joseph Dancer, was one of the founders of and a lecturer at the Liverpool Mechanical Institution. Dancer often assisted his father, and his interest in science grew. One instrument constructed by Josiah was a large solar microscope, which had a 30cm (12in) condensing lens. Dancer used this equipment to view aquatic animals and he soon became an expert. On his father's death he took over control of the family business and the public lectures.

Dancer was a popular lecturer and he soon improved many of the standard laboratory practices of the period. He introduced unglazed porous jars in voltaic cells to separate the electrodes (previously the division was made of membranes from animal bladders and ox gullets). During the nineteenth century they were adopted as standard in Daniell and Leclanche cells, but unfortunately Dancer had not patented his invention.

He also devoted a lot of time to electrolysis during the 1830s; he became particularly expert in the electrodeposition of copper. He perfected a method of preparing a sheet of electrodeposited copper which retained features of a 'master' on which it was plated. Unfortunately for Dancer the invention was developed by Thomas Spencer into an early form of electrotype. He also improved on the Daniell cell by crimping or corrugating its copper plates. The power of the cell was considerably increased because of the greater electrode surface area.

Dancer was particularly interested in electrical circuits - in fact, in anything spectacular for inclusion in his lectures. Dancer used a Faraday voltameter with large platinum electrodes to prepare gases (hydrogen and oxygen) from water by electrodecomposition. By slight modification of the conditions he was able to prepare a colourless gas with a strong odour which caused coughing. The gas was not named initially, but was later (1839) identified as ozone by Christian Schonbein (Professor of Chemistry at Basle). The induction coil was a popular piece of equipment which was often claimed to have spurious medical benefits. Dancer incorporated the 'magnetic vibrator', similar to the spring make-and-break contact used in electric bells. He again did not patent his invention.

He began a series of experiments in 1839 based on Daguerre's and Fox Talbot's photography methods. By July 1840 Dancer had developed a method of taking photographs of microscopic objects, such as fleas, using silver plates. The photographic image was capable of magnification up to 20 times before clarity was lost. Dancer also gave 'magic lantern' shows, and these new plates were a considerable improvement over the painted slides then available. In the 1850s Scott Archer introduced a new process, the collodian method, and Dancer was not slow to realize its benefits in improving on his earlier techniques.

By 1856 Dancer had prepared many microphotographs and his work was exhibited throughout Europe. The clarity was excellent and by 1859 he was showing slides which carried whole pages of books 'in one-sixteenth hundredth part of a superficial inch'. Microdot photography was born. In all, the Dancer business produced for sale 512 different microphotographs, mounted on standard microscope slides. They included photographs of distinguished scientists of the era and portraits of the British royal family.

Dancer was an active member of the Manchester Literary and Philosophical Society, at whose meetings he presented many papers on a variety of scientific topics. He was a fellow of the Royal Astronomical Society and optician in Manchester to the Prince of Wales. He also constructed the apparatus with which James Joule determined the mechanical equivalent of heat.

In his later years he suffered from diabetes, which led to glaucoma of his eyes. Dancer died in November 1887, leaving behind a technique which has led to a method of storing huge quantities of data in a small space - microfilm and microfiche.

Darby, Abraham *(1677-1717)*, was an English ironmaster and engineer who devised a new way of smelting iron using coke rather than the much more expensive charcoal.

Darby was born at Wren's Nest near Dudley, Worcestershire, the son of a farmer. He served an engineering apprenticeship with a malt-mill maker in Birmingham, and on completing this in 1698 he set up in business on his own. In about 1704 he visited Holland and brought back with him some Dutch brass founders, establishing them at Bristol (at the Baptist Mill Brass Works) using capital from four associates who left to him the management of the business.

Believing that cast iron might be substituted for brass in some products, he tried with his Dutch workmen to make iron castings in moulds of sand. At first the experiment failed but proved eventually successful when he adopted a suggestion made by a boy in his employment, named John Thomas, who consequently rose in his service and whose descendents were for about 100 years trusted agents of the Darby family. In April 1708 he took out a patent for a new way of casing iron pots and other ironware in sand only, without loam or clay, a process which cheapened utensils much used by poorer people and at that time largely imported from abroad. This decision led to protracted arguments with his associates, who finally refused to risk more money on the new venture. Darby dissolved his connection with them and, drawing out his share of the capital, he took a lease on an old furnace in Coalbrookdale, Shropshire, moving to Madely Court in 1709. There he prospered until his death on 8 March 1717.

In the seventeenth century the development of the iron industry in Britain was limited by two technical difficulties. Firstly, the growing demand for charcoal - then the only satisfactory fuel for blast furnaces - had forced up the price very considerably. The shortage of wood for conversion into charcoal had been caused by the heavy demands of shipbuilders and a rapid growth in the demand for iron-made objects (resulting in the denuding of the large areas of forest which had been a feature of the English landcape for thousands of years). The second difficulty was due to the attempts to improve efficiency by using bigger furnaces; these were frustrated by the fact that charcoal is too soft to support more than a relatively short column of heavy ore. Attempts were made to use coal in place of charcoal, but the presence in most coals of sulphur, which spoils the quality of the iron, resulted in only limited success; the claim put forward by Dud Dudley (1599-1684) that in 1619 he had successfully smelted iron by using coke is not now generally accepted.

Attention was therefore directed to coke - already used in the smelting of copper and lead - since the coking process eliminates the sulphur. Darby had considerable experience of smelting copper with coke at Bristol and had also used coke in malting during his apprenticeship days in Birmingham. (In malting, for different reasons, the presence of sulphur prevents the use of raw coal.) The old furnace which Darby converted to house the Bristol Iron Company was ideally situated on the River Severn, close to good local supplies of iron ore and good coking coal. Initially much of the iron was used for making pots and other hollow-ware. The quality of the molten iron made it possible for him to make thin castings which competed satisfactorily with the heavy brassware then in common use.

The advent of the Newcomen steam engine

gave an important new market; some of the cylinders required for mine-pumping engines weighed as much as six tonnes with a length of 3m (10ft) and a bore of 1.8m (6ft). By 1758 more than 100 such cylinders had been cast. The steam engine, in turn, improved the manufacture of iron by giving a more powerful and reliable blast for the furnaces than water-power could supply.

The Coalbrookdale Works were much enlarged, their processes improved and increased and their operations extended under the second Abraham Darby. His son and successor, the third Abraham Darby, took over the management of the Coalbrookdale Works when he was about 18 and is memorable as having constructed the first iron bridge ever erected, the semicircular cast-iron arch acrosss the river Severn near the village of Brosely at Coalbrookdale, opened for traffic in 1779 (and still standing today).

Da Vinci, Leonardo *(1452-1519)*, was a famous Italian artist, inventor and scientist, and is regarded as one of the greatest figures of the Italian Renaissance for the universality of his genius.

Da Vinci was born on his father's estate, in Vinci, Tuscany. The illegitimate son of the Tuscan land-owner Ser Piero and a peasant girl, he was taken into his father's household in Florence, where he was the only child. He received an elementary education and in about 1467 was apprenticed to the artist Andrea del Verrocchio. There he trained in artistic as well as technical and mechanical subjects. He left the workshop in about 1477 and worked on his own until 1481. He went to Milan the following year and was employed by Ludovico Sforza, the Duke of Milan, as 'painter and engineer of the duke'. In this capacity he advised the duke on the architecture of proposed cathedrals in Milan and nearby Pavia, and was involve in hydraulic and mechanical engineering. After Milan fell to the French in 1499, he fled and began a long period of wandering. In 1500 he visited Mantua and then Venice, where he was consulted on the reconstruction and fortification of the church San Francesco al Monte. Two years later he went into the service of Cesare Borgia as a military architect involved in the designing and development of fortifications. In 1503 he returned to Florence to investigate, on Cesare Borgia's behalf, the possibility of re-routing the river Arno so that the besieged city of Pisa would lose its access to the sea. It was at about this time that he painted his internationally renowned portrait the *Mona Lisa*. He was invited that year by the Governor of France in Milan, Charles d'Amboise, to work for the French in Milan, and in 1506 he took up the offer. There he devised plans for a castle for the governor and for the Adda Canal to connect Milan to Lake Como. In 1513 the French were defeated and forced to leave Milan; Da Vinci left with them and went to Rome to look for work. He stayed with Cardinal Giulano de' Medici, the brother of Pope Leo X, but there was little for him to do (although both Michelangelo and Raphael were working there at that time) other than to advise on the proposed reclamation of the Pontine Marshes. Three years later he left Italy for France on the invitation of King Francois I, and he lived in the castle of Cloux, near the king's summer residence at Amboise. Da Vinci spent the rest of his life there, sorting and editing his notes. He died on 2 May 1519.

Da Vinci's training in Verrocchio's workshop developed his practical perception, which served him well as a technical scientist, a creative engineer and as an artist. In the years of his first visit to Milan, principally between 1490 and 1495, he produced his well-known notebooks, in mirror-writing. The illustrated treatises deal with painting, architecture, anatomy and the elementary theory of mechanics. The last was produced in the late 1490s and is now in the Biblioteca Nacional, Madrid. In it Da Vinci proposes his theory of mechanics, illustrated with sketches of machines and tools such as gear, hydraulic jacks and screw-cutting machines, with explanations of their functions and mechanical principles and of the concepts of friction and resistance.

Da Vinci's interest in mechanics developed as he realized how the laws of mechanics, motion and force operate everywhere in the natural world. He studied the flight of birds in connection with these laws and, as a result, designed the prototypes of a parachute and of a flying machine.

During this time, he also developed his ideas about the Renaissance Church Plan, which later were considered favourably by the architect Bramante in connection with the building of the new St Peter's in Rome.

In about 1503, when Cesare Borgia's plan for the diversion of the river Arno failed, Da Vinci also devised a project to construct a canal, wide and deep enough to carry ships, which would bypass the narrow portion the Arno so that Florence would be linked to the sea. His hydrological studies on the properties of water were carried out at this time.

The variety of Da Vinci's inventions reflect his passionate absorption in biological and mechanical details and ranged from complex cranes to pulley systems, lathes, drilling machines, a paddle-wheel boat, an underwater breathing apparatus and a clock which registered minutes as well as hours. As a military engineer he was responsible for the construction of assault machines, pontoons, a steam cannon and a tortoise-shaped tank. For a castle in Milan he create a forced-air central heating system and also a water-pumping mechanism. His notes and diagrams established him, beyond dispute, as the greatest descriptive engineer and scientist of his age. Despite these achievements, he remains most famous as an artist, unique in the history of the world's greatest painters.

De Forest, Lee *(1873-1961)*, was an American inventor and pioneer of wireless telegraphy, and is sometimes known as the Father of Radio.

Born in Council Bluffs, Iowa, on 26 August 1873, De Forest was raised in Alabama, to which his family moved in 1879. Even as a child, De Forest was keenly interested in machinery, building model trains and a blast furnace while still in his early teens. Despite pressure from his father (a Congregational minister who made great efforts to bring education to the local black people), he decided to follow his scientific inclinations, enrolling at the Sheffield Scientific School of Yale University in 1893. He was forced to supplement his scholarship and meagre allowance from his parents by taking menial jobs, but succeeded in gaining his doctorate in 1899. Called 'Reflection of Hertzian Waves from the Ends of Parallel Wires', this thesis was probably the first American dissertation to deal with radio.

De Forest's first appointment was with the Western Electric Company in Chicago. In the company's experimental laboratories, he devised ways of rapidly transmitting wireless signals, his system being used in 1904 in the first wireless news report (of the Russo-Japanese War).

Following this and other successes De Forest set up his own wireless telegraph company, but by 1906, following a number of bad misjudgements (he was twice defrauded by business partners), the firm went bankrupt. Then came his biggest breakthrough: the 'Audion' detector, which he patented in 1907. This thermionic grid-triode vacuum tube was based on the two-element valve device patented by John Ambrose Fleming in 1904. By adding a grid for a third electrode, De Forest had turned Fleming's valve into an amplifier as well as a rectifier. It made possible both radios, radar, television and even the earliest computers.

Even with such a major development behind it, De Forest's second company started to fold in 1909, again through internecine wrangling. He was indicted for attempting to use the US mail to defraud, by seeking to promote the 'worthless' audion tube, a charge of which he was later acquitted. He achieved much more favourable attention in 1910, however, by using his invention to broadcast the singing of Enrico Caruso, at the Metropolitan Opera. In 1912 De Forest realized that by cascading the effect of a series of audion tubes, it would be possible to amplify high-frequency radio signals to a far higher degree than that achieved using single tubes. The use of this effect made possible long-range (consequently weak-signal) radio and telephonic communication. The same year saw his discovery of a way of using feedback to produce a means of transmission capable of sending both speech and music, and in 1916 he set up a radio station and was broadcasting news.

De Forest eventually sold his audion triode to American Telephone and Telegraph for $290,000, which used it to amplify long-distance communication. This company was to purchase many of De Forest's best inventions at very low prices, yet further proof of his lack of business acumen.

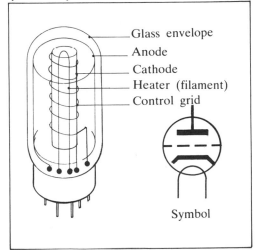

De Forest developed the triode valve, a three-electrode vacuum tube in which a control grid allows the current flowing through the valve to be controlled by the voltage at the grid. The triode was used in amplifying circuits for radio and early computers until largely superseded by transistors and other solid-state devices.

In 1923 De Forest demonstrated an early system of motion pictures carrying a soundtrack called phonofilm. Unfortunately its poor quality, and lack of interest from film makers, led to its demise, despite the fact that the system, which later succeeded commercially, was based on the same principles.

Even in the scientific world, De Forest suffered bad luck, being strongly recommended for the Nobel Prize but failing to be awarded it. He ended his days quietly, with his third wife Marie, and died in Hollywood, California, on 30 June 1961.

De Havilland, Geoffrey *(1882-1965)*, was an English pioneer of the early aircraft industry. He built his own aircraft six years after the Wright Brothers' first flight, and then produced a line of mainly successful machines which culminated in the *Comet*, the first pure jet passenger airliner and the *Comet 4*, the first jetliner to fly the Atlantic.

De Havilland was born on 27 July 1882, near High Wycombe, where his father was a curate. As a schoolboy he was an enthusiastic builder of model engines. He graduated to the design and construction of racing steam cars, designed and built motor cycles, one of which became the basis of successful production machines, and in 1905 joined the Wolseley company in Birmingham.

In 1908 de Havilland was a draughtsman at the Motor Omnibus Company of Walthamstow, fascinated by news from abroad of flying. Now that flight had become a reality in the hands of the Wright brothers and Farman, de Havilland became convinced that he could design his own engine and aeroplane and teach himself to fly. He asked his friend and former marine engineering apprentice, Frank Hearle, to give up his job as a mechanic at another bus company and to join him in this project. Having obtained his legacy of $1,000 in advance from his grandfather, de Havilland rented a room and set about designing his first aero engine.

It was a flat-four water-cooled design giving 34kW (45hp) at 1,500rpm for a dry weight of 113kg (250lbs). The Iris Car Company agreed to make a prototype for £220 and de Havilland rented the attic of a builder's workshop in Fulham, barely big enough for the span of the biplane wings he contemplated. The two men began construction of the aircraft which was based on a tapering white wood space frame fuselage projecting almost equally in front and behind the 11m (36ft) wings. It was to carry a 4.3m (14ft) pair of elevators each side of the nose and a 3m (10ft) plane at the tail, above which a rudder was stayed by a thin outrigger from the flat radiator forming the top wing centre-section. The front spar of the main planes differed noticeably in location from all previous biplanes, being more than 300mm (1ft) back from the leading edge. Earlier biplanes, such as those of Wright, Farman and Cody, had used the leading edge as a spar but this gave a high drag entry and a weak spar for the weight. De Havilland's design, using a location at a point of greater wing thickness in a better aerodynamic shape was to prove the ultimate standard.

By November 1909 work was nearly finished. De Havilland hired a lorry to transport the 4 wings, engine, fuselage and other components to the Hampshire Downs where sheds had been bought at Seven Barrows from Moore-Brabazon

(later Lord Brabazon).

De Havilland had never flown before (indeed, he had only ever seen one aircraft flying in the distance), and his first flight rather inevitably ended in the aircraft being wrecked. However, the salvaged aircraft Number One was the basis of the successful Number Two, even though only the engine had been left intact. In 1910 the Downs south of Newbury saw De Havilland flying consistently for as long as 40 minutes around the countryside. He had done away with the twin propellers and mounted a single wooded screw direct on the crankshaft. The landing gear had been lightened and the main structure made lighter, simpler and more robust.

To raise more money for further trials, de Havilland sold Number Two to the Army Balloon Factory (later called the Army Aircraft Factory) for £4000, its two builders being taken on the staff. Although officialdom favoured balloons, de Havilland's aircraft was awarded an airworthiness certificate and officially designated FE1. (This stood for 'Faman Experimental No 1' because, like Faman's machine, it had a pusher propeller.) De Havilland produced FE2 with a Gnome rotary engine, then BE1 ('Bleriot Experimental' because it had a tractor propeller like Bleriot's machine) and a number of other designs.

As the war clouds were gathering in 1914, de Havilland joined the Aircraft Manufacturing Company, or Airco, as chief designer and produced DH1, a two-seater pusher, and DH2, a single-seat fighter with a single Lewis gun in the nose which went into quantity production. Then came the DH4, a fast two-seat bomber that could hold its own against most fighters.

After World War I, de Havilland established his own company at the famous Stag Lane Works at Edgware and during the inter-war period produced a series of extremely successful light transport aircraft. The DH50, a civil version of the DH4, won a competition at Gothenburg, with Alan Cobham at the controls, but it was the *Moth* series, starting with the *Cirrus Moth*, which opened up aviation as no other aircraft had done before. To power these new machines de Havilland designed the 75kW (100hp) *Gipsy 1* engine, followed by the 97kW (130hp) *Gipsy Major*, and established his own Engine Division. The *Tiger Moth* became the standard RAF trainer and De Havilland won the 1933 Kings Cup air race in the three seat *Leopard Moth* at 224kph (140mph).

Many records were established in DH aircraft, with the all-wood DH88 *Comet* racer monoplane, built in 1934 for the MacRobertson England-Australia Air Race, covering the 19,680km (11,300 miles) to Melbourne in 79 hours 59 minutes.

As a private venture, the de Havilland Company designed the famous all-wood *Mosquito*, which was at first rejected by the Air Ministry, losing six months of precious time. The highly versatile aircraft went into squadron service in September 1941 and a total of 7,781 were built. It was about 30kph (20mph) faster than the *Spitfire* and so, like the DH4, could out-fly virtually anything in the air.

After World War II the De Havilland company put a range of jet-powered aircraft into production, many of which used the company's own engines. The world's first jet trainer was the de Havilland Vampire fighter and fighter-bomber, built under licence in Europe. The final development of this twin-boom jet fighter was the Sea Vixen.

The dangers facing pioneers in aeronautics were made tragically apparent to De Havilland on several occasions. On 27 September 1946, the experimental tail-less DH108 Swallow broke up over the Thames Estuary, killing his eldest son, Geoffrey. His second son John, had been killed three years earlier in a mid-air collision in a Mosquito. A re-built Swallow subsequently captured the world air speed record, averaging 968.37kph (605.23mph) on a 100km (62 mile) closed circuit with John Derry at the controls. Derry died when a wing of his DH110 folded during a display at the Farnborough Air Show; 28 spectators were killed in the wreckage.

The world's first production jet airliner, the Comet, first flew on 27 July 1949, but after a triumphant entry into service in May 1952, a Comet crashed after take off from Rome in January 1954. A second crashed under the same circumstances in April, and caused the Comets to be withdrawn from service. After the most exhaustive investigation ever carried out on an aircraft, it was established that the pressurized cabin had ruptured due to the then unsuspected problems of low-cycle fatigue. The Comet eventually surmounted its problems, Comet IIs entering service with the Royal Air Force while the Comet 4 became the first jet airliner to operate Transatlantic scheduled services, beating the Boeing 707 by a narrow margin.

Other civil projects, however, enjoyed notable success. De Havilland died in 1965 having seen the company he had founded absorbed into the Hawker Siddeley conglomerate, which had also swallowed Armstrong Whitworth, Avro, Blackburn, Folland, Gloster and Hawker.

De Laval, Carl Gustaf Patrik *(1845-1913)*, was a Swedish engineer who made a pioneering contribution to the development of high-speed steam turbines.

De Laval was born at Orsa into a family that had emigrated to Sweden from France in the early 17th century. He was educated at the Stockholm Technical Institute and at Uppsala University. In the vigour and variety of his interests - and of his inventive talent - he has been likened to Thomas Edison. In 1878 he invented a high-speed centrifugal cream separator that incorporated a turbine, and of the machine was successfully marketed and used in large dairies throughout the world. He also invented various other devices for the dairy industry, including a vacuum milking machine, perfected in 1913. De Laval's greatest achievement, however, lay in his further contribution to the development of the steam turbine, which he completed in 1890 after several years of experiments. In the absence of reliable data on the properties of steam, de Laval solved the problem of the high velocity by special features in the design of the wheel carrying the vanes of the turbine, and that of direction of the stream of particles by the form given to the nozzle through which the steam jet was produced. The turbine disc had a hyperbolic profile and was mounted on a flexible shaft, which ran well above the critical whirling speed. The machine had a convergent-divergent ('condi') exit nozzle.

De Laval's other interests ranged from electric lighting to electrometallurgy in aerodynamics. In the 1890s he employed more than 100 engineers in developing his devices and inventions, which are exactly described in the 1,000 or more diaries he kept.

The history of turbines goes back to ancient times, when man first began to use water and wind to perform useful tasks. The first device that could be classified as a steam turbine is generally attributed to Hero of Alexandria in about the first century AD. Operating on the principle of reaction, this device achieved rotation through the action of steam issuing from curved tubes, or nozzles, in a manner similar to that of water in a rotary lawn sprinkler. Another steam-driven machine, described in about 1629, used a jet of steam impinging on blades projecting from a wheel, causing it to rotate. This 'motor', in contrast to Hero's reaction machine, operated on the impulse principle.

The first steam turbines having any commercial significance appear to have been those built in the United States by William Avery in 1831. His turbines consisted of two hollow arms attached at right-angles to a hollow shaft, through which the steam could issue. The steam vents were openings at the trailing edge of the arms, so that rotation was achieved by the reactive force of the steam. Although about 50 of these turbines were made and used in sawmills, wood-working shops and even on a locomotive, they were finally abandoned because of their difficult speed regulation and frequent need of repair. Among the prominent later inventors working in the steam-turbine field was Charles Parsons (1854-1931). He soon recognized the advantages of employing a large number of stages in series, so that the release of energy from the expanding steam could take place in small steps. This principle opened the way for the development of the modern steam turbine. Parsons also developed the reaction-stage principle, in which pressure drop and energy release are equal, through both the stationary and moving blades.

In 1887 de Laval developed his small high-speed turbines with a single row of blades and a speed of 42,000 revolutions per minute. Although several of these were later employed for driving cream separators, he did not consider them practical for commercial application. De Laval turned to the development of reliable, single-stage, simple-impulse turbines. He is credited with being the first to employ a convergent-divergent type of nozzle in a steam turbine in order to realize the full potential energy of the expanding steam in a single-stage machine. During the period from 1889 to 1897 he built a large number of turbines (ranging in size from about 5 to several hundred horse-power), and it was de Laval who invented the special reduction gearing which allows a turbine rotating at high speed to drive a propellor or machine at comparatively slow speed, a principle having universal application in marine engineering.

De Lesseps, Ferdinand *(1805-1894)*, was a French civil engineer who is remembered as the designer and builder of the Suez Canal, the strategic importance of which, as a trade route between Europe and the East remains until the present day.

De Lesseps had the distinction of being born at the Palace of Versailles, being a cousin of the Empress Eugénie. As befitted his noble birth (he was a Vicomte), he was brought up to regard diplomatic service as the natural choice for a career and from 1825 he held posts in various capitals including Lisbon, Tunis and Cairo.

He also had other interests in life, and these centred around engineering and construction, especially where canal building was concerned. When it was suggested in 1854 that a passage should be cut to link the Mediterranean with the Red Sea, De Lesseps was the ideal man to take charge of the work.

In 1856 permission was granted by the Viceroy of Egypt, Muhammad Said, and the actual canal was begun in 1860, financed mainly with money put up by the French Government and Ottoman Empire. Ten years later the canal opened for traffic, shortening the route between Britain and India by 9,700m (6,000 miles).

De Lesseps received many honours for his achievement, an English knighthood, the Grand Cross of the Legion of Honour and election to the French Academy of Science being chief among them. Unfortunately, all these were rather overshadowed by the disaster of the Panama Canal, the construction of which he reluctantly undertook in 1881. The project met with failure and bankruptcy. De Lesseps was sentenced to five years' imprisonment for breach of trust, but was too ill to leave his house. A broken and sick old man, he was allowed to remain there and died on 7 December 1894.

Since Roman times, thoughts of cutting across the Isthmus of Suez had been discussed at various intervals. Napolean I, on his visit to Egypt in 1799, saw the possibilities and advantages of a canal, but no practical steps were taken until 1854 when the Suez Canal Scheme was conceived. A technical commission met in 1855 and mapped out a suitable route. It then remained for permission to be granted by the Viceroy and a for a company to be formed to finance the operation. All this was achieved by 1860 when work began in earnest.

As there was no great difference in the levels of the two seas at either end of the isthmus, locks were unnecessary and the construction, although long - more than 16km (100 miles) - was relatively simple. It linked the cities of Port Said and Suez and initially measured 8 metres deep, 22 metres wide at the bottom and 70 metres across at the surface. When it was finished on 17 November 1869 it reduced the journey from the Mediterranean to the Indian Ocean by thousands of miles and removed the necessity for weeks at sea traversing of the Cape of Good Hope.

Originally Britain owned none of the shares in the Suez Company, but in 1875 the Khedive of Egypt, Ismail Pasha (who succeeded Muhammad Said in 1863) sold his stock to the British government. From then on the company was mainly controlled by the British and the French, and in 1888 it was agreed that the Canal should be opened to all nations, at all times. Constructed in the beginning as a one-lane canal, it has been widened and deepened in recent years to accommodate the increase of traffic, particularly from the oil fields of the Arab countries. At one time, tankers made up 70 per cent of shipping recorded as passing through the canal.

The Suez Canal was a brilliant piece of engineering carried out efficiently under the watchful eye of De Lesseps. The advantages to trade were obvious to our Victorian forefathers, and in the modern world that narrow strip of man-made waterway has proved vital to the Western economy.

Diesel, Rudolph Christian Karl *(1853-1913)*, was a German mechanical engineer whose name will always be associated with the compression-ignition internal combustion engines he invented.

Diesel was born in Paris on 18 March 1853, of parents who came from the Bavarian town of Augsburg. His father was a bookbinder. While receiving his early education in Paris Diesel spent much of his spare time in the city's museums. He was particularly attracted to the Museum of Arts and Crafts, which had on permanent display Joseph Cugnot's steam-propelled gun carriage of 1769.

At the outbreak of the Franco-Prussian War in 1870, the Diesel family travelled to England and took up residence in London. Rudolph, however, was sent to Augsburg to continue his education with a relative who was a teacher at the local trade school. He progressed so well that he qualified for the Munich Polytechnic, where he proved to be a brilliant scholar. He shared part of his time there with Carl von Linde, the founder of modern refrigeration engineering, from whom he learnt the basic theory of heat engines.

Diesel became fascinated by engines and came to the conclusion that an engine four times as effective as a steam engine could be made by designing it to carry out the combustion within the cylinder while utilizing as large a temperature range as possible. Because the temperature obtained depends to a great extent on the pressure, a very high pressure must be used to compress the air before fuel injection to avoid premature explosion.

His ideas were published in a paper of 1893, one year after he had taken out his first patent in Berlin. In the early stages of his experiments he was lucky to escape being killed when a cylinder head blew off one of his prototype engines, but this did not deter him and he carried on to perfect a model which was capable of commercial exploitation. In 1899 he founded his own manufacturing company at Augsburg, which flourished despite Diesel having little or no business sense. He was, however, talented at putting over his ideas, and he gave a series of lectures in the United States in 1912 which were well attended. In 1913, at the height of his success, he vanished from the decks of a steamer crossing from Antwerp to England while on his way for consultations with the British Admiralty. His body was never found.

Like the petrol engine, the diesel engine is a form of internal combustion engine but it differs in not having a carburettor to pre-mix air and fuel; nor does it require a spark for ignition. In the diesel engine, as the piston moves down, pure air is drawn into the cylinder and on the up stroke this air is compressed by a ratio of between 12:1 and 25:1 (much higher than that of the petrol engine, which is usually between 6:1 and 10:1). Compression, by increasing pressure, raises the temperature of the air to in excess of $540^{\circ}C$. When the piston nears the top of the compression stroke, an injector admits through a nozzle a fine spray of fuel which mixes with the heated air and ignites spontaneously, the explosion moving the piston downwards. As the rate of inflow of air remains constant in a diesel engine, its power output is governed by the amount of fuel injected.

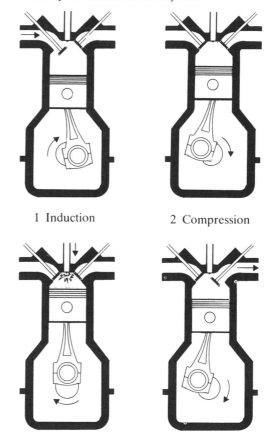

1 Induction   2 Compression

3 Combustion   4 Exhaust

In a diesel engine, fuel is injected on the combustion stroke into hot compressed air at the top of the cylinder, where it ignites spontaneously. The four stages are exactly similar to those of the four-stroke Otto cycle.

In his first engine, Diesel is thought to have used coal dust as a fuel, but he later discarded this along with several other types in favour of a form of refined mineral oil. Diesel engines will in fact run on many fuels but the most widely used today is distilled from petroleum closely related to kerosene.

Until the 1920s further development of the diesel engine took place mainly in Germany (principally by Karl Bosch), where it proved particularly useful during World War I for powering submarines. Designers such as Cummins of the United States and Gardner in Britain eventually adapted the invention for small boats, and later work by Cedric Dicksee and Harry Ricardo put it into a practical form for road use.

Diesel's death remains a mystery but his work lives on. A century after his birth more than half the world's tonnage of ships and a large proportion of the railways were diesel driven. The engine has been adapted for buses, tractors and trucks as well as servingas an alternative to coal-burning boilers and fast-flowing water for driving alternators in the generation of electricity.

Dicksee, Cedric Bernard *(1888-1981)*, was the British engineer who was a pioneer in developing the compression ignition (diesel) engine into a suitable unit for road transport.

Dicksee received his technical education at the Northampton Engineering College (1906-1910). He was chief designer at the Aster Engineering Company Ltd, Wembley, and in 1918 he joined the Austin Motor Company Ltd. The following year he went to Westinghouse Electric and Manufacturing Company in charge of design and development of engines for generating plants.

After 7 years in the USA, Dicksee returned to Britain and joined the Association Equipment Company (AEC) Ltd in 1928 as engine designer, later becoming research engineer. When in 1929 the development of a compression ignition engine suitable for road transport was started, this became his major activity and was the work for which he is best known.

During World War II Dicksee worked on combustion chamber design for the de Havilland series of jet engines. He returned to AEC at about the time the war ended and after leaving became a consultant to Waukesha for several years. He retired to Seaford where he died.

When Dicksee began work, the London General Omnibus Company (LGOC) had two lorries at their depot fitted with massive 3-cylinder Junkers oil engines. These were unsuitable for automotive use and within a year, he had his first engine running. It was a six-cylinder 8.1 litre (c.40 cu in) unit with an aluminium crankcase and it entered service with the LGOC just before Christmas 1930.

After development with Ricardo and Com-

pany an improved version took to the road in September 1931. A smaller - 7.7 litres (35cu in) - engine followed in 1933 and soon became the standard for AEC (LGOCs manufacturing subsidiary) chassis. A further development of this engine used combustion chambers of a toroidal shape and was also highly successful. This feature was subsequently adopted for larger engines in the company's range.

Dicksee's engines ran at speeds ranging from 1,800 to 2,400 (governed) rpm which were higher than comparable engines of the day. With this performance, the way was opened for the adoption of compression ignition engines instead of petrol engines for road transport. As a result, in the early 1980s there was scarcely a commercial vehicle of any size which did not have a high-speed compression-ignition engine as its power unit.

Donkin, Bryan *(1768-1855)*, was a British engineer who made several innovations in paper-making, printing and food preservation.

Little is known of Donkin's childhood. He was born in Northumberland and later apprenticed to John Hall, a paper-maker of Darford, Kent. He went on to work for Hall and perfected a new type of paper-making machine which had been devised in 1798 by the Frenchman Nicolas Robert and later patented in England by Henry and Sealy Fourdrinier. This success led Donkin to investigate another recent invention from France, the preservation of food by bottling. He established his own company, even gaining royal approval by presenting samples to the Prince Regent in 1813. With this security behind him, he returned to the printing and paper trade, and invented the forerunner of the rotary press. By 1815 he had turned to civil engineering, and became a founder member of the Instition of Civil Engineers. When he died in London on 27 February 1855, he was remembered as much for his role in founding such official groups as for his engineering skills.

Donkin made his first practical Fourdrinier paper-milling machine at Frogmore Hill, Hertfordshire, in 1803. He set up a factory in Bermondsey, South London, where he manufactured nearly 200 machines in all. Donkin's contribution to food preservation was to take Appert's bottling process and modify to use metal cans instead of glass bottles. In printing, he tackled the problem of increasing the speed of presses. The original flat-bed press, with its back-and-forth movement, was too slow. Donkin arranged 4 (flat) formes of type around a spindle - a rudimentary rotary press. He introduced a composition of glue and treacle for the inking rollers, an innovation which was still widely used long after his press had been superseded.

Dowty, George *(1901-1975)* was the engineer and industrialist who exploited the concept of supplying specialized components to a large number of industries. His expertise in hydraulics began in the aircraft industry and led to the formation of a group of companies world-wide with a turnover in excess of £350.8 million in the year to March 1982.

Dowty was born in Pershore, Worcestershire, on 27 April 1901. He was 10 years old when his father died. There was no engineering background in the family but he idolized early aviators such as Bleriot and Cody. He attended Worcester Royal Grammar School and served his apprenticeship with the Heenan and Froude company from 1915 to 1918. As a journeyman he gained experience with aircraft development, instrument design, mechanical handling equipment, compression rubber research and aircraft design.

Initially he concentrated on improving the shock-absorbing qualities of aircraft landing gear, using hydraulic principles, and floated a company for design and manufacture of an improved strut in 1931. After initial struggles to gain acceptance of his ideas, he obtained his first large order in 1934. Other hydraulic products followed and during World War II the Dowty organization grew to a wartime peak of 3,000 employees, and many thousands more with the 250 subcontractors dispersed throughout England, Canada and the USA.

After the War, Dowty looked for ways to diversify to avoid a traumatic run-down of the company. He turned to advanced seals to contain the ever-increasing hydraulic pressures being used and then conceived the idea of hydraulic pit props for mines. He formed companies within the Group to exploit hydraulics in many industries and other concerns joined the Group until, in 1982, there were 47 companies under the Dowty umbrella. He was elected Fellow of the Royal Aeronautical Society in 1937 and President for the 1952-1953 term. He was awarded a knighthood in the 1956 Birthday Honours List. He was President of the Society of British Aircraft Constructors for the 1960-1961 term. Dowty died at his home in Cheltenham while still chairman of the group he founded.

In the 1920s aircraft design had made great strides due to the impetus given by World War I but landing gear was crude. When an aircraft landed, it was virtually uncontrollable. At low speeds this is not too important but as flying (and landing) speeds increased landing became increasingly hazardous. In 1931 Dowty judged that the aircraft industry had reached a stage where there was scope for the design and production in large quantities of some components. He thought that if a firm could establish a reputation for specialized skill and knowlege it would be recognized by the whole industry. He decided to concentrate on landing gear.

His first order was from pioneer Don Cierva for the de Havilland autogiro and the second was from Nevil Shute Norway for the Airspeed Ferry. These struts were manufactured by friends in the evenings on an old treadle lathe in a cellar and assembled in a small wooden hut. Dowty then resigned from Gloster Aircraft, where he was a draughtsman, to concentrate on his own projects. He designed an internally sprung and braked wheel and soon afterwards received an order for 6 wheels from Kawasaki, the Japanese firm of aircraft manufacturers. Later than year he rented his first premises in Cheltenham and sold the Japanese manufacturing rights to Kawasaki for £1,000.

Orders for struts for prototype aircraft followed but production quantities were needed to keep the company solvent. Few aircraft were being built in the 1930s recession, so Dowty marketed a photographic print-glazing press and metal garden labels to obtain funds. At last, in 1934, he obtained an order for struts to be fitted to 25 Gloster Gauntlets. Later Dowty internally sprung wheels were fitted to the Gladiator, which was developed from the Gauntlet. Also in 1934 he received an order for 250 Bristol Bulldog tail wheels.

During the War Dowty companies built 87,000 undercarriages and nearly 1 million hydraulic units fitted to nearly every type of British aircraft that flew. In addition there was a sizeable reconditioning and repair factory at Aschurch where components from crashed aircraft were put back into service.

In the diversification phase after the war, acceptance of the hydraulic pit props was slow but from 1948 sales grew and in 1957 the millionth prop came off the production line. Success with props led to the automation of roof supports for mines. Then came hydraulic railway buffers, couplings and wagon control systems. Back in aviation, there were aircraft engines. Then there was electronic and electrical equipment and marine water jets. Dowty-Rotol manufactures variable-pitch propellers, ducted fans, auxiliary drive gearboxes, hovercraft lift and propulsion fans and many other products. It is the largest company in the Dowty Group.

Engineering encompasses not only the conception, design and production of ideas, but also the exploitation of those ideas - including marketing and personnel and financial management.

Dowty's genius lay in the skill with which he blended these different facets and built up a world-wide organization from an idea.

Dunlop, John Boyd *(1840-1921)*, was a Scottish veterinary surgeon who is usually credited with the invention of the pneumatic tyre (originally for bicycles).

Dunlop was born at Dreghorn, Ayrshire, on 5 February 1840. He studied veterinary medicine at Edinburgh University, before setting up practice in Ireland near Belfast in 1867. He devised a pneumatic tyre 10 years later in an attempt to improve the comfort of his son's tricycle. It was so successful that in the following year (1888) he applied for the British patent and within 3 years he had founded his own company, with the encouragement of Harvey du Cros (whose sons were keen racing cyclists).

When Dunlop's business was already established, it was discovered that the tyre had previously been patented by another Scotsman, R.W. Thomson of Stonehaven, Kincardineshire. He had made a set of tyres as early as 1846 and fitted them to a horse- drawn carriage. They had been tested over 1,600km (995 miles) before they had needed replacing. Thomson's invention had gone practically unnoticed, whereas Dunlop's arrived at a crucial time in the development of transport. The bicycle was fast becoming recognized as more than a hobby, and the motorcar was about to make its spectacular appearance on the roads. In 1896, after trading for only about 5 years, Dunlop sold both his patent and his business for £3 million, and Arthur Philip du Cros took over as managing director.

The key to Dunlop's invention was rubber. The rubber industry had become established in Europe in around 1830 with the development of vulcanization (the blending of india-rubber with sulphur to produce a workable substance). In 1876 the Englishman Henry Wickham travelled to the Amazon and collected seeds of wild rubber plants, which he brought back to Kew Gardens for propagation. The young plants were taken to Ceylon (Sri Lanka) and Malaya, where they formed the nucleus of the new rubber plantations.

Dunlop realized that rubber was the most suitable material for making tyres because it could stand up to wear and tear while retaining its resilience. His first simple design consisted of a rubber inner-tube, covered by a jacket of linen tape with an outer tread also of rubber. The inner tube was inflated using a football pump and the tyre was attached by flaps in the jacket which were rubber-cemented to the wheel. Later he incorporated a wire through the edge of the tyre which secured it to the rim of the wheel. Whether or not Dunlop's

invention was the first, he certainly pioneered the mass production of tyres and Fort Dunlop, the Dunlop Rubber Company's factory in Birmingham, remains today.

E

Eads, James Buchanan *(1820-1887)*, was an American engineer who made various contributions to canals and waterworks. He is probably best known, however, for building a bridge across the River Mississippi at St Louis.

Eads was born in Lawrenceburg, Indiana on 23 May 1820. As a child he used to watch the steamboats on the river Mississippi, and after leaving school at the age of 13 he found work on them. He had a flair for business (despite his lack of education) and in 1842 he set up a successful company for salvaging wrecks from the river. As a result, he become knowledgeable in hydraulics and mechanics; he also designed and patented a diving bell.

After a brief, and unsuccessful, period as a glassmaker, Eads turned his attention to shipbuilding. At the beginning of the American Civil War in 1861, Abraham Lincoln asked for his advice on protecting the Mississippi and its system of canals. Eads suggested a fleet of armour-plated gunboats, and was awarded the contract to build them. By the end of the war, his reputation had grown to such an extent that he was consulted about building a bridge across the Mississippi at St Louis - a task that 27 other leading engineers had said was impossible. Eads produced a design, and built his bridge (which still stands) between 1867 and 1874.

In 1875 he was given an even more diverse contract - to clear the silted ship channel at the mouth of the great river. Again he used his ingenuity, and the project was completed 4 years later. Towards the end of his life he devised a scheme to build a railway that could carry ships across the Isthmus of Tehuantepec, Mexico, in competition with the Panama Canal, but the project never came to fruition. Eads died at Nassan, in the Bahamas, on 8 March 1887.

The grounding for Eads' engineering knowledge was acquired during his years in the salvage business and, not surprisingly, when he turned to shipbuilding it was an easy transition. The Civil War gave him the opportunity to prove his management skills, and he deployed his 4,000 workers so that they built 7 600-tonne (590 ton)

Eads' bridge over the River Mississippi at St Louis (built between 1867 and 1874) had three steel arches and two decks. Road vehicles and pedestrians used the upper deck, while the lower deck carried a twin-track railway line.

gunboats in 65 days, the first being launched after only 45 days. He built a total of 25 vessels during the war, for serving and protecting the river Mississippi and the Gulf of Mexico.

His most famous achievement, brought off despite all predictions that it was an impossibility, was the construction of a steel arch bridge at St Louis. The specification was for a 158.5m (520 ft) span with a height of 15m (50 ft) above water level for clearance for ships. The work was difficult and hazardous but Eads' company completed the contract in 7 years.

Eads' understanding of the river and its currents brought him the task of clearing the mouth of silt and mud to be scoured away - he made the river do the work. The method was so effective that when a similar project was suggested for the estuary of the river Mersey near Liverpool in Britain he was called upon to give his expert opinion.

From a simple education to engineering brilliance, Eads was a fine example of that nineteenth-century phenomenon, the self-taught and self-made man. Whatever he tackled he treated with a determination that refused to be beaten by technical problems, and he always managed somehow to find an answer. His love of the Mississippi and understanding of all its aspects brought him wealth and success, and the St Louis bridge still stands as a monument to his fame.

Eastman, George *(1854-1932)*, was the American inventor, businessman and benefactor who founded the Kodak company. He started the 'press button' end of photography and brought it within range of virtually everybody's skill and pocket.

Born on 12 July 1854, in Waterville, New York, Eastman left school at 14 to earn a living and ease his family's financial hardships. He started as a messenger boy, studying accounting in the evenings. He saved $3,000, in 1879 patented a photographic emulsion coating machine, and the following year began mass production of dry plates.

Eastman had started experimenting with photographic emulsion in 1878. At that time, there were large numbers of photographic processes in use, the most popular of which was collodion-coated glass plates. These had to be pre-

pared, sensitized, exposed and developed in rapid succession which meant that landscape photographers had to carry a complete darkroom about with them. Enlargement was not practicable so negatives had to be the size of the finished print - thus some cameras were the size of soap boxes.

Various methods to preserve the collodion were used but most were complicated and reduced the sensitivity of the plate. The first practical dry process introduced in 1855 was the collodion albumen plate which needed 6 times the exposure of the wet plate. Gelatine emulsion, usually attributed to Maddox, appeared in 1871 and Burgess's gelatino-bromide prepared dry plates appeared in 1873. This ushered in a new era of photography in which the mobile darkroom was no longer required. Eastman began production of his own dry plates in 1880 in a rented loft of a building in Rochester, New York.

Stripping film, in which paper was used only to support the emulsion and was not destined to be part of the negative, was patented in 1855 by Scott Archer, but the technique was not used to any great extent until Eastman introduced it for the Eastman/Walker roller slide in 1886. Eastman's system consisted of a paper base, a layer of soluble gelatine, a layer of collodion and a layer of sensitized gelatine emulsion.

After exposure, the roll was cut up into individual negatives, developed and fixed. The emulsion side was then attached to glass plates and coated with glycerine. Hot water dissolved the gelatine so the paper could be stripped off. The image on the glass had to be transferred to a gelatine sheet for printing.

Eastman's roller slide fitted into existing cameras and he confidently expected that users of glass plates would soon change over to the new film. But this was not to be. He therefore decided to reach the general public with the Kodak camera, launched in 1888. This camera was loaded with a large enough roll of the stripping film for 100 exposures and sold, with shoulder strap and case, for $25. After use, the camera was sent to Rochester, where the film was developed by the complicated process and a new film loaded for $10.

Eastman followed this up in the next year with the first commercially available transparent nitro-cellulose (Celluloid) roll films. These had been produced since the mid 1850s, but until the advent of Celluloid, none were successful. Unfortunately, on 2 May 1887 the Rev Hannibal Goodwin applied for a patent for a transparent roll film made of Celluloid but the patent was not granted until September 1898. Meanwhile Eastman's company had captured the market with its own roll film. A long and complicated law suit between the company which had acquired Goodwin's interests (he had died in 1900), and Eastman's company was finally settled in March 1914 with the Eastman company paying $5 million to the owners of Goodwin's patent. Virtually the only change there has been since then is the replacement of the flammable nitro-cellulose by non-flammable cellulose acetate. Eastman's roll-film replaced his stripping film in the Kodak camera and ushered in the era of press-button photography.

Eastman continued the popularization of photography by spooling his film so that the camera could be daylight loaded, and did not have to be returned to the Rochester factory. A pocket-sized box camera was marketed for $1 in 1900. The 8mm movie camera, (which appeared in 1932), colour film, panchromatic film, automatic exposure control, sound film, instant cameras - all these and many more innovations followed.

Eastman was the first man to recognize the importance of the amateur market in photography, which until 1880 had been restricted by the need for darkroom work. Other manufacturers tried to produce rival cameras but due to Kodak's virtual roll film monopoly, for two or three decades a hand camera, of whatever make, was simply known as a 'Kodak'.

Despite all these successes, Eastman still had severe private problems that led to his suicide on 14 March 1932.

Eastwood, Eric *(1910-   )*, is a British electronics engineer who has made major contributions to the development of radar for both military and civilian purposes.

Eastwood was born on 12 March 1910 and educated at Oldham High School, Lancashire. He went to Manchester University and studied physics under Lawrence Bragg (1890-1971), and then moved to Cambridge University to take his PhD. He taught physics for a while at the Collegiate School, Liverpool, before entering the Signals branch of the Royal Air Force during World War II, and becoming involved with the solution of technical problems concerning radar.

At the end of the War (1945), Eastwood joined the Nelson Research Laboratory of the English Electric Company. In 1948 he transferred to the Marconi Research Laboratory and was its

director for many years.

In 1962 he accepted the appointment of Director of Research for the English Electric Group of Companies and, with the merger in 1968 of GEC and AEI, became Director of Research for the new company, General Electric, a position he held until his retirement in 1974. He now lives at Little Baddow, near Chelmsford in Essex, and still maintains a part-time interest in Marconi's as a director and scientific consultant.

Radar is a system using pulsed radio waves transmitted to and reflected back from a 'target' to measure its distance and direction. It was developed as a result of research carried out in the late 1800s and early 1900s. Heinrich Hertz (1857-1894) first discovered radio waves in 1888 and found they could be focused into a beam. Over the next 20 years several other scientists and inventors experimented with their potential, the most successful being Guglielmo Marconi (1874-1937) who in 1901 used these 'Hertzian waves' to send a message in Morse code across the Atlantic.

Further research on radio waves led to the first 'wireless' (radio) programmes of the early 1920s, but it took the probability of a war to rekindle interest in radio waves as a possible means of early detection of hostile aircraft. In 1935 the British Air Ministry asked Robert Watson-Watt (1892-1973) to investigate the concept of pulse radar. By the outbreak of World War II in 1939 there were radar stations along Britain's eastern coast, and these played a major part in the subsequent Battle of Britain.

Eastwood's part in the development of this system, and in the solving of its technical problems, left him ideally qualified to continue in this field of research. At the Marconi Research Laboratory he concentrated on the extension of the laboratory's interest in telecommunications, radar and applied physics. He soon realized that the new radar systems, which the laboratory had been commissioned to develop, could also be used as powerful tools in research. With the aid of the Marconi experimental station at Bushy Hill, Essex, he applied radar methods to the study of various meteorological phenomena (such as the aurora) and carried out extensive investigations into the flight behaviour of birds and migration; his book *Radar Ornithology* was published in 1967.

Eckart, John Presper *(1919-   )*, is an American electronics engineer who is best known for his pioneering work on the design and construction of digital computers. He also holds patents on numerous other electronic devices.

Eckart was born in Philadelphia, Pennsylvania on 9 April 1919. He attended the William

Pema Charter School and went on to graduate in 1941 from the Moore School of Electrical Engineering at the University of Pennsylvania. He remained at the Moore School for 5 years as a research associate. During this time he worked on the design of radar ranging systems and then, to help with the complex calculations that these involve, turned to the design of electronic calculating devices. From 1942 to 1946, with John William Mauchly, he devised the Electronic Numerical Integrator And Calculator (ENIAC), one of the first modern computers.

ENIAC was first used in 1947, and proved to be successful although open to various improvements. Eckart had left Pennsylvania University the year before to become a partner in the Electric Control Company, and in 1947 began a 3-year term as a Vice-President of the Eckart-Mauchly Computer Corporation. During this period design improvements were incorporated into new computer models.

In 1950, the company was incorporated in Remington Rand. Eckart became Director of Engineering within the Eckart-Mauchly Division, becoming Vice-President in 1954. A year later the company came under the control of the Sperry Rand Corporation, and Eckart stayed on as Vice-President of the UNIVAC (Universal Automatic Computer Division).

Eckart's important contributions to computer design have been recognized with awards and honorary degrees from various organizations and universities. He lives in Philadelphia, where he continues to supervise research in his field.

The need for improved accuracy and, particularly speed in routine calculations became most apparent during World War II, when ballistic firing tables had to be rapidly recalculated to suit new weaponry and battle conditions. Eckart realized that normal calculators were ineffective and inefficient. With the assistance of Mauchly he used electronics to construct an integrator, and produced a flexible digital computer which could be used for calculating firing tables and much more.

The ENIAC, although only a prototype of present-day computers, incorporated many modern design features and could perform mathematical functions. It lacked a memory, but could store a limited amount of information. Its major drawbacks were its size (it weighed many tonnes and included thousands of resistors and valves) and its high running cost (it consumed 100KW of electric power). Nevertheless it formed applications to various military, meteorological and research problems.

ENIAC was superseded by BINAC, also designed in part by Eckart, which (by virtue of even more sophisticated design) was smaller and faster. In the early 1950s Eckart's group began to produce computers for the commercial market with the construction of the UNIVAC I. Its chief advance was the capacity to store programs.

Edison, Thomas Alva *(1847-1931)*, was an American electrical engineer and inventor. He took out more than 1,000 patents, the best known of which were the phonograph, the precursor of the gramophone, and the incandescent filament lamp.

Edison was born in the small town of Milan, Ohio, on 11 February 1847 and brought up in Michigan. Most of his tuition was provided by his mother - he received only three months' formal public elementary education. His lifelong interest in things technical was soon apparent - by the age of 10 he had set up a laboratory in the basement of his father's house. By the age of 12, he was selling newspapers and candy on trains between Port Huron and Detroit, and three years later (1862) he had progressed to telegraph operator, a job he maintained throughout the Civil War (1861-1865) and for a couple of years thereafter. During this period, in 1866 (at the age of 19), he took out a patent on an electric vote recorder, the first of a total of 1,069 patents.

Perceiving the need for rapid communications, made apparent by the recent war, he turned his inventive mind to problems in that field. His first success came with a tape machine called a 'ticker', which communicated stock exchange prices across the country. He sold the rights in this and other telegraph improvements to the Gold and Stock Telegraph Company for $30,000, using the money to equip an industrial research laboratory in Newark, New Jersey, which he opened in 1869.

From telegraphy, the transmission of coded signals across long distances, he then turned his attention to telephony, the transmission of the human voice over long distances. In 1876 he patented an electric transmitter system which proved to be less commercially successful than the telephone of Bell and Gray, patented a few months later. Typically, he was undeterred and not for the first time he applied his keenly inventive mind to improving someone else's idea. His improvements to their systems culminated in the invention of the carbon granule microphone, which so increased the volume of the signal that despite his deafness he could hear it.

With the money made from this invention he moved to Menlo Park, where he bought a house and equipped the laboratory that was to remain the centre for his research. In the following year, 1877, he invented the phonograph, a device in which the vibrations of the human voice were engraved by a needle on a revolving cylinder coated with tin foil. Thus began the era of recorded sound.

In the 1870s gas was the most advanced form of artificial lighting, the only successful rivals being various clumsy and expensive types of electrically powered arc lamp. While experimenting with the carbon microphone, Edison had toyed briefly with the idea of using a thin carbon filament as a light source in an incandescent electric lamp, an idea he returned to in 1879. His first major success came on 19 October of that year when, using carbonized sewing cotton mounted on an electrode in a vacuum (one millionth of an atmosphere), he obtained a source which remained aglow for 45 hours without overheating, a major problem with all other materials used. Even this success was not enough for him, and he and his assistants tried 6,000 other organic materials before finding a bamboo fibre which gave a bulb life of 1,000 hours. In 1883 he joined forces with Joseph Wilson Swan, a chemist from Sunderland to form the Edison and Swan United Electrical Company Ltd.

To produce a serious rival to gas illumination, a power source was required as well as a cheap and reliable lamp. The alternatives were generators or heavy and expensive batteries. At that time the best generators rarely converted more than 40 per cent of the mechanical energy supplied into electrical energy. Edison made his first generator for the ill-fated Jeannette Arctic Expedition of 1879. It consisted of a drum armature of soft iron wire and a simple bi-polar magnet, and was designed to operate one arc lamp and some incandescent lamps in series. A few months later he built a much more ambitious generator, the largest built to date; weighing 500kg, it had an efficiency of 82 per cent. Edison's team were at the forefront of development in generator technology over the next decade, during which efficiency was raised above 90 per cent. To complete his electrical system he designed cables to carry power into the home from small (by modern standards) generating stations, and also invented an electricity meter to record its use.

Edison became involved with the early development of the film industry in 1888. After persuading George Eastman to make a suitable celluloid film, he developed the high-speed camera and kinetograph, viewing the picture through a peep hole. Although he had referred to the possibility of projecting the image, he omitted it from his patent - a rare error. He had dropped his interest in kinematography by 1893, but three years later resumed it when Thomas Armat developed a projector. They joined forces but Armat was commercially naive and the machine was advertised as

Edison's latest triumph; the resulting split caused considerable patent litigation.

His later years were spent in an unsuccessful attempt to develop a battery-powered car to rival the horseless carriages of Henry Ford. During World War I he produced many memoranda on military and naval matters for the Department of Operational Research.

When he died, aged 84, on 18 October 1931, Edison had come a long way from the ten-year-old boy with a laboratory in his father's basement to being probably the most prolific and practical inventive genius of his age. He was a man whose work has greatly influenced the world in which we live, particularly in the fields of communication and electrical power. On the day following his death, his obituary in the *New York Times* occupied four-and-a-half pages, an indication of the importance of Edison to the twentieth century world.

Edwards, George *(1908-)*, is the British aircraft engineer who was responsible for a number of major aircraft projects and became chairman of the British Aircraft Corporation from 1963-1975.

Edwards was born on 9 July 1908 and educated at South West Essex Technical College and London University. After general engineering experience, he joined the Design Office of Vickers-Armstrongs (Aircraft) Ltd at the age of 27 and was later appointed the company's experimental manager.

From 1940 to 1941 he was seconded (part-time) to the Ministry of Aircraft Production and at the end of World War II (1945) he was appointed chief designer of the Aircraft Section of Vickers-Armstrongs. In 1953 he was appointed director, general manager and chief engineer of the company, of which he later became managing director.

When the British Aircraft Corporation (BAC) was formed in 1960, Edwards became its executive director and, 3 years later, chairman. He retired from the chairmanship in December 1975. In recognition of his work Edwards has received many decorations, medals, awards and honorary degrees, including the MBE (1944), CBE (1952), Knight Batchelor (1957) and OM (1971). His Fellowship of the Royal Aeronautical Society came in 1947 and of the Royal Society in 1968.

At the end of World War II, there were large numbers of surplus DC3 Dakatos which were refitted to form the backbones of many airlines. The DC3, however, first flew in 1935. It had evolved from the DC1 and 2, so it was a 15-year-old concept, and it normally carried only 21 passengers. With Edwards at the head of the design team,

Vickers produced the VC1 Viking which was the first British postwar civil transport to enter service. The Viking was faster and had greater range, but it was also an interim design seating 21 passenger. The fuselage was lengthened to carry 36 and the aircraft became the workhorse of BEA until it was replaced by Viscounts in 1954.

The Valetta, an RAF transport version of the Viking, and the Varsity, an RAF trainer, emerged from the Vickers stable where Edwards was design chief, and in 1953 the world's first scheduled service with turboprop aircraft began. This machine was the Viscount Type 701 which could cruise at 499kph (310mph) with 53 passengers.

The Valiant was the first of Britain's V-bombers to fly, entering service in 1955. It was built to a less advanced specification than the Victor and Vulcan but nevertheless had a maximum speed of Mach 0.84 above 9144 metres (30,000ft) and a service ceiling of 16,459m (54,000ft). It provided the first effective striking force for Britain's nuclear deterrent.

Continuing overall technical direction of Vickers after becoming managing director, Edwards was responsible for the Vanguard, a 139-seater, second-generation turboprop, followed by the VC10 and Super VC10 airliners and the TSR2 (tactical strike/reconnaissance) aircraft, which was cancelled in April 1965.

As executive director BAC, Edwards fostered the BAC 1-11 short-haul 'bus-stop jet' which started as a project by Hunting Aircraft Ltd, absorbed into BAC. This 99-seater, tee-tailed, twin jet was produced in Europe. Technically, the products which came from the design and manufacturing Edwards headed were of the highest order.

Eiffel, Alexandre Gustav *(1832-1923)* was the French engineer now known chiefly for the 300m (98ft) high edifice he erected for the 1889 exhibition commemorating the hundreth anniversary of the French Revolution.

Eiffel was born at Dijon in 1832. After attending the Ecole des Arts et Manufactures in Paris he won early fame by specializing in the design of large metal structures, notably the iron railway bridge over the Garonne at Bordeaux. Here he was one of the first to use compresssed air for underwater foundations. in 1867, he set up his own firm which constructed bridges, viaducts, harbour works and other large projects. His great arch bridges include the 159m (530ft) span over the Douro river in Portugal, and the 165m (550ft) span of the Garabit Viaduct in France. Other projects included the immense roof which covers the central station at Budapest, the Machinery Hall for the Paris Exhibition of 1867, the protective

ironwork for the Statue of Liberty in New York Harbour, designed by Bartholdi, and the 84m (277ft) dome for the observatory at Nice.

In the Eiffel Tower, completed for the Paris Exhibition of 1889, each stage has to be suffiently strong to support all those above it, hence the shape which takes the form of an exponential curve.

Eiffel began work on the famous wrought-iron tower for the Champs de Mars in 1886, using his experience of building high-level railway bridges. From a detail set of plans, the 12,000 metal parts of the tower were all prefabricated and numbered for assembly. The majority of the 2.5 million rivets used were put in place before the structure was erected on the site. Work proceeded so smoothly that not one worker's life was lost through accidents on the scaffolding, and was completed (except for the lifts) in two and a quarter years.

The tower's cross-braced, latticed girder structure offers minimum wind resistance: the estimated movement of the structure with hurricane-force winds is only 22cm (9in). It is constructed from over 7,000 tonnes (6,900 tons) of wrought iron, resting upon 4, 2.25sq.m (252ft) masonry piers. The piers are set in 2m (7ft) of concrete on foundations carried down by the aid of caissons and compressed air to about 15m (44ft) on the side next to the Seine and about 9m (30ft) on the other side.

The Tower has three well-marked stages. Below the first platform, which is placed at a height of 57m (183ft) the four quadrilateral legs are linked by arches. At the second platform, 115m (380ft) high, the legs join and the third platform is at a height of 276m (911ft). Above this platform are the lantern and the final terrace.

Originally, the Tower was intended to be dismantled at the conclusion of the exhibition. Many writers and artists deplored its construction, describing it as 'a hideous hollow candlestick'. However the newly discovered possibilities of the tower as a radio transmitting station finally won the day and it was left standing. For some time it was by far the highest artificial structure in the world. It also showed what could be achieved by correct engineering design and paved the way for yet higher structures in the future.

With subsequent disaster for himself and his country, Eiffel participated in the Panama Canal enterprise, in the course of which he designed and partly constructed some huge locks. When the entire project collapsed in 1893, Eiffel was implicated in the scandal; he went to prison for 2 years and received a fine of 200,000 francs. In 1900 he took up meteorology and later, using wind tunnels, carried out extensive research in aerodynamics at the Eiffel Tower and afterwards at Auteuil where he constructed the first laboratory for the new science. He died in Paris in December, 1923.

Elkington, George Richards *(1801-1865)*, was a British inventor who pioneered the use of electroplating for finishing metal objects.

Elkington was born in Birmingham and in 1818 he became an apprentice in the local small-arms factory; in due course he became its proprietor. With his cousin Henry Elkington he explored the alternatives to silver-plating from about 1832. The fire-gilding process of plating base metals, or more often silver, with a thick film of gold had been practised from early times. The article was first cleaned and then placed in a solution of mercurous nitrate and nitric acid, so that it acquired a thin coating of mercury. The surface was next rubbed with an amalgam of gold and mercury, in the form of a stiff paste held in a porous fabric bag, until a smooth coating of the pasty mixture had been applied. Finally, the article was heated on a charcoal fire to drive off the mercury, and the residual gold was burnished.

The process of plating base metals with silver and gold by electro-deposition was announced in a patent taken out by the Elkington cousins in 1840. This proposed the use of electrolytes prepared by dissolving silver and gold, or their oxides, in potassium or sodium cyanide solution. The articles to be coated were cleaned of grease and scale and immersed as cathodes in the solution, current being supplied through a bar of metallic zinc or other electropositive metal (anode); later silver or gold anodes were used, brass and German silver were suggested as the most suitable metals for plating.

A second patent, granted in 1842 to Henry Beaumont (an employee of the Elkingtons), covered some 430 additional salts of silver which it was thought might have application to electroplating. In the same year, John Stephen Woolrich obtained a patent for the use of a magneto-electric machine which depended on Michael Faraday's discovery of electromagnetism in 1830, the plating solution being the soluble double sulphate of silver and potassium. Licences were first issued to the Elkingtons in 1843, but Thomas Prime of Birmingham appears to have been the first to use such plate commercially, by employing Woolrich's patented machine; Dr Percy, a famous metallurgist, claims to have conducted Faraday himself round Prime's works in 1845. Subsequently the Elkingtons took over Woolrich's patent, for which they paid him a royalty, and they were thereafter able to command a minimum royalty themselves of £150 from all who practised electroplating. In spite of this, however, electroplate rapidly supplanted Old Sheffield plate; the Sheffield directory of 1852 contained the last entry under this heading, with only a single representative remaining from the many who had practised the art five years previously.

Taking into partnership Joseph Mason, the founder of Mason College (subsequently Birmingham University), the Elkingtons established a large workshop in Newhall Street, Birmingham, which after a seven-year battle against the older methods of silver plating at last won acceptance. The Elkingtons also successfully patented their ideas in France. George Elkington established large copper-smelting works in Pembrey, South Wales, additionally providing houses for his workers and schools for their children but the chief centre for his activities remained in Birmingham. He died in Pool Park in North Wales in 1865.

Ellet, Charles *(1810-1862)*, was an American civil engineer who designed the first wire-cable suspension bridge in the United States and became known as the 'American Brunel'.

Ellet's career began when he was appointed as a surveyor and assistant engineer on the Chesapeake and Ohio Canal in 1828, where he remained for three years. He then went to Europe and enrolled as a student at the Ecole Polytechnique in Paris, and continued to gather experience by studying the various engineering works taking place in France, Germany and Britain.

He returned to the United States in 1832 and submitted to Congress a proposal for a 305m (1,000ft) suspension bridge over the Potomac River at Washington DC, but the plan was too advanced for its time and failed to receive government support. In 1842, over the Schuylkill River at Fairmount, Pennsylvania, he built his first wire-cable suspension bridge. Ellet introduced there a technique that was common in France, that of binding small wires together to make the cables; five of these latter supported the bridge at each side, the span being 109m(858ft).

Between 1846 and 1849 he designed and built for the Baltimore and Ohio Railway the world's first long-span wire-cable suspension bridge, crossing the Ohio River at Wheeling, West Virginia. The central span of 308m (1,010ft) was then the longest ever built. However, the bridge failed under wind forces in 1854 because of its overall aerodynamic instability. Ellet's towers remained standing, and the rest of the bridge was rebuilt
by John Roebling (1806-1869), who later achieved fame by his own record-breaking activities in building long-span suspension bridges of wire cable of his own manufacture. (In 1956 the Wheeling Bridge was again under repair; Ellet's towers and anchorages and Roebling's cables and suspenders were retained, but the deck was entirely renewed.)

In 1847 Ellet received a contract to build a bridge over the Niagra River, only 3.2km (2 miles) below the falls. The result was a light suspension structure, and Ellet subsequently claimed to be the first man to cross the Niagara Gorge on the back of a horse (thanks to the bridge). This was, however, to prove to be another enterprise which turned sour for its promoter. A dispute over money led Ellet to resign in 1848, leaving the project uncompleted.

Following the outbreak of the American Civil War in 1861, Ellet produced a steam-powered ram which was used by the Union (Northern) forces with decisive effect against the Confederate army on the Mississippi river. In June 1862 Ellet personally led a fleet of nine of these rams in the Battle of Memphis. The Union side was victorious, but in the course of the fighting Ellet was fatally wounded.

Ericsson, John *(1803-1889)*, was a Swedish-born American engineer and inventor who is best known for his work on naval vessels.

Ericsson was born on 31 July 1803 at Langban Shyttan in Varmland, Sweden, and between the ages of 13 and 17 served as a draughtsman in the Gotha Canal Works. He was then commissioned into the Swedish Army, where he did map surveys. In 1826 he moved to London to seek sponsorship for a new type of heat engine he had invented (which used the expansion of superheated air as the driving force). This forerunner of the gas turbine was not successful, and Ericsson turned his attention to steam engines.

In 1829 he built the *Novelty*, a steam locomotive which competed unsuccessfully against Stephenson's *Rocket* at the Rainhill Trials for adoption on the Liverpool and Manchester Railway. In 1839 Captain Stockton of the United States Navy placed an order for Ericsson to supply a small iron vessel fitted with steam engines and a screw propellor. The vessel was built and sailed to New York, Ericsson himself sailed out a few months later. He became an American citizen in 1848.

In 1851 he resumed his interest in the heat or 'caloric' engine. It was found to be too heavy for the ship he built for it (immodestly called the *Ericsson*), making the vessel too slow. Only towards the end of his life did Ericsson construct small, efficient engines of this type.

A more successful line of development resulted from his work on the helical screw propellor, an interest he shared with his contemporary Isambard Kingdom Brunel. Realizing that the paddle steamer was incapable of further development, Ericsson had built two small screw-driven ships in Britain in 1837 and 1839. In 1849 he built the *Princeton*, the first metal-hulled, screw-propelled warship and the first to have its engines below the waterline for added protection.

It was the outbreak of the American Civil War in 1861 which finally gave Ericsson the opportunity to demonstrate his skill as a naval engineer. His turreted iron clad ship, the *Monitor*, was first offered to Napoleon III and only after he refused it did it go to Ericsson's adopted country. Equipped with a low freeboard and heavy guns, it was the first warship to have revolving gun turrets - a practice soon to be adopted universally. In the Battle of Hampton Roads in 1862, the *Monitor* defeated the Confederate ship *Morrimack*.

After the Civil War Ericsson continued to design warships, torpedoes and a 35.6cm (14-inch) naval gun, but he also devoted time to more peaceful pursuits. Among his inventions were an apparatus for extracting salt from seawater, fans for forced draught and ventilation, a shipboard depth-finder, a steam fire engine and surface condensers for marine engines. Between the years

1870-1885, he also explored the possiblity of using solar energy and gravitation and tidal forces as sources of power.

Not always successful in the realization of his ideas, Ericsson was a wilful and impetuous man, often far ahead of other engineers of the day. He died on 8 March 1889 in New York City, and in 1889 the VSS *Baltimore* took his body back to Sweden, in accordance with his last wishes.

Eyde, Samuel *(1866-1940)*, was a Norwegian industrial chemist who helped to develop a commercial process for the manufacture of nitric acid which made use of comparatively cheap hydroelectricity. He was a member of the Norwegian Parliament, and in 1920 Norwegian Minister in Poland.

Eyde was born at Arendal in Norway and received his higher education in Germany at the Charlottenburg High School in Berlin, where he gained a diploma in constructural engineering. He then worked as an engineer in various German cities, principally Hamburg. In partnership with the German engineer C.O Gleim, he returned to Scandinavia to work on the construction of various railway and harbour installations. But increasingly his interest turned to the possibiltity of developing the electrochemical industry in his native Norway, where hydroelectric schemes were beginning to make cheap electrical energy available.

In 1901, while studying the problem of the fixation of nitrogen (the conversion of atmospheric nitrogen into chemically useful compounds), he came to know his compatriot Kristian Birkeland. The two men set up a small laboratory where they combined their efforts to discover the conditions necessary for the economic combination of nitrogen and oxygen (from air) in an electric arc to produce nitrogen oxides and, eventually, nitric oxide. Their method, known as the Birkeland-Eyde process, can be summarized by the following chemical equations:

$$N_2 + O_2 \rightleftharpoons 2NO$$

(nitrogen and oxygen combine to give nitric oxide)

$$2NO + O_2 \longrightarrow 2NO_2$$

(nitric oxide combines with oxygen to form nitrogen dioxide)

$$4NO_2 + O_2 + H_2O \longrightarrow 4HNO_3$$

(oxidation of nitric oxide in the presence of water produces nitric acid)

Their experiments resulted in the first commercial success in this area of research. The key to the process was an oscillating disc-shaped electric arc, produced by applying a powerful magnetic field to an arc formed between two metal electrodes by an alternating current. The electrodes

were copper tubes cooled by water circulating inside them. In 1903 the Norwegische Elektrishe Aktiengeswllschaft constructed a small-scale plant at Ankerlökken, near Oslo. Two years later full-scale operation began at Notodden. Then interest in the work was shown by the company of Badische und Anilin Soda Fabrik which, following on from German research on the thermodynamic equilibrium of nitrogen oxides, had employed O. Schonherr to study the nitrogen-oxygen reaction in 1897. In 1904 he patented a method of producing a steadier arc than had been attained by Birkeland and Eyde.

By this time Eyde had obtained the hydroelectric rights on some waterfalls, and in 1904 he became administrative director of an electrochemical company, financed partly from a Swedish source which supported the Birkeland-Eyde process. In the following year he obtained extensive support from French financiers to found a hydroelectric company, which he directed with great skill until he retired from active participation in 1917.

Eyde died at Aasgaardstrand in Norway in 1940, shortly after writing his autobiography.

Evans, Oliver *(1755-1819)*, was an American engineer who developed high-pressure steam engines and various machines powered by them. He also pioneered production-line techniques in manufacturing.

Evans was born on 13 September in 1755 in Newport, Delaware, and at the age of 16 he was apprenticed to a wagon-maker. He read books on mathematics and mechanics, and became interested in steam engines. His first invention was a machine for cutting and mounting wire teeth in a leather backing to make devices for carding textile fibres before spinning; his machine produced 1,500 cards a minute. In 1780 he joined his two brothers at a flour mill at Wilmington, where he helped to build the machinery that used water power to drive conveyors and elevators. As a result, he attained a degree of automation that allowed one man to operate the whole mill as a single production line. Other millers remained unimpressed by his invention, however.

Evans then moved to Philadelphia, where he spent more than ten years trying to develop a steam carriage. For some time he tried to couple one of James Watt's steam engines to a wagon and as early as 1792 he was working on internally fired boilers for steam engines. But he had to abandon the enterprise because of lack of financial support, and eventually he turned his attention to the manufacture of stationary steam engines.

In 1786 and 1787 he successfully petitioned the legislatures of Pennsylvania and Maryland for exclusive patent rights to profit from his inventions, and by 1802 he had developed a high-pressure steam engine with a 15cm (6in) cylinder, 95cm (18in) stroke and a 2.3m (7.5ft) flywheel. It employed a 'grass hopper' beam mechanism and had an internally fired boiler and provision for exhausting spent steam into the air. It worked at a pressure of 3.5kg sq.cm (50psi) and ran at 30 revolutions per minute.

Two years later Evans built a steam dredger for use on the Schuylkill river. It had power-driven rollers as well as a paddle so that it could be moved on land under its own power. This amphibious machine, the *Orukter Amphibole*, was the forerunner of some 50 or so steam engines which he built in the next 15 years.

In 1806 Evans began to develop the Mars works for the manufacture of steam engines. In 1817 he completed his last work, a 17.4 kW (24 hp) engine for a waterworks. On 11 April 1819 his principal workshop was destroyed in a fire started by a grudge-bearing apprentice. The consequent shock to Evans probably hastened his death in New York City a few days later on 15 April 1819.

Like many engineers Evans died with many bold dreams unrealized. In March 1815 he claimed, in the *National Intelligencer* (although many seriously question the claim), that he could have introduced steam carriages as early as 1773 and steam paddle boats by 1778. Less controversially, Evans published the *Young Millwright* and *The Miller's Guide* in 1792 and, in 1805, a book called *The Abortion of the Young Steam Engineer's Guide*.

F

Fairbairn, William *(1789-1874)*, was a Scottish engineer who designed a riveting machine which revolutionized the making of boilers for steam engines. He also worked on many bridges, including the wrought iron box-girder construction used first on the bridge across the Menai Straits in Wales.

Fairbairn was born into a poor family on 19 February 1789, at Kelso. He received little early education, although he did learn to read at the local parish school. He started work when he was 14 years old when his family moved to a farm owned by the Percy Main colliery near Newcastle-upon-Tyne; Fairbairn became apprenticed to a millwright. He learned mathematics in his spare

time and displayed his engineering ingenuity by constructing an orrery (a working model of the Solar System).

He finished his apprenticeship in 1811 having, in the meantime, become a friend of the Stephensons. He worked as a millwright at Bedlington, then took a series of jobs in London, Bath, Dublin and Manchester. During this time he invented a sausage-making machine and a machine for making nails. In Manchester he worked on the construction of the Blackfriar's Bridge and then set up as a manufacturer of cotton-mill machinery. In 1824 Fairbairn erected two watermills in Zurich, and later turned his attention to ship-building and, finally, bridge-building.

In 1862 he invented a self-acting planning machine for dealing with work up to 6m (20ft) by 1.8m (6ft). He became an authority on mechanical and engineering problems and received many honours and awards, including a baronetcy in 1869. Fairbairn died on 18 August 1874, at Moor Park in Surrey and was buried at Prestwick, Northumberland.

From very humble beginnings, Fairbairn used his inventive skills and engineering ability to earn a fortune by the time he was 40 years old. He had acquired a sound reputation for producing machinery for the cotton mills and by that time employed about 300 workmen. His reputation abroad had been enhanced when he solved the problem of an irregular water supply with his watermills in Switzerland.

In 1830 he was commissioned by the Forth of Clyde Company to build a light iron boat to run between Glasgow and Edinburgh. He then concentrated on ship-building, first in Manchester (where he built ships in sections) then from 1835 in Millwall on the river Thames, where his Millwall Iron Works employed some 2,000 people.

Fairbairn returned to Manchester, and in 1844 designed and built the first Lancashire shell-boiler. It was constructed of rolled wrought-iron plates rivetted together by a machine of his own design. It was this expertise that led Robert Stephenson to consult Fairbairn over the building of the Menai railway bridge, which was constructed of wrought-iron plates. Built between 1846 and 1850, it was the longest railway bridge at the time with a continuous box girder (in which the trains ran) 461m (1,511ft) long. Fairbairn's participation ended in 1849 after a misunderstanding about his position (he and Stephenson were both termed Superintendent), and he published his own account of the construction.

Ferranti, Sebastian Ziani de *(1864-1930)*, was a British electrical engineer who pioneered the high-voltage AC electricity generating and distribution system still used by the National Grid and other power networks. He also designed, constructed and experimented with many other electrical and mechanical devices, including high-tension cables, circuit breakers, transformers, turbines and spinning machines.

Ferranti was born in Liverpool, Lancashire, on 9 April 1864. From his youth he was fascinated by machines and the principles by which they operate. After moving south he attended St Augustine's College in Ramsgate, Kent, and so impressed his teachers with his mechanical ideas that they set aside a room in which he could experiment. During this time he constructed an electrical generator. He left school in 1881 and took a job at the Siemens works in Charlton near London. He discovered that he could rotate and therefore mix the molten steel in a Siemens furnace by applying an electric current, and within a year he was supervising the installation of electric lighting systems for the company. A year after that - still only 18 years old - he was engineer to his own company which designed and manufactured the Thompson-Ferranti alternator and installed lighting systems. The company was formed in partnership with Lord Kelvin (Joseph Thompson) and a solicitor named Ince.

In 1886 Ferranti became engineer to the Grosvenor Gallery Company in London. The gallery had its own electricity generating system for lighting, and was also selling electricity to outside customers. Ferranti modified the system considerably to meet extra demand and, realizing the business potential, led the Grosvenor Company into the formation of a separate enterprise, the London Electric Supply Corporation Ltd and suggested building a large generating station at Deptford. Extending an electricity supply to such a large area would, he argued, eventually become more economical and practicable than hundreds of small electrical enterprises serving limited areas. Most of the small systems used direct current of 200 to 400 volts together with storage batteries, and were suitable only over short distances and when the demand for electricity fell within suitable limits. To achieve large-scale distribution, Ferranti proposed using alternating current as 10,000 volts which was fed by mains to London, where step-down transformers reduced it to a voltage suitable for its purpose. The idea was revolutionary, because electricity at more than 2,000 volts was considered to be extremely dangerous. The cable for the mains was made to Ferranti's design, and produced in 6m (20ft) lengths which were spliced together without the use of solder. The Deptford power station and its associated distribution network became the basic model for the future of electricity generation and supply.

In 1888 Ferranti married Gertrude Ince, the daughter of his solicitor partner. Three years later he left the London Electric Supply Corporation and concentrated on work as a consultant and on the development of his own company. This firm went on to design and build all kinds of electrical equipment, most of which was designed by Ferranti himself. He was also involved with heat engines of various kinds, turbines, cotton-spinning machines and, during World War I, the design and manufacture of steel casings.

He became President of the Institution of Electrical Engineers in 1911 and a year later was awarded a DSc degree by the University of Manchester. In 1929 he was elected a Fellow of the Royal Society. He enjoyed motoring and was very proud of his fast journey times. He died after an illness while on holiday in Zurich, Switzerland, on 13 January 1930.

Ferguson, Henry George *(1884-1960)*, was the British inventor and engineer who developed automatic draught control for farm tractors. This improved performance so dramatically that farmers world-wide could buy the small, inexpensive machines, thus precipitating a revolution in farming methods. Virtually every modern tractor incorporates some form of automatic draught control.

Ferguson was born near Growell, near Belfast. He left school at 14 to work on his father's farm. In 1902 he joined his brother in a car and cycle repair business in Belfast. He started to build his own aeroplane in 1908 and flew it on 31 December 1909, becoming one of the first Britons to do so.

He started his own motor business, imported tractors from the United States and in 1917 he and William Sands designed their first plough. Another went into production in the United States, and on 12 February 1925 Ferguson patented the principle of draught contol. The Brown-Ferguson tractor, manufactured by David Brown, was launched in May 1936 and a redesigned version, built by Henry Ford in the United States, was launched in June 1939.

In 1946, with British government backing, the famous TE20 Ferguson tractor, made by the Standard Motor Company in Coventry, was launched. In the United States, Ferguson and Ford fought a massive anti-trust suit, largely over a similar machine produced by Ford. Ferguson set up his own US plant, the first machine coming off the line on 11 October 1948.

After selling out to Massey-Harris in 1953, Ferguson entered into various negotiations and tried to interest motor manufacturers in a revolutionary design of car produced by Harry Ferguson

Research. These attempts came to little, and Ferguson died at his home at Abbotswood, Stow-on-the-Wold, on 25 October 1960.

Tractive effort on smaller farms around the turn of the century was provided almost exclusively by draught animals. In addition to ploughs and harrows, there were horse-drawn binders and mowers and some barn machinery was driven by oil engines. Mechanized ploughing was carried out by traction engines, such as those produced by Fowler, one at each end of a field pulling a balance plough between them. This and other mechanized equipment was generally affordable only by large landowners.

In the 1880s two mobile steam engines for the farm appeared. They were small by the standards of the time but weighed 2 tonnes (2.5 tons). Both were expensive, however, and farmers that could afford them preferred the steam-driven tackle. In Canada 10-tonne (9.8 ton) traction engines were being used. These heavy machines compacted the soil and produced a 'pan' which prevented proper drainage and inhibited root formation.

Lighter, petrol-engined tractors were being made by 1910, but they were simply mechanical horses used to pull trailed equipment. Driving them was dangerous because, if a plough hit an obstruction, they tended to rear up and could crush the driver. For the first Fordson tractor, Ferguson designed a plough that coupled to the back of the tractor with the 'Duplex' hitch. This overcame the rearing problem, but there was little transfer of plough draught to the rear wheels. It was the principle of draught control which was the complete answer to the problem. The Ferguson System plough was built with two hitching points at about the normal level and a third hitch about a 1m (c.3ft) above the ground connecting via a top link to a point about the same height on the tractor. When the plough hit an obstruction, the top link went into compression and tended to push the front of the tractor on to the ground instead of the reverse.

Ferguson incorporated a hydraulic system in the tractor for raising or lowering the plough out of or into work. This system was not new but using it to keep the plough at the correct working depth without the use of a depth wheel was a revolutionary step. The compression in the top link operated a sleeve valve in the hydraulic system, admitting varying amounts of oil to the pump. When the plough bit deep, it tended to tilt forwards, putting the top link in compression and opening the valve. This allowed more oil to be pumped into the hydraulic cylinder.

The cylinder raised the two bottom links, keeping the plough at an even depth. Thus the weight of the furrow slice was transferred to the tractor's back wheels, enabling it to exert greater effective traction. If the plough had a depth wheel, the draught was transferred to this wheel and not to the tractor's wheels. Ferguson's system meant that expensive, heavy machines were no longer necessary.

Fessenden, Reginald Aubrey *(1866-1932)*, was a Canadian-American physicist whose invention of radio-wave modulation paved the way for modern radio communication.

Born in East Bolton, Quebec, Canada on 6 October 1866, Fessenden studied at Trinity College School, Port Hope, Ontario and Bishop's University at Lennoxville, Quebec. It was only after he had moved to Bermuda, to take up the position of Principal at the Whitney Institute there, that his interest in science really came alive. With little opportunity to follow up such interests in Bermuda, he left to go to New York, where he met Thomas Edison (1847-1931). By his early twenties, Fessenden had become the chief chemist at Edison's laboratories at Orange, New Jersey.

In 1890 he left to join Edison's great rival, the Westinghouse Electric & Manufacturing Company, where he stayed for two years before returning to academic life, first a Purdue University, Lafayette, as Professor of Electrical Engineering and then at the Western University of Pennsylvania (now the University of Pittsburgh). It was there that Fessenden began major work on the problems of radio communication.

By 1900 he had overcome some major technical difficulties and succeeded in transmitting speech by radio, taking out the first patent for voice transmission the following year. Two key inventions of Fessenden's turned his 1900 experiment into the forerunner of modern radio communication. The first was that of modulation. In the early days of radio, experimenters such as Guglielmo Marconi (1874-1937) had sent messages using short bursts of signals to mimic Morse code. Fessenden realized that the amplitude of a continuous radio wave could be varied to mimic the variations of more complex wave patterns. By converting sound waves into variations of amplitude, it would therefore be possible to transmit voices and music. This is the principle of amplitude modulation.

Fessenden's other major invention was that of the heterodyne effect. In this, the received radio wave is combined with a wave of frequency slightly different to that of the carrier wave. The resulting intermediate frequency wave is easier to amplify before being demodulated to generate the original sound wave.

Two years after his initial broadcast, Fessenden organized the building of a 50kHz alternator for radiotelephony by the General Electric Company. This was followed by his building a transmitting station at Brant Rock, Massachussetts. On Christmas Eve, 1906, the first amplitude-modulated radio message was broadcast; both words and music were transmitted. In the same year he established two-way radio communication between Brant Rock and Scotland.

By his death in Bermuda on 22 July 1932, Fessenden held 500 patents, a figure surpassed only by his former employer Edison. Amongst his patents are those for the sonic depth finder, the loop-antenna radio compass and submarine signalling devices.

Fleming, John Ambrose *(1849-1945)*, was a British electrical engineer whose many contributions to science included the invention of the thermiomic diode valve, which proved to be a key electronic component in the early development of radio.

Fleming was born in Lancaster, Lancashire, on 29 November 1849, the son of a parson. When he was 4 years old his family moved to London, where his father continued his ministry in Kentish Town. Fleming was educated at University College School, and later at University College, London where he was awarded his BSc in 1870. His studies at the University were only part-time because for 2 years he worked as a clerk with a firm of stockbrokers. From 1872 to 1874 he studied at South Kensington, first under Edward Frankland and later under Frederick Guthrie.

For the next three years, he was a science master at Cheltenham College, then in 1877 he entered St John's College, Cambridge, having won an entrance exhibition (and having saved £400 to pay the fees). At Cambridge he worked in the Cavendish Laboratory and studied electricity and advanced mathematics under James Clerk Maxwell, author of the famous treatise on electricity and magnetism. In 1879 Fleming obtained his DSc (London) and researched into electrical resistances. Three years later he was appointed to the newly created chair of Mathematics and Physics at University College, Nottingham, but resigned his post the following year to take up consulting work with the Edison Electric Light Company.

In 1883 Fleming was elected Fellow of St. John's and in 1885 he was appointed Professor at University College, London. Between 1889 and 1898 he published several important papers on the practical problems of the electrical and magnetic properties of materials at very low temperatures. During part of this time he made a careful study of the 'Edison effect' in carbon-filament lamps. In 1904 he produced experimental proof that the known rectifying property of a thermionic valve

was still operative at radio frequencies, and this discovery led to the invention and production of what was first known as the 'Fleming valve'.

In 1905 Fleming described his electric wave measurer or cymometer, and demonstrated it to the Royal Society. In 1874, he read the very first paper to the Physical Society on its foundation in that year; 65 years later in 1939, at the age of 90, he read his last paper to the same Society. Fleming died on 18 April 1945 at his home in Sidmouth, Devon.

The value of Fleming's work was widely recognized. In 1892 he was elected an FRS and received the Hughes Medal from the Royal Society in 1910. In 1921 he was awarded the Albert Medal of the Royal Society of Arts and, in 1928, the Faraday Medal from the Instition of Electrical Engineers. He was knighted in 1929.

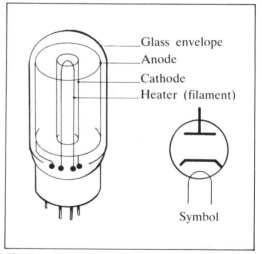

Glass envelope
Anode
Cathode
Heater (filament)

Symbol

Fleming's work on electric lamps led him to invent the diode valve, a two-electrode vacuum tube in which a heated filament causes thermionic emission of electrons from the cathode. The valve was used as a rectifier and a dectector in radio receivers until largely superseded by the semiconductor diode.

Although an avid experimenter, Fleming did not concern himself merely with the theoretical aspects of electrical science but took an active part in its practical application. As engineer and adviser to the Edison, Swan and Ferranti electric lighting companies between 1882 and 1889, he was responsible for improvements in incandescent lamps, meters and generators. For 26 years he was scientific consultant to the Marconi Wireless Telegraph Company and he designed many parts of their early radio apparatus - particularly those used by Marconi in his pioneering transatlantic transmission in 1901.

In the early 1880s, Fleming investigated the

phenomenon known as the Edison effect - the escape of electrons or ions from a heated solid or liquid - but had abandoned the project as being of no practical value. In 1904 this early work on the 'one-way' conductance of electricity in an incandescent lamp led to Fleming's most important practical achievement - the invention of the two-electrode thermionic rectifier which became known as the Fleming valve or diode.

Fleming was searching for a more reliable detector of weak electric currents. He recalled his earlier experiments and made a new 'lamp' that had a metal cylinder surrounding the filament in a high vacuum. He found that it was very useful in detecting the very weak currents in radio receiving apparatus because it responded to currents alternating at very high frequencies. Previous instruments he had employed had been unable to do this because the electric 'waves' produced forces that tended to produce additional alternating currents.

He called his invention a valve because it was the electric equivalent of a check valve in a water supply system which allows water to pass in one direction only. In a like manner, the Fleming valve allowed electrical currents to pass in only one direction. It worked by allowing one of the electrodes - the cathode - to be kept hot so that electrons could evaporate from it into the vacuum. The other electrode - the anode - was left cool enough to prevent any appreciable evaporation of electrons from it. It was thus a device that permitted currents to flow essentially in one direction only when an alternating current was applied to it, and it revolutionized the early science of radio.

The Fleming valve has now been superseded by the transistor diode, an electronic device which utilizes the properties of single-crystal semiconductors. However, because he made possible a very significant advance in radio and television, Fleming's work will always remain an important milestone in electronic engineering. And despite the comparative relegation of the importance of his most famous practical contribution, his work in the theoretical and teaching aspects of electrical science remains undiminished.

Ford, Henry *(1863-1947)*, was an American automotive engineer and industrialist who, in the early twentieth century, revolutionized the motorcar industry and manufacturing methods generally. His production of the Model-T popularized the car as a means of transport and made a considerable social and economic impact on society. His introduction of the assembly line (bringing components to the workers, rather than vice versa) gave impetus to the lagging Industrial Revolution.

Ford was born at Springwells, Michigan, on 30 July 1863. He attended rural schools and soon displayed a mechanical and inventive skill. Moving to Detroit at the age of 16, he obtained a job as a machinist's apprentice. During the next few years he worked for several different companies, and repaired watches and clocks in his spare time. After his apprenticeship Ford worked on the maintenance and repair of Westinghouse steam engines. In 1891 he was appointed chief engineer to the Edison Illuminating Company.

In about 1893 he constructed a one-cylinder petrol (gasoline) engine and went on to build his first car in 1896. Three years later he resigned from Edison's and joined the Detroit Automobile Company. He left there in March 1902 and, with some financial backing, formed the Ford Motor Company on 16 June 1903.

The first Ford car sold almost as soon as it was produced; further orders came in, and production rose rapidly. In 1906, because of a disagreement with his business associates (the Dodge brothers), Ford became the majority shareholder and president of the company, and by 1919 he and his immediate family held complete control of it.

Despite his success with the motorcar, Ford's non-industrial activities met with little success. An expedition to Europe he organized in December 1915 aimed at ending World War I, proved to be a fiasco. His attempt to run as a democrat for a Senate seat in Michigan and subsequent defeat left him bitter about alleged irregularities in his opponent's campaign.

However, other of his activities have brought him a great deal of credit as a benefactor. He created Greenfield Village as a monument to the simple rural world - a world that his automobiles had done so much to destroy. In it, he reconstructed the physical surroundings and the crafts of an earlier era. Near the village is the Henry Ford Museum containing his fine collection of antiques. Ford also restored the Wayside Inn of Longfellow's poem, and his important collection of early motion pictures were donated to the National Archives. He endowed the Ford Foundation, established in 1936, as a private, non-profit-making corporation 'to receive and adminster funds for scientific, educational and charitable purposes'. Ford finally gave up the Presidency of his company in 1945. He died in Dearborn on 7 April 1947.

Motorcars were in their infancy when Henry Ford produced his first automobile in 1896 and decided to make his reputation in the field of racing cars. His determination to do this led him to leave the Detroit Automobile Company and to work on his own. In a memorable race at Grosse Point, Michigan, in October 1901, his victory brought him the publicity he sought. Barney Oldfield, also driving a Ford racer, added to Ford's reputation and in 1904 Ford himself drove his '999' to a world record of 39.4 seconds for a mile (1.6km) over the ice on Lake St Clair in January 1904.

The success of Ford's family cars was immediate. From the low-priced Model-N he went on to produce the Model-T, which first appeared in 1908. Over 19 years, 15 million were sold, and the car is regarded as having changed the pattern of life in the United States. It was one of the first cars to be made using assembly-line methods, and Henry Ford's name became a household word the world over.

The car itself was a sturdy black vehicle with a 4-cylinder 20 hp engine with magnetic ignition. A planetary transmission eliminated the gear-shift (and the danger of stripping the gears). 'Splash' lubrication was used and vanadium steel, of high tensile strength but easy to machine, was employed in many of the car's parts. Ford himself was responsible for the overall concept, and many of the basic ideas embodied in the construction of the Model-T were his own. In 1914 Ford became the first employer of mass labour to pay $5 a day minimum wage to all his employees who met certain basic requirements.

Dictatorial in his attitude, he later dismissed many key individuals who had helped to build the company's early success. He relinquished presidency of the company in 1909 to his son Edsel but strongly resisted changes in production despite an increasing loss of the market to up-and-coming competitors like the General Motors Corporation and Chrysler. Eventually, Ford acknowledged the inroads the newcomers were making on his Model-T. Characteristically, he set out to beat them with a new design, and in January 1928 he produced the Model-A.

The new car was the first to have safety glass in its windscreen as standard equipment. It was available in four colours and 17 body styles. Four-wheel brakes and hydraulic shock absorbers were incorporated in the car and it became a worthy successor to the Model-T. But Ford's previously undisputed leadership in the industry was not restored. Even the introduction of the V-8 engine - an engineering innovation at the time - did not halt the steady deterioration of Ford's share of the market.

When Edsel Ford died in 1943, Henry Ford resumed presidency of the company but in 1945 he surrendered it, for the last time, to his grandson and namesake, Henry Ford II.

Fourneyron, Benoit *(1802-1867)*, was a French engineer who invented the first practical water turbine.

Fourneyron was born on 31 October 1802 in Saint-Etienne, Loir. As the son of a geometrician, he was well prepared in mathematical sciences before entering the New School of Mines at Saint-Etienne at 15 years of age. He graduated at the top of his class. His early activities were devoted to developing the mines at Le Creusot, prospecting for oil, laying out a railway and, finally, initiating the fabrication of tin-plate - until then an English monopoly - at Pont-sur-l'Ognon, Haute Saone.

Because the process involved the use of a water wheel, whose efficiency was very low, Fourneyron became obsessed with the idea of producing a high-efficiency water wheel and, in 1827, he succeeded. In 1855, he produced an improved version and went on to build more than a thousand hydraulic turbines of various forms and for use in different parts of the world. He died in Paris on 8 July 1867.

The idea of using a stream of water to drive a wheel is very old and it is thought that the water wheel was invented in the first century BC. The first device that operated on the principle of reaction was a steam 'turbine' of Hero of Alexandria in the first century AD.

Improvement in the design and efficiency of water wheels came slowly. By the early part of the nineteenth century, with the application of mathematics and a growing knowledge of hydraulics, the first reaction wheels of Leonhard Euler and those of Claude Burdin were produced - but it was Fourneyron, one of Burdin's pupils, who first achieved success. His 1827 reaction turbine was 80 per cent efficient and could develop about 6 horsepower.

Fourneyron's machine is generally recognized as opening the modern era of practical water turbines. It was essentially an outward flow turbine. Water passed through fixed guide passages and hence into guide passages in the moveable outer wheel. When the water impinged on these wheel vanes, its direction was changed and it escaped round the periphery of the wheel. But the outward-flow turbine was essentially unstable because, as water flowed through the fixed and moveable vanes it entered a region of successively increasing volume. The speed regulation of the turbine also presented difficulties.

Fourneyron patented an improved design which incorporated a three-turbine installation in 1832. However, his machine lost favour, being superseded in 1843 by the Jonval axial-flow machine.

Fourneyron's machines were still used in large commercial undertakings. All his earlier designs were of the free-flow efflux type, but he foresaw the advantages of allowing the efflux to flow into a diffuser and, in 1855, he patented an outflow diffuser in the form of the present-day inflow scroll case. Two turbines, each consisting of Fourneyron wheels keyed to one shaft, were used by the Niagra Falls Power Company in 1895. They were built into 49m (160ft) wheel-pits dug into the supply channel at the top of the Falls.

Fowler, John *(1817-1898)*, was a British engineer who designed the Forth railway bridge and built the first railway bridge across the river Thames in London.

Fowler was born in Sheffield on 15 July, 1817, and educated at Whitley Hall private school. After leaving school he became a pupil of J.T. Leather, engineer of the Sheffield waterworks. He then undertook work on railways, first on the London–Brighton line, then on the proposed Morecambe Bay railway, and finally as engineer, general manager and locomotive superintendent of the Stockport–Hartlepool line.

In 1844 he set up as a consulting engineer in London, designing the Pimlico railway bridge over the Thames. From 1857 he worked on the Metropolitan Railway, being responsible for most of the extensions to the original line from Edgware Road to King's Cross. In 1869 he went to Egypt to advise the Khedive on railway matters, and a year later he was in Norway on behalf of the Indian government to studying narrow-gauge railways. His recommended gauge of 1.07m (3ft 6in), instead of the Norwegian 0.84m (2ft 9in) was adopted for the Indian railways. In 1875 he took Benjamin Baker as a partner, with whom he designed the Forth Bridge. He twice (unsuccessfully) stood for Parliament and died on 20 November 1898, in Bournemouth.

Fowlers best-known works are probably the Metropolitan Railway and the Forth Bridge. By 1846, the nineteenth-century railway mania was in full spate and Fowler took an active part in the struggles of the various Railway Acts being promoted in Parliament. The Metropolitan received its first Act in 1853, the first section of the line was opened in 1863, and Fowler worked on its extensions and branches to the London suburbs. When a bridge over the river Forth was proposed in the 1870s, its design was first entrusted to Thomas Bouch. But when his Tay Bridge collapsed disastrously in 1879, the task was given to Harrison, Barlow, Fowler and Baker, the consulting engineers of the four railway companies involved. Their report (1881) advocated a cantilever bridge.

The great structure was begun in 1883 and successfully completed seven years later, being opened by the Prince of Wales on 4 March 1890. Fowler received a baronetcy for his work on the bridge, and Baker was knighted.

Foyn, Svend *(1809-1894)*, was a Norwegian who modernized the technology of whaling with his invention of the explosive harpoon and the introduction of the steam-powered whaler.

Foyn was born in Tonsberg on 9 July 1809. He married twice (in 1839 and, after a divorce, again in 1849) and had a son and a daughter by each marriage. He died in Ramdal on 29 November 1894.

The hand-throw harpoon was improved and developed by Dutch whalers in the 1730s and was in general use until 1864, when Foyn introduced guns to fire harpoons with explosive heads. These heavy guns were mounted on the fore-deck of the faster steam-powered boats and made it possible, for the first time, to successfully hunt the elusive fin, sei and blue whales.

Foyn's version of the old-fashioned harpoon had a set of hinged barbs which spread out within the whale and, as they opened, broke a small glass tube of sulphuric acid that ignited a fuse which then set off a charge of gunpowder. Foyn also introduced the steam-driven whaling boat and the bow mounted harpoon gun. These inventions were followed, in 1890, by the first factory ship and the first Atlantic whaling expedition which Foyn organized in 1893.

The new techniques - and consequently larger catches - gave the industry a new impetus just when, in the 1860s, the numbers of grey whales were seriously in decline. The larger catches encouraged the development of massive shore stations where entire carcasses could be processed. The whale oil formed the basis for the manufacture of soap, perfumes, glycerine and varnish.

Friese-Greene, William *(1855-1921)*, was a British inventor and one of the early pioneers of cinema photography.

Friese-Greene was born on 7 September 1855 in Bristol where he was educated at the Blue Coat School. He became interested in philosophy and in about 1875 opened a portrait studio in Bath. In the early 1880s he met a mechanic J.A.R. Rudge, who asked him to produce slides for a magic lantern (forerunner of the modern slide projector). This work awakened Friese-Greene's interest in moving pictures. In 1885 he opened a studio in London and met Mortimer Evans, an engineer. They decided to collaborate, and in 1889 Friese-Greene patented a camera that could take ten photographs per second on a roll of sensitized paper. Using his own apparatus, he was able to project a jerky picture of people and horse-drawn vehicles moving past Hyde Park Corner - probably the first time a film of an actual event had been projected on a screen. In 1890 he substituted celluloid film for the paper in the camera, and in the next few years he patented improved cameras and projectors. Friese-Green died in London on 5 May 1921.

The early story of moving pictures is obscure, complicated by claims and counter-claims. Certainly several inventors were working on similar lines at about the same time. In 1824, Peter Roget lectured to the Royal Society on the subject of persistance of vision, and projected onto a screen a series of still pictures at the rate of 24 per second which gave the illusion of smooth and continuous movement. In the 1860s and 1870s there were various inventions for similarly projecting a series of stills, such as that of Heyl (in which transparencies were mounted on a glass disc and rotated). Faster camera shutter speeds and improved photographic emulsions enabled people to take sharper pictures of moving objects. Eduard Muybridge took a series of photographs of a racehorse by placing 24 cameras along a track, then projecting the pictures using an apparatus similar to Heyl's. Thomas Edison designed a motion-picture machine that recorded pictures in a spiral on a cylinder, but it was unsatisfactory. In 1889 George Eastman, founder of the Kodak company, produced roll film which solved part of Edison's problem, but the pictures could still be viewed only through a lens and not projected. Edison's invention was improved by others, and in france the Lumiere Brothers developed a machine that functioned both as a camera and a projector. They arranged a show in London in 1896, the first time the public had been able to see moving pictures.

Although Friese-Greene's films were but short fragments and consisted of only ten pictures per second - inadequate to produce a convincing effect of movement - he had taken and projected 'moving' pictures before Edison and his patent was judged by a United States court to be the master patent. This brought him neither success nor financial gain, however. The same seems to have been true of his other inventions: a three-colour camera, moving pictures using a two-colour process, and machinery for rapid photographic processing and printing.

Froude, William *(1810-1879)* was the English engineer and hydrodynamiscist who first formulated reliable laws for the resistance that water offers to ships and for predicting their stability. He also invented the hydraulic dynameter for measuring the output of high-power engines. These achievements were fundamental to marine development.

Froude (pronounced 'Frood') was educated at Buckfastleigh, Westminster School and Oriel College, Oxford, where he obtained (1832) a first in mathematics and a third in classics. He remained at Oxford working on water resistance and the propulsion of ships and in 1838 became an assistant to I.K Brunel on the building of the Bristol and Exeter Railway.

In 1839 he married Katherine Holdsworth of Widdicombe. He probably worked on the South Devon Railway and was intimately connected with the ill-fated atmospheric railway. In 1846 he went to live with his father at Dartington Parsonage and began work in earnest on marine hydrodynamics. Brunel consulted him on the behaviour of the *Great Eastern* at sea and, on his recommendation, the ship was fitted with bilge keels.

When his father died in 1859 Froude moved to Paignton where he began his tank-testing experiments. In 1863 he started to build his own house, known as Chelston Cross, at Cockington, Torquay, and helped the local water authority with its supply problems. In 1867 he began his experiments with towed models. After grudging financial assistance from the Admiralty, he built another experimental tank near his home in 1871.

He described his hydraulic dynameter in a paper to the Institution of Mechanical Engineers in 1877 but did not live to see his machine work. It was built in 1878, the year in which Froude's wife died and in which he became seriously ill. He went on a voyage of recuperation to the Cape but caught dysentry and died on 6 May 1879 in Simon's Town, where he was buried.

Froude was elected a Fellow of the Royal Society in 1870 and his work was continued by his sons Richard and Robert. Robert built the towing tank for the Admiralty at Haslar, near Portsmouth, and Richard joined Hammersley Heenan to manufacture the dynamometer commercially.

Generally there are two modes in which vessels can travel: by displacement, in which they force their way through the water, and by planing, or skating on top of the water. In the displacement mode, the propulsive power is absorbed in making waves and in overcoming the friction of the hull against the water.

Froude's first successful experiments started in 1867 when he towed models in pairs, balancing one hull shape against the other. Initially he incorporated his findings into a single law, now known as Froude's Law of Comparison. This stated that the entire resistance of similar-shaped models varies as the cube of their dimensions if their speeds are as the square root of their dimensions.

As Froude himself realized, this law becomes increasingly unreliable as the difference in size between the models increases. This is because the frictional resistance and the wave-making resistance follow different laws. His Laws of Comparisons is now only applied to the wave-making component.

To estimate frictional resistance, Froude carried out tests in his tank at Torquay, where he towed submerged (to eliminate wave-making resistance) planks with different surface roughness. He was able to establish a formula which would predict the frictional resistance of a hull with accuracy.

With these two analytical results, using only models and mathematics, Froude had found a reliable means of estimating the power required to drive a hull at a given speed. Model testing had been tried before but was considered unreliable because previous workers had failed to appreciate that the two major components of ship resistance varied differently. Opponents of model testing maintained that the only way to gather the required information was to work on full-sized hulls. It was this anti-model lobby which was largely responsible for Froude's difficulties in pursuading the Admiralty to part with £2,000 for building the Torquay tank.

Froude had done a large amount of theoretical work on the rolling stability of ships and when the Torquay tank had been built, he was able to carry out model experiments, relating them to observations made on actual ships. His general deductions were challenged at the time but they were found to be correct and to this day are the standard exposition of the rolling and oscillation of ships.

Engine builders usually need to test their machinery before installation. The friction brake is useful only for lower-power applications, so Froude employed hydrodynamic principles to absorb 1,491kW (2,000hp) at 90rpm. His brake consisted of a rotor and stator, both of which were shaped in a series of semi- circular cups angled at 45° but of opposite pitch. The change is momentum when water passes from rotor to stator and back again creating a braking reaction. By measuring this braking reaction and the shaft speed, the power of the engine could be calculated.

Froude was a tireless experimenter who put one of the most powerful analytical tools into the hands of marine architects. Sometimes he is credited as 'the father of ship hydrodynamics'. If any one man can be said to father anything in engineering, this handle is probably accurate.

Fulton, Robert *(1765-1815)*, was an American artist and engineer and inventor who built one of the first successful steamboats, propelled by two paddle-wheels.

Fulton was born on 14 November 1765 in Lancaster County, Pennsylvania. His artistic talent was evident at an early age, and he was employed by local gunsmiths to draw designs for their work. At the age of 17 he moved to Philadelphia, where he became a successful portrait painter and miniaturist. Four years later, in 1786, he decided to go to London to study under the American artist Benjamin West. England changed Fulton's life. The country was involved in the Industrial Revolution; roads, canals and bridges were being built, factories were springing up and mining enterprises were getting under way. He was fascinated by all he saw and eventually, in 1793, he gave up art as a vocation in favour of engineering projects.

When Fulton was 14 he designed a small paddleboat and now he considered designing one with a steam engine to power it. In 1786 John Fitch (1743-1798) had demonstrated a steamboat in the United States, but it had not proved to be a success. The British government had placed a ban on the export of steam engines, but Fulton nevertheless contacted a British company about the possibility of purchasing an engine suitable for boat propulsion. Meanwhile he designed and patented a device for hauling canal boats over difficult country. He also patented machines for spinning flax (for linen), saving marble and twisting hemp (for rope), and he built a mechanical dredger for canal construction.

In 1796 Fulton went to France, where he experimented with fitting steam engines to ships, and by 1801 he had also carried out tests with the *Nautilus*, a submarine he had invented. But he failed to interest the French in his inventions, so by 1804 he tried the British government, again without success. In 1802 Fulton had met Robert Livingstone, a former partner in another steamboat invention and then American Minister to the French government. He and Fulton joined forces and in 1803 a steam engine was obtained from the British firm of Boulton and Watt; but it took three years to get permission to export it to the United States.

In New York, Fulton worked to install the new engine in a locally-built vessel. Livingstone favoured designing a propulsion system using a jet of water forced out at the stern under pressure, but Fulton settled on a paddlewheel on each side. In 1807, the paddlesteamer *Clermont*, with a 24hp engine fitted into its 30m (100ft) hull, made its first successful voyage up the Hudson river at an average speed of 8km/h (5mph). A large boat works was built in New Jersey, and steamboats came into use along the Atlantic Coast and later in the West. In 1815, Fulton began to build a steam-powered warship for the United States navy.

Fulton died on 24 February 1815 in New York City.

Francis, James Bicheno *(1815-1892)*, was the British born hydraulics engineer who spent most of his working life in the USA and played a crucial role in the industrial development of part of New England. He made significant contributions to the understanding of fluid flow and to the development the Francis-type water turbine for which he is remembered.

Francis was born on 18 May 1815 at Southleigh, Oxfordshire, the son of a railway superintendent and builder. After a short education at Radleigh Hall and Wantage Academy, he became assistant to his father on canal and harbour works. Two years later, he was employed by the Great Western Canal Company.

He travelled to the USA in search of greater opportunities arriving in New York City in the Spring of 1833. There he was employed by Major George Washington Whistler (1800-1849) on building the Stonington Railroad, Connecticut. A year later when Whistler became chief engineer to 'The Proprietors of the Locks and Canals on the Merrimack River' a corporation known simply as 'The Proprietors' Francis went with him to Lowell, Mass.

In 1837 Whistler resigned and Francis became his successor. In the same year Francis married Sarah Wilbur Brownell of Lowell on 12 July. When The Proprietors decided (in 1845) to develop the river's water-powered facilities, Francis was made chief engineer and general manager. He travelled to England (1849) briefly to study timber preservation methods and on his return turned his attention to developing water turbines. In 1855 his famous work, The Lowell Hydraulic Experiments, was published.

Francis wrote more than 200 papers for learned societies and was president of the American Society of Civil Engineers in 1880. He advised on a number of important dam projects, was a member of.the Massachusetts state legislature president of the Stonybrook Railroad for 20 years and for 43 years a director of the Lowell Gas Light Company.

He retired from active business in 1885, and was succeeeded by one of his sons. Francis died on 18 September and was survived by his wife and six children.

The industrialization of New England resulted initially from water power rather than steam. The leading part Francis played in the exploitation of the Merrimack River was thus at the time more important than the work he did on turbines.

The Proprietor's corporation had been formed in 1792, originally to improve navigation. Realizing the potential, a Boston group purchased 400 acres near the Pawtucket Falls, a site which soon developed into the town of Lowell. The company built a 289.56m (950ft) dam on the river which produced a 10.67m (35ft) head and 29km (18 miles) of backwater, the pondage feeding 11 independent mills.

One of Francis' responsibilities was the measurement of the flows used by each of the manufacturing companies along the river to assess costs. He made numerous tests on sharp-crested weirs, and determined the numerical values in the Francis weir formula, the form of which was suggested by his colleague, Uriah Atherton Boyden (1804-1879). The second (1868) edition of Francis' work included his studies of measurements with weighted floats.

Francis' work on turbines started when The Proprietors acquired, in the late 1840s, an interest in the patent turbine designed by Samuel B Howd. This was a radial inflow (or 'centre-vent') machine which was effective but inefficient. Significantly, however, Francis had built (in 1847) a model wheel similar to Howd's, and it, too, was not very efficient. Two years later several inward-flow wheels of 172kw (230hp) each were built from Francis' design. Tests showed peak efficiencies of nearly 80 per cent.

The Francis wheels of the development days were an improvement over those of Howd, but only to a small degree do the so-called Francis turbines of today resemble Francis' original designs. At the outset they utilised purely radial flow runners and they had neither the familiar scroll case nor the draught tube of modern units. Later engineers developed the design into the forerunner of the modern mixed flow unit.

The reason Francis' name continues to be associated with the design presumably stemmed initially from the wide-spread attention attracted by his book and then from the adoption of the designation by the German and Swiss firms which led in its scientific development later in the century.

Francis also devised a complete system of water supply for fire protection and had it working in the Lowell district for many years before anything similar was in operation anywhere else. He designed and built hydraulic lifts for the guard gates of the Pawtucket Canal and between 1875 and 1876 he reconstructed the Pawtucket Dam.

Francis was to a large part responsible for Lowell's rise to industrial importance. In retrospect, however, this is less notable than the experimental work he did in connection with the flow of fluids over weirs, and the establishment of the Francis Formula. His work on the inward-flow turbine was significant and after his death the Canadian Niagra Power Company installed Francis turbines developing 10,250hp (7,643kW) at the famous falls.

G

Gabor, Dennis *(1900-1979)*, was a Hungarian-born British physicist and electrical engineer, famous for his invention of holography - three-dimensional photography using lasers - for which he received the 1971 Nobel Prize for Physics.

Gabor was born on 5 January 1900 in Budapest. He was educated at the Budapest Technical University and then at the Technishe Hochschule in Charlottenburg, Berlin. From 1924 to 1926 he was an assistant there, and for the next three years he held the position of Research Associate with the German Research Association for High-Voltage Plants. He was a Research Engineer for the firm of Siemens and Halske in Berlin from 1927 until he fled Nazi Germany in 1933 to Britain. He then worked as a Research Engineer with the Thomson-Houston Company of Rugby from 1934 to 1938, and later became a British subject. In 1949, he joined the Faculty of the Imperial College of Science and Technology, London University as a Reader in Electronics. He was Professor of Applied Electron Physics from 1958 to 1967, when he became a Senior Research Fellow. From 1976 until his death he was Professor Emeritus of Applied Electron Physics of the University of London. He died in London on 8 February 1979.

Gabor first conceived the idea of holography in 1947 and developed the basic technique by using conventional filtered light sources. Because conventional light sources provided too little light or light that was too diffuse, his idea did not become commercially feasible until the laser was demonstrated in 1960 and was shown to be capable of amplifying the intensity of light waves.

Holography is a means of creating a unique photographic image without the use of a lens. The photographic recording of the image is called a hologram. The hologram appears to be an unrecognizable pattern of shapes and whorls, but when it is illuminated by coherent light (as by a laser beam), the light is organized into a three-dimensional representation of the original object. Gabor coined the name from the Greek *holos* meaning whole and *gram* meaning message, because the image-forming mechanism which he conceived recorded all the optical information in a wavefront of light. In ordinary photography, the photographic image records the variations in light intensity reflected from an object, so that dark areas are produced where less light is reflected and light areas where more light is reflected. Holography records not only the intensity of light, but also its phase, or the degree to which the wavefronts making up the reflected light are in step with each other. The wavefronts of ordinary light waves are not in step - ordinary light is incoherent.

When Gabor began work on the holograph, he considered the possibility of improving the resolving power of the electron microscope, first by using the electron beam to make a hologram of the object and then by examining this hologram with a beam of coherent light. It is possible to obtain a degree of coherence by focusing light through a very small pin-hole, but the resulting light intensity is then too low for it to be useful in holography. In 1960, the laser beam was developed. This has a high degree of coherence and also has high intensity. There are many kinds of laser beam, but two have special interest in holography, the continuous-wave (CW) and the pulsed laser. The CW laser emits a bright continuous beam of light of a single, nearly pure colour. The pulsed laser emits an extremely intense, short flash of light that lasts only about 10^{-8} second. Two American scientists, Emmett Leith and Juris Upatnieks have applied the CW laser to holography with great success, opening the way to many research applications. To achieve a three-dimensional image, the light streaming from the source must itself be photographed. If the waves of this light with its many rapidly moving crests and troughs, are frozen for an instant and photographed, the wave pattern can then be reconstructed and will show the same three-dimensional character as the object from which the light is reflected.

Pulse laser holography is used in the study of chemical reactions, where optical properties of solutions often change. It is also used in wind-tunnel experiments, where it can be used to record refractive index changes in the air flow, created by pressure changes as the gas deflects around the aerodynamic object. This recording is done interferometrically (by observing interference fringes).

Apart from the invention of holography, Gabor's other work included research on high-speed oscilloscopes, communication theory, physical optics and television. He took out more than 100 patents for his invention and became renowned as an outstanding engineer and physicist of the twentieth century.

Gatling, Richard Jordan *(1818-1903)*, was a prolific American inventor who is best remembered for his invention of the Gatling gun, one of the earliest successful rapid-fire weapons.

Gatling was born in Hertford County, North Carolina, on 12 September 1818. Son of a well-to-do planter, he showed mechanical aptitude early in life and collaborated with his father on the invention of a machine for sowing cotton and for thinning out the young plants. He followed a varied career, his first job being in the county clerk's office. He then taught for a brief period before becoming a merchant.

In 1844, Gatling moved to St Louis, adapted his cotton sowing machine for sowing rice and other grains and established his manufacturing centre there. Other factories were later set up in Ohio and Indiana.

Gatling's career took a new turn after an attack of smallpox. He entered Ohio Medical College, in Cincinnati, to study medicine, qualifying in 1850 but never practising. Instead, for a time he was concerned with railway enterprises and property, but he was still inventing - a hemp-breaking machine (1850), a steam plough (1857) and a marine steam ram (1862).

Forms of rapid-fire weapons were in use as early as the 16th century, but not until about 1860, when breech loading became firmly established, did effective machine guns become possible. One of the first was the Reffye, which had 25 barrels round a common axis.

Gatling's gun, which he patented in 1862, consisted of 10 parallel barrels arranged round a central shaft, each barrel firing in turn as it reached the firing position. An operating cam, driven through a hand-cranked worm gear, forced the locks forward and backward. On a single barrel, loading took place in the first position. The 2nd, 3rd and 4th positions were used to force the cartridge into the breech, and the gun was fired in to the 5th position. The 6th, 7th, 8th and 9th positions were used for extraction of the empty case, which was rejected at the 10th.

The gun was fed from a drum on top which dropped the cartridges into the locks. Each barrel therefore fired as it approached the bottom of its circular journey. In 1862, the year of Gatling's patent specification, the gun was capable of firing 350 rounds a minute. There was no official interest in his invention, however, so he made further improvements to it, extending its range and increasing its firing rate. This still failed to attract official interest, but a few commanders during the Civil War purchased some with private funds. It was not until 1866, after the end of the War, that the Army Ordnance Department ordered 100. Meanwhile, they were being manufactured by the Colt Company and sold overseas to England, Russia, Austria and South America, and were used in

the war of 1870.

In that year, Gatling moved to Hartford, Connecticut, to supervise manufacture and by 1882 his gun could fire 1,200 rounds a minute. Gatling continued to develop his invention producing greater rates of fire and driving it by different methods.

The Gatling was one of the earliest successful rapid-fire weapons but it cannot be regarded as the forerunner of the modern machine gun as it needed an external power source to drive the loading, firing, extraction and ejection mechanism. The laurels for the first workable, truly automatic machine gun must go to Maxim. The main contribution Gatling made to history was to alert the military mind to the possibilities of such weapons. Indeed, special tactics were developed in the Franco-German war of 1870 to counter Gatling-type weapons by massive artillery barrages. It thus failed to make any serious impact.

Gatling died, aged 84, in New York City on 26 February 1903.

Giffard, Henri *(1825-1882),* was a French aeronautical engineer, famous for building the first steerable powered airship and making a successful flight in it.

Giffard, who studied engineering, was particularly interested in balloon flight, which had been pioneered in his native France. In the early 1850s he began to experiment with methods for steering balloons, which hitherto had been entirely at the mercy of the wind. In 1852 Giffard built his airship. It was a sausage-shaped gas bag 44m (144ft) long and 12m (52ft) in diameter, with a hydrogen capacity of 2,500 cu. metres. The gondola was strung from a long pole or keel attached to the gasbag by ropes. It was powered by a small 3-horsepower steam engine driving a 3-bladed propellor - itself an innovation at the time. The airship was steered using a rudder, a canvas sail stretched over a bamboo frame and hinged to the keel. On 24 September 1852 Giffard took off from the Hippodrome in Paris and flew to Elancourt, near Trappes. His average speed was only about 5km/h (3mph) and he had problems with the steering.

Giffard gave up his experiments with airships but went on to other inventions, such as an injector to feed water into a steam engine boiler to prevent it running out of steam when not in motion. But his historic flight marked the real beginning of man's conquest of the air.

Gilchrist, Percy Carlyle *(1851-1935),* was a British metallurgist who devised an inexpensive steel-making process.

Gilchrist was born in Lyme Regis, Sussex, on

27 September 1851, the son of a local barrister. He was educated at Felsted School, Essex, and later at the Royal School of Mines, where he acquired a sound knowledge of metallurgy. Between 1875 and 1877, together with his cousin Sydney Gilchrist Thomas, he developed a method of producing low-phosphorus steel from high-phosphorus British ores (reducing·the need - and cost - of using special imported ores). Thomas died soon afterwards but Gilchrist, who lived on for more than 50 years, became famous. He was Vice President of the Iron and Steel Institute and in 1891 was elected a Fellow of the Royal Society. He died on 16 December 1931.

Steel was a comparatively rare commodity until the 1850s, because its production was difficult and costly. Then in 1855 Henry Bessemer invented his convector (in which air blown through molten pig iron oxidized impurities to produce a brittle, low-carbon steel). The addition of ferromanganese gave a tougher product, but even so only low-phosphorus iron could be used, and most British ores were too high in phosphorus.

In 1870 Sidney Gilchrist Thomas was a junior clerk working in London for the Metropolitan Police but, like his cousin, he had an intense interest in natural science and metallurgy. After attending a series of lectures at the Birkbeck Institute, he joined Percy Gilchrist in trying to manfacture cheap steel from high-phosphorus ores. They used an old cupola to make a Bessemer-type convector and lined it with a paste made from crushed brick, sodium silicate and water. The pig iron was added and melted before being subjected to prolonged 'blowing'. The oxygen in the blast of air oxidized carbon and other impurities, and the addition of lime at this stage caused the oxides to separate out as a slag on the surface of the molten metal. Continued blowing then brought about oxidation of the phosphorus, raising the temperature of the metal still further. When oxidation was complete (as judged by the colour of the flames coming from the convector), the cupola was tilted and the slag run off, leaving the molten steel to be poured into ingot moulds. The product became known at first as 'Thomas steel', and the age of cheap steel had arrived.

Goddard, Robert Hutchings *(1882-1945)*, was the US physicist who pioneered modern research into rocketry. He developed the principle of combining liquid fuels in a rocket motor and the technique has been used subsequently in every practical space vehicle. He was the first to prove by actual test that a rocket will work in a vacuum and he was the first to fire a rocket faster than the speed of sound.

Goddard was born on 5 October 1882 in Worcester, Massachusetts. He was 17 when he began to speculate about conditions in the upper atmosphere and in interplanetary space. He considered the possibility of using rockets as a means of carrying research instruments.

In 1901, while studying for his BSc at Worcester Polytechnic Institute, he wrote a paper suggesting that the heat from radioactive materials could be used to expel substances at high velocities through a rocket motor to provide power for space travel. Two years later, after making his first practical experiments to determine the efficiency of rocket power, he proposed the use of high-energy propellants, such as liquid oxygen and hydrogen.

At Clark University in his home town, and at Mount wilson, California, Goddard carried out experiments with naval signal rockets. He went on to design and build his own rocket motors. As an instructor in physics at Worcester Polytechnic, Goddard directed his experiments towards the development of rockets to explore the upper atmosphere. It was not until 1917 that he received financial aid from the Smithsonian Institute.

On the USA's entry into World War I, he turned his energies to investigating the military application of rockets, whereupon the US Army provided funds. At Clark University, teaching physics in the early 1920s, Goddard switched his practical research from solid fuel to liquid propellants. On 1 November 1923 he fired the first liquid rocket in a test stand. Two years of development were rewarded with the historic first launching of a liquid-propelled rocket on 16 March 1926 at Auburn, Massachusetts.

During the next 3 years he improved engine performance and reduced the weight his design. Instruments, and a camera to record them, were carried aloft for the first time on 17 July 1929. This significant flight attracted funds for a fuel-scale rocket-testing programme.

The greater altitudes and speeds his rocket attained dictated the need for a precise method of flight control and on 28 March 1935 Goddard successfully fired a rocket controlled by gyroscopes linked to vanes in the exhaust stream.

It was in 1937 that one of his rockets reached 3km (1.8 miles), then the greatest altitude for a projectile. His work in New Mexico continued until the World War II. In 1942, with the USA in the War, he joined the Naval Engineering Experimental Station at Annapolos, Maryland, continuing his research until his death on 10 August 1945.

Unlike his contemporaries at the dawn of the space age, Goddard pioneered the science of rocketry by practical experiment. He proved that liquid oxygen and a hydrocarbon fuel, such as petrol or kerosene, was the mixture which would provide the considerable thrust necessary. He built a motor in which to fire the fuels and used it in the first rocket of its kind, nearly 5 years before the first German experimental flights.

His rocket designs which flew in 1940, although smaller, were more advanced than the menacing V2 missile which was to fly 2 years later and was to be launched against European cities. Goddard's development of gyroscopically controlled steering vanes also predated German work by a number of years.

Goddard's other practical work led to the development of the centrifugal propellant pump. While in his early years he foresaw the use of the rocket for high altitude research and wrote about space exploration. He was also aware of the military applications of his work. A rocket he developed for the US Army was fired from a launching tube, but the War ended a few days after its successful demonstration and the need disappeared.

Through much of his career Goddard worked as a 'loner', many of his achievements being made single-handedly. As one of the few practitioners of space research, in a world which was still trying to grasp the significance of air travel, his work and writings were not taken seriously until 1929 and the flight of his first instrumented rocket. The finance which this achievement attracted (initially from the industrialist, Daniel Guggenheim) enabled Goddard and his small team to undertake research during a period of 12 years. This was surpassed only (because it had practical military application) by the achievement of the army of German scientists under Dornberger, in their 5 years' work at Peenemunde to put the V2 strategic missile into service.

The full significance of the German work was not appreciated until the war's end, when Goddard was amazed to find such similarity with his designs. He died only months later and the military and space rocket programmes of both the USA and USSR were to be founded upon this German work.

It was not until 1960 that the US government recognized the value of Goddard's work. It admitted to frequent infringement of many of his 214 patents during the evolution of missile and satellite programmes. In that year his widow received $1,000,000 from Federal funds.

In view of the USA's failure to recognize the significance of his work, at a time when its enemy was almost in a position to influence the course of the War with the rocket, it is ironic to record that Robert Goddard received more financial support for one project than any other single scientist up to World War II.

Gooch, Daniel *(1816-1889)*, was the Northumbrian engineer who at the age of only 21, became the first locomotive superintendent of the Great Western Railway. One of the great practical locomotive engineers of the 19th century and among the greatest locomotive designers of all, he became disillusioned with overall management at the GWR, and resigned. He was knighted for his work on the first trans-Atlantic cable, successfully accomplished in 1866. Only one year after leaving the GWR he was invited back as chairman - the office of which he held from 1865 until his death in 1889.

Gooch was born in Bedlington, Northumberland on 24 August 1816 and was educated at the village school. When he was 15, the family of ten moved to Tredegar, Monmouthshire, his father having taken a post at the local ironworks. It was there that Gooch got his first job, in the foundry and pattern shop. After his father's death in August 1833, Gooch left Tredegar and in January 1834 started work at the Vulcan Foundry which was newly-established by Robert Stephenson and Charles Tayleur at Newton-le-Willows. Ill-health forced him to leave after a few monts. He then worked briefly with his elder brother, Thomas, in surveying the London & Birmingham Railway.

In July 1837, hearing that Brunel, the builder of the Great Wester Railway, was looking for a locomotive superintendent, Gooch applied and was appointed. His initial task was daunting. Brunel was a civil engineer but his directors had given him sole charge for producing the locomotives. He had done his best to specify piston speeds, steam pressures and engine weights, leaving the manufacturers to comply as best they could. For the opening of his 2.14m (7ft) gauge railway he had ordered 19 locomotives from no fewer than six different manufacturers, calling for piston speeds and axle weights far below those of most contemporary standard-gauge engines. The performance of the fleet was deplorable, the engines being so inefficient that timetable working was impossible. These were the circumstances that faced Gooch.

Fortunately there was one star performer in the locomotive fleet - the 2-2-2 *North Star*, built by Robert Stephenson, and delivered in November 1837. It incorporated none of Brunel's specifications but was a straightforwards design ordered originally by the US 1.68m (5ft 6in) gauge New Orleans Railway who had been unable to pay for it. Brunel bought it and made suitable modifications. Extended axles and driving wheels enlarged to 2.1m (7ft) diameter, enabled it to haul the first GWR passenger train.

Gooch was ordered, over the head of Brunel, to produce engines. Being a practical and cautious man who valued reliability in service above all, but possessed great foresight for future requirements, he took the *North Star* as his basic model. He retained its main design features, enlarging some of its dimensions but maintaining the closest attention to detail. He insisted on standardization and quality control from the locomotive manufacturers, who were held liable for their engines' first 1609km (1,000 miles) of running with normal load.

His first locomotive, was *Fire fly* (1840), a 2-2-2 with 2.1m (7ft) wheels and 380x460mm (15x18in) cylinders. It was the forerunner of a class of 62 engines built during the next two years. They were the most powerful engines of their time averaging start-to-stop speeds of 80km/h (50mph) - and lasted at least 30 years. they were closely followed by the slightly smaller 1.8m (6ft) wheel diameter *Sun* class, 21 of which were built for passenger work. Then there were 18 2-4-0s for goods work and 4 0-6-0s of the *Hercules* class. These early locomotives were the first examples of standardization on a grand scale by any railway company.

In 1840 Gooch had chosen Swindon, at the junction of the line to Gloucester and South Wales, as the site for his locomotive works. From there emerged (1846) his colossal locomotive - the 2-2-2 *Great Western*. with 2.4m (8ft) driving wheels and a boiler developing 690kN/sq. m (100psi) pressure, it was built to out-perform any then existing locomotive of any gauge. An early feat was to cover the 85km (53 miles) from Paddington to Didcot in the incredible time of 47 minutes, an *average* speed of 107km/h (67mph).

Development continued, and in 1847 Gooch launched his first eight-wheeled engine, the 4-2-2 *Iron Duke*. It was of the classics of early Victorian locomotive designs and first of the standard 4-2-2 express locomotives that would so ably serve the remaining 45 years of the broad-gauge era. Altogether 29 were built, of which 24 were rebuilt in the 1870s. These were huge engines, weighing 35.6 tonnes (35 tons) without tender. Built for fast running, they often reached speeds in excess of 113km/h (70mph) and were the pinnacle of broad gauge locomotive design.

In 1840 Gooch took out a patent for cladding iron wheels with a steel surface for harder wearing. In 1843, however, he launched, but never patented, his stationary link motion - an important advance used by many other locomotive builders over the next 20 years.

He became a director the Great Eastern Steamship Company in 1860, one year after Brunel's death. In 1864, by which time the GWR. was in deep financial trouble, the price of two decades of rapid expansion, Gooch resigned to

join the Telegraph Construction Company, which chartered Brunel's great iron ship *Great Eastern* to lay the first cable under the Atlantic ocean.

In 1865 he was invited to rejoin the GWR as Chairman and a major accomplishment of this was the boring of the 7.2m (4.5 mile) Severn Tunnel (the longest in Britain) which significantly shortened the route to South Wales. Commenced in 1973 and costing 2 million, it opened for traffic on 9 January 1886. Gooch died a tired old man, three years later on 15 October 1889, aged 73 and was buried in Clewer Churchyard, near Windsor.

Gooch was not a man for experiments. He was a strict puritan and firm disciplinarian but nonetheless a far-sighted engineer ahead of most of his contempories. In 27 years as locomotive superintendent he had designed 340 engines, none of them a failure, and among them, in his day, the fastest and largest passenger engines in the world.

Goodyear, Charles *(1800-1860)*, was an American inventor who is generally credited with inventing the process for vulcanizing rubber.

Goodyear was born in New Haven, Connecticut, on 18 December 1800. When he came of age he entered his father's hardware business at Naugatuck, Connecticut, where he worked with enthusiasm, inventing various implements, including a steel pitchfork to replace the heavy iron type.

The firm became financially unstable, and by 1830 Goodyear realized that he would have to turn to something else. He chose to investigate india-rubber and the problems associated with it, particularly how to make the rubber remain strong and pliable over a range of temperatures. He thought he had found the solution by mixing nitric acid with the rubber, and in 1836 secured a government order for a consignment of mail bags. But they would not stand up to high temperatures and were therefore useless. Goodyear was forced to start again.

In 1837 he bought out the rights of Nathaniel Hayward, who had had some success by mixing sulphur with raw rubber. After much patient experiment - and a deal of luck - Goodyear finally perfected the process he called vulcanization.

He obtained United States patents in 1844, but both Britain and France refused his applications because of legal technicalities. His attempts to set up companies in both countries failed, and for a while he was imprisoned for debt in Paris. Eventually he returned to the United States, where many of his patents had been pirated by associates. Even his son, who had been working for him, decided to leave the ailing firm and Goodyear was forced to face his heavy debts alone. He died lonely and poverty-striken in New

York City on 1 July 1860.

Various people throughout the western world tried to make rubber a more commercially viable material. Goodyear discovered the vulcanization process by accident. One day he was mixing rubber with sulphur and various other ingredients when he dropped some on top of a hot stove. The next morning the stove had cooled, the rubber had vulcanized, and he thought that all his problems had been solved.

The invention was highly significant at a time of industrial advancement. The new process made rubber a suitable material for such applications as belting and hoses, for which strength at high temperatures was the governing factor. It was also particularly valuable once the idea of rubber tyres was conceived, at first for bicycles and then for motorcars.

Goodyear's process was eventually superseded by more refined methods and by the development of synthetic rubbers. And although he failed to find wealth in his lifetime, his name still lives on and can be seen on motor tyres throughout the world.

Gresley, Nigel *(1876-1941)*, was a British steam locomotive engineer who introduced design innovations for the Great Northern Railway, and later the London and North Eastern Railway.

The son of a Derbyshire rector, Gresley was educated at Marlborough School. In 1893 he began his engineering career at Crewe in 1893 as an apprentice under Francis Webb (1836-1906), but after completing his initial 5 years training he left and joined the Lancashire and Yorkshire Railway as a pupil draughtsman under Aspinall. He married and became foreman at the Blackpool depot and, because of a series of retirements by his more senior colleagues, quickly rose to the position of assistant superintendent of the Lancashire and Yorkshire carriages and wagons department. While still only 29 he sought further promotion by joining the Great Northern Railway, where he became carriage and wagon superintendent under Ivatt.

He used his position to demonstrate his flair for design and introduced elliptical-roof coaches and steam heating to the prestige Anglo-Scottish East Coast trains. When Ivatt retired in 1911, Gresley was appointed his successor and began a 30-year period during which he was Britain's best-known locomotive designer.

Gresley's first design was for a mixed-traffic locomotive which abandoned the usual wheel arrangement of 0-6-0 in favour a 2-6-0. He also patented what was to become known as the 'Gresley conjugated valve gear', which he incorporated into some of his later designs for the railway.

Gresley's *Great Northern* appeared in 1922, the main difference in design being the use of 3 cylinders, 2m (6ft 8in) driving wheels and a boiler pressure of 180psi. This all made for a smooth-riding locomotive and in early trials over the Great Northern main line out of London the 150 tonne (147.5ton) locomotive hauled a train of 600 tonnes (590 tons).

In the railway amalgamation of 1923, the Great Northern was incorporated into the new London and North Eastern Railway (LNER) and Gresley was offered the position of chief mechanical engineer in charge of 11 locomotive works and more than 7,000 locomotives. During the next 20 years he was to establish himself as one of the foremost engineers in the history of locomotives, with famous names like the *Flying Scotsman*, *Cock of the North,* the record-breaking *Mallard* and the celebrated *Silver Jubilee* to his credit. Much progress was made in stream-lining, reducing running costs and introducing safety factors, Gresley being particularly concerned with giving each new type of engine stringent trials to ascertain its stresses and weaknesses.

As a result of the success of the *Silver Jubilee*, built to honour the jubilee of King George V, Gresley was knighted in 1936. World War II brought its own problems for Gresley, who strived to maintain the railways under difficult circumstances. He was associated with various organizations and was greatly overworked, which in the end brought the inevitable result. He died of a heart attack in April 1941, 2 months before he was officially due to retire.

Gutenberg, Johann *(c.1397-1468)*, was a German printer who invented moveable type, often regarded as one of the most significant technical developments of all time.

Gutenberg was born in Mainz, a small town on the river Rhine. His exact birthdate is not known, although it is believed to have been between 1394 and 1399. He served an apprenticeship as a goldsmith, but his interest soon turned to printing. In partnership with his friend Andreas Dritzehn he set up a printing firm in Strasbourg some time in the late 1430s. Dritzehn died soon afterwards, and his brother sued for admission to the partnership in his place. Gutenberg was exposed to legal proceedings and from evidence given during the hearing it is thought that the two men may have already invented moveable type by 1438, although no printed work has survived to substantiate this assumption.

Gutenberg returned to Mainz and persuaded the goldsmith and financier Johann Fust to lend him the money to set up a new press. With the security of financial backing he produced the so-called Gutenberg Bible, now regarded as the first major work to come from a printing press. His security was short-lived, however, when Fust brought a lawsuit to recover his loan. In November 1455 Gutenberg's printing offices were taken over in lieu of payment, and Fust installed his son-in-law Peter Schoeffer to operate the press.

Gutenberg may or may not have set up another press. Certainly an edition of Johann Balbus' Catholicon printed in Mainz in 1460 is often attributed to him, along with other lesser works. In 1462 Mainz was involved in a local feud, and in the upheaval Gutenberg was expelled from the city for five years before being reinstated, offered a pension and given tax exemption. He died there on 3 February 1468.

The art of printing using moveable type is thought to have been originally invented nearly four centuries earlier in China, then a much more advanced civilization, but was unknown in the western world until the work of Gutenberg. Previously books had to be printed by the laborious method of carving out each page individually on a wood block, and this meant that only the very wealthy were able to afford them. Gutenberg made his type individually, so that each letter was interchangeable. After a page had been printed, the type could be disassembled and used again. He punched and engraved a steel character (letter shape) into a piece of copper to form a mould which he then filled with molten type metal. The letters were in the Gothic style, nearest to the handwriting of the day, and of equal height.

Using paper made from cloth rags and vellum sheets he printed the famous '42-line' (42 lines to a column) Gutenberg Bible, thought to be the first major work to come from a press of this kind. There are 47 surviving copies of the book, of which 12 are printed on vellum. Many bear no printer's name or date, but from evidence found in two copies in the Paris Library it is concluded that they were on sale before August 1456. By 1500 more than 180 European towns had working presses of this kind, including William Caxton's in Westminster, London, set up in 1476.

H

Hadfield, Robert Abbott *(1858-1940)*, was a British industrial chemist and metallurgist who invented stainless steel and developed various other ferrous alloys.

Hadfield was born in Sheffield, Yorkshire, on 29 November 1858; his father owned a small steel foundry. He received a good education and was trained locally as a chemist before taking up an appointment as an analyst. After a while he joined his father's firm (founded in 1872) and by the age of 24 was its manager. His father died in 1888 and Hadfield became chairman and managing director. He also continued his research into various steel alloys, which he had begun in the early 1880s, eventually publishing more than 150 scientific papers. His findings proved productive and commercially successful, and in recognition of his contribution to the British steel industry he was knighted in 1908; elected a Fellow of the Royal Society a year later, and created a Baronet in 1917. He died in London on 30 September 1940, leaving the well-known company of Hadfields in Sheffield as reminder of the family name.

The basic ingredient of steel is pig iron, the product of iron smelting in a blast furnace, which contains 2.5 to 4.5 per cent carbon. In making ordinary mild steel, carbon (and other impurities) are oxidized, to lower the carbon content. Hadfield carried out many experiments in which he mixed other metals to the steel. He found, for example, that a small amount of manganese gave a tough, wear-resistant steel suitable for such applications as railway track and grinding machinery. By adding nickel and chromium he produced corrosion-resistant stainless steels. Within 20 years silicon steels were available. Again the basic metal with the addition of 3-4 per cent silicon produced an ideal metal for making transformer cones, for which high permeability is required. Today steels and other alloys can be tailor-made to suit almost any requirements.

Hall, Charles Martin *(1863-1914)*, was an American chemist who developed an economic way of making aluminium. His exact contemporary, **Héroult, Paul Louis Toussaint,** *(1863-1914)*, was a French metallurgist who simultaneously developed the electrolytic manufacturing process for aluminium. He also invented the electric arc furnace for the production of steels.

Hall was born on 6 December 1863 in Thompson, Ohio, and educated at Oberlin, where he was influenced by F.F Jewett, a former pupil of the German chemist Friedrich Wohler (1880-1882) who had succeeded in producing impure aluminium under laboratory conditions.

As a result, Hall became interested in the commercial manufacture of aluminium while still a student, perhaps attracted by the prospect of becoming wealthy and famous by bringing this versatile metal to the industrialized world. Just 8 months after graduating in 1855, Hall had found that electrolysis was the best route to achieving his goal, had built his own batteries and, in his home laboratory, had isolated the best compound for commercial production of aluminium: cryolite (sodium aluminium fluoride). By adding aluminium oxides to this compound in its molten state, and using small carbon anodes, a direct current gave a deposit of free molten aluminium on the carbon lining of the electrolytic cell. On 23 February 1886, the 22-year-old Hall was able to present his professor with buttons of aluminium he had himself prepared; these are still preserved by the Aluminium Company of America.

Despite this astonishing achievement, Hall had both financial and technical difficulties in achieving commercial success. A firm which took out a 1-year option on the process found that the electrolytic cells failed after just a few days. Financial backing eventually came from the wealthy Mellon family, and the Pittsburgh Reduction Company (later to become the Aluminium Company of America) was formed to build commercially viable units, requiring no external heating during operation.

Meanwhile, in Europe, Héroult the French metallurgist had arrived at the same process and was achieving similar success, the first British plant being based at Patricroft in 1890. Héroult was born at Thury-Harcourt, Normany, in November 1863. He was still a student when he read Henri DeVille's account of his efforts to isolate aluminium by chemical reactions. Following a year spent at the Paris School of Mines, Héroult began to study the use of electrolysis to extract aluminum from compounds. Like Hall in the United States, Héroult used direct-current electrolysis to find the best combination of material for the production of aluminium, dissolving aluminium oxide in a variety of molten fluorides, and finding cryolite (sodium aluminium flouride) the most promising. Unlike Hall's apparatus, however, Héroult used one large, central graphite electrode in the graphite cell holding the molten material. As with Hall, Héroult succeeded in producing aluminum using his electrolytic appartus at the age of 23. He patented the system in 1886. He also met with the same subsequent difficulty in commercializing the process. The system was taken up, however, by a joint German-Swiss venture at Neuhausen, and large-scale production got underway. Héroult also patented a method for the production of aluminium alloys in 1888.

By 1914 the Hall-Héroult process had brought the price of aluminium down from tens of thousands of dollars a kilogram to 40 cents in the space of 70 years.

As Hall had been told as a student, the process which he had suceeded in making commercial resulted in him becoming a multi-millionaire. On his death at Daytona Beach, Florida, on 27 December 1914, Hall recognized his debt to Oberlin by leaving several million dollars as a gift. Eight months earlier, on 10 April 1914, Héroult had died near Antibes.

Hancock, Thomas *(1786-1865)*, was a British inventor who was influential in the development of the rubber industry.

Hancock,the son of a timber merchant and brother of Walter Hancock, one of the pioneers of steam road-carriages was born in Marlborough, Wiltshire. Both brothers were enterprising in their own particular fields. Thomas travelled to London in 1820 and took out a patent for applying caoutchouc, (now known as India rubber) to various articles of dress. Having secured the patent, he opened a factory in Goswell Road, London, and began manufacturing on a large scale, assisted at a later date by his brother.

It was a successful venture, and from 1820 to 1847 he took out a further 16 patents connected with working rubber. He also collaborated with Charles Macintosh (1766-1843) of Glasgow, famous for his waterproof cloth, over some aspects of manufacturing.

The Goswell Road factory was transferred to his nephew James Lyne Hancock in 1842, and Hancock himself applied his talents to reseach in his own private laboratory, which he had set up in Stoke Newington. Like Charles Goodyear (1800-1860) in the United States, he too was interested in solving the problems of rubber's tackiness and inconsistency at different temperatures. After seeing some samples of Goodyear's products and reading an article about his work, Hancock adopted the heat process of vulcanization. In 1857 he published *Personal Narrative of the Origin and Progress of the Caoutchouc or India Rubber Manufacture in England.*

Joseph Priestley (1733-1804), the discoverer of oxygen, introduced the term 'rubber' after using a small piece of the substance to erase a pencil mark on his notes. The prefix 'India' came from the place where it was first found, the West Indies. The first description of rubber in use came to Europe via Charles de la Condamine, who in 1735 was commissioned by the Academy of Sciences, Paris, to carry out some research in South America. He noted that the local people made items from a watertight material which they had previously prepared from a milky liquid spread out in the sun to cure.

One of Hancock's earliest and most important inventions was a 'masticator', a machine which kneaded the raw rubber to produce a solid block. He nick-named this his 'pickle machine'.

He worked continuously on improvements to

rubber, seeking the help and advice of Charles Macintosh. Like Goodyear in the United States, he found that the real problems lay in maintaining the strength and pliable nature of the substance under changing temperatures. Hancock finally mastered the technique after experimenting with sulphur additives and reading an article on Goodyear's work.

Handley Page, Frederick *(1885-1962)*, was a British aeronautical engineer who founded a company that achieved a world-wide reputation for constructing successful military aircraft.

Handley Page was born at Cheltenham and as a boy determined to become an electrical engineer; by the age of 21 he was chief designer of an electrical company. In 1907 he presented a paper on the design of electrical equipment to the Institute of Electrical Engineers, and such was the interest created that he was offered a tempting post by the Westinghouse Company in the United States. But Handley Page was fascinated with the potential of the aeroplane and he became an early member of the (later Royal) Aeronautical Society. In 1908 he set up as an aeronautical engineer and a year later, with a capital of £10,000, he established the first private British company of this kind, using some sheds at Barking, Essex as workshops and nearby waste ground as an aerodrome.

The outbreak of World War I in 1914 determined the line he was to follow. The need of the British Admiralty for an aircraft capable of carrying a heavy load of bombs led to his design of the first 2-engined bombers. Igor Sikorski in Russia and Giovanni Caproni (1886-1957) in Italy had been thinking along similar lines, but Handley Page produced the first large aircraft. It first flew in December 1915 and before the War had ended had been enlarged into a 4-engined bomber with a fully-laden weight of 13 tonnes (13 tons). More than 250 of these aircraft were produced although the War ended before many saw active service.

After the War (1918) Handley Page turned his attention to civil aircraft. For 4 years another company bearing his name used his machines to operate a service on routes from London to Paris and Brussels, later extended to Zurich. All that this experience proved commercially, however, was that civil aviation was not viable without government subsidies, and these were only to be had when Handley Page lost its identity by merging with Imperial Airways, the forerunner of BOAC. The manufacturing side of Handley Page's business continued, due largely to his development of the automatic slot safety device.

During the inter-war years, in 1930, Handley Page produced the first 40-seat airliner. This was the Hercules, a 4-engined plane which arose at about 145km/h (90mph). It was extremely comfortable - often being compared with Pullman trains - but the aircraft failed to attract overseas orders.

During World War II Handley Page produced another bomber, the Halifax, of which 7,000 were constructed. Work on the bomber continued after the end of the war in 1945, resulting in a four-engined jet of unusual design, the Victor, which made its first flight in 1952. For his services to the aircraft industry in peace and war, Handley Page was knighted in 1942. In 1960 he was awarded the Gold Medal of the Royal Aeronautical Society.

Hargreaves, James *(1720-1778)*, was a British weaver who invented the spinning jenny, a machine that enabled several threads to be spun at once.

Virtually nothing is known of Hargreaves's early life. He was probably born in about 1720 in Blackburn, Lancashire, and from 1740 to 1750 seems to have been a carpenter and hand-loom weaver at nearby Standhill. In about 1760 his skill led Robert Peel (grandfather of the statesman) to employ him to devise an improved carding machine. He is supposed to have invented the spinning jenny in about 1764 when he observed that a spinning-wheel, accidentally overturned by his daughter, continued to revolve, together with the spindle, in a vertical position. Seeing the machine in this unfamiliar up-ended state apparently made him think that if a number of spindles were placed upright and side by side, several threads might be spun at the same time.

At first the resulting jenny was used only by Hargreaves and his children to make weft for the family loom. But in order to supply the needs of a large family he sold some of his new machines. Spinners with the old-fashioned wheel became alarmed by the possibility of cheaper competition and in the spring of 1768 a mob from Blackburn and its neighbourhood gutted Hargreaves's house and destroyed his jenny and his loom. Hargreaves moved to Nottingham, where he formed a partnership with a Mr James who built a small cotton mill in which the jenny was used.

Throughout his life Hargreaves was handicapped by having had virtually no formal education nor what has often proved to be an adequate compensation for it, a sound business sense. He was, however, at least aware of his deficiencies in the latter and with the aid of his partner took out a patent for the spinning jenny in 1770. And when he found out that many Lancashire manufacturers were using the machine, he brought actions for infringement of patent rights. They offered him £3,000 for permission to use it, but he stood out for £4,000. The case continued until his lawyer learned that Hargreaves had sold a number of jennies in Blackburn, and the lawyer withdrew his services.

Hargreaves continued his business partnership until James died in April 1778. Six years later there were 20,000 hand-jennies in use in England compared with 550 of the mechanized (spinning) mules. Hargreaves is said to have left property worth £7,000 and his widow received £400 for her share in the business. But after her death some of the children were extremely poor and Joseph Brotherton sought to raise a fund for them and found great difficulty in getting from the wealthy Lancashire manufactures sufficient money to save them from destitution.

The spinning jenny came, like so many successful inventions, at a time when the need for it was at a maximum. The flying shuttle, invented by John Ray and first used in cotton weaving in about 1760, had doubled the productive output of the weaver, whereas that of the worker at the spinning-wheel had remained much the same. The spinning jenny at once multiplied eightfold the output of the spinner and, because of its simplicity, could be worked easily by children. It did not, however, entirely supersede the spinning-wheel in cotton manufacturing (and was itself overtaken by Crompton's mule). But for woollen textiles the jenny could be used to make both the warp and the weft.

There is as about as much uncertainty surrounding the origins of the spinning jenny and its name as there is about its inventor. Some maintain that it was Thomas Highs, and not Hargreaves, who invented the jenny and that Richard Arkwright (another contender in this confused history) stole part of Highs's idea in order to claim the invention was his own. But there is little conclusive evidence that it was Highs or Arkwright, rather than Hargreaves, who invented the jenny. As to the name of the machine, it is said that Highs had a daughter named Jane whereas Hargreaves definitely did not, and that Jane Highs gave her pet name - Jenny - to the machine. Were this so, it is difficult to believe that Hargreaves would have accepted without comment or protest the widespread use of a name that virtually branded his claim to be 'father' of the jenny as nothing less than imposture.

Heathcoat, John *(1783-1861)*, was a British inventor of lace-making machinery. His contribution was acknowledged by Marc Isambard Brunel who said that Heathcoat (then aged 24) had devised 'the most complicated machine ever invented'.

Heathcoat was born at Duffield, near Derby. He received an average education and, after completing his apprenticeship as a journeyman in the hosiery trade, he became a master mechanic at Hathorn in about 1803. He then set himself the task of constructing a machine that would do the work of the pillow, the multitude of pins, thread and bobbins, and the finger of the hand lacemaker and supersede them in the production of lace - just as the stocking loom had replaced knitting needles in stocking-making.

Analysing the component threads of pillow-lace he classified them into longitudinal and diagonal. The former he placed on a beam as warp. The remainder he reserved as weft with each thread worked separately, twisted around the warpthread to close the upper and lower sides of the mesh. He then devised the necessary mechanical features: bobbins to distribute the thread, the carriage and groove in which they must run, and their mode of twisting round the warp and travelling from side to side of the machine. The first square yard (0.83sq. m) of plain net from the machine was sold for £5. By the end of the nineteenth century its price had fallen to one shilling .

In 1805 Heathcoat settled in Loughborough - as a consequence his improved machine became known as the 'Old Loughborough'. Four years later he went into partnership with the aptly named Charles Lacy, a former point-net maker at Nottingham. Following this amalgamation the machine's capacity was so increased that by 1816 there were as many as 35 frames at work in the Loughborough factory. They also made much money from royalties paid by other companies with permission to use the machines.

On the night of 28 June 1816 an angry crowd of Luddites, fearful that the new machines would deprive them of their jobs, attacked Heathcoat's Loughborough factory and destroyed 35 frames, burning the lace that was on them. The company sued the county for damaged and received £10,000 in compensation, on condition that the money was spent locally. Heathcoat refused to accept the condition; he had already received threats to his life and wanted to leave the district for good. He dissolved his partnership with Lacy and left for Tiverton in Devon, forfeiting his right to compensation.

At Tiverton events took a more favourable turn. With a former partner, John Boden, he bought a large water-powered mill on the river Exe. Heathcoat devised new frames which were wider and faster, and by using rotary power he lowered the cost of production. He patented a rotary, self-narrowing stocking frame and put gimp and other ornamental threads into the bobbin by mechanical adjustment.

In 1821 the partnership with Boden was ended. Year by year Heathcoat took out patents for further inventions, continuing to make improvements in the textile trade until he retired in 1843. Also in 1832, with Henry Handley, he patented a steam plough to assist with agricultural improvements in Ireland. On 12 December of that year he was elected to represent Tiverton in the new reformed Parliament and remained MP for the borough until 1859. He died at Tiverton 3 years later, in his 78th year.

Hero of Alexandria *(c. AD 60)*, variously described as an Egyptian scientist and a Greek engineer, was the greatest experimentalist of antiquity. His numerous writings describe many of his inventions, formulae and theories, some of them centuries ahead of their time. His famous aeolipile which demonstrated the force of steam generated in a closed chamber and escaping through a small aperture (the first rudimentary steam turbine) was not developed further for another 18 centuries.

A gifted mathematician, he adopted the division of the circle into 360 degrees, orginally brought to the Western World by Hipparchus of Bithynia. He was also a famous teacher and at Alexandria founded a technical school with one section devoted entirely to research.

He regarded air as a very elastic substance which could be compressed and expanded, and successfully explained the phenomenon of suction and associated apparatus, such as the pipette and cupping glass; he also used a suction machine for pumping water. His writing on air compressibility and density and his assumption that air is composed of minute particles able to move relative to one another preceded Robert Boyle by 1500 years.

In mechanics he devised a system of gear wheels which could lift a 1,000kg (2,200lb) weight by means of a mere 5kg (11lb) of force. His work entitled *Mechanics*, the only existing copy of which is in Arabic, contains the parallelogram of velocity, the laws of levers, the mysteries of motion on an inclined plane and the effects of friction, and much data on gears and the positions of the centre of gravity of various objects. His construction of a variable ratio via a friction disc has been used to build a motor vehicle with a semi-automatic transmission.

Civil and construction engineers owe him a debt for his tables of dimensions used in building arches and in drilling tunnels and wells. Another of his famous books, *On The Dioptra*, describes a diversity of instruments, including a type of theodolite that employs a refined screw-cutting technique for use in boring tunnels; the book also describes a hodometer for measuring the distance travelled by a wheel.

Hero's book *Metrica* explains the measurement of plain and solid geometrical figures and discusses conic sections, the frustum of a cone, and the five regular or Platonic solids. It includes a formula for calculating the area of a triangle from the lengths of its sides, and a method of determining the square root of a non-square number.

Pneumatics, another of his books describes numerous mechanical devices operated by gas, water, steam, or atmospheric pressure, and siphons, pumps, fountains and working automata in the likeness of animals or birds devised, it seems, just for amusement.

Hero was a genius in the techniques of measurement of all kinds and in founding the science of mechanics. After his death there was no further progress in physics for centuries. But for the Arabs, it is extremely likely that all record of his works would have vanished.

Herzog, Bertram *(1929-)*, is a German-born computer scientist who became one of the major pioneers in the use of computer graphics in engineering design.

Herzog was born in Offenburg, Germany, on 28 February 1929. He went to the United States and became an American citizen, and began his university education at the Case Institute of Technology, from which he graduated with a bachelor's degree in engineering in 1949. In the early 1950s he worked as a structural engineer before taking up appointments as an associate professor, first at Doanbrook and then at the University of Michigan, where he obtained a doctorate in engineering mechanics in 1961.

In 1963 Herzog joined the Ford Motor Company as engineering methods manager, where he extensively applied computers to tasks involved in planning and design. During this time he was engaged in bringing the developing field of computer graphics to the requirements of design problems in the motor industry. Herzog remained as a consultant to Ford, while returning to academic life in 1965 as Professor of Industrial Engineering at the University of Michigan. Two years later he became Director of the computer centre and Professor of Electrical Engineering and Computer Science at University of Colorado.

Heyman, Jacques *(1925-)*, is a British civil engineer whose chief interests include the structures of modern buildings as well as the restoration of old masonry ones.

Heyman was born on 8 March 1925. From 1934 to 1941 he attended Whitgift School in South Croydon, Surrey, before going for 3 years to Peterhouse College, Cambridge, where he studied mathematics and mechanical science. He worked as a research engineer before returning to Cambridge in 1946 as a research student. He spent 3 years in the United States (1949-1951) at Brown University in Province, Rhode Island, before finally returning to Cambridge to take up an academic post which was to lead to his appointment in 1971 as Professor of Engineering. He also became a consultant engineer to various historic buildings, including Ely Cathedral (1972) and St Albans Cathedral (1978).

Much of Heyman's work has concerned the theory of structures, and during the course of 20 years he has published 5 books on various aspects of the subject. He was one of the original members of the Cambridge team which developed plastic theory, and published research papers on the optimum design of structures, the design of tall buildings, and the design of turbine discs (for this Heyman was awarded a James Clayton Prize by the Institution of Mechanical Engineers). He has also applied the plastic principles of structural theory to the analysis of masonry, and has been consulted about the restoration of medieval bridges and old churches.

Hodgkinson, Easton *(1789-1861)*, was a British civil engineer who worked to introduce scientific methods of measuring the strength of materials.

Hodgkinson was born on his father's farm at Anderton, Cheshire, in February 1789. After showing distinct ability in mathematics during his schooldays because of the early death of his father and his mother's consequent penury he was obliged to give up hopes of a professional education and instead to assist his mother in running the family farm. He had little aptitude for this work and pursuaded his mother to invest her limited capital in a pawnbroking business in Salford, Manchester.

He also found time to develop his interest in natural science and became acquainted with the chemist John Dalton (1766-1844) and other gifted men then living in Manchester. In March 1822 he read a paper on 'The Transverse Strain and Strength of Materials' before the Literary and Philosophical Society. In this contribution he recorded a factor which became important in all his subsequent experiments, namely 'set' or the original position of a strained body and the position it assumes when the strain is removed. He fixed the exact position of the 'neutral line' in the section of rupture or fracture and made it the basis for the computation of the strength of a beam of given dimensions. His conception of the true mechanical principle by which the position of the line could be determined has long been generally accepted.

In 1828 he read before the same society an important paper on the forms of the catenary links in suspension bridges, and in 1830 one on his research into the strength of iron beams, one of the most valuable contributions ever made to the study of the strength of materials.

From a theoretical analysis of the neutral line, he devised experiments to determine the strongest beam which resulted in the discovery of what is known as 'Hodgkinson's beam'.

Hodgkinson rendered important services to Robert Stephenson (1803-1859) in the construction of the Britannia (Menai) and Conway tubular bridges by fixing the best forms and dimensions of tubes. He edited the fourth edition of Tredgold's work on the strength of cast iron (1842) and published a volume of his own: *Experimental Researches on the Strength and other Properties of Cast Iron* (1846).

He worked from 1847 to 1849 as one of the Royal Commissioners to inquire into the application of iron to railway structures. Also in 1847 he was appointed Professor of the Mechanical Principles of Engineering at University College, London, where his lectures were somewhat impaired by his hesitancy of speech. He did not live to see an authoritative publication of all his collected papers, dying in Manchester in 1861.

Hoe, Richard March *(1812-1886)*, was an American inventor and manufacturer, famous for inventing the rotary printing press.

Hoe was born in New York City on 12 September 1812. He was the eldest son of Robert Hoe (1784-1833), a British-born American who, with his brothers-in-law Peter and Matthew Smith, established in New York a firm manufacturing printing presses. Richard Hoe was educated in public schools before entering his father's firm at the age of 15. When his father retired in 1830, Richard and his cousin Matthew took over the business. Richard proved to have the same mechanical genius as his father, and the application of his ideas revolutionized printing processes. He discarded the old flat-bed printing press and placed the type on a revolving cylinder. This was later developed into the Hoe rotary or 'lightning' press, patented in 1846 and first used by the *Philadephia Public Ledger* in 1847.

Under Hoe's management the company grew at a rapid rate. In 1859 he built Isaac Adams's Press Works in Boston. After the Civil War, new premises were built in Grand Street, New York, and the old buildings in Gold Street were abandoned. Between 1865 and 1870, a large manufacturing branch was built up in London, employing 600 people.

In 1871, with Stephen D Tucker as a partner,

Hoe began experimenting and designed and built the Hoe Web Perfecting press. This press enabled publishers to satisfy the increasing circulation demands of the rapidly growing American population.

While Richard Hoe was the leading influence in the company, he spent much time and money on the welfare of his employees. Quite early in his career he started evening classes for apprentices, at which free instruction was given in those aspects of their work most likely to be of practical use to them. He was addressed by them as 'the Colonel', which dated from his early service in the National Guard.

He died suddenly while on a combined health and pleasure trip to Florence with his wife and a daughter, on 7 June 1886. He was succeeded in the business by his nephew, Robert Hoe.

At the time when Richard Hoe was made responsible for the company, it was making a single small cylinder press. Its capacity was 2,000 impressions per hour and there was demand for a greater speed of output. This prompted Hoe to concentrate on improvements to meet the demand and, in 1837, a double small cylinder press was perfected and introduced. In the next ten years, he designed and put into production a single large cylinder press. This was the first flatbed and cylinder press ever used in the United States. Hundreds of these machines were made in subsequent years and were used for book, job, and wood-cut printing. During 1845 and 1846 Hoe was busily engaged in designing and inventing presses to meet the increased requirements of the newspaper publishers. The result was the construction of the revolving machine based on Hoe's patents. The basis of these inventions was a device for securely fastening the forms of type on a central cylinder placed in a horizontal position. The first of these machines, installed in the *Public Ledger* office, had four impression cylinders grouped around the central cylinder. With one boy to each cylinder to feed in blank paper, 8,000 papers could be produced per hour.

Almost immediately newspaper printing was revolutionized, and Hoe's rotary press became famous throughout the world. In 1853, he introduced the cylinder press which had been patented in France by Dutartre and improved on it in the following years for use in lithographic and letterpress work. In 1861 the curved stereotype plate was perfected, and in 1865 William Bullock succeeded in producing the first printing machine that would print on a continuous web or roll of paper. Spurred on by this latest development, Hoe and his partner began experimenting and designed and built a web press. The first of these to be used in the United States was installed in the office of the *New York Tribune*. At maximum speed, this press printed on both sides of the sheet and produced 18,000 papers per hour. Four years later, Tucker patented a rotating, folding cylinder which folded the papers as fast as they came off the press.

In 1881 the Hoe Company devised the triangular former-folder which, when incorporated into the press, together with approximately twenty additional improvements, gave rise to the modern newspaper press. It was with the introduction of this that the 1847-type revolving press was superceded.

Hollerith, Herman *(1860-1929)*, was an American mathematician and mechanical engineer who invented electrical tabulating machines. He was probably the first to automate the large-scale processing of information, and as such was a pioneer of the electronic calculator, particularly its application to data handling in business and commerce.

Hollerith was born on 29 February 1860 in Buffalo, New York. After his schooldays he attended the School of Mines at Columbia University, from which he graduated in 1879. The following October he became an assistant to W.P Trowbridge, one of his university lecturers, in the work for the United States census of 1880.

Hollerith worked on the statistics of manufacturing industries, especially those concerned with steam and water power in the iron and steel industries. The physician and librarian John Billings (1838-1913) and Hollerith came into close contact with him. In the course of processing the many census returns, they became aware that an automated recording process would have considerable labour-saving advantages. Whether it was Hollerith who had the idea of punching holes into cards to indicate quantities or whether Billings made the initial suggestion is not known. What is important is that later Hollerith developed the idea of punching first a continuous roll of paper, and later individual cards the same size as a dollar bill, with holes to represent information. The quantities indicated by the holes were counted when the tape or cards passed through a device in which electrical contact was made through the holes. The passage of an electric current caused electromechanical counters, to advance one place for each hole. The realization of these ideas in practical terms did not however come about in time for the processing of the 1880 returns.

In 1882 Hollerith obtained a position as instructor in mechanical engineering at the Massachusetts Institute of Technology (MIT). He preferred experimental work to teaching, and after a year he left MIT and went to St Louis until 1884 where he worked on the development of electro-mechanically operated air-brakes for railways. He was then employed by the Patent Office in Washington DC, and until the next census in 1890 he developed his recording and tabulating machines.

By 1889 he had developed not only his electrical machines for recording the information on punched cards, but also machines for punching the cards and for sorting them. But by this time he was not the only inventor of data-processing equipment, and a trial was held to decide which system was to be adopted for the 1890 census. The Hollerith system proved to be twice as fast as the best of the other two and was used to handle the returns of 63 million people. In 1891 the Hollerith system was used in the censuses in Austria, Canada and Norway (and in Britain in 1911). The machines were later successfully adapted to the needs of government departments and businesses which handled large quantities of data, and particularly to the tabulating of railway statistics.

Hollerith soon realized that the age of large-scale data handling had begun, and in 1896 he formed the Tabulating Machine Company, to manufacture the machines and the cards they used. With the growth of business in this area, Hollerith's company was soon merged with two others into the Computing-Tabulating-Recording Company, which later became the International Business Machines Corporation (IBM). IBM has remained one of the foremost companies in the development and manufacture of data-processing systems, and has been an important producer of electronic computers for many years.

Hollerith stayed with IBM as a consultant engineer until his retirement in 1921. He died from heart disease in Washington on 17 November 1929, aged 69.

Hooker, Stanley *(1907-   ),* is the British engineer responsible for major aircraft engine development projects which culminated in the successful *Proteus* turboprop, *Orpheus* turbojet, *Pegasus* vectored thrust turbofan, *Olympus* turbojet and *RB211* turbofan.

Hooker was born in Sheerness, Kent, on 30 September 1907 and educated at Imperial College, London, and Brazenose College, Oxford. He joined the Admiralty Scientific and Research Department in 1935, working on anti-aircraft rocket development. In 1938 he moved to Rolls-Royce in charge of the Performance and Supercharger Department.

In 1940 he met Sir Frank Whittle and the following year, as chief engineer of the Rolls-Royce Barnoldswich Division, he was responsible for the development of the Whittle *W2B* turbojet. In the

period 1944-1945 the *Nene* and *Derwent* engines emerged from Barnoldswick and in 1946 the *Meteor*, powered by two *Derwent V* engines, established a world speed record of 603mph.

Hooker joined the Aero Engine Division of the Bristol Aeroplane Company, becoming chief engineer in 1951 and a director the following year. When Bristol Siddely Engines was formed in 1959, he became technical director of the Aero Division and, following the merger with Rolls-Royce in 1966, technical director of the Bristol Engine Division.

In January 1971 Hooker was appointed group technical director and seconded to Derby in charge of *RB211* development. The same year he took his seat on the main board as group technical director. At the end of 1976 he retired from the main board and is now technical advisor.

In his distinguished career Hooker has received many honorary degrees, decorations, medals and awards, including the OBE (1946), CBE (1964) and a Knighthood (1974). His FRS came in 1962 and Fellowship of the Royal Aeronautical Society in 1947.

The *Merlin* engine, which was to power so many Allied aircraft in the 1939-1945 war, started life in 1935 developing under 671.1kW (900hp). As the need for greater engine power increased, particularly at high altitudes, supercharging was one of the most effective ways of meeting the demand. The *Merlin* supercharger, developed under Hooker, was so successful that special versions of the engine were delivering up to 1968.65kW (2640hp) by the end of the War.

A turboprop engine uses the exhaust efflux from a turbo jet (usually called a gas generator, in this application) to drive a conventional propeller. The *Proteus* turboprop in its Mark 705 version entered service in the 100 Series *Britainnia* airliner in January 1957 at 2,900kW (3,890tehp) (total equivalent hp, being the shaft power delivered to the propeller plus the equivalent of the residual jet

The turbojet engine passes all the air it draws in through the combustion chambers and expels it in a hot high-velocity jet; it uses the energy of the jet alone to drive the aircraft. It is inefficient at low speeds, but as the aircraft passes through about 1500km/h (900mph) its rating improves and it is the preferred power unit for military and supersonic applications. The *Orpheus* turbojet, for which Hooker had overall responsibility, was chosen to power the Fiat *G91*, selected under the NATO mutual weapons development programme, entering service in May 1958 as the *Mark 801* at 18kM (4,050lb) thrust.

The turbofan engine passes only a proportion of the air through the combustion chambers. This air emerges as a hot high-velocity jet and is mixed with the air which by-passed the core of the engine. The amount of by-pass air varies in different engines.

The *Pegasus* vectored thrust engine was conceived after discussions between Hooker and Sir Sydney Camm. It is the power unit for the *Harrier* V/STOL (vertical/short take-off and landing) combat aircraft and is a unique design of turbofan. Its by-pass air is ducted through 2 forwards nozzles and the gas coming from the core of the engine is ducted through 2 rear nozzles. All 4 nozzles can be rotated downwards to provide vertical thrust and rearwards to provide forwards thrust. Intermediate settings give the aircraft its short take-off capability. Rotating the nozzles in flight, even forwards to give reverse thrust, makes the Harrier the most manoeuvrable combat aircraft flying in the early 1980s.

The *Olympus* turbojet, eventually to power the supersonic *Concorde* airliner, started life in 1946 when Bristol submitted designs to the Ministry of Supply in answer to a tender for an engine of about 35.6kN (8,000lb) thrust. The design was then unique, because it was the first time the two-spool concept had been proposed. This layout uses two independent compressors driven by two independent turbines, giving the engine high compression (important for fuel economy) and great adaptability.

The engine underwent extensive development under Hooker and then flew in the prototype and pre-production aircraft, designated *593B*, with a thrust of 169kN (35,080lb) thrust. In the series aircraft designated 600, it flies with 169kn (38,000lb) thrust.

The *RB211* turbofan was designed with one of the highest by-pass ratios of any engine in the early 1980s. This and other design features makes it the quietest and most economical in airline service. Economy encompasses every aspect of operating an engine, not just the fuel consumption. One of the most important aspects of the *RB211* operating economics is its modular design. In older concept engines, changing a turbine at the end of its service life needed a complete engine strip-down; the *RB211* has a turbine module, a compressor module, etc., so that replacement is comparatively simple and swift.

From the *Merlin* supercharger to the *Olympus* and *RB211*, Hooker has led design teams which have introduced some of the most advanced aeroengine concepts in the world, operating to the rigid requirements of aviation.

Horlock, John *(1928-   ),* is a British research engineer and Vice-Chancellor of the Open University.

Horlock was born on 19 April 1928 and educated at Latymer School, in Edmonton London . He planned to take an engineering apprenticeship on leaving school, but instead accepted his teacher's advice to go to St John's College, Cambridge, from which he graduated in medical sciences in 1948.

On leaving Cambridge Horlock joined the design department of Rolls Royce, Derby. There, under the guidance of Geoffrey Wilde, the chief compressor designer, he became part of a team which was exploring the potential of jet engineering. After two years, however, he felt it would be in his best interests to return to Cambridge to study for his PhD. He was offered a place by the professor of applied thermodynamics, William Hawthorne (1913-   ) who not only encouraged him to follow this course but persuaded Rolls Royce to lend Horlock an expensive item of equipment to assist him with his research.

Horlock was awarded his PhD in 1955 and initially planned to return to Rolls Royce, this time working on research with A.A Griffith. But instead he began an academic career, which has led him to hold some of the most demanding academic and adminstrative posts.

He began simply as a demonstrator at Cambridge, became a Fellow of St John's and a lecturer at the college, and then spent some time in the United States at the Massachusetts Institute of Technology, working as a visiting assistant professor. On his return to Britain, while still only 30 years old, he was appointed a professor and head of the mechanical engineering department of Liverpool University, where he instigated a new and impressive research programme.

In 1967 he returned to Cambridge as Professor of Engineering, became Deputy Head of the Department of Engineering in 1969 and also head of the Whittle Laboratory. Even with such success he was restless, and in 1974 he accepted the position of Vice-Chancellor of the recently created University of Salford. He found the university still in its infancy, but realized that it had great potential. During the six years he spent there he raised it from little more than a college of technology to a thriving university with broad-based ideas.

Horlock has the ability to bring new energy and motivation to whatever he tackles. his appointment as Vice-Chancellor of the Open University on 1 January 1981 has been seen as a move to project this zeal for administration into an organization which needs his kind of determined enthusiasm.

Hounsfield, Godfrey Newbold *(1919-   ),* is a British research scientist whose part in the invention and development of computerized axial tomography (the 'CAT' scanner) was recognized by the award of the 1979 Nobel Prize in Medicine.

Hounsfield was born on 28 August 1919 and educated at the Magnus Grammar School, Newark, and later at the City and Guilds College, London and the Faraday House Electrical Engineering College.

After serving with the Royal Air Force during World War II, he joined the Medical Systems Section of EMI in 1951 and has been actively engaged in research with the company ever since. He was made Professorial Fellow of Manchester University (for Imaging Sciences) in 1978 and has been awarded some of the most coveted prizes in the scientific world including the Nobel Prize, the Price Phillip Medical Award (1975), the Lasker Award (1975) and the Churchill Gold Medal (1976).

Hounsfield's long career in medical research and engineering has culminated in the invention of the EMI scanner, formerly a computerized transverse axial tomography system for X-ray examination. Its development, using all the most advanced technology available, has led to major improvements in the field of X-ray, enabling the whole body to be screened at one time. It is proving particularly valuable in the detection of cancer.

Howe, Elias *(1819-1867)*, was an American engineer who invented a sewing machine, one of the first products of the Industrial Revolution that ultimately eased the burden of domestic work.

He was born on 9 July 1819 in Spencer, Massachusetts. As a boy, Howe worked on the farm his father ran, and in his grist-mills and saw-mills where he took particular interest in the machinery. He trained to be a machinist, and having conceived the idea of a sewing machine, spent much of his life developing and patenting one. He died in Brooklyn, New York, on 3 October 1867.

Howe began work on the design of a sewing machine in about 1843. Within a year he had a rough working model, and in September 1846 he was granted a US patent for a practical machine. He was the first to patent a lock-stitch mechanism, and his machine had two other important features: a curved needle with the eye (for the thread) at the point, and an under-thread shuttle (invented by Walter Hunt in 1834).

Howe immediately went to Britain and sold the invention for £250 to a corset manufacturer named William Thomas of Cheapside, London. In December 1846 Thomas secured the English patent in his own name, and engaged Howe (on weekly wages) to adapt the machine for his needs. Howe worked with Thomas from (1847 to1849), but his career in London was unsuccessful. He

pawned his US patent rights, and returned in poverty to the United States, where he found his wife dying.

While Howe had been away, the sewing machine was beginning to arouse public curiosity, and he found that various people were making machines which infringed his patent. The most prominent of these - an inventor in his own right - was Isaac Singer (1811- 1875), who in 1851 secured a US patent for his own machine. Howe now became aware of his rights, redeemed his pawned patent, and took out law suits against the infringers. After much litigation, the courts found in his favour and from that time (about 1852) until his patent expired in 1867, Howe received royalties on all sewing machines made in the United States. When he died, he left an estate worth $2 million, an enormous sum in 1867.

The basic invention in machine sewing was the double-pointed needle, with the eye in the centre, patented by C.F Weisenthal in 1755 which enabled the sewing or embroidery stitch to be made with the needle being inverted. Many of the features of the sewing machine are distinctly specified in a patent secured in England in 1790 by Thomas Saint. The machine he described was for stitching, quilting or sewing but seems to have been chiefly intended for leather-work. If Saint had hit upon the eye-pointed needle, his machine would have completely anticipated the modern chain-stitch machine. A real working machine was invented in France by a poor tailor, Barthélemy Thimmonier, and a patent was obtained in 1830. By 1841 about 40 of these machines were being used in Paris to make army clothing, although the machines were clumsy, being largely made of wood. An ignorant crowd wrecked his establishment and his machines, but undeterred he patented vast improvements on it. The troubles of 1848, however, blasted his prospects and his patent rights for Britain were sold. A machine of his shown at the Great Exhibition of 1851 did not attract any interest and Thimmenier died in 1857, unrewarded.

In about 1832, Walter Hunt of New York constructed a machine with a vibrating arm, at the extremity of which he fixed a curved needle with an eye near its point. The needle formed a loop of thread under the cloth to be sewn, and an oscillating shuttle passed a thread through the loop, thus making the lock-stitch of all ordinary two-thread machines. Howe was apparently unaware of Hunt's invention.

Since that time, thousands of patents have been issued in the United States and in Europe, covering improvements in the sewing machine. Although these numerous attachments and accessories, have improved the machine's efficiency and usefulness the main principles are still the same as they were in the basic machine. There are well over 2,000 types of modern sewing machine, designed for making up garments, boots and shoes, hats, for working embroidery, for edging lace curtains and for sewing buckles on shoes. Most machines are now powered by electricity, although treadle-operated machines are still seen in specialized fields such as shoe-mending. Microelectronics are now providing push-button controls on home sewing machines, but the basic mechanism remains the same as that devised by Howe.

Hussey, Obed *(1792-1860)*, was an American inventor who developed one of the first successful reaping machines and various other agricultural machinery.

Hussey was born into a Quaker family in Maine. The family moved to Nantucket, Massachusetts, and like most boys living there at that time, the young Hussey wanted to go to sea when he grew up. He was a quiet and studious boy, always thoughtful and modest. He liked studying intricate mechanisms and became a skilled draughtsman and inventor. In addition to the reaper, he invented a steam plough, a machine for making hooks and eyes, a grinding mill for maize and a horse-powered husking machine, a sugar-cane crusher and an ice-making machine. On 4 August 1860, while travelling on a train from Boston to Portland, Maine, he got off at a station to fetch a drink of water for a child. The train started as he was getting back on, and he fell beneath the wheels and was killed.

Hussey began work on a reaping machine early in 1833 in a room at the factory of Richard Chenoweth, a manufacturer of agricultural implements in Baltimore, Maryland. The finished prototype was tested later that year near Cincinnati, Ohio, where it so impressed a local businessman, Jarvis Reynolds, that he provided the finance and a factory for manufacturing the reaper. It was patented in December 1833 and pictured in the *Mechanics Magazine* of April 1834 as 'Hussey's Grain Cutter'.

At first Hussey used a reel to gather the grain up to the cutter and throw it on to the platform, but after trials he decided that the reel was an encumbrance and discarded it. The main frame containing the gearing was suspended on 2 wheels about a metre (1yd) in diameter; the platform was attached to the rear of the frame and extended nearly two metres (c.2yd) on each side. A team of horses attached to the front of the frame walked along the side of the standing grain. The cutting knife consisted of 7.5cm (3in) wide steel plates, tapered towards the front, rivetted to a flat iron bar to form a sort of saw with very coarse teeth sharpened on both edges. The knife was supported on what Hussey called guards attached to the front of the platform every 7.5cm (3in) across the whole width of the machine. They projected forwards and had long horizontal slits in which the cutter oscillated from side to side. They thus supported the grain while it was being cut and protected the blades from damage by large stones and other obstructions. The cutter was attached by means of a Pitman rod to a crank activated by gearing, connected to one or both or the ground wheels. This arrangement gave a quick vibrating motion to the cutter as the machine was pulled along.

The point of each blade oscillated from the centre of one guard, through the space between, to the centre of the next, thus cutting equally both ways.

In his next modification to the machine, Hussey used one large ground wheel instead of two and moved the platform to a position along side the frame, providing a seat for an operator who faced forward and raked the cut grain off the back of the platform.

During the harvest of 1834 Hussey successfully demonstrated his machine to hundreds of farmers and began to sell the reapers for $150 each. The fame of the machine spread, slowly at first, and it was eventually used in the far West. In September 1851 he went to Britain and demonstrated the reaper at Hull and Barnardscastle. He was invited to show it to Prince Albert who bought two (at £21 each), one for the estate at Windsor and one for Osborne House on the Isle of Wight.

An earlier rival design of reaper had been developed by Cyrus McCormick in 1831, although Hussey's was patented first. Both machines used the principle of a reciprocating knife cutting against stationary guards or figures, although McCormick's design employed a division between the cut and uncut grain and a reel to topple the cut grain on to the platform. Hussey's contribution was summed up succinctly in the title of a book which relates the story: *Obed Hussey: Who of all inventors, made bread cheap.*

I

Issigonis, Alec *(1906-   )*, is a naturalized British automotive engineer and the first person to exploit scientific component packaging in the design of small volume-produced motorcars. His designs gave much greater space for the occupants together with greatly increased dynamic handling stability and improved small-car ride.

Issigonis was born on 18 November 1906 in what was then Smyrna, and came to Britain with his widowed mother after the 1922 war between Turkey and Greece. He studied engineering at Battersea Polytechnic, and began his career working for a small engineering firm which was developing an automatic gearchange.

This work introduced Issigonis to the Humber division of the Rootes Group in 1934, and in 1936 he joined Morris Motors to work on suspension design. During this pre-war period he built the ingenious Lightweight Special hill climb and sprint single seater, which demonstrated the potential of all independent suspension with rubber springs. His first complete production motorcar was the Morris Minor, launched in 1948, which brought new standards of steering and stability to small motorcars - and went on to become the first British motorcar to pass the million mark (in 1961). After a spell (1952-1956) working at Avis on an experimental 3.5 litre car with hydrolastic suspension, he returned to what had now become BMC to face, within a short while, his greatest challenge.

Sir Leonard Lord (later to become Lord Lambury), chairman of BMC, asked him to design and produce a small and economical car to counteract the flood of 'bubble cars' which followed the Suez crisis. A period of intensive design and development led to the launch of the Mini in 1959. His other major designs were the 1100 (1962), the 1800 (1964) and the Maxi (1969). He was made CBE in 1964, became a fellow of the Royal Society in 1967, and received a knighthood in 1969.

The main significance of his work was in taking on car design as a 'vehicle architect', overseeing the separate approaches of styling, interior packaging, body engineering and chassis layout. In this way he conceived the overall package from his knowledge and experience the major factors affecting the product; specialists in his team then designed and engineered the subsystems of the vehicle. The approach was to make the human factor paramount in selecting design criteria.

This approach was particularly recognizable in the 'wheel at each corner' layout on the Morris Minor and its effect on handling. The vehicle's polar moment of inertia (a measure of directional stability), was made small compared with the magnitude of the tyre's cornering forces. This improved the speed of response to change in direction, and designed-in nose-heaviness allowed

quick correction of the car after a side-gust disturbance.

With the layout of the Mini a degree of interior spaciousness was achieved beyond that available in previous cars of similar exterior size. The technique included repositioning the dash panel to follow the projected line of the curved lower edge of the windscreen, using single skinned doors and rear quarter panels, with large open lockers on the inside. By adopting a transverse engine-over-gearbox/final-drive layout with front wheel drive, and independent suspension of all wheels, considerable gains were made in front knee-room and space at the rear of the seat base.

The use of compact wheel-location lever-arms acting on rubber suspension springs also gave a substantial packaging advantage, besides giving a well-damped ride, free of static friction. In arranging for fluid correction of the springs, the suspension could be tuned to separate motions of pitch and bounce of the vehicle; tuning virtually eliminated pitch as a prime factor in ride discomfort.

The Mini, for which Issigonis is best known, reigned supreme among small cars until the late 1970s. At the beginning of its life the car attracted a considerable cult following and all through its life it was the basis for a great diversity of modification by specialist firms. In the early 1980s, despite the competition, this 25-year-old design was actually increasing its market share, following an intial dip when the Mini-Metro was introduced.

J

Jacquard, Joseph Marie *(1752-1834)*, was a French engineer who developed a loom (originally for carpets), whose complicated patterns were 'programmed' on to punched cards.

Jacquard was born in Lyons on 7 July 1752, the son of a weaver. He was apprenticed when he was quite young, first to a bookbinder and later to a cutler. Throughout his time in these trades he considered ways of improving the crafts and lessening the labour needed. When his parents died, they left him their small weaving business and Jacquard took up that trade. He attempted to weave patterned fabrics which brought a relatively high profit, but he was not successful at this intricate craft which required long hours of hard, patient toil to finish even the most modest piece of material. He returned to the cutlery trade after becoming bankrupt as a weaver.

He continued his efforts to devise an improved weaving machine, but his first loom was not made until 1801. It combined a number of innovations which had been used before on various other machines with some ideas of his own. In 1804 he went to Paris to demonstrate a new machine for weaving net. This was welcomed and, as well as receiving a patent, he was allocated a small pension, which enabled him to work on improving looms and weaving at the Conservatoire des Arts et Métiers.

Jacquard's attachment for pattern weaving, which was developed during this time and later improved by others, allowed patterns to be woven without the intervention of the weaver. Weavers had always had to plan the pattern they wished to weave before they began their task. This planning now became the essential feature of the weaver's job. Part of Jacquard's invention was a series of cards with holes punched in them through which tools could come up and pull the warp threads down, so that the shuttle could pass over them. If there was no hole the shuttle went underneath the warp. In this way the correct threads were brought into conjunction to weave an intricate pattern.

During the first decade of the nineteenth century many Jacquard looms were installed in weaving mills. As Jacquard intended, his loom saved a great deal of physical labour, and because of this it was not kindly received by the workers in the weaving trade. In Lyons and elsewhere his machines were smashed, and Jacquard himself suffered violence at the hands of the angry weavers. Even angry workers, however, could not halt mechanical progress and by 1812 it is recorded that there were 11,000 Jacquard looms working in France. During the next few years they were introduced into many other countries, including England.

One pattern, when punched onto cards, could be used over and over again, which gave the new machine a tremendous advantage over the traditional one, but the preparation of the cards was a difficult and tedious task and it was only with the coming of the electronic computer that this labour was reduced.

The idea of the Jacquard cards was to feed a machine with instructions, and it was applicable in principle, at least, to many kinds of machine. One direct application of the cards was in the mechanical computing machine called the 'Analytical Engine' designed and partly constructed by Charles Babbage in the years following 1833. In this machine the cards directed a sequence of arithmetical operations and the transfer of numbers to and from the store. Other pioneers of automatic computing have also used punched cards and punched tape as a means of storing, sorting and transferring information. Herman Hollerith, for example, used a vast mechanical tabulatory system which relied on punched cards with holes in 288 positions for his 1890 census of the United States.

Only now with the rapid modern development of electronic computers and magnetic storage systems are the descendants of the Jacquard cards declining in use as representations and stores of information. The principle of the Jacquard loom still survives in weaving, even though the machinery and programming are somewhat different.

Jacquard was highly honoured, and eventually even the weavers appreciated his invention. He survived the violence of his times and died at Oullines, France, on 7 July 1834.

Jessop, William *(1745-1814)*, was a British civil engineer, a builder of canals and early railways.

Jessop was born in January 1745 in Devonport, Devon, the son of a foreman and shipwright at the local naval dockyard. His father had been associated with John Smeaton in the building of the Eddystone lighthouse. When his father died in 1761, William Jessop, aged 16, became a pupil of Smeaton, who was appointed his guardian.

Jessop worked with Smeaton on the Calder and Hebble, and the Aire and Calder navigations in Yorkshire. Jessop later became England's greatest builder of large waterways; he was responsible for the Bransley, Rochdale and trent navigation, the Nottingam and the Grand Junction (Grand Union) canals. The only narrow one he worked on was the Ellesmere canal. In 1773 Smeaton went to Ireland, taking his pupil with him, and the Grand Canal of 50km (80 miles) from Dublin the Shannon (which had been started in 1753) was completed in 1805, just 2 months after the Grand Junction Canal in England.

It was his work on the building of the Cromford Canal to link Arkwright's Mill at Bromford with the Derbyshire coalfield and Nottingham which led Jessop, together with Benjamin Outram, John Wright and Francis Beresford, to found the Butterley Iron Works Company in 1790. This Company later became responsible for many iron bridges. This was the main reason why the canal engineers Jessop and Outram became much in demand for the development of the iron railways in the Midlands, especially in Nottinghamshire and Derbyshire. The first all-iron rail was laid in the 1790s. In 1792, fish-bellied cast-iron rails were designed by Jessop. He was also involved in some spectacular iron bridges, particularly the Pontcysyllte aqueduct, completed in 1805. His son Josias was trained by him and became an important engineer in his own right. William Jessop was held in very high reputate and for 16 years from 1774 served as Secretary of the Society of Civil Engineers. He died at Butterley Hall, Derbyshire, on 18 November 1814.

Jessop was the chief engineer, appointed in 1793, on the construction of the Grand Union Canal (which was then called the Grand Junction Canal). This canal was 149.5km. (93.5 miles) long from the Oxford Canal at Braunston, via Wolverton, Leighton Buzzard, Tring, King's Langley, to the Thames at Brentford. The canal was completed in 1800, apart from the 2.79km (1 mile) long tunnel at Blisworth, which was not finished until 25 March 1805. While this tunnel was being completed, Jessop built a railway over the hill - the first in Northamptonshire - to enable traffic to operate on the canal in 1799. The canal provided a vital link between London and the Midlands.

Jessop's first tunnel was the 2.84km (1.74 mile) long Butterley Tunnel on the Cromford Canal, and led to the forming of the Butterley Iron Works. The Cromford and High Peak Railway engineered by Jessop's son Josias in 1825, was built to connect the Cromford Canal with the Peak Forest Canal at Whaley Bridge.

The Surrey Iron Railway grew out of a proposal of 1799 to open a part railway/part canal route from London to Portsmouth. The Thames at Wandsworth to Croydon was to have been canal, but Jessop and Rennie, retained as consultants, decided that a canal would be harmful to the industries of the Wandle Valley. The Surrey Iron Railway was incorporated by an Act of Parliament on 21 May 1801, and Jessop was appointed Chief Engineer. The railway was opened in 1802.

The first all-iron rails were laid in the 1790s and spread over the country during the first years of the nineteenth century, coinciding with the Revolutionary and Napoleonic Wars. These wars caused the cost of wood to soar and the price of iron to fall with the intensification of industry.

The fish-bellied iron rails which Jessop designed had a broad head on a thin web, deepest in the centre. One end had a flat foot, nailed with a peg on to a stone block. The other end had a round lug which was fitted into the the foot of the next rail. It was the true ancestor of the modern rail.

Jessop is not given enough credit for his involvement with Telford in the construction of the Pontcysyllte aqueduct. This crossed the river Dee and was completed in November 1805. In 1795, Jessop and Telford decided on a 302.4m (1,007ft) iron trough, standing on a series of slender stone piers, each solid at the base but hollow from about 21m (70ft) upwards. The work involved building 19 arches, each with a span of 13.5m (45ft). The work must have been extremely dangerous, carried out high above the swirling river Dee, with huge blocks of stone. A mixture of ox blood, water and lime was used as mortar. The flanged iron plates to make the trough were cast at Plaskynaston Foundry (within view of the aqueduct) and were bolted together, the joints being made watertight with Welsh flannel and lead dipped in boiling sugar! In November 1805, 8,000 people watched the opening. The bridge cost £47,000 with labourers paid 8 to 12 shillings (40-60p.) per week. When Telford wrote later about the achievement, he gave himself all the credit, with no mention of Jessop's contribution. Pontcysyllte is the finest aqueduct in Britain and is certainly the most spectacular piece of aerial navigation in the world. Jessop also built the Derwent aqueduct with 24.3m (80ft) span, and a less successful three-arch masonry aqueduct near Cosgrove.

He worked on the construction of a large wet-dock area on the Avon at Bristol, on the West India Docks and the Isle of Dogs Canal in London, on the harbours at Shoreham and Littlehampton, and on many other projects.

By 1799 or 1800, he had abandoned the fish-bellied rails in favour of cast-iron sockets fixed to the sleepers in which the rails were supported in the upright position. He produced what is equivalent to the flanged wheel of today, with flanges inside the rails.

The work of Jessop forms the link between that of Smeaton and Rennie. He achieved an incredible amount in a relatively short lifetime and was always ready to help his fellow professionals, for many of whom he acted as a consulting engineer on their projects, and his opinion was frequently sought because of his vast experience.

K

Kaplan, Viktor *(1876-1934)*, was an Austrian engineer, famous for inventing the turbine that bears his name.

Kaplan was born on 27 November 1876 at Murz, Austria. He was educated at the Realschule in Vienna and then at the Technische Hochschule, where he studied machine construction and gained his engineer's diploma in 1900. After a year's voluntary service in the Navy, he became a constructor of diesel engines for the firm of Ganz and Company of Leobersdorf, in Austria. In 1903 he was appointed to the chair of kinematics, theoretical machine studies and machine construction at the Technische Hochscule in Brunn. In 1918, he became Professor of Water Turbine Construction. He became debilitated and retired early in 1931. He died on 23 August 1934 at Unterach on the Attersee, Austria.

Kaplan published his first paper on turbines in 1908, writing about the Francis turbine and basing it on work that he had done for his doctorate at the Technische Hochschule in Vienna. In connection with this paper, he set up a propeller turbine for the lowest possible fall of water. In 1913 the first prototype of the turbine was completed. The Kaplan turbine was patented in 1920 as a water turbine with adjustable rotor-blades the runner blades can be varied to match the correct angle for a given flow of water. (The Francis-type turbine corresponds to a centrifugal pump, whereas the Kaplan-type turbine resembles a propeller pump.)

The Kaplan turbine in its traditional form has a vertical shaft, although one power-generator design uses a horizontal shaft and an alternator mounted in a 'nacelle' (metal shell) in the water flow. This is particularly suitable for lower output machines operating on very low heads of water, in which an almost straight water passage is possible. This type of turbine was designed for a French project on the river Rance estuary on the Gulf of St Malo, Brittany, France. Construction was begun in January 1961, on the world's first large-scale tidal plant, and completed late in 1967. It was designed to be made up of 24 hydroelectric power units. Each consisted of an ogive-shaped shell of metal containing an alternator and a Kaplan turbine. These units were installed in apertures in a dam through which the water flows. Each turbine acts both as a turbine and a pump, in both directions of tidal flow and in both directions of rotation, with each hydroelectric power unit generating 20,000kw.

The physical size and the operating head for which a Kaplan turbine can be used have increased considerably since 1920 when it was first patented. Runner diameters of 9.1m (30ft) have been employed. British manufacturers have developed designs operating at heads of 57.8m (190ft), but it is likely that further progress in increased heads will be limited due to the advent of the Deriaz turbine.

Kay, John *(1704-c.1780)*, was an English inventor of improved textile machinery, the most important of which was the flying shuttle of 1733.

Kay was born in July 1704 at Walmersley, near Bury in Lancashire. Little is known of his early life, although he is thought to have been educated in France. It is thought that on finishing his schooling he was put in charge of a wool fac-

tory owned by his father in Colchester, Essex. By 1730 he was established in his home town of Bury as a reed-maker (for looms). In that year he was granted a patent for an 'engine' for twisting and carding mohair, and for twining and dressing thread. At about the same time he improved the reeds for looms by manufacturing the 'darts' of thin polished metal, instead of cane, which were more durable and better suited to weaving finer fabrics.

In 1733 Kay patented his flying shuttle, which was probably the most important improvement that had been made to the loom. Up to that time the shuttle had been passed by hand from side to side through alternate warp threads. In weaving broad cloth two men had to be employed to throw the shuttle from one end to the other.

The weft was closed up after each 'pick' or throw of the shuttle by a 'layer' extending across the piece being woven. Kay added to the layer a grooved guide, called a 'race-board', in which the shuttle was rapidly thrown from side to side by means of a 'picker' or shuttle driver. One hand only was required, the other being employed in beating or closing up the weft. Kay's improvement allowed the shuttle to work with such speed that it became known as the flying shuttle. The amount of work a weaver could do was more than doubled, and the quality of the cloth was also improved. A powerful stimulus was thus given to improve spinning techniques, notably the inventions of James Hargreaves.

The patent of 1733 also included a batting machine for removing dust from wool by beating it with sticks. Kay's next patent (granted in 1738) was for a windmill for working pumps and for an improved chain-pump, but neither of these proved to be of any practical importance. In this last patent Kay described himself as an engineer.

Kay's biographer, Woodcroft, states that he moved to Leeds in 1738. The new shuttle was widely adopted by the woollen manufacturers of Yorkshire but since they were unwilling to pay royalties an association called The Shuttle Club was formed to defray the costs of legal proceedings for infringement of the patent. Kay found himself involved in numerous law suits and, although he was successful in the courts, the expenses of prosecuting these claims nearly ruined him.

In 1745 Kay was again in Bury and in that year he obtained a patent (in conjuction with Joseph Stell of Keighley) for a small loom actuated by mechanical power instead of by manual labour. This attempt at a power loom does not seem to have been successful, probably because of his financial difficulties and the hostility of the workers.

In 1753 a mob broke into Kay's house at Bury and destroyed everything they could find, Kay himself barely escaping with his life. Not surprisingly he lost his enthusiasm for working in England under such trying conditions, and he left for France where he remained for the next ten years, introducing the flying shuttle there with fair success.

In 1765 Kay invented a machine for making the card-cloth used in carding wool and cotton. The last years of his life are poorly documented. He is said to have been ruined by suits to protect his patents and is believed to have returned to France in 1774 and to have received a pension from the French court in 1778. After this nothing more is known of him.

Kelly, William *(1811-1888)*, was an American metallurgist, arguably the original inventor of the 'air-boiling process' for making steel, known universally as the Bessemer process. Kelly remained in relative obscurity in spite of his invention, whereas his rival (Bessemer) received $10 million in the USA and was knighted.

Kelly was born in Pittsburgh, Pennsylvania, on 21 August 1811, the son of a wealthy landowner said to have built the first two brick houses in Pittsburgh. Kelly was educated at local schools. He was inventive and fond of metallurgy, but at the age of 35 found himself working for a dry-goods business in Philadelphia as a junior member of the firm McShane and Kelly. He was sent out to collect debts to Nashville, Tennessee, and it was there that he met his wife and her father, who was a wealthy tobacco merchant. Kelly settled there and with his brother bought nearby iron-ore lands and a furnace known as the Cobb furnace in Eddyville.

Kelly patented his steel-making process in 1857, and in 1871 had his patent renewed for 7 years. Steel under the Kelly patent was first blown commercially in Autumn 1864 at the Wyandotte Iron Works near Detroit.

Kelly then moved to Johnstown, Pennsylvania, where he was acclaimed as a genius, and after 5 years he moved to Louisville, where he founded an axe-making business. He retired from active business at the age of 70 and died in Louisville on 11 February 1888. His axe-manufacturing business was carried on by his son in Charlestown, Western Virginia. On 5 October the American Society for Steel Treating erected a bronze tablet to Kelly's memory at the site of the Wyandotte Iron Works.

In Eddyville, Kelly developed the Suwanee Iron Works and the Union Forge. He manufactured sugar kettles, which were much in demand by farmers in the area. To do this he used wrought iron made from pig iron, which involved the burning out of the excess carbon. This needed lots of charcoal, and the local supply soon ran low.

One day he noticed that although the air-blast in his 'finery fire' furnace was blowing on molten iron with no charcoal covering, the iron was still becoming white hot. When he experimented further, he found that contrary to all iron-makers' beliefs, molten iron containing sufficient carbon became much hotter when air was blown on to it. 3 to 5 per cent of carbon contained in molten cast iron can be burnt out by the air-blast. Here the carbon itself is acting as a fuel, and makes the molten mass much hotter.

Kelly became so obsessed with his discovery that his wife called the doctor, thinking he was ill. Unfortunately, his customers could not be convinced that the steel made by this new, cheaper process was as good and so he had to revert to using charcoal. Meanwhile, with two other iron-makers, he started building a converter secretly. His first attempt was a 1.2-metre (4ft) high brick kettle. Air was blown through holes in the bottom into and through molten pig iron. The method was only partly successful. Between 1851 and 1856 he secretly built 7 of these converters. In 1856, he heard that Henry Bessemer of England had been granted an American patent on the same process. Kelly immediately applied for a patent and managed to convince the Patent Office of his priority. On 23 June 1857 he was granted a patent and declared to be the original inventor. Four years later, his patent was renewed for a further 7 years, whereas Bessemer's patent renewal was refused.

The financial panic of 1857 had bankrupted him, however, and he sold his patent to his father for $1,000. His father, thinking his son to be an incompetent businessman, bequeathed the patent to his daughters and would not return it to Kelly. Kelly therefore moved away to Johnstown, where a Daniel J. Morrell of the Cambria Iron Works listened to his plight. Kelly built his 8th converter there (the first of a tilting type), and it is still preserved in the office of the Cambria Works, now part of the Bethlehem Steel company. His second attempt at Johnsville was a success and it produced soft steel cheaply for the first time and in large quantities. It was used for rails, bars and structural shapes and marked a milestone in the Steel Age which was just beginning.

Kelly's patent eventually came under the control of Kelly Pneumatic Process Company, with which Kelly had nothing to do. This Company later merged with the Company of Alex. L. Holley, which was Bessemer's sole American licensee. Bessemer's name came into exclusive use for the Kelly-Bessemer steel-making process, and Kelly remained in relative obscurity.

Korolev, Sergei Pavlovich *(1906-1966)*, was the Russian engineer who designed the first manned spacecraft, interplantetary probes and soft lunar landings. As such, he was one of the founders of practical space flight.

Korolev was born on 30 December 1906 at Zhitomir in the Ukraine, the son of a Russian schoolmaster. His early technical training was received at a building trades school in Odessa; he graduated from there in 1924. Three years later he entered the aviation industry, but continued with his studies at the Moscow School of Aviation. He graduated from the Baumann Higher Technical School in 1930 and, in June of that year, he became a senior engineer at the Central Aerodyamics Institute. After successfully developing a number of gliders he became interested in rocket-type aircraft. In 1931, with Tsander, he formed a group for the study of jet propulsion. This became an official body, and in 1932 Korolev became its head. The group eventually trained many of the men responsible for the subsequent Soviet triumphs in space. It was this group that built the first Soviet liquid-fuel rocket, which was launched in 1933. Korolev was appointed deputy director of the new Institute for Jet Research, which was formed by combining the original Korolev group and the Gas Dynamics Laboratory in 1933. In 1934 he was appointed head of the rocket vehicle department.

Korolev was responsible for designing a number of rockets and, from 1924 to 1946, he worked as deputy chief engine designer in the Specialized Design Bureau. Later, Korolev was appointed head of the large team of scientists who developed high-power rocket systems.

Korolev received many honours. In 1953 he was made corresponding member of the Academy of Sciences of the USSR and a member of the CPSU. He was twice named Hero of Socialist Labour, the first time in 1956 and the second time in 1961. In 1958 he was made full member of the Academy of Sciences, having been awarded the Lenin Prize in 1958. In addition, his name is commemorated for all time: the largest formation on the hidden side of the moon is named after him. On his death on 14 January 1966 his body was buried in the Kremlin Wall in Red Square, Moscow - one of the highest honours which can be conferred on a Soviet citizen.

Korolev published his first paper on jet propulsion in 1934. By 1939 he had designed and successfully launched the Soviet 212 guided wing rocket. This was followed in 1940 by the RIP-318-1 rocket glider, which made its first piloted flight in 1940. From then on, Korolev was responsible for a large number of historical first achievements in space exploration.

He was responsible, in an executive and scientific capacity, for directing the early research and design work which later led to vast Soviet achievements in space flight. Korolev initiated many scientific and technological ideas which have since been widely used in rocket and space technology, including ballistic missiles, rockets for geophysical research, launch vehicles and manned spacecraft. The most famous of these is the Vostok series of Soviet single-seater spaceships designed for close-earth orbit in which Soviet cosmonauts made their first flights.

Vostok 1, manned by Yuri Gagarin, made the first manned space flight in history, which took place on 12 April 1961. Launched from the Baikonur space-launch area, Gagarin and Vostok 1 completed one orbit of the earth in just under two hours. This flight was followed by Vostoks 2,3,4,5 and 6 (which was manned by Valentina Tereshkova, who became the first female astonaut in history). The technological improvements made by Korolev and his team were such that Tereshkova and Vostok 6 were able to make 48 orbits in a total time of just over 70 hours.

These close-earth flights were followed by the launching of Sun satellites and the flights of the unmanned interplanetary probes into the solar system - including the Elecktron and Molniia series. Korolev was also responsible for the Voskhod spaceship, from which men made their first space-walks.

Krupp, Alfred *(1812-1887)*, was a German metallurgist who became known as the Cannon King because of his success in manufacturing cast-steel guns. He also invented the first weldless steel tyre for railway vehicles.

Krupp was born in Essen on 26 April 1812. At 14 years of age he was obliged to leave school to help his mother run the small family steel works. The firm remained small until Krupp made his first gun in 1847. In 1851, at the Great Exhibition in London, he exhibited a solid flawless ingot of cast steel weighing 2 tonnes (1.95 tons). Soon afterwards Krupp produced the first weldless steel tyre for railway vehicles. The works expanded its operations in the manufacture of artillery, eventually becoming the largest armaments firm in the world. Krupp was also humanely interested in the social welfare of his workers, and introduced low-costhousing and pension schemes for all his employees. He died in Essen on 14 July 1887.

In 1811 Alfred Krupp's father, Frederick, had founded a firm in Essen for the purpose of making cast steel of a superior quality. His experiments had produced a formula for making a high-quality product and, when he died prematurely in

1826, the secret was left to his son. The firm remained small, however, and for a while production almost came to a standstill. At age 14 Alfred Krupp took full charge of his father's company. Four years later he extended production to include the manufacture of steel rolls. He also designed and developed new machines. He invented the spoon roll for making spoons and forks, and manufactured rolling mills for use in government mints. In 1847 the firm cast its first steel cannon, a small 3-pounder muzzle-loading gun, but it still specialized in making fine steel suitable for dies, rolls and machine-building.

At the Great Exhibition of 1851 in London, Krupp exhibited his solid flawless ingot of cast steel. In 1852 he manufactured the first seamless steel railway tyre and was the first to introduce the Bessemer and Open-Hearth steel-making processes in Europe. The advent of the railways caused the firm's fortunes to increase. At first, railway axles and springs were the only cast steel products in use, but Krupp's seamless tyre greatly contributed to the speed and safety of railway travel and became extensively used. Then mass production of rails began and the company expanded still further to become a vast organization with collieries, ore-mine, blast furnaces, steel plants and manufacturing shops.

In 1863 Krupp established a physical laboratory for the testing of steels. To prove the quality of his own steel, Krupp turned to making guns and was the first to produce a successful all-steel gun. Drilled out of a single block of cast metal it was the marvel of its day, and in the Franco-German war of 1870-1871 the performance of Krupp guns won him world renown.

By this time, the firm employed 16,000 workers and had developed into a vast integrated industrialized empire - one of the first ever to arise in Germany. Although Krupp's reputation is mainly built on the manufacture of weapons of war, the output of goods from his works - even in wartime - was predominatly for peaceful purposes.

Krupp was also a philanthropist. Recognizing early the human problems of industrialization, he created a comprehensive welfare scheme for his workers. As early as 1836 he instituted a sickness fund and, in 1855, he established a pension fund for retired and incapacitated workers. Low-cost housing, medical care and consumer co-operatives all enjoyed company backing. These institutions proved so successful that they acted as models for the social legislation enacted in Germany under Bismark from 1883-1889.

Krupp built housing settlements, hospitals, schools and churches for his employers. His social paternalism minimized serious labour troubles and fostered the Krupp employee's pride in being Kruppianer. Krupp at one time had only seven employees in his steel plant. At his death in Essen on 14 July 1887, the enterprise employed 21,000 persons.

L

Laennec, René Théophile Hyacinthe *(1781-1826)*, was the French physician who invented the stethoscope in 1816.

Laennec was born at Quimper, Brittany, on 17 February 1781. Because his mother died early, he was sent to live with his uncle who was a physician in Nantes, and there he was introduced to medical work. The French Revolution struck the town with some ferocity and Laennec, only just in his teens, worked in the city hospitals. In 1795 he was commissioned as third surgeon at the Hôpital de la Paix, and shortly afterwards at the Hospice de la Fraternité - he was then just 14 years old. It was there that Laennec became acquainted with clinical work, surgical dressings and the treatment of large numbers of patients.

Because his own health was not good, he abandoned medicine until 1799, when he returned to his medical studies and became a pupil of J.N Corvisart. He was appointed surgeon at the Hôtel Dieu in Nantes. From there, he entered the Ecole Pratique in Paris and studied dissection in Depuytren's laboratory.

Between June 1802 and July 1804, Laennec published a number of papers on anatomy. His 1804 thesis 'Propositions sur la doctrine d'Hippocrate relativement à la médecin-pratique' resulted in the award of a doctor's degree.

Laennec became particularly interested in pathology. Appointed an associate of the Société de l'Ecole de Médecine in 1808, he founded the Athenée Médical which later merged with the Société Academique de Médecine de Paris. Laennec was appointed personal physician to Cardinal Fesch, uncle of Napoleon I. In 1812-1813, with France at war, Laennec took charge of the wards in the Salpetrière reserved for Breton soldiers. On the restoration of the monarchy, he took the post of physician to the Necker Hospital but, by February 1818, poor health obliged him to retire to his country estate where he lived the life of a gentleman farmer in Brittany. At the end of that year, however, he returned to Paris, but in 1819 he was again forced to retire to his estates at Kerbourarnec, where he assumed the role of country squire.

In 1822 Laennec was appointed to the chair and a lectureship at the Collège de France. In 1823 he became a full member of the Académie de Médecine and, in 1824, he was made a Chevalier of the Légion d'Honneur. He became internationally famous as a lecturer. However, his health failed him again and he left Paris for the last time in May, 1826. He died on 13 August of the same year.

Laennec's important contribution to medical science was his invention of the stethoscope. In 1816, while walking in a courtyard in Louvre, he noticed two small children with their ears close to the ends of a long stick. They were amusing themselves by tapping lightly on the stick and listening to the transmitted sound. He immediately realized the diagnostic possibilities and quickly developed an instrument based on the children's activities. It was essentially a wooden tube some 30cms (12in) long and he used it to listen to sounds in the human body. As it was particularly useful for sounding the lungs and heart, he called it a stethoscope (from the Greek *stethos*, meaning chest).

Laennec was now deeply interested in emphysema, tuberculosis and physical signs of chest diseases. Although auscultation had been known since the days of Hippocrates, it was always done by the 'direct' method - which was often inconvenient. Laennec introduced the 'mediate' method by using his hollow tube for listening to the lungs, and a solid wooden rod to listen to the heart.

By February 1818 he was able to present a paper on the subject to the Académie de Médecine and, by 1819, he was able to classify the physical signs of egophony, rales, rhonchi and crepitations. His book *De l'auscultation médiate* was published in August 1819. This was much more than a book on the use of the stethoscope; it was an important treatise on diseases of the heart, lungs and liver, and was acknowledged to represent a great advance in the understanding of chest diseases.

Laithwaite, Eric Robert *(1921-   )*, is a British electrical engineer, most famous for his development of the linear motor.

Laithwaite was born on 14 June 1921 at Atherton, Yorkshire. He was educated at Kirkham Grammar School and then at Regent Street Polytechnic, London. He read for his BSc at the University of Manchester, but his studies were interrupted by World War II. From 1941 to 1946 he served in the Royal Air Force; for 4 years he worked at the Royal Aircraft Establishment, Farnborough, researching into automatic pilots for aircraft. He gained his BSc in 1949 and an MSc in the following year. He remained at the University of Manchester until 1964, holding positions of Assistant Lecturer, Lecturer and Senior Lecturer. During that time he was awarded a PhD in 1957, and a DSc in 1964. In that same year he was appointed Professor of Heavy Electrical Engineering at the Imperial College of Science and Technology at the University of London, and it is this position that he has continued to hold. From 1967 to 1976 he was External Professor of Applied Electricity at the Royal Institution, and in 1970 he became President of the Association for Science Education.

Laithwaite is unusually able to put his ideas across to laymen and to children. He is one of the most popular contributors to the Christmas Lectures at the Royal Institution. In 1966 the title of his lectures was 'The Engineer in Wonderland' which he followed in 1974 with 'The Engineer Through the Looking Glass'. He has also participated in radio and television broadcasts on general science including: 'Young Scientists of the Year', 'It's Patently Obvious' and 'The Engineer's World'. He has also made a number of films, several of which have won major awards.

The idea of a linear induction motor had been suggested in 1895, but a new principle has been discovered and worked on by Laithwaite: that it is possible to arrange two linear motors, back-to-back, so as to produce continuous oscillation without the use of any switching device. The important feature of the linear motor is that it is a means of propulsion without the need for wheels. This in itself is nothing remarkable. Yachts, rowing boats, surf-boards, ice-skates, skiis, canoes, gliders - all are examples of propulsion methods without wheels. Even swimming and walking are mechanisms requiring no rotary movement in a pure sense. Man's early propulsion systems were designed to use either his muscular power or natural power sources such as air currents or the wave energy of a sailing yatch in a steady wind. It is possible to continually extract power from a source, although often continuous motion has to be made up from reciprocating motion - achieved by the use of a ratchet, for example.

Linear motion is very common in industrial processes. Planing machines, looms, saws, knitting machines and pumps all make use of motion in a straight line. In 1947 Laithwaite began research into electric linear induction motors as the shuttle drives in weaving looms. Further investigations were carried out into the use of linear motors for conveyers and as propulsion units for railway vehicles. By 1961, his research had aroused sufficient interest for it to be included in a BBC television programme which added to public interest in the linear induction motor, and development was further stimulated by a lecture which Laithwaite gave to the Royal Institution in March 1962 entitled 'Electrical Machines of the Future'

Probably the project which has aroused the greatest interest in the Press and on television is the high-speed transport project, in which hovering vehicles, moving on air cushions or jets, are powered by linear induction motors, used as high-speed propulsion units. These systems are in use in the United States, France, Japan and the Soviet Union for high-speed railways, and for a while the Tracked Hovercraft Project in Cambridge, England, aroused great interest. There is also speculation on the possiblity of using linear motors for the assisted take-off of space vehicles.

Lanchester, Frederick William *(1868-1946)*, was the English engineer who created the first true British motorcar of reliable design and produced the first comprehensive theory of flight.

Lanchester was born at Lewisham, London on 28 October 1868. Two year later his family moved to Hove, where his father set up business as an architect. In 1883 Lanchester went to the Hartley Institution (which later became University College, Southampton). From here he won a scholarship to what is now Imperial College.

After a brief period as a Patent Office draughtsman, he joined the Forward Gas Engine Company of Birmingham as assistant works manager in 1889, becoming works manager within a year.

It was in 1893, following his return from an unsuccessful trip to America to sell his gas engine patents, that Lanchester set up a workshop next to the Forward Company. By 1896 his first motor car had emerged, with a single cylinder 4kW (5hp) engine and chain drive. He rebuilt it the following year with an 6kW (8hp) flat twin engine and a worm gear transmission for which he designed both the worm form and the machine tool to produce it. His second car, built at his Ladywood Road factory, was a 6kW (8hp) Phaeton with flywheel ignition, roller bearings and cantilever springing.

The car won a gold medal for its performance and design at the Royal Automobile Club trials at Richmond in 1899, and the following year it completed a 1600km (1,000 mile) tour. The company then went into production with 7.5 to 9kW (10 to 12hp) motorcars, of which some 350 were built between 1900 and 1905. A 15kW (20hp) 4 cylinder and 21kW (28hp) 6 cylinder models were produced in 1904 and 1905 respectively.

As early as 1891 Lanchester had acquired an interest in manned flight and soon began experimenting with powered and gliding models. He showed that a well-designed aircraft could be inherently stable, a concept that underpins modern airworthiness requirements. On 19 June 1894 he marshalled his theories of flight in a paper of fundamental importance: The soaring of birds and the possibilities of mechanical flight', which was given at a meeting of the Birmingham Natural History and Philosophical Society.

Lanchester revised and amplified his paper, and submitted it to the Physical Society, only to have it rejected in September 1897. Nothing daunted, he resurrected his theories and incorporated them in his great work, *Aerial Flight* which was published in 2 volumes, *Aerodynamics* in 1907 and *Aerodonetics* in 1908. The first volume won Lanchester instant acclaim.

Lanchester and his collaborator Norman A Thompson designed an experimental aircraft whose wings were covered by an aluminium skin and a sheet steel fuselage. Sadly, the undercarriage collapsed on the first trial flight in 1911, and Lanchester decided to quit the practical side of aviation. A second aircraft, with broadly similar design, did fly successfully in the summer of 1913, and in the following year a seaplane, also incorporating many of Lanchester's ideas, took to the air. This machine was the prototype for a batch of 6 built for the Admiralty and used during World War I to counter the German submarine menace.

In 1900 Lanchester acquired the Armourer Mills in Montgomery Street, Sparbrook which were to house the Lanchester Engine Company until 1931. However, the company went into receivership in 1904 and was reconstructed the following year as the Lanchester Motor Company. This was a financial success.

The publication of Aerial Flight led to Lanchester's joining Prime Minister Asquith's advisory committee for Aeronautics at its formation on 30 April 1909. The same year he was appointed consulting engineer and technical advisor to the Daimler company.

With the outbreak of World War I, Lanchester's involvement in military work became so great that he moved to London. On 3 September 1919 he married Dorothea Cooper, daughter of the vicar of Field Broughton, near Windermere.

After the War he left the Committee, and his work in the capital tailed off. Having become increasingly busy in the Daimler business in Coventry, Lanchester decided to move back to Birmingham. He founded Lanchester's Laboratories Ltd in 1925, intending to provide research and development services, but the economic depression meant there was little call for his expertise.

Lanchester was also interested in radio and, having patented a loudspeaker and other audio equipment he went into production. Again he hit difficulties, and these, combined with his failing health, forced him finally to close down his Laboratories in January 1934.

His health improved towards the end of the year, and he began to write prolifically both on technical and non-technical subjects. His works included a collection of poems (under the pseudonym of Paul Netherton-Herries), an explanation of relativity and a treatise on the theory of dimensions.

When World War II broke out, the symptons of Parkinson's disease had become clear. Although his mind was still lively, Lanchester was forced to effectively retire. Finally, plagued by financial worries and losing his sight, Lanchester died, on 8 March 1946.

Lanchester's work with motorcars is remarkable not only because of the number of new ideas which were incorporated into them, but also because he produced them with interchangeable parts. This was the concept later adopted so successfully by mass production manufacturers. In his study of flight he was the first engineer to depart from the empirical approach and to formulate a comprehensive theory of lift and drag. His work on stability was fundamental to aviation.

Lanchester received many honours and awards, including the presidency of the Institute of Automobile Engineers (1910), Fellowship of the Royal Aeronautical Society (1917) and of the Royal Society (1922), and the Gold Medal of the RAS in 1926. Birmingham University made him an honorary doctor of law in 1919.

Lebon, Phillipe *(1767-1804)*, was a French engineer who was the first person to successfully use 'artificial' gas as a means of illumination on a large scale.

Lebon was born in the charcoal-burning town of Bruchay, near Jonville. He received a sound scientific education, first at Chalon-sur-Saone and later at the Ecole des Ponts et Chaussées, a famous school for engineers. He graduated in 1792 and received the rank of major, serving as a highway engineer. For a time in Angouleme, near Bordeaux, From Angouleme, he was recalled to Paris to teach mechanics at the Ecole des Ponts et Chaussées.

In about 1797, Lebon became interested in the process of using 'artificial' gas, produced from wood, for heating and lighting purposes. He also made some attempts at perfecting the steam engine and received a national prize of 2,000 livres for the improvements he accomplished. In 1799, he read a paper on his experiments with gas to the Institut de France and was granted a patent on his invention later that year. Further patents were granted in 1801. Lebon's work was, however, cut short by his sudden death on 2 December 1804. He was attacked and stabbed on the Champs Elys-

sée in Paris, and died of his wounds.

Lighting on a large scale was demonstrated when the streets of Paris were first lit in 1667 using large lanterns containing candles and metal reflectors. An oil lantern was developed in 1744 and, in 1786, Argand completed his invention of an oil lamp with a glass chimney. Carcel introduced an oil pump and such oil lamps continued to be popular for lighting streets and houses. Lebon was the first person to consider using gas as a lighting medium.

In 1797, at Bruchay, he became interested in the extraction of gas from wood for this purpose and began experimenting with the use of sawdust. He placed some sawdust in a glass tube and held it over a flame. The gas given off caught alight as it emerged from the tube - but it smoked badly and emitted a strong resinous smell. On his return to Paris, Lebon discussed his work with several scientists, including Fourcroy. They encouraged him and, in 1799, he read a paper on the subject before the Institut de France. He patented his invention in that year and called his new lamp the Thermolampe (heat lamp) because he intended to use it for heating as well as lighting purposes.

Approaches to the government to interest them in using his invention for public heating and lighting proved of no avail. To publicize his Thermolampe, Lebon leased the Hotel Seignelay in Paris in 1801 and, for several months, he exhibited a large version of the lamp which attracted huge crowds. But, although they admired Lebon's successful attempt to illuminate a fountain in the hotel, because he had been unable to eliminate the repulsive odour given off by the gas the public decided that his invention was not a practical one.

Further work by Lebon was curtailed by his early death and it was left to William Murdoch (working independently at about the same time in Scotland) to succeed where Lebon had failed, and it was Murdoch who has received the credit for the invention of gas lighting.

Lenoir, Jean Joseph Étienne *(1822-1900)*, was a Belgian-born French engineer and inventor who in the early 1860s produced the first practical internal combustion engine and a car powered by it. He also developed a white enamel (1847), an electric brake (1853) and an automatic telegraph (1865). Lenoir was born at Mussy-la-Ville, Belgium, on 12 January 1822; he died in Varenne-St-Hilaire, France, on 4 August 1900.

The first self-propelled road vehicles were steam cars - using an external-combustion steam engine. The French army captain Nicolas Cugnot built a three-wheeled steam tractor for hauling cannon as early as 1769, and a passenger carrying vehicle was constructed in England in about 1801.

By 1830, steam carriages were in regular use but they were noisy, dirty and the smoke and hot coals often caused fires along the route, making them unpopular with farmers who feared for their crops.

Several people had claimed to have invented an internal combustion engine before Lenoir. The Reverend W. Cecil read a paper to Cambridge University in 1829 about his experiments, and William Barnett in 1838 also laid claims, but not until Lenoir in 1859 did a practical model become a reality. His engine consisted of a single cylinder with a storage battery (accumulator) for the electric ignition system. Its two-stroke cycle was provided by slide valves, and it was fuelled by coal gas, as used then for domestic purposes and street lighting. Lenoir built a small car around one of his prototypes in 1863, but it had an efficiency of less than 4 per cent and although he claimed it was silent, this was only true when the vehicle was not under load.

The real value of his engine was for powering small items of machinery, and by 1865 more than 400 were in use in the Paris district driving printing presses, lathes and water pumps. Its use for vehicles was restricted by its size and not until some 20 years later, when Gottlieb Daimler and Karl Benz independently devised the four-cycle engine, that internal combustion engines were successful in vehicles.

Lilienthal, Otto *(1848-1896)*, was a German engineer whose experiments with gliders helped to found the science of aeronautics. But for his premature death in a flying accident, he might well have beaten the Wright brothers to the achievement of powered flight.

Lilienthal was born in Pomerania (then part of Prussia), and trained as an engineer just before the outbreak of the Franco-Prussian War in 1870. He made exhaustive studies of the flight of birds, especially of the stork, but was aware that it was 'not enough to acquire the art of the bird' it was also necessary to put the whole problem of flight on a scientific basis. From these studies he learnt that curved wings allow horizontal flight without an angle of incidence to the wind, and that soaring is related to air thermals. In 1889 he published his famous book *Der Vogelflug als Grundlage der Fliegekunst* (Bird Flight as a Basis for Aviation), which was to have a great influence on the work of the pioneers of the next vitally important years. He was one of the few who showed conclusively that birds produce thrust by the action of their outer primary feathers. It was perhaps this that kept Lilienthal on the path of the ornithopter - a machine which simulated the winged flight of a bird as the ultimate means of powered flight.

Lilienthal flew the first of his famous series of gliders in 1891, and continued, until his final fatal glide in 1896 to hold to his fundamental conviction that the key to eventual powered flight was in glider-flying, in which men could master the elements of control and design. Its relative safety - sadly not safe enough for Lilienthal - allowed the pioneers of flying to come to terms with problems of movement and airflow. The step to powered flight was a straightforward progression from advanced gliding. The Wrights' breakthrough was a simple extension of their own work with gliders, which in turn was greatly helped by Lilienthal's many glides and careful observations. Among other things he had demonstrated the superiority of cambered wings over flat wings - the principle of the aerofoil.

By 1893 he was flying a cambered-wing monoplane from a springboard near his home. It had a wingspan of 7 metres (23ft) and a surface area of about 14 sq. metres (17sq. yds); its wings folded for transport. Other gliders included two biplanes, with tailplanes in front of the vertical tail fin (the first gliders were tail-less). His 1894 model (Number 11 in the offical biographies) became his standard machine. With a wing surface of 13 sq. metres (15sq. yds) this glider had the tailplane integral with the fin and achieved glides of more than 300 metres (1,000 ft). By this time his activities had given a boost to gliding as a sport, and enthusiasts began 'sailing' in many countries.

1894 also saw the introduction of a shock-absorbing hoop which, on 9 November, certainly helped to save his life in a crash. A detailed description of this incident caused other workers, including the Wrights, to build elevators in front of their machines, the idea being to prevent damage in the event of a nose-dive. By 1889 Lilienthal had introduced leading-edge flaps to counteract the tendency to nose-dive. Also in that year he introduced the biplanes referred to above found to possess increased stability with reduced wingspan, but he did not develop these machines. (The Wrights' successful flights were with biplanes.) Lilienthal's later machines were flown from an artificial earthwork which he had constructed outside Berlin. These gave a launching height of about 15m (50ft) and, being conical, allowed independence of wind direction.

In 1895 Lilienthal resumed some earlier work on the idea of a powered machine with moving wing-tips, using a carbon dioxide motor despite the fact that petrol engines had been made by that time. The machine was not tested. Only in that year did he consider means of control other than body swinging. Up to then the 'pilot' was suspended by his arms - like a modern hang-glider- the rest of him dangling free after the running take-off. Movement was produced by swinging the body, altering the centre of gravity. The idea of the body harness was introduced, an echo of something Leonardo da Vinci had sketched some 500 years previously.

The influence of Lilienthal, both before and after his death, was enormous, helped greatly by the developments in photography and printing of that period - the dry-plate negative and the half-tone printing process. These advances allowed a magnificent series of pictures to be given world-wide circulation. They had a tremendous and important impact at a time when even a scientist like Lord Kelvin was saying that he had 'not the smallest molecule of faith' in flying, other than in balloons!

On a fine summer's day in 1896, after several trouble-free glides, an unexpected gust caused Lilienthal's Number 11 to stall and fall to the ground. His spine was broken and he died the following day. His gravestone carries a favourite saying of his: 'Sacrifices have to be made'.

Locke, Joseph *(1805-1860)*, was a British railway engineer, a contemporary and associate of Isambard Brunel and the Stephensons.

Lock was born on 9 August 1805, the youngest of four sons of a colliery manager at Attacliffe Common, Sheffield, Yorkshire. His father was a man of strong views and for various reasons changed employers several times while Joseph was still a child. He did, however, receive a 'sort of an education' at the grammar school in Barnsley and left at the age of 13 knowing a little but, as he said, 'knowing that little well'.

Locke found employment carrying letters at Pelaw, County Durham, under the watchful eye of William Stobart, colliery viewer for the Duke of Norfolk, but after two years he returned to Barnsley. He was then sent to Rochdale work for a land surveyor named Hampson. The situation looked promising until he was asked to look after the Hampson baby. He gave up the job and once again returned home - this time after only a fortnight.

The family resigned themselves to the fact that he was rather idle and left him to find work for himself. He might well have remained unsettled had not luck interceded. His father's old friend from the Attacliffe colliery days called to see them - George Stephenson, the civil engineer. When he saw the plight of his friend's young son he suggested Joseph should be sent to work for him, and this began what was to prove a fortunate career as an apprentice railwayman.

From 1823 to 1826 Locke learnt much about surveying, railway engineering and construction. He loved the life and learnt with enthusiasm, something which had been lacking in his earlier attempts at a career. After three years he was to emerge as one of the foremost engineers of the railway era.

Locke's first task undertaken alone was the construction of a railway line from the Black Fell colliery to the River Tyne. This he managed so successfully that Stephenson confessed to have 'complete confidence' in Locke's ability. He was immediately asked to begin surveys for lines running between Leeds and Hull, Manchester and Bolton, and Canterbury and Whitstable.

The hectic era of railway expansion was under way when George Stephenson (now joined by his son Robert), Brunel and Locke were in great demand. By 1842 more than 2,988km (1,857 miles) of track had been laid and Locke had made a reputation for himself as a man who built as straight as possible, used the terrain, and avoided the expense of tunnels whenever he could. He was asked to tackle the London to Southampton line and although others favoured tunnelling through the chalk downs, he chose to cut into it, leaving steep embankments on each side of the line. His method proved successful and gave few problems after the line was opened on 11 May 1840.

Locke took over part of the construction of the Grand Junction railway from Stephenson and the Sheffield-to-Manchester route from Vignoles. The latter was a complicated operation which cut a 4,850 metre (5,300 yard) bore through the millstone grit of the Pennines. In 1841 he began work as Chief Engineer on the Paris to Rouen line and completed it on schedule in May 1843. This was to be the first of several contracts in France and it added even more prestige to his name.

Turning once more to work in Britain, he carried out construction of lines on behalf of the Lancaster and Carlisle Railway and the Caledonian Railway, but during 1846 he made some important decisions regarding his own life. He bought the manor of Honiton in Devon and fulfilled a boyhood ambition to enter Parliament. Many accused him of buying his way in, although he did in fact stand for election in 1847 and remained Liberal member for Honiton until his death 13 years later.

All three of the railway 'giants' spent their remaining years in well-earned comfort while yet being fully employed. The construction of new railways continued relentlessly, and their skills were always in great demand. Contemporaries to the point of all being born within the same three-year period, strangely they all died within the same space of time: Brunel on 14 September 1859, Robert Stephenson, his friend of long-standing, on 12 October 1859, and Locke himself on 18 September 1860.

Lumière, Auguste Marie Louis Nicolas *(1862-1954)* **and Lumière, Louis Jean** *(1864-1948)*, were two brothers who became famous as inventors of the cinematograph.

Louis Lumière, the younger of the two and ultimately the one who spent his whole career in photography, was born on 5 October 1864 at Besançon in eastern France. The family owned and operated a photographic firm in Lyons. When the brothers were old enough to join the business they did so with enthusiasm and contributed several minor improvements to the developing process, including in 1880 the invention of a better type of dry plate.

In 1894 their father purchased an Edison Kinetoscope (a cine viewer) which impressed them greatly, although more for the potential it represented than for itself. They borrowed some of the ideas and developed a new all-in-one machine - camera and projector - which they patented in 1895, calling it a cinematograph. To advertise their success they filmed delegates arriving at a French photographic congress and 48 hours later projected the developed film to a large audience.

When the brothers ultimately separated, August went on to do medical research leaving Louis to continue in the photographic industry. He was associated with several other improvements, among them a photorama for panoramic shots and in 1907 a colour printing process using dyed starch grains. During World War I he worked on aircraft equipment and afterwards carried on with photography, branching out into stereoscopy and three-dimensional films. He died at Bandol, France, on 6 June 1948.

Edison had patented his design for the kinetograph in 1888 after persuading George Eastman to make suitable celluloid film. Unfortunately the pictures could be viewed only through a peep-hole and, although Edison had seen the possibility of projecting them so they could be viewed by a large audience, he had omitted this from his patent, which was for him a rare error.

The Lumière brothers took the best of Edison's ideas and developed them further, inventing a combined camera and projector which weighed much less than the Edison model. The film passed through the camera at the rate of 16 frames per second, slower than the modern equivalent, while a semicircular shutter cut off the light between the lens and the film. By the end of 1895 the brothers had opened their first cinema in Paris, attracting large crowds to see the real-life films. Other establishments soon followed and a whole new industry was founded, bringing entertainment within the reach of the working man.

In the United States, Edison had seen how the error in his patent had been exploited and had resumed his interest in the moving-picture phenomenon, joining forces with Thomas Armat who had devised a projector. To the Lumières in France and Edison in the United States can be attributed the honours for the origin of the motion picture industry of the twentieth century.

M

Mannesman, Reinhard *(1856-1922)*, was a German ironfounder who invented a method of making seamless steel tubes.

Mannesman was born on 13 May 1856. Both he and his brother Max were ironmasters and, like other inventors in the second half of the nineteenth century, they increasingly turned their attentions from machine tools to heavy equipment for the production of metals. They perfected a way of making a seamless tube, which was much more accurate than the welded tube. The idea behind the invention had been conceived by their father in 1860, while he was working at Remscheid.

The Mannesman process, as it was later to be called, involved the passing of a furnace-heated bar between two rolls which rotated. Because of their geometrical configuration, the rolls drew the bar forward and at the same time produced tensions in the hot metal that caused it to tear apart at the centre. A stationary, pointed mandrel caused the ingot of metal to open out and form a tube. The tubes were later forged to size - again on mandrels in rolling mills with grooved rolls that varied in diameter like cams. Between the compression phases, in which the tube is advanced by the rolls, the activating mechanism rotates and then partially returns the tubes. Thus the process is intermittent, taking place in a series of short steps. This later technique involved the tube stock being fed to pilger mills from the Mannesman machines; thus the process was called pilgering.

The first Mannesman plant and pilger mills were installed in Swansea in 1887 and operated by the Landore Siemens Steel Company of Swansea. The plant consisted of six Mannesman machines, the largest being capable of piercing solid billets of up to 25cm (10 in) in diameter. In 1891 the process was granted a patent. It was this invention that most impressed the American inventor Thomas Edison during his visit to the World Exhibition in Chicago in 1893.

The Landore Siemens Steel Company remained the major manufacturer of seamless steel tubes until near the end of the last century. Then a plant designed and created at Youngstown, Ohio, took over as the most important manufacturer in the world.

Reinhard Mannesman died in 1922.

Marconi, Guglielmo *(1874-1937)*, was a physicist who saw the possiblity of using radio waves-long waves-length electromagnetic radiation - for the transmission of information. He was the first to put such a service into operation a service on a commercial scale, and was responsible for many of the developments which have made radio and telegraph services into major industries.

Marconi was born in Bologna into a wealthy family on 25 April 1874. His education consisted largely of private tutoring, although he was sent for a brief period to the Technical Institute in Leghorn where he received instruction in physics. He studied under a number of prominent Italian professors but never enrolled for a university course.

His studies of radio transmission began on his father's estate in the 1890s. By 1897 he had established a commercial enterprise in London, based on developments from his early work. He became famous in 1901 when he succeeded in sending a transatlantic coded message.

In 1909 he was awarded, jointly with K.F Braun, the Nobel Prize in Physics, and was honoured by the receipt of the Albert Medal from the Royal Society of Arts in 1929. He was also being made a Knight Grand Cross of the Royal Victorian Order, and was given the title of Marchese by the Italian Government. From 1921 he lived aboard his yacht *Elettra*, which served as a home, laboratory and receiving station. Marconi was given a state funeral after his death in Rome on the 20 July 1937.

Marconi's researches began in 1894, the year of Heinrich Hertz's death, when he read a paper on the possible technical applications of the electromagnetic waves discovered by Hertz in 1886. Marconi realized that the waves could be used in signalling and began experiments with Professor Righi of the University of Bologna to determine how far the waves would travel.

Marconi based his apparatus on that used by Hertz, but used a coherer to detect the waves. (The coherer was designed to convert the radio waves into electric current.) Marconi improved Hertz's design by earthing the transmitter and receiver, and found that an insulated aerial enabled him to increase the distance of transmission. During 1895 he slowly increased the distance over which he was able to transmit a signal, first from

the house into the garden and eventually to about 2.5km (1.5 miles) - the length of the family estate.

The Italian government was not interested in the device, so Marconi travelled to London where he enlisted the help of relatives to enable him to obtain a patent and to introduce his discovery to the British government. He obtained his patent in June 1896 for the use of waves similar to those discovered by Hertz but of longer wavelength, for the purpose of wireless telegraphy. Marconi enabled Queen Victoria to send a message to the Prince of Wales aboard the Royal yacht, and increased his transmission distance to 15km (about 9 miles), then to 30km. The first commercial 'Marconigram' was sent from Lord Kelvin to Stokes.

The Wireless Telegraph Company was founded in London in 1897, and later became the Marconi Wireless Telegraph Co. Ltd in Chelmsford in 1900. In 1899 Marconi went to the United States and sent reports about the presidential election taking place there. On 12 December 1901, after many hold-ups, Marconi succeeded in sending a radio signal in Morse across the Atlantic Ocean from Pondhu in Cornwall to St Johns in Newfoundland, Canada.

Marconi became increasingly involved with the management of his companies from 1902, but he attracted many distinguished scientists to work with him. Some of the important developments were: the magnetic detector (1902), horizontal direction telegraphy (1905) and the continuous wave system (1912).

During World War I Marconi worked on the development of very short wavelength beams, which could be used for many purposes including enabling a pilot to fly an aircraft 'blind'. After the War these short wavelength beams contributed to communication over long distances. In 1932 Marconi discovered that he could detect microwave radiation, that is waves with very high frequencies. These wavelengths were soon to form the basis of radar.

Martin, James *(1893-1981)*, was the Ulster-born British aeronautical engineer whose pioneering work in the design and manufacture of ejection seats has saved the lives of thousands of military jet aircrew since 1949.

Martin was born on 11 September 1893 at Crossgar, County Down. The son of a farmer, he had designed, made and sold various machines while still a teenager. He scorned conventional education, but by practical work and study he had become an accomplished engineer before the age of 20.

In his early 20s he designed a three-wheeled enclosed car as a cheap runabout. Small oil engines and specialized vehicles were among his first products when he set up a one-man business in Acton, London. In 1929 Martin established the works at Denham, Middlesex that have served as a permanent home for his company until the present day. His first aircraft, a two-seater monoplane, which had the engine mounted amidships, driving a propeller through an extension shaft, did not reach completion.

In the early 1930s he designed and built a small, cheap, two-seater monoplane which used an ingenious construction - round-section thin-gauge steel tubing throughout. The designation of this machine, Martin Baker MB1, marked the start of the partnership between Martin and Captain Valentine Henry Baker, the company's chief test pilot. During the next 10 years to 1944 Martin was to design 3 significant fighter aircraft, each of which could have been developed into an outstanding machine for the RAF - but no orders were forthcoming.

Martin is remembered best for his devices that help to save the lives of aircrew. The first of these devices was a barrage-balloon cable cutter, designed before World War II, which was produced in large quantities and employed with great success by most RAF Bomber Command aircraft.

Martin's quick response to an urgent need during the Battle of Britain heralded his pioneering work on ejection seats. This was to make it possible to jettison the cockpit canopy of the Spitfire to improve the pilot's chances of escape by parachute. In 1943 increasing aircraft speeds, and the prospect of even greater speeds with the jet engine, led to considerable interest in means for improving the chances of escape for aircrew.

Martin's first response was demonstrated in model form in 1944. Using a powerful spring and a swinging arm to lift the pilot from his aircraft, this scheme generated sufficient official interest to enable Martin to pursue the much more elegant solution of the seat and its occupant being forceably ejected from the aircraft by means of an explosive charge.

The first successful dummy ejections took place in May 1945 and Martin developed his seat until it reached the level of sophistication, reliability and universal application that it has today. Most notable landmarks were the first live ejection on 24 July 1946, the first live ground-level ejection on 3 September 1955, ejection from an aircraft with rearwards facing seats on 1 July 1960, and a zero speed, zero altitude ejection on 1 April 1961.

Martin was appointed a Commander of the British Empire in 1957 and made a Knight Bachelor in 1965. He continued to develop the ejection seat for use at higher speeds, greater altitudes, vertical take-off, multiple crew escape and underwater ejection.

When he died in January 1981 he was Managing Director and chief designer of the company he founded. About 50,000 seats had been delivered and in February 1983, the 5,000th life was saved.

Martin's MB2 fighter of 1938 had a performance as good as that of contemporary fighters. It could be produced quickly and cheaply, because of the simplicity of its structure and easy assembly - features not shared by the Spitfire. The MB5, developed at the War's end, attained the highest standards in piston-engined fighter aircraft. Despite the praise it attracted from fighter pilots, it is thought to have been viewed officially as 'decadent', and was never put into production.

Martin's development of the ejection seat was pioneering because there was no previous knowledge of the effects on the human body of violent acceleration. He experimented first with sand bags and then human volunteers, firing them up test rigs. So successful and significant was this work that the decision was taken to install Martin-Baker seats in new British military jet aircraft as early as June 1947. The experience from their service pointed the way for the numerous improvements, such as automatic separation of pilot from seat and automatic parachute deployment.

In the mid 1950s, when most US carrier-borne aircraft were fitted with US ejection seats, ejection at take-off was usually fatal. So convinced was the US Navy that the Martin-Baker seat would increase the chances of pilot survival that, against great opposition from politicians and industrialists, it brought Martin and a team to the USA in August 1957 to demonstrate conclusively the efficiency of the ground-level ejection system. level ejection system.

Martin-Baker seats were then fitted retrospectively to the whole inventory of US carrier-borne aircraft. Similarly, Martin-Baker was called in to fit its seat to existing NATO aircraft, including the F-86 *Sabre*, RF *Thunderstreak* and F-100 *Super Sabre*.

Like Rolls-Royce, Martin-Baker's is one of the few British companies to leave its mark on the US aerospace industry. At the time of his death it was reckoned that about 35,000 ejection seats were in service with the air forces and navies of 50 countries.

Mauchly, John William *(1907-1980)*, was an American electronics engineer who, with John Eckart, became co-inventor of one of the first electronic computers (the ENIAC). He played an active role in the development of more advanced machines (EDVC, BINAC and UNIVAC) and in encouraging the appreciation of their enormous potential for government, military, scientific and business purposes.

Mauchly was born in Cincinnati, Ohio, on the 30 August 1907. He attended Johns Hopkins University, entering as an engineering student but transferring into the physics department. He was awarded his PhD in physics in 1932 and went into teaching. He became Professor of Physics at Ursinus College in Collegeville, Pennsylvania. He attended a course in electronics at the Moore School of Electrical Engineering of the University of Pennsylvania in the summer of 1941. The faculty there requested him to stay on as an instructor. He learnt of the work being done at the Moore School under contract from the Ballistics Research Laboratory as part of the war effort. He submitted a memorandum in 1942 on the design of a computing machine, and the Moore School was awarded a contract for its construction. The project lasted from 1943 until 1946, with Mauchly as principal consultant and Eckart as chief engineer. A.W Burks, T.K Sharpless and R Shaw were three of the many other scientists involved in the project.

The ENIAC (Electrical Numerical Integrator and Computer) was announced in 1946 and put into operational service a year later. A dispute over patent policy with the Moore School caused Mauchly and Eckart to leave the institute, although they had been in the middle of the development of the EDVAC (Electronic Discrete Variable Automatic Computer). Their departure greatly hindered the development of this machine, which did not make its debut until 1951. Mauchly and Eckart set up a partnership, which became incorporated in 1948 (the Eckart-Mauchly Computer Coroporation). An unfortunate accident in 1949 meant that they lost their financial backing, so in 1950 they sold the company to Remington Rand Inc., which merged with the Sperry Corporation in 1955. From 1950 unti 1959 Mauchly served as director of UNIVAC (Universal Automatic Computer) applications research. He left the Sperry Rand Corporation in 1959 in order to set up a consulting company called Mauchly Associates, and set up a second consulting organization (Dynatrend) in 1967. Mauchly returned to the Sperry Rand Corporation as a consultant in 1973.

The importance of Mauchly's work is so great that it is all the more surprising that he is not better known outside the ranks of his own profession. He received many awards and honours, but was not famous with the general public. He died during surgery for a heart ailment in Abington, Pennsylvania, on 8 January 1980.

Mauchly's early research, at Collegeville, was on meteorology. It involved many laborious calculations, so he was deeply interested in finding methods of speeding up the process. He realized the possibility of using an electronic apparatus, constructed with vacuum tubes (valves), and this was why he attended the course in 1941 at the Moore School; to improve his understanding of electronics.

The United States Army found that new battle conditions and new types of weapons required that its artillery range tables (which enabled the gunners to aim and fire effectively) needed to be recalculated. This was a mammoth task, and so Mauchly and the Army had a community of interest: both needed methods for rapid calculation. Mauchly's 1942 memorandum on computer design initiated the project which culminated in 1946 with the ENIAC.

The ENIAC was one of the first electronic computers. It could perform addition in 200 microseconds and multiplication in 300 microseconds. Although it was primarily designed for trajectory calculation, it could also be used for other purposes, including the solution of partial differential equations. Its drawbacks were that it was huge, and had vast power requirements and running costs. Its input and output consisted of punched cards; it had limited storage, and no memory.

Work on the EDVAC began in 1944. It had improved storagee, J. von Neumann helping with the design of the storage system.

The ENIAC was first tested in 1947 at the Aberdeen Proving Ground in Maryland, for ballistics purposes.

In 1947 Mauchly and Eckert obtained a contract from the Northrop Aircraft Company to design a small-scale binary computer. The BINAC (Binary Automatic Computer) was completed in 1949, and was more economical to use as well as being faster and more compact. A new feature was the replacement of punch cards with magnetic tape, and the computer's capacity to use internally stored programs.

The UNIVAC was designed during the early 1950s, and was first tried out in 1951 by the US Bureau of Census; it was designed to serve the business community. Mauchly's role in its development was primarily in the design of the software.

Maudslay, Henry *(1771-1831)*, was a British engineer and toolmaker who, in an age when mechanical engineering lagged behind other crafts, improved the metal-working lathe to the point that it could be employed for precise screw cutting. He also desiged a bench micrometer, which became the forerunner of the modern instrument.

Maudslay was born on 22 August 1771 at Woolwich, London where his father was a joiner at the Royal Arsenal. He had little formal education and at the age of 12 he went to work at the Arsenal filling cartridges, but after two years went first to the joiner's shop and then to the metal-working shop as an apprentice. By the time he was 18 his skill as a craftsman was renowned. He joined the firm of Joseph Bramah, the pioneer of hydraulics and the inventor of the Bramah press and lock. Maudslay eventually became manager of the workshop but after a disagreement over pay he left to start his own business.

In his works, just off Oxford Street, London, he developed a method of cutting screw threads on a lathe. Previously large threads had been forged and filed, and small threads had been cut by hand by the most skilled of craftsmen. Maudslay's new screw-cutting lathe gave such precision as to allow previously unkown interchangeability of nuts and bolts and standardization of screw threads. He was also able to produce sets of taps and dies.

Using his new device he cut a long screw with 50 threads per inch (about 20 per cm) and made this the basis of a micrometer, which came into daily use as an instrument to check the standard of the work he produced. In the period 1801 to 1808, in conjunction with Marc Brunel, he constructed a series of machines for making wooden pulley blocks at Portsmouth dockyard. The A3 special-purpose power-driven machines, operated by 10 unskilled workers, did the work formerly done by 110 skilled men using hand methods.

Maudslay's firm, with him as its chief working craftsman, went on to produce marine steam engines. The first was a 17hp model; later, engines of 56hp were built. In 1838, after Maudslay's death, the company built the engines for the first successful transatlantic steamship, Isambard Brunel's *Great Western*, which developed 750hp. Early in 1831 Maudslay caught a chill on his return to Britain after a trip to France and he died on 15 February that year. He was buried in a cast-iron tomb at Woolwich.

Maxim, Hiram Stevens, *(1840-1916),* was an American-born British inventor, chiefly remembered for the Maxim gun, the first fully automatic, rapid-firing machine gun.

Maxim was born on 5 February 1840 in Sangerville, Maine the son of a farmer and wood-turner. He spent his early life in various apprentiships before exhibiting his talent for invention at the age of 26 with a patent for a curling iron in 1866. More significant ideas followed, and in 1878 he was appointed chief engineer to the United States Electric Lighting Company. While working for this company he came up with a way of manufacturing carbon-coated filaments for the early light bulbs that ensured that each filament was evenly coated.

It was during a trip to the Paris Exhibition of 1881 that Maxim made the statement that was to change his life. He declared that work on armaments would prove the most profitable sector of invention. Taking his own advice, he left the United States to settle in Britain, where he thought the most opportunity for his work existed. He set up a small laboratory at Hatton Garden, London, and set to work on improving the design of current guns.

In 1884 he had produced the first fully automatic machine gun, which used the recoil from the shots to extract, eject, load and fire cartridges. With a water-cooled barrel, the Maxim gun used a 250-round ammunition belt to produce a rate of fire of 10 rounds a second. Its efficiency was further improved by Maxim's development of a cord-like propellant explosive, cordite. His own company, set up on the unveiling of the Maxim gun, became absorbed into Vickers Limited. By 1889 the British Army had adopted the gun for use, and not until the appearance of tanks on the battlefront was the power of the Maxim weapon eclipsed significantly. Maxim became a naturalized British subject in 1900, was knighted by Queen Victoria in 1901, and later also became a Chevalier of the Legion of Honour of France.

Although chiefly remembered for the gun, Maxim is responsible for many other, lesser, inventions, having taken out well over a 100 patents in both the United States and Britain for devices ranging from mousetraps to gas-powered engines. He was particularly interested in powered flight, his experiments being described in his book *Artificial and Natural Flight*. In 1889 he started investigations into the relative efficiencies of aerofoils and airscrews driven by steam-powered engines. Five years later he had produced a steam-driven machine whose engine produced 6hp for every pound weight. After three trials the aircraft succeeded in leaving the tracks along which it ran. Although impressive, it was clear that the massive amount of feed-water needed for longer flights would add an impossible weight burden to the craft.

Maxim wrote an autobiography in 1915, a year before his death in Streatham, South London, on 24 November 1916. He was survived by his inventor son, Hiram Percy Maxim (1869-1936), who developed a 'silencer' for rifles.

Maybach, Wilhelm *(1847-1929)*, was a German engineer and inventor who worked with Gottlieb Daimler on the development of early motor cars. He is particularly remembered for his invention of the float-feed carburettor which allowed petrol (gasoline) to be used as a fuel for internal combustion engines - most of which up to that time had been fuelled by gas.

From 1862, when Maybach was still a teenager, he was a great friend and associate of Daimler. In 1882 they went into partnership at Cannstatt, where they produced one of the first petrol engines. In 1895, Maybach became technical director of the daimler Motor Company. While working with daimler, in 1901, Maybach designed the first Mercedes car - named after Mercedes Jellinec, the daughter of their influencial associate the Austro-Hungarian consul in Nice.

Maybach invented the spray-nozzle or float-feed carburettor in 1893. An adjusting screw controlled the rate of maximum fuel flow and a second screw varied the area of the choke. When the inlet valve was opened, air sent along the choke passage caused a drop in pressure, making the fuel enter through a jet as a fine spray. The vaporized fuel mixed with air to produce a combustible mixture for the engine's cylinders.

Maybach's other inventions included the honeycomb radiator - still used in some Mercedes cars - an internal expanding brake (1901) and an axle-locating system for use with independent suspensions. He left Daimler's in 1907 to set up his own factory for making engines for Zeppelin's airships.

McAdam, John Loudon *(1756-1836)*, was a British civil engineer whose system of road-building - and particularly, surfacing - made a major contribution to the improvement of road transport during the nineteenth century. Indeed, his methods continued to be used after the development of motorized road vehicles, well into the twentieth century.

McAdam was born in Ayr, Scotland, on 21 September 1756. At the age of 14 he emigrated to the United States, where he settled in New York City. He went to work for his uncle, and eventually became a successful businessman in his own right. McAdam returned to Ayrshire in 1783, and 15 years later moved to Falmouth in Devon. He was appointed Surveyor-General of the roads in Bristol in 1816, and of all the roads in Britain in 1827. He died on 26 November 1836.

The success of McAdam's technique came not so much from making wide, straight roads but from the excellent road surfaces, the method that was to become known as 'macadamizing'. He also drew up basic rules for highway management. Before McAdam's time there was some organization of roads repairs in Britain, but it seldom worked well. Each parish was responsible for its own repairs, but the parishes were small (and sometimes poor) and often not particularly interested in maintaining roads largely for the use of travellers from outside the parish. Also there was

little skill and experience among either the labourers or the supervisors.

Towards the end of the eighteenth century the usual method of making a road was to plough the area, smooth the surface, and put down loose sand, gravel or pebbles. McAdam raised the road above the surrounding terrain, compounding a surface of small stones bound with gravel on a firm base of large stones. A camber, making the road slightly convex in section, ensured that rainwater rapidly drained off the road and did not penetrate the foundation. By the end of the nineteenth century, most of the main roads in Europe were using this method.

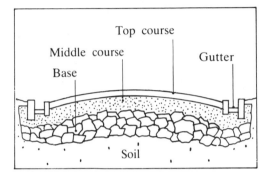

In McAdam's method of building roads, a base course of large stones was laid on a compacted, cambered soil footing. A middle course of smaller stones was capped by a top course of small ones or gravel which traffic made into a fairly smooth, (but still cambered) surface. Gutters at each side carried away rainwater.

McAdam was also responsible for reforms in road administration which were as important as his innovatory road surfacings. He encouraged men to enter the profession of road-making by offering them suitable salaries, thus ensuring that more able and intelligent workers would be attracted to the task. He was in a better position to wield such influence after he was appointed Surveyor-General of metropolitan roads in 1827.

It was, in fact, many years before this that McAdam began to take an interest in road construction - indeed it became almost an obsession with him. In the ten years from 1810 he had spent his fortune on his 'hobby' and he petitioned Parliament for reward. The roads he had made in Bristol and other areas, and the three books he had written on road-making, had ensured that his name was very well-known. At the time of his appointment as Surveyor-General he was also granted £10,000 by a grateful government.

Prior to the ultimate job in highways maintenance, McAdam became (in 1816), Surveyor to the Bristol Turnpike Trust; he re-made the roads there and his advice was widely sought. Further to his belief in the importance of good road administration, he recommended the strengthening of turnpike trusts - but under the control of Parliament - and was advisor to many of these trusts. Turnpike roads were introduced in the late seventeenth century to provide better roads, but the costs were transferred to the road-users. McAdam ensured that public roads became the responsibility of the Government, financed (out of taxes) for the benefit of everyone.

McCormick, Cyrus Hall *(1809-1884)*, was an American inventor who is best known for developing the first successful mechanical reaper.

Son of the inventor Robert McCormick, Cyrus McCormick was born in Virginia on 15 February 1809. Under the guiding influence of his father, he was encouraged to use the talents of his own inventive mind, and in 1831 produced a hillside plough, the first of several agricultural implements with which he was associated. In the same year he invented the prototype for his reaping machine, and although it was another nine years before it was perfected, when the machine was put into production a ready market existed.

With the Midwest opening up there was a need for mechanization to cope with the huge acreages involved. McCormick was invited to Chicago to demonstrate his machine and, as a result, began manufacturing there in 1847. But in 1848, when his patent expired, he had to face strong competition and only his good business sense kept him from being overwhelmed by other manufacturers who had been waiting to encroach on his markets. He survived and prospered, introduced his reaping machine into Europe and opened up an entirely new market, winning several prizes (including one at the Great Exhibition of 1851).

An inventor first and foremost, he also had the intelligence to spread his interests in other directions, including mining, railways and newspaper publishing. He died in Chicago on 13 May 1884.

McCormick's reaping machine consisted of seven basic mechanisms which were principally the same as in its modern equivalent: the divider, reel, straight reciprocating knife, guards, platform, main wheel and gearing, and side-draft propulsion. The working was simple. A pulley at the side of the one road-driving wheel was connected by a band to another pulley above, turning the circular wooden frame. The blades of this were slightly twisted so that they gradually bent the corn down. Bevelled gears turned a small cranked shaft, which gave the movement to the cutting knife, working it backwards and forwards.

The machine was designed purely as a reaper, and it left the corn lying flat, ready to be raked up and tied into sheaves. In the original machine the raker had to walk backwards while carrying out his work to avoid standing on the corn; in later models a seat was incorporated into the machine so that the raker could sit.

It was estimated that a McCormick reaper operated by a two-man crew and drawn by a single horse could cut as much corn as could 12 to 16 men with reap hooks. In a nation like the United States, with a rapidly expanding population (from 13 to 60 million in 40 years) needing to be fed, it was essential that agriculture should be lifted from the manual to the mechanical wherever possible. McCormick's invention was the first of many which were to increase the production of cereals and guarantee enough food for all.

McNaught, William *(1813-1881)*, was a Scottish mechanical engineer who invented the compound steam engine. This type of engine extracts the maximum energy from the hot steam by effectively using it twice - once in a high-pressure cylinder (or cylinders) and then, when exhausted from this, in a second low-pressure cylinder.

The evolution of the steam engine had been taking place for nearly 100 years when McNaught developed his method of compounding at his Glasgow works in 1845. The technique became known as 'McNaughting', and was to prove to be a valuable energy-saving system for many years to come. The firm of J. and W. McNaught was eventually established in 1860, and in 1862 acquired premises at St George's Foundry, Rochdale, in Lancashire where they set about manufacturing small steam engines. Later the business branched out into the construction of larger types and moved to a bigger building, where it remained in operation until 1914.

In all the McNaughts' were responsible for making of some 95 engines, many of which were for used in the northern textile industry. At least 2 of the engines have been preserved as fine examples of their type, one at the Glasgow Kelvingrove Museum and the other at the Bradford Industrial Museum.

The forerunner of the steam engine was invented by Thomas Savery, an English military engineer, in 1698. The idea was taken up in 1712 by Thomas Newcomen, a blacksmith, and became known as an atmospheric engine. But the first real 'steam engine' is credited to James Watt, a Scottish instrument maker, in 1765. Watt unfortunately met with various technical problems after his initial success and, faced by lack of resources, was about to give up when he met Matthew Boulton. Together they formed the partnership of Boulton and Watt and in all were concerned with the making of more than 500 engines which supplied power to all manner of equipment duringthe crucial years of the Industrial Revolution.

Many steam engines were used to power the textile mills of the cotton and wool trade in the north of England. By 1845, the majority of these mills found that even by the introduction of higher steam pressures, their engines (most of which were the Boulton and Watt design) could no longer keep up with the increasing demand for more power. This meant to the mill owners that they faced the costly business of replacing the engines, but naturally they were reluctant to do so. It was at this point that McNaught supplied a very acceptable answer, by offering a conversion to compound action.

His conversion consisted of a high-pressure cylinder exhausting into the original low-pressure cylinder. The new cylinder was connected to the opposite end of the 'beam', halfway between its pivot and the connecting-rod end, making it necessary for the stroke to be shorter than on the original cylinder. Three types of new engine were to emerge using McNaught's principle. The first used cylinders mounted side by side, the second had cylinders in a line (a tandem compound), and the third and rarer type had the high-pressure cylinder enclosed by the low-pressure one. As a measure of the success of the McNaught's design, the last beam engine made for use in a mill in 1904 was partly based on his principles. It can be said, therefore, that he was responsible for a vast and enduring improvement in the performance of the factory of 'steam giants'.

Mergenthaler, Ottomar *(1854-1899)*, was a German-born American inventor who devised the Linotype machine, which greatly speeded typesetting and revolutionized the world of printing and publishing.

Mergenthaler was born in Germany on 11 May 1854 and was apprenticed to a watchmaker before he immigrated to the United States in 1872. He settled in Washington DC and found employment in a factory manufacturing scientific instruments. In 1876 he moved to Baltimore and began working for James O. Clephane, remedying faults in a recently invented prototype of a writing machine. Although a full-sized machine was constructed, it was not a success and the two men abandoned the idea. They combined their talents and in 1884 produced what was to become known as the Linotype machine.

By 1886, the first machines were in use and a company was formed to spearhead their production with Mergenthaler as one of the directors. He resigned from the position in 1888 but continued to show an interest in the firm, contributing over the years as many as 50 new modifications to the original design. He died in Baltimore on 28 October 1899.

Before Linotype, printing was carried out by hand-setting, a long and laborious process. Mergenthaler's invention speeded this operation and made printed matter, from books to penny news sheets, cheaper to produce. The design of the machine enabled a line of type (hence the name) to be composed at one time and cast as a single piece of metal. The machine was rather like a large typewriter, about two metres high, with a store of matrices (moulds) at the top. The operator selected the letters by means of rods controlled by the 'typewriter' keys, and these letters fell through tiny trapdoors to drop into position in a line setting. As each line was completed it was passed on to the 'metal pot' area where a cast was made to form a 'slug' with the letters in relief on one side. This then fitted into a page of type ready for printing, while the matrices were returned to the store at the top of the machine for re-use.

A man operating one of Mergenthaler's keyboards could set type up to three or four times faster than by hand-setting, cutting the labour cost of production to a fraction of before. The machine heralded a new age for printing in which books became something most people could afford, and newspapers could really claim to carry up-to-the-minute information for the Linotype meant it was possible to change and re-set copy to within minutes of going to press.

Messerschmitt, Willy Emil *(1898-1978)* was the German aircraft designer and industrialist, the foremost of only a handful of people who shaped the development of the aircraft industry in his country from the early 1920s to the early 1980s.

Messerschmitt was born in Frankfurt am Main on 26 June 1898. In Bamberg, in 1909, he attended the Realschule, a secondary school with a scientific bias. He was fascinated by the fast-developing world of aviation, and in 1912 met the architect and gliding pioneer Friedrich Harth. It was their building and experimentation with primitive canard (tail first) gliders that decided Messerschmitt on his future career.

As a student at the Oberealschule in Nuremburg during 1915, Messerschmitt undertook the detailed design and construction of his first glider. Given a military discharge on medical grounds in 1917, he continued his education at the Technische Hochschule in Munich.

A glider he designed with Harth achieved an unofficial world duration record in 1921. The following year they set up a flying school and in 1923, while still a student, Messerschmitt formed his own company in Bamberg. Its first product, the S14 cantilever monoplane glider, formed the subject of his Dipl Ingenieur thesis.

After experiments with gliders powered by auxiliary engines, he produced his first powered aircraft in 1925, the ultra-light sports two-seater *M17*. In 1926 came the flight of the *M18* small transport, the production version of which was adapted to largely metal construction.

Working in a country in which the manufacture of military aircraft was forbidden under the Treaty of Versailles, Messerschmitt pursued designs for light sporting aircraft, none of which attracted many orders. When the Nazis came to power in 1933, however, the German air ministry gave great stimulus to aviation, and an order to Messerschmitt to develop a new touring aircraft.

The resulting design, the *M37* (or *Bf108* in production) became the archetypal low-wing four-seater cabin monoplane, with retractable landing gear and flaps. It was the success of this aircraft which kept Messerschmitt in the industry, for in 1934 he had given serious thought to taking up a professorship in Danzig Technical College.

In taking part in the German air ministry's 1934 design competition for a fighter aircraft to equip the 'secret' Luftwaffe, Messerschmitt risked all by building a machine of advanced concept and employing the most modern techniques. The resulting *Bf109* was to become the standard fighter of the Luftwaffe and several other air forces. It was to be equated with the legendary *Spitfire*.

By 1938, firmly established as a designer of advanced fighter aircraft, Messerschmitt was appointed chairman and general director of the company manufacturing his designs - Bayerische Flugzeugwerke - which was then renamed Messerschmitt AG. He and his company went on to produce numerous designs for fighter, bomber and transport aircraft, many of which served the Luftwaffe in large numbers throughout World War II.

At the war's end Messerschmitt was taken prisoner by the British who with the French and Americans, asked him to work for them as an adviser, but he declined all proposals. On return to Germany he was arrested by US troops and held in custody for two years. Banned from manufacturing aircraft in Germany, Messerschmitt went on to design and produce components for prefabricated houses, sewing machines, and a popular tandem, two seat, three-wheel 'bubble' car.

He took up aircraft design again in 1952 under an advisory contract with the Spanish manufacturer Hispano, which was already building his '109' fighter under licence. His HA200 *Saeta*, first flown in 1955, served in the early 1980s

as the standard advanced trainer of the Spanish Air Force.

Between 1956 and 1964 Messerschmitt worked in association with the German Bolkow and Heinkel companies and developed the *VJ101* supersonic V/STOL (Vertical/Short Take-off and Landing) combat aircraft. His company merged with Bolkow in 1963 and they were later joined by Hamburger Flugzengbau. In 1969 Messerschmitt became chairman of the supervisory board of the resulting Messerschmitt Bolkow Blohm (MBB) group.

MBB is identified today with the *Tornado* multi-role combat aircraft being built for NATO countries, and the A300 *Airbus* airliner, both designs being initiated before Messerschmitt's death on 15 September 1978, when he was honorary chairman.

Many of the great names in aircraft manufacture were from the generation before Messerschmitt's. They built their companies on the sales of vast numbers of military biplanes for World War I. Messerschmitt, however, never willingly designed biplanes. To him they were a retrograde step. The efficient cantilever monoplanes he designed from the early 1920s failed to secure large sales mainly because they were launched on to a market convinced of the need for visible struts and bracing wires.

The *M18* small transport and the *M19* sporting aircraft, both of the mid-1920s, embodied characteristics to be found in any aircraft designed or supervised by him. These were: simple concept, minimum weight and aerodynamic drag, and the possibility of continued development.

The last-mentioned characteristic was taken to the extreme in his '109' fighter which, in 20 years and more than 35,000 examples (making the second largest production of any aircraft), was developed in more than 50 variants. Messerschmitt's devotion to innovation in construction was exemplified by the hundreds of personal patents that were used throughout his designs.

Many of Messerschmitt's aircraft, when first flown, were the most advanced of their kind, having considerable performance advantage over competitors. Performance, coupled with elegance, characterizing his earlier designs, was to be seen also during World War II in the *Me 262* twin-jet fighter. In operation at the same time as the Gloster *Meteor* jet, Messerschmitt's machine featured triangular minimal cross-section fuselage, high aspect ratio swept wings, heavier armament and a 210km/h (130mph) speed advantage over the staid British design.

Messerschmitt's '109' fighter, which gave employment to (or forced it upon) as many as 81,000 people in 25 plants, was the backbone of the Luftwaffe fighter force for the whole of the war. Production topped an incredible 2,000 per month by the end of 1944. Messerschmitt's name and work live on in what is today Germany's largest aerospace enterprise, Messerschmitt Bolkow Blohm. Employing more than 20,000 people, MBB makes satellites, helicopters, missiles and transport systems, as well as the *Tornado* and *Airbus* aircraft.

Mitchell, Reginald Joseph *(1895-1937)*, was a British aeronautical engineer who, in Britain at least, was largely responsible, for the development of the high-speed monoplane. His early work on the design of seaplanes for the Schneider Trophy competition led to ideas for the construction of a single-engined fighter; this became the *Spitfire*.

Mitchell was born in Talke, near Stoke-on-Trent, on 20 May 1895. His father was a schoolmaster and later a printer. His early childhood was spent at Longton, a few miles from his birthplace, and he went first to the village school; and later to Hanley High School. On leaving school he became apprenticed to a firm of locomotive builders in Stoke. Mitchell realized the importance of sound scientific principles in engineering, and continued his own education in the evenings at technical colleges. It was not an easy way to get the scientific and practical expertise needed to become a design engineer, but he succeeded. He soon passed from the work bench to the drawing office, and in 1916 he moved to the Supermarine Aviation Company at Southampton. He had always had an interest in aeroplanes and had built models to test his own theories. Now he was able to test his ideas on a larger scale.

Aviation was still in its infancy, but was rapidly developing. Jacques Schneider, the son of a wealthy armaments manufacturer was impressed by the flights of Wilbur Wright in France in 1908, and decided at the Aero Club of France in 1912 to offer a trophy (Le Coupe d'Aviation Maritime Jacques Schneider) to the national aero club of the country which produced the fastest seaplane. If a country won the trophy three times within five years, then it was to retain it.

Mitchell first became involved with producing aeroplanes for the trophy for the 1919 race (the third contest). Partly under his direction, the *Supermarine Sea Lion* (G-EALP) was adapted from a standard design. No aeroplane completely finished the course, Mitchell's *Sea Lion* having retired during the first lap.

A year later Mitchell became chief engineer for *Supermarine*. The firm at that time specialized in flying boats, and later models of the *Sea Lion* flew with distinction in the 1922 race, when *Sea Lion II* came first with a speed of 234.4km/h (45.7mph) and in 1923 when *Sea Lion III* came

third at 252.9km/h (157.17mph). For the next contest, in 1924, Mitchell was allowed to design his own aeorplane. This was the *Supermarine S4*. It was a monoplane and the whole wing section was made in one piece. The radiator for the engine was on the underside of the wing and the fuel was carried in the floats. The *S4* looked fast and elegant and, was probably too fast for its design for it crashed during the trial before the race, previously having captured the world seaplane speed record at 365.055km/h (226.752mph). In the 1927, 1929 and 1931 contests, Mitchel's *S5*, *S6* and *S6B* - the direct decendents of the ill-fated *S4* - took the trophy with speeds finally increased to 547.30km/h (340.08mph). The Schneider Trophy was won for ever for Britain and it now has a place of honour in the Science Museum, London. This was not quite the end of the story: the *S6B* S1585 set a speed record of 668.19km/h (415.2mph) on the 29 September 1931 with George Stainforth at the controls.

To fulfil an Air Ministry contract for a single-engined fighter, Mitchell used and extended the ideas that had been embodied in the Schneider Trophy winners. This was not a simple task because he had to develop a reliable aeroplane that could fly time and again carrying a heavy load of fuel and ammunition at high speeds. His first aeroplane built directly to the specifications is said to have been mediocre, but when he was allowed full rein for his own ideas he produced the prototype of the *Spitfire* (K 5054). This was first flown by Captain J Summers on the 5 March 1936.

The *Spitfire* came into being when the storm clouds of war were gathering and it proved to be Britain's most important, but by no means only, fighter aeroplane. The early *Spitfires* had a top speed of 556.8km/h (346mph), but the later ones were capable of about 740km/h (460mph). More than 19,000 *Spitfires* were built, adapted to every role and circumstance appropriate to a high-speed single-engined aeroplane. Although faster single-engined fighters were eventually built, the manoeuverability and all-round adaptability of the Spitfire made it one of the most successful aeroplanes ever.

Mitchell saw very little of his greatest creation after its first flight. When it took to the air he was already seriously ill with tuberculosis. He died on 11 June 1937, aged 42 years.

Montgolfier, Joseph Michel *(1740-1810)*, and **Montgolfier, Jacques Etiènne** *(1745-1799)*, pioneered manned flight by building the first hot-air balloons.

The Montgolfier brothers were sons of a paper manufacturer from Annonay, near Lyons, France. The eldest, Joseph, was born on 26 August 1740 and although he was given to playing truant from school, he developed a strong interest in chemistry, mathematics and natural science, even to the point of setting up his own small laboratory. Jacques, the younger by nearly 5 years, was born at Vidalon on 7 January 1745. He became a successful architect before joining his father's company, but once involved with it invented the first vellum paper.

The first manned balloon flight, in a Montgolfier hot-air balloon, took place in Paris in November 1783. Burning straw heated about 2,000m³ of air in the 15m balloon, which was made of paper lined with linen.

Both brothers were fascinated by the views and theories on the possibility of flight by early scholars like the fourteenth century Augustine monk Albert of Saxony and the seventeenth century Jesuit priest, Father Francesco de Lana de Terzi, who designed a 'ship of the air' supported by evacuated copper spheres. But neither made any attempt at invention until 1782. It was then, purely by chance, they noticed the effects rising smoke had on particles of unburnt paper. Using this as a basis for their work, they progressed within 2 years from inflating paper bags to the first

manned free balloon flight in history.

Their success story really began in June 1783, when the brothers demonstrated their invention ot an admiring crowd in the market place of Annonay. A large fire of straw and wood was built and the brothers placed over it a sphere of their own design made of paper and linen, allowing the heat to lift it gently into the air. Encouraged by their achievement, they took their invention to Versailles and in the grounds of the Palace before a large audience (which included Louis XVI and Marie Antionette) their balloon ascended, carrying a sheep, a cock and a duck, and made an 8-minute flight of approximately 3km (2 miles).

A month later, on 15 October 1783, the first manned ascent was made by Francois Pilâtre de Rozier (1757-1785) in a tethered balloon, paving the way for the first manned free balloon flight on 21 November of that year. The crew of two, *Pilâtre de Rozier* and the *Marquis d'Arlandes*, ascended from the gardens of the Château la Muette, near Paris, and travelled over the city, completing a journey of 9km, (12 miles)

Originally the brothers thought they may have discovered a new gas, but this was obviously not so and they discarded the idea. The success of their invention could not be denied, however, and other people were quick to set up in competition, the main rivals being the Robert brothers, who used hydrogen to inflate their balloon under the instructions of the French scientist Jacques Charles (1746-1823). The first manned flight in this type of balloon took place on 1 December 1783.

Jacques Montgolfier died at Servières on 2 August 1799 and, after his death, his brother Joseph devoted himself entirely to scientific research with varying degrees of success. He developed a type of parachute, a calorimeter and hydraulic ram and press. He was elected to the French Academy of Science and honoured by Napolean when he was created Chevalier of the Legion of Honour. Outliving his brother by 11 years, he died at Balaruc-les-Bains on 26 June 1810.

Morse, Samuel Finley Breese *(1791-1872)*, was an American artist who invented an electric telegraph and gave his name to Morse Code.

Morse was born on 27 April 1791, in Charlestown, Massachusetts, the eldest son of a clergyman. Brought up to appreciate all forms of culture, he chose to devote himself to art and after studying at Yale University, from which he graduated in 1810, he studied at the Royal Academy in London.

On returning to the United States he achieved a fair amount of success, particularly in sculpture and in the painting of miniatures on ivory. Unfortunately the financial rewards brought him no more than a bare living, and in 1829 he returned once more to Europe in the hope of establishing a firm artistic reputation. From 1829 to 1832 he travelled widely, but after three years he once more set sail for home aboard the ship *Sully*. It was on this voyage that fate took a turn in the shape of fellow passenger Charles Jackson, who had recently attended lectures on electricity in Paris. He had with him an elctromagnet and Morse, having made his acquaintance, became fascinated with the talk of electricity and the possiblities of this new idea.

For the remainder of the voyage he spent hours making notes and became fired with the concept of communication by electric current 'telegraph'. As soon as he landed he set about turning his theories into working models and became so obsessed with the invention that he more-or-less abandoned his art career, relying for means of support on his appointment as Professor of the Art of Design, at the University of New York.

By 1836 he had devised a simple relay system and having enlisted the help of Professor Gale, a chemist, and Alfred Vail, he improved his apparatus to the point where it became a commercial proposition.

After a further four years of political wrangling, his invention was finally given the backing of Congress and with a salary to give him freedom from money problems, Morse undertook the superintending of the first line between Baltimore and Washington. A trial run was telegraphed on 23 May 1843 and the line was eventually opened for public use on 1 April 1845.

Morse's basic idea hinged on the conception that an electric current could be made to convey messages. The signal current would be sent in an intermittent coded pattern and would cause an elctromagnet to attract intermittently to the same pattern on a piece of soft iron to which a pencil or pen would be attached and which in turn would make marks on a moving strip of paper. Once a suitable code had been worked out and batteries with sufficient power located, the technical problems mainly concerned the conductors, which on the first line were carried above ground on poles. Although underground conductors were envisaged, telegraph poles became a familiar feature of the countryside for the next 100 years.

The original receiver recorded signals by indentation. The Morse inker was a later innovation, invented mainly because Morse disliked the operators 'reading' the messages by ear (they became so adept they could identify letters from the sound of the clicks made by the machine), and

also because he felt a written proof of receipt by the machine was a necessity.

Murdock, William *(1754-1839)*, was a British engineer who introduced gas lighting and was a pioneer in the development of steam engines and their application. Murdock was born in Auchinleck, Ayrshire. In 1777 he entered the engineering firm of Matthew Boulton & James Watt at their Soho works in Birmingham, and two years later was sent to Cornwall to supervise the fitting of Watt's engines in mines. He lived in Redruth and proved an invaluable help to Watt, and references to him are numerous in the Soho correspondence. According to documents at Soho he signed an agreement on 30 March 1800 to act as an engineer and superintendant of the Soho foundry for a period of 5 years. He was, however, constantly despatched to various parts of the country, and he frequently visited Cornwall after he had ceased to reside there permanently. His connection with Boulton and Watt's firm continued until 1830, when he virtually retired. He died in 1839 at his house at Sycamore Hill, within sight of the Soho foundry.

An industrious but modest man, Murdock's subsequent fame has been somewhat overshadwed by that of his employers, Matthew Boulton (1728-1809) and James Watt (1736-1819). In about 1782, while residing in Cornwall, he began experiments on the illuminating properties of gases produced by distilling coal, wood, peat and so on. He lighted his house at Redruth by this means, and in 1892 the centenary of gas lighting was duly celebrated, but on the evidence now available it appears that the decisive breakthrough came several years later than 1792. Murdock succeeded in producing coal gas in large iron retorts and conveying it 21m (70ft) through metal pipes. After returning to Birmingam in about 1799 he perfected further methods for making, storing and purifying gas.

In 1802, in celebration of the Peace of Amiens with France, part of the exterior of the Soho factory was illuminated by gas, and a year later the factory interior was similiarly lit. Thereafter apparatus was erected ensuring that a part of the Soho foundry was regularly lighted this way, and the manufacture of gas-making plant seems to have been commenced about this period, probably in connection with apparatus for producing oxygen and hydrogen for medical purposes. In 1804, George Lee of the firm of Phillips & Lee, cotton-spinners of Manchester, ordered an apparatus for lighting his house with gas. Subsequently Phillips & Lee decided to light their mills. On 1 January 1806, Murdock wrote informing Boulton & Watt that 'fifty lamps of the different kinds' were lighted that night with satisfactory results. There was, Murdock added, 'no Soho Stink' - an expression which seems to show that the method of purification used at the foundry was somewhat primitive.

In February 1808 Murdock read a paper before the Royal Society in which he gave a full account of his investigations, and also by the saving effected by the adoption of gas lighting at Phillip & Lee's mill. The paper is the earliest practical essay on the subject. The Rumford Gold Medal, bearing the inscription *Ex fume clare lucem*, was awarded to Murdock for his paper, which concludes with these words: 'I believe I may, without presuming too much, claim both the first idea of applying and the first actual application of the gas to economical purposes.'

Murdock also made important improvements to the steam engine. He was the first to devise an oscillating engine, of which he made a model about 1784. In 1786 he was bringing to the attention of Boulton & Watt, who both remained highly sceptical of such possibilities, the idea of a steam carriage or road locomotive, an enterprise which was not successful. In 1799 he invented the long-D slide-valve. He is generally credited with inventing the so-called Sun and planet motion, a means of making a steam engine give continuous revolving motion to a shaft provided with a fly wheel. Watt, however, patented this motion in 1781. Murdock also experimented with compressed air, and in 1803 constructed a steam gun.

N

Nasmyth, James *(1808-1890)*, was a British engineer who contributed greatly to the design and production of tools. He is particularly known for his invention of the steam hammer and powered milling, shaping, slotting and planing machines. One of his lesser-known inventions, which he did not choose to patent, is the flexible drive shaft for drilling and other machines.

Nasmyth was born in Edinburgh on the 19 August 1808; his father was a well-known Scottish painter and amateur engineer. He attended Edinburgh High School, and on leaving there at the age of 12 he devoted his time to building engines and other mechanical devices. His success was such that he attempted to build a steam road carriage. When he was 21 he travelled to London with his father, and there met Henry Maudslay

(1771-1831), himself famous for work in tool and engine construction. Nasmyth showed Maudslay a model steam engine he had built, and so impressed him that he was taken on as his assistant. Over the next 2 years he learned Maudslay's techniques and developed his own accurate and rapid means of producing hexagonal-heading nuts. Also during this period he devised a flexible shaft of coiled spring steel for drilling holes in awkward places. (Later in life, during a visit to his dentist, he was told that this was the latest American invention.) Shortly after the death of Maudslay he returned to Edinburgh and built his own small workshop, which included a Maudslay lathe and a number of other machine tools.

On seeing better prospects for an engineer in Manchester, he moved there in 1834 to a small workshop in which power was available. With the success of his machine tool business he moved to a site on the Bridgwater Canal at Patricroft. In his Bridgwater foundry Nasmyth continued to manufacture machine tools and began to build railway locomotives and other machinery. His famous steam hammer was invented there in 1839, initially to forge the driving shaft of the steamship *Great Britain*. This device speeded up the production of large forgings without the loss of accuracy. It was a very successful tool in the great age of machine building.

Nasmyth devised many other tools, including a vertical cylinder-boring machine which speeded up the production of steam engines, and all sorts of milling, shaping, slotting and planing machines. Apart from the obvious effect these had on the accurate repetition of old techniques at an increased rate, they handled metal in new ways: all manner of lateral, transverse and rotating cutting machines were devised. His shaping machines in particular were a financial success. Generally these devices speeded up the rate of production in the engineering industry in an unprecedented manner. Even with his hand-held tools, such as taps, he devised means of producing more accurate work with increased ease.

As the building of locomotives, and other heavy engineering projects, overshadowed the machine-tool aspect of his business, his personal interest declined and in 1856, at the age of 48, he retired from engineering. This was not the end of his scientific curiosity, for he devoted more time to astronomy, a hobby which he pursued in a serious way. At his foundry he had built a number of telescopes, the largest being a reflector with a 50cm (20inch) mirror. During his retirement he lived at Penshurst in Kent, and used this instrument to make an extensive study of the Sun and Moon. In the course of his solar observations he was particularly concerned with sunspots. He chartered the lunar surface and developed his own volcanic theory of the origin of the craters. In 1851 his maps of the Moon received a prize at the Great Exhibition in London. Later he wrote a book about his lunar discoveries and theories. He died in London on 7 May 1890.

Newcomen, Thomas *(1663-1729)*, was an English blacksmith who developed the first really practical steam engine, which was principally to power pumps in the tin mines of Cornwall and the coal mines of northern England.

Newcomen was born in Dartmouth in 1663, and christened there on the 24 February of that year. His family were probably merchants. His education was probably obtained from a Noncomformist called John Favell. It is thought that he was eventually apprenticed to an ironmonger in Exeter, and on completion of his training went to Lower Street, Dartmouth, where he established his own business as a blacksmith and ironmonger. Newcomen is known to have been an ardent Baptist and a lay preacher.

In his trade Newcomen was assisted by a plumber called John Calley. It is not known exactly when they built the first steam engine. The first authenticated Newcomen engine was erected in 1712 near Dudley Castle, Wolverhampton. This engine was, however, much more than a prototype and it is believed that a number of earlier machines must have been operated to develop the engine to this point. The whole situation is confused by a patent granted to Thomas Savery to 'raise water by the force of fire' and most steam machines of the time were referred to as 'Saverys'. Also Newcomen may have infringed Savery's patent and deliberately not advertised the fact. During later years Newcomen paid royalties to Savery and, after his death, to a syndicate which bought up the patent.

The Newcomen engine was used to draw water from mines and so operated a pump. The engine consisted of a boiler and cylinder, with the cylinder mounted above the boiler. In the cylinder was a piston, sealed as closely as possible to the wall with a leather flap. The piston was, in turn, attached to one end of a large wooden beam, the other end being attached to the water pump. Steam from the boiler entered the cylinder at little more than atmospheric pressure when the piston had been pulled to the top of the cylinder by the weight of the beam. The steam valve was shut and water injected into the cylinder to condense the steam. As the steam condensed a vacuum was created, and the pressure of the atmosphere pushed the piston to the bottom of the cylinder, thus operating the pump. Gravity operating on the beam again raised the piston ready for the next

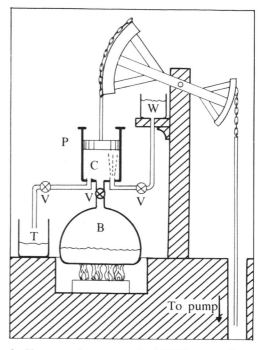

In Newcomen's steam engine (1712), steam from the boiler (B) entered the cylinder (C) while the weight of the pump-rod pulled the piston (P) to the top of the cylinder. Water from a header tank (W) was sprayed into the cylinder, condensing the steam and creating a vacuum so that air pressure forced down the piston and activated the pump. Condensed water flowed into a second tank (T). The various inlet and outlet stages were controlled by valves (V).

stroke.

Newcomen's engine consumed an enormous amount of coal because fresh hot steam had to be raised for each stroke. This made the machine more popular in the coal mines. The early engines were very expensive because the cylinder was made of brass which could be founded and machined more accurately than iron. Later iron cylinders were produced, but they were thick-walled and consequently much less efficient in terms of coal consumed. This was, of course, of little importance as long as they were used in coal mines. As mining operations changed, the pumps were moved to new locations and sometimes modified. The practical success and usefulness of the Newcomen engine was such that after later refinements, several of which were introduced by Watt in the 1800s, they became popular for adoption anywhere water was to be raised. Some are known to have remained in operation until the early part of the 20th century when they were superceded by the electric pump.

It was with the Newcomen engine that the art and science of steam was begun. Tables were drawn up in 1717 by Henry Beighton to show the size of cylinder required to raise a particular quantity of water through a particular height. For water drawn from great depths several lifts could be used in series, one raising through the first level and then another taking it from there upwards, and so on.

Thomas Newcomen did not live to see the widespread adoption of his long serving engine or its effect on developing British industry. He died of a fever in Southwark, London on the 5 August 1729.

O

Otis, Elisha Graves *(1811-1861)*, was an American engineer who pioneered the development of the lift (elevator). Although mechanical lifts and hoists had been known since early in the nineteenth century, it was the invention by Otis of a safety device which caused them to be generally adopted in commerce and slightly later as passenger-carrying machines. He also invented and patented a number of other important machines.

Otis was born on 3 August 1811 on his father's farm in Halifax, Vermont. His father was a Justice of the Peace and seved four terms in the Vermont State Legislature. Elisha's education was received in Halifax. When he was 19 he went to Troy, New York, to work as a builder. Illness and enterprise led him to take up a haulage business. As he accumulated capital he engaged in other businesses with varying degrees of success: first as a miller, and when this failed he converted his mill into a factory to make carriages and wagons. Again ill health caused him to abandon his livelihood. This time he became employed in Albany, New York, as a master mechanic in a factory making beds. Again he acquired capital and opened his own machine shop, which was successful for a time. Misfortune struck again when the Albany authorities diverted the stream which drove the water turbine he had invented to supply the workshop with power. He returned to his old

job as a master mechanic, in another factory making beds, this time in New Jersey, where after a time he was put in charge of the preparation of a new factory at Yonkers, New York. During the construction of the building, in 1852, he had to make a hoist and, as many serious accidents had been caused by out-of-control lifting platforms, he sought a way of making this one absolutely safe.

Otis built the frame of his hoist with a ratchet into which could be slotted a horizontal wagon spring attached to the 'cage' of the lift. The rope of the hoist was fixed to the centre of the spring and kept it in tension, so preventing it from engaging with the ratchet. If, however, the rope broke, the spring was released and jammed into the ratchet, immediately immobilizing the lift.

Interest was shown in his lifts, or elevators as he called them, and when the bed factory went out of business he took over its plant to fulfill the initial three orders he received for his invention. Further orders came slowly until Otis exhibited his patented lift at the second season of the Crystal Palace Exposition in New York in 1854. As part of his demonstration he climbed onto his elevator, was hoisted into the air, and then a mechanic cut the hoisting rope. This was a grand advertisement and the orders started to come in. In 1857 the first public passenger lift was opened by the New York china firm of E.V Haughwout and Company. Generally the lifts were powered by steam engines and in 1860 Otis patented and improved the double oscillatory machine specially designed for his lifts. Also from the workshops of his elevator company, Otis invented and patented railway trucks and brakes, a steam plough and a baking oven.

Otis was married twice and had two sons. By the time of his death on 8 April 1861 his business was fairly profitable. Later it was developed to massive proportions with the help of his sons.

Otto, Nikolaus August *(1832-1891)*, was a German engineer who developed the first commercially successful four-stroke internal combustion engine. even today, the four-stroke cycle is still sometimes referred to as The Otto Cycle.

Otto was born at Holzhausen, Nassau, the son of a farmer. He left school at the age of 16 to work in a merchant's office, and later moved to Cologne where he became greatly interested in the gas engines developed by Jean Lenoir (1822-1900). In 1861 he built a small experimental gas engine, and three years later joined forces with Eugen Langen, an industrialist trained at the Karlsruhe Polytechnic, to form a company to market such engines. He received valuable help also from a former fellow student, Franz Reuleaux. At the Paris Exhibition of 1867 the firm's product won a gold medal in competition with 14 other gas engines. Further capital was raised, and a new factory, the Gasmotorenfabrik, was built at Deutz near Cologne in 1869. Otto concentrated on the administrative side of the business, leaving Langen, with his new recruits Gottlieb Daimler (1834-1900) and Wilhelm Maybach (1847-1929), to develop the engineering side.

In 1876, Otto described the four-stroke engine for which his name is famous. Unfortunately his patent was invalidated in 1886 when his competitors discovered that Alphonse Beau de Rochas had described the principle of the four-stroke cycle in an obscure pamphlet. In the period 1860 to 1865 Lenoir sold several hundred of his small double-acting gas engines, but technical

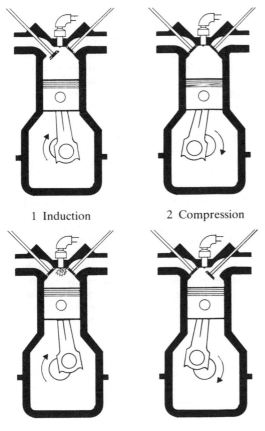

1 Induction   2 Compression

3 Combustion   4 Exhaust

The Otto cycle, devised originally for a gas engine, is the basis of all four-stroke internal combustion engines.

weaknesses - especially low compression - limited their potential. Otto's much more efficient and relatively quiet engine, the so-called 'silent Otto'

was well received and sold extensively in the first ten years of manufacture. Otto died in Cologne in 1891.

Otto first designed a successful vertical atmospheric gas engine in 1867. Some ten years later he introduced a horizontal engine, the operation of which was closely similar to the cycle of Beau de Rochas. Almost certainly, however, Otto reached his results independently of Rochas and the system has ever since been referred to as 'The Otto Cycle'.

In the Otto four-stroke cylinder cycle the explosive mixture, in the first stroke of the piston towards the crankshaft, is drawn into the cylinder (the induction stroke). It is compressed on the return (compression) stroke. Ignition is then effected at or about the top dead centre position and the burning mixture drives the piston during the third stroke of the cycle. Finally, on the fourth (exhaust) stroke, the burnt gases are driven out of the cylinder. The cycle is then repeated.

The superiority of Otto's new engine over other types was soon apparent. Thousands of them, manufactured by Otto and Langen, were installed throughout the world in a very few years. Other types of engine were still made, such as the low-power vertical Bischop engine, in which expansion of the exploded gases raised the piston which was then driven downwards by atmospheric pressure during its downward stroke (in accordance with Huygen's conception).

Following steam-engine practice to a large extent, the early gas-engine designers naturally adopted the ideas of the slow-speed horizontal engine, but this proved to be a serious mistake. A few engines used electric ignition, but most relied upon ignition by means of a flame drawn into the cylinder at the correct moment. An internal flame was kept burning inside the body of a cock-key, in front of a slot in the cylinder wall. When the firing-point arrived a slide-valve was so arranged as to open the slot, enabling the flame to ignite the mixture, and the slot was then closed again. The internal flame was at once extinguished by the explosion and so it was necessary to have a second, external flame outside the body of the cock in order to reignite the internal flame. At the moment of ignition the external flame was shut off from the internal one.

A later idea was the hot-tube method, in which a small tube of platinum or other noncombustible material was inserted in the cylinder, its outer end being closed. The tube was kept at a bright red heat by an external gas flame, and upon compression a portion of the charge was forced into the tube and promptly ignited. Finally the invention of the free-float carburettor by Maybach allowed petrol (gasoline) to be used as a fuel instead of gas, and electric ignition - using sparking plugs (developed by Bosch) - became standard.

P

Papin, Denis *(1647-c.1712)*, was a French physicist and technologist, who invented a vessel which was the forerunner of the pressure cooker or autoclave.

Papin was born in Blois, France, on 22 August 1647 and studied medicine at Angers University, where he obtained his MD in 1669. His first job was as an assistant to Cristiaan Huygens in Paris, and then in 1675 he went to London to assist Robert Hooke (then responsible for the running of the Royal Society), to write letters for a payment of two shillings (10p) each. Papin was not appointed a Fellow of the Royal Society until late in the 1680s. In 1680, he returned to Paris to work with Huygens and in 1681 he went to Venice for three years as Director of Experiments at Ambrose Sarotti's academy. In 1684 he tried to secure the position of Secretary of the Royal Society, but Edmund Halley got it and Papin was appointed 'temporary curator of experiments' with a salary of £30 a year. In November 1687 he was appointed to the Chair of Mathematics at Marburg University and stayed there until 1696 when he moved to Cassel to take up a place in the Court of the Landgrave of Hesse. He returned to London in 1707, but by then his friends had gone and there was no position for him at the Royal Society. He drifted into obscurity and died in about 1712 (certainly not later than 1714).

Papin's first scientific work as Huygens' assistant was to construct an air pump and to carry out a number of experiments. Later, with Robert Boyle, he introduced a number of improvements to the air pump and invented the condensing pump. In 1680 they published *A Continuation of New Experiments*. It was while he was with Boyle that he invented the steam digester - a closed vessel with a tightly fitting lid in which water was heated. This was the prototype of the modern pressure cooker, but it is used more extensively in the chemical industry as the autoclave. In Papin's prototype, the steam was prevented from escaping so that a high pressure was generated, causing the boiling point of the water to rise considerably. Papin invented a safety valve to guard against excessive rises in pressure. This safety valve was of technical importance in the development of steam power. He showed his invention to the Royal

Society in May 1679.

In the early 1680s, when he was employed by the Royal Society, he carried out numerous experiments in hydraulics and pneumatics, which were published in *Philosophical Transactions*.

In 1690 Papin suggested that the condensation of steam should be used to make a vacuum under a piston previously raised by the expansion of the steam. This was the earliest cylinder-and-piston steam engine. His idea of using steam later took shape in the atmospheric engine of Thomas Newcomen. His scheme was unworkable, however, because he proposed to use one vessel as both boiler and cylinder. He proposed the first steam-driven boat in 1690 and in 1707 he built a paddle-boat, but the paddles were turned by man power and not by steam.

Also during this period, he considered the idea of a piston ballistic pump with gunpowder and discussed the project with Huygens. In a letter to Leibniz on 6 March 1704, he claimed the idea as his own. In 1705, Leibniz sent him a sketch of Thomas Savery's high-pressure steam pump for raising water. In 1707 Papin devised a modification of this, which was workable but not as productive as the original piston model.

Parsons, Charles Algernon *(1854-1931)*, was a British mechanical engineer who designed and built the first practical steam turbine and developed its use as the motive power for the generation of electricity in power stations, in centrifugal pumps and, particularly, as a source of power for steamships. In most areas of its application it replaced the much less efficient reciprocating steam engine. To accompany this invention Parsons developed more efficient screw propellers for ships and suitable gearing to widen the turbine's usefulness, both on land and sea. In his later life he designed searchlights and optical instruments, and developed methods for the production of optical glass. The firm of Grubb Parsons is still of world renown in the design and servicing of the optical systems for large telescopes.

Parsons, the 6th and youngest son of the Earl of Rose, was born in London on 13 June 1854. He came from a talented family. His grandfather had been Vice-President of the Royal Society and his father was its President. During his youth in Ireland, Parsons was educated by private tutors. When he was 17 he spent 2 years at Trinity College, Dublin. From there he went to St John's College, Cambridge, where he gained high honours in mathematics. He began his training in engineering on leaving Cambridge by becoming an apprentice at William Armstrong and Company near Newcastle-upon-Tyne. After further experience as an engineer he went to the firm of Clarke,

Chapman and Company at Gateshead as a junior partner, in charge of their electrical section. It was there that he succeeded in making a practical steam turbine and applied it to the generation of electricity.

In a steam turbine a cylindrical bladed rotor is enclosed within a casing with static blades, and the steam passes between the two, contacting first one set of turbine blades then being directed on to another set designed to work with the same steam at a slightly lower pressure. At the same time the work done by the expansion of the steam aids the rotation produced. Parsons's first machine was used as a turbo-generator for electricity and can now be seen in the Science Museum, London.

In 1889 he formed his own company, which still exists, near Newcastle-upon-Tyne. He developed turbo-generators of various kinds and, as time went on, increasing capacities, which formed the basic machinery for national (and much of international) electricity production.

From about 1894 Parsons, with the formation of a new company at Wallsend-upon-Tyne, applied his turbine to various uses. His first venture, the 48m (100ft) vessel *Turbinia* (displacement 44 tonnes (4.3 tons) achieved initially a speed of 20 knots. Even at this high speed he calculated that the output from the turbine (about 2,000 hp) was not being used efficiently. He designed a propulsion system which incorporated 3 shafts, each with 3 propellers. From this new machinery the *Turbinia*, with Parsons, at the controls, created quite a stir when it sailed up and down the assembled rows of British and foreign warships at the Naval Review of 1897, to celebrate the Diamond Jubilee of Queen Victoria. *Turbinia* can still seen in the Museum of Science and Industry at Newcastle-upon-Tyne.

Prompted by the difficulties of realizing the full power output from the turbine at sea, Parsons investigated the loss of efficiency of screw propellers and the phenomenon of cavitation caused by the water not adhering to the propeller blades at high speeds - and the accompanying damage to the blades. Use steam turbines instead of reciprocating steam engines, high speeds - with less vibration - were to be had by ocean liners, and greater efficiency - with increased fuel economy - was obtained by the slower trading vessels. Parsons turbines fitted to the liners *Lusitania* and *Mauritania* developed some 70,000hp.

Parson's work on searchlights and specialist marine and other optical instruments was taken up by the Royal Navy and various maritime trading companies. He also revitalized the British optical glass industry and safeguarded its production for possible military applications at a time when it was about to be eclipsed by German companies. Throughout most of his lifetime he attempted, without success, to make artificial diamonds by the crystallization of carbon at high pressures and temperatures.

Parsons was a man of considerable courage in so far as he often undertook to produce machines far beyond the current limits of design and expertise. He was, without a doubt, one of the greatest engineers of the late nineteenth and early twentieth centuries and was recognized as such by his election to the Royal Society, the award of a knighthood and various honourary degrees and in being the first engineer to be admitted to the Order of Merit.

His ingenuity has lasted and benefitted mankind in that now there are turbines in use in a large variety of roles, providing the most convenient, useful and efficient means of converting power into motion. Parsons died while on a cruise to the West Indies on 11 February 1931, aged 76 years.

Pelton, Lester Allen *(1829-1918)*, was an American engineer who developed a highly efficient water turbine used to drive both mechanical devices and hydro-electric power turbines using large heads of water.

After spending his youth in Vermillion, Ohio, the 20-year-old Pelton, then a carpenter, went to California in search of gold. He failed (like thousands of others) in his quest, but it was while involved in gold-mining that he made a discovery which led him to his invention.

Waterwheels were used at the mines to provide power for machinery. The energy to drive these wheels was supplied by powerful jets of water which struck the base of the wheel on flat-faced vanes. In time, these vanes were replaced by hemispherical cups, with the jet striking at the centre of the cup. Pelton noticed that one of the water wheels appeared to be rotating faster than usual. It turned out that this was because the wheel had become loose on its axle, and the water jet was striking the inside edge of the cups, rather than the centre.

Pelton went away to reconstruct what he had seen, finding again that the wheel rotated more rapidly, and hence developed more power. Working on the construction of stamp mills at Camptonville in California, Pelton found that using split cups the effect could be enhanced, and by 1879 he had tested a prototype at the University of California. This was so successful that he was awarded a prize. A patent was granted in 1889, and he later sold the rights to the Pelton Water Wheel Company of San Francisco.

By 1890, Pelton wheels developing hundreds of horsepower at efficiencies of more than 80 per

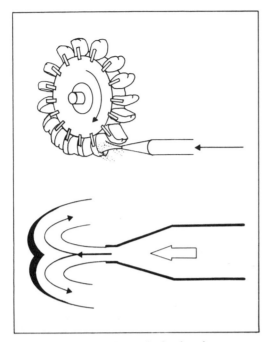

In a Pelton water turbine, the buckets have a two-curved section which completely reverses the direction of the water jet striking them.

cent were in operation. Efficiencies of more than 90 per cent were being achieved using the wheel in hydro-electric schemes of thousands of horsepower by the time of Pelton's death in 1910. The Pelton wheel remains the only hydraulic turbine of the impulse type in common use today.

Porsche, Ferdinand *(1875-1951)*, was the Bohemian engineer who designed and built the first mass-produced European people's car and later helped to develop small, high-performance luxury cars destined for series production. He also invented synchronizing gearboxes and torsion-bar suspension.

Porsche was born the son of a tinsmith in Bohemia. From 1923 to 1929 he served as technical director of the German Daimler company which became Daimler Benz in 1926. During that period his most notable contribution was the *Mercedes SSK* racing car. He rose from relative obscurity to form a limited liability company on 25 March 1931, registered in Stuttgart in the name of Dr Ing h c F Porsche Ltd.

From 1931 to 1933, Porsche developed his first small-car prototypes for Zündapp and NSU, under contract. In 1932 he devised the first torsion-bar suspension system and in the same year visited Russia to make an extensive study trip through all centres of the Soviet vehicle industry

of that period. He was allowed to visit any factory which interested him and was said to have been shown all their designs for vehicles, aircraft and tractors. Probably no other European has gained the insight into the Russian industry which Porsche possessed at that time. At the end of this journey, the Russians in Moscow offered him the job of chief national designer for the land, to be accompanied by a wealth of authority and privilege. But Porsche declined; the language barrier, in particular, deterred him.

In 1936 he received a contract from the German government to develop the *Volkswagen* and plan the factory where it would be built. Just prior to this he conceived a racing car, without contract. The project was taken over by Auto Union and the car subsequently claimed victories on virtually every race track in Europe between 1934 and 1937, as well as many class records.

The first *VW* prototypes were on the road by the end of 1935; the years to follow, up to the outbreak of World War II, were years of the utmost concentration on the *Volkswagen* for Porsche. Some other design jobs, however, had appeared alongside the major *Volkswagen* contract to cause Porsche to expand his company. During June 1938 the design offices moved from Kronenstrasse 24 in Stuttgart to Spitalwaldstrasse 2 in Suffenhausen, where he led the development of light tractor. Those tractors built to Porsche license and under the firm's supervision after World War II can be traced to these designs. Concepts were also developed by him for aviation engines as well as plans and designs for wind-driven power plants - large windmills with automatic sail adjustment which delivered electric current via generators.

The War cut short further development of the *Volkswagen* so Porsche designed the *Leopard* and *Tiger* tanks used by German Panzer regiments and helped to develop the *V-1* flying bomb. During this period he was awarded an honorary professorship.

After internment following the end of the War, Porsche joined his son in Gmünd, Carinthia, with the firm which had been moved from Zuffenhausen to help develop the first *Type 256* Porsche roadster, later to become the *911* model. He was considerably weakened by his 22 month term of imprisonment, however, and his health caused him to withdraw from engineering by the end of the 1940s. He died in 1951.

The *Volkswagen* was conceived in 1934 as a utility car of low weight to be 'achieved by new basic measures'. The first prototypes were built in 1935 and 1936, prior to obtaining the contract to build. A lightweight 'flat-four' cylinder air-cooled engine of substantial magnesium alloy construction was rear-mounted in the vehicle. It was un-

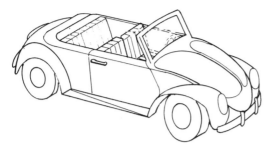

In 1934 Porsch designed the 'people's car' or Volkswagen, *later to become popular throughout the world as the VW 'Beetle'.*

ited with a similarly constructed gearbox. Independent suspension of all 4 wheels was by swing axles with torsion-bar springing.

Substantial weight-savings resulted in the absence of axle beams and the combined weight of the rear-mounted engine and gearbox unit was insufficient to cause handling instability. The disposition of major components allowed an aerodynamically efficient saloon car body of light-weight chassis-less construction to be fitted, giving adequate leg room within the small exterior envelope.

Porsche's first production *Volkswagen* rolled off the assembly lines in 1945 at the Wolfsburg plant. On 17 February 1972 it became the car with the longest and biggest production run in the history of the automobile, outpacing the *Model T Ford* at 15,007,033 units.

Porsche was a brilliant engineer whose genius reached into many disciplines. It has been said that the torsion-bar suspension alone would have sufficed to establish a monument to his name in the automotive industry. He can be considered one of the pioneers of air-cooled engines in the industry. The sports cars bearing his name were developed by his son Ferry and the first, the *356*, was based on the incredibly versatile *VW Beetle.*

R

Rankine, William John Macquorn *(1820-1872),* was a Scottish engineer and physicist who was one of the founders of the science of thermodynamics, especially in reference to the theory of steam engines.

Rankine was born in Edinburgh on 5 July 1820, the son of an engineer. He trained as a civil engineer under John Benjamin MacNeil, and was eventually appointed to the chair of civil engineering and mechanics at the University of Glasgow in 1855, a position he continued to hold until his death on 24 December 1872. In 1853 he became a Member (and later a Fellow) of the Royal Society, whose official catalogue credits him with 154 papers.

One of Rankine's earliest scientific papers, on metal fatigue in railway axles, led to improved methods of construction in this field. In about 1848 he commenced the series of researches on molecular physics which occupied him at intervals during the rest of his life and which are among his chief claims to distinction in the realm of pure science. In 1849 he delivered two papers on the subject of heat. His first work, 'On an Equation between the Temperature and the Maximum Elasticity of Steam and other Vapours' was published in the Edinburgh New Philosophical Journal and at the end of the year he sent to the Royal Society of Edinburgh his paper, 'On a Formula for Calculating the Expansion of Liquids by Heat'.

In 1853, together with James Robert Napier, he projected and patented a new form of air-engine, but this patent was afterwards abandoned. It was in 1859 that he produced what is perhaps his most influential work, *A Manual of the Steam Engine and other Prime Movers*, the thirteenth attempt at a treatment of the steam engine theory. In it he described a thermodynamic cycle of events (the so-called Rankine cycle) which was used as a standard for the performance of steam power installations where a considerable vapour provides the working fluid. Rankine here explained how a liquid in the boiler vapourized by the addition of heat converts part of this energy into mechanical energy when the vapour expands in an engine. As the exhaust vapour is condensed by a cooling medium such as water, heat is lost from the cycle. The condensed liquid is pumped back into the boiler. This concept of a power cycle is useful to engineers in developing equipment and designing power plants.

Besides writing in various newspapers, Rankine contributed many papers to scientific journals, the most significant ones being on the subject of thermodynamics. The application of the doctrine that 'heat and work are convertible' to the discovery of new relationships among the properties of bodies was made about the same time by three scientific men, William Thomson (afterwards Lord Kelvin), Rankine and Clausius. Lord Kelvin cleared the way with his account of Carnot's work on *The Motive Power of Heat* and pointed out the error of Carnot's assumption that heat is a substance and therefore indestructible. Rankine in 1849 and Clausius in 1850 showed the further modifications which Carnot's theory required.

Lord Kelvin in 1851 put the foundations of the theory in the form they have since retained.

Rankine also made an important contribution to soil mechanics and his work on earth pressure and the stability of retaining walls was a notable advance. He contributed with others to produce *The Imperial Dictionary of Universal Biography* and was the corresponding and general editor of *Shipbuilding, Theoretical and Practical* (1866).

Ransome; James Edward *(1839-1905)*, was the British engineer and businessman who produced the first commercial motor lawn mower. This simple development forged an essential link in the chain of events which has made gardening one of the most popular pastimes in the world and changed the appearance of the countryside and the suburbs in most developed countries.

Ransome was born in Ipswich on 13 July 1839 and served an engineering apprenticeship at the Orwell works of Ransomes and Simms, as it was then known. The works were founded in 1789 by his grandfather, Robert Ransome (1753-1830), the inventor of the chilled ploughshare. Ransome managed the plough and implement department for 20 years, becoming a partner in 1868 and a managing director in 1884.

From 1886 Ransome was company chairman in alternate years with John Robert Jefferies until the latter's death in 1900, when Ransome became sole chairman until his own death. He was an active member of many agricultural societies and a Justice of the Peace. He died in London on 30 January 1905.

Until the invention of the lawnmower by Edwin Beard Budding (1796-1846) and its patenting in 1830 by John Ferrabee, the only way to cut grass was by scythe. Not even the best men could obtain an even finish and the work was slow and laborious. As a result, lawns were only for the rich and even they had relatively small areas, most grassland being grazed by livestock.

Budding went into partnership with Ferrabee, who developed and patented the idea and issued the first manufacturing licence to Ransomes in 1832. Pushing the early mowers was extremely hard work and soon horse-drawn machines were in action (the horses wore boots to avoid marking the turf). The steam mower appeared in 1892, built by James Sumner, but it weighed about 1.5 tons.

It was in 1902 that the Orwell works, under Ransome's personal direction, produced a 1050mm (42inch) cut machine powered by a Simms 6hp (4.5kW) 4-stroke, water-cooled petrol engine. It was not the first motor mower (Stephenson-Peach and Messrs Grimsley were probably about 5 years earlier) but it was certainly the first successful one.

The following year the company was offering a choice of 4 machines. In 1905 came a competitive demonstration between a steam-powered machine produced by the Leyland Steam Motor Company (the predecessor of British Leyland) and a Ransomes 30-inch (762mm) model at Eaton Hall, seat of the Duke of Westminster. From this time on, the motor mower reigned supreme, two 30 inch models being ordered by King Edward VII after a demonstration at Buckingham Palace.

Ransome was not cast in the mould of the innovator/engineer who struggles for fame and fortune throughout his life. He was a sound businessman/engineer with a long list of improvements to agricultural equipment to his credit. The lawnmower side of the Ipswich business was under his personal direction and it is to his foresight and calculated investment that the world owes the millions of acres of lawns which grace suburban and country houses today.

Remington, Philo *(1816-1889)*, was an American mechanical engineer largely responsible for perfecting the Remington breech-loading rifle and the Remington typewriter.

Born in Litchfield, New York State, the son of a small-arms manufacturer, Remington entered his father's business, spending 25 years as superintendent of the manufacturing department. It was in this post that he did the work for which he is now remembered.

During the American Civil War, business boomed for the Remingtons but, following the victory of the Union in 1865, the firm looked to diversification to meet the future. In 1873 a perfect answer materialized. After work carried out in the Kleinstuber machine shops in Milwaukee, Wisconsin. The American inventor Christopher Sholes had designed a typewriter capable of being mass-produced, This development attracted the attention of two businessmen, who bought Sholes' patent and then went to Remington with a proposal that the typewriter be manufactured by the company.

The contract was signed in 1873, and what soon became known as the Remington typewriter - based on Sholes' original design - was marketed the following year. This first typewriter had no facility for upper and lower case type; only capitals were available. This was soon solved by the simple device of putting both types on each typebar, and providing a mechanism (the shift key) for lifting the key to make contact with the paper. The first typewriter carrying the shift key, the Remington Mark II, appeared in 1878.

To overcome initial market inertia, the Remington machine was loaned to over 100 firms free of charge. Mark Twain bought one, becoming the first author to provide his publisher with a typewritten manuscript.

Together with his father Eliphalet, Remington made many improvements to guns and their manufacture. This work went back to 1816, when Remington's father had made a flintlock rifle at his own father's forge in Utica, New York, with an accuracy that soon attracted great attention. That led to the setting up of E. Remington & Son at Ilion, beside the Erie Canal. Among the advances made by the father-and-son team was a special lathe for the cutting of gunstocks, a method of producing extremely straight gun barrels, and the making of the first American drilled rifle barrel from cast steel.

Rennie, John *(1761-1821)*, was one of the foremost British engineers during the Napoleonic era in Europe, building or improving canals, docks, harbours and bridges both in the United Kingdom and in Ireland.

Rennie was born in June 1761 at Phantassie in Haddingtonshire, the son of a farmer. From an early age he showed great mechanical aptitude. He was allowed to spend many hours in the workshop of Andrew Meikle, millwright, the inventor of a threshing machine, who lived on the Phantassie estate.

In 1780 Rennie went to Edinburgh University, where he remained for the next three years. During his time there he spent the vacations working as a millwright and is said to have established a business in this trade on his own account. His awareness of new possibilities was shown at this time by his introduction of cast-iron pinions instead of wooden trundles.

Rennie journeyed southwards in 1784 to visit James Watt at his Soho works near Birmingham. For a short while he worked under Watt and then in the same year left for London to take charge of the Albion Flour Mills, Blackfriars, for which Boulton and Watt were building a steam engine. The machinery was all designed by Rennie and was the most perfect of its kind, a characteristic feature being the replacement of wood by iron for the shafting and framing. In about 1791 he started in business on his own account as a mechanical engineer in Holland Street, Blackfriars, where he and his successors conducted engineering works of great importance.

The first subject of Rennie's attention was canals. He carried out his works in connection with the Kennet and Avon Canal, which was his first civil engineering undertaking in England. This was succeeded by the Rochdale Canal which traverses some difficult country between Rochdale and Todmorden. The Lancaster Canal followed, and in 1802 Rennie revised the plans for the Royal Canal of Ireland from Dublin to the Shannon near Longford. For many years he was engaged in extensive drainage operations in the Lincolnshire fens and in the improvement of the river Witham.

Among the docks and harbours constructed or improved by Rennie are the London docks, East and West docks, Holyhead harbour, Hull docks, Ramsgate harbour and the docklands at Sheerness and Chatham. He devoted much time to plans for a government dockyard at Northfleet, but these were never implemented.

Rennie also achieved a high reputation as a builder of bridges. In the early part of his career he built bridges at Kelso and Musselburgh in Scotland, the latter structure showing a remarkable innovation in the flatness of the roadway - previously bridges of any length had shown a distinct rise in the centre. His later constructions show that Rennie had developed a keen sense of the beauty of design. His London bridges were indeed his greatest achievements. Waterloo Bridge (1810-1817), a replica of Kelso Bridge, was constructed of masonry arches (it was replaced 1937-1947). The Old Southwark bridge (1814-1819) consisted of three cast-iron arches. London Bridge, built from his designs but not completed until 1831, ten years after his death, consisted of multiple masonry arches. More than 130 years later it was taken down and re-erected at Lake Havasu, Arizona.

Of all Rennie's works, that which appeals most strongly to the the imagination is probably the breakwater at Plymouth, constructed in deep water, and consisting of a wall 1.6km (1 mile) in length across the Sound, and containing 3,670,000 tonnes of rough stone, besides 22,000 cubic metres of masonry on the surface. This colossal work was first proposed in a report by Rennie, dated 22 April 1806; an order in council authorizing its commencement was issued on 22 June 1811, and the first stone was deposited only two months later on 12 August. After Rennie's death the work was completed by his son, also named John Rennie.

Reynolds, Osborne *(1842-1912)*, was a British research engineer, one of the first people to approach engineering as an academic rather than a practical subject. He is particularly remembered for his investigation into turbulent flow in fluids.

Reynolds was born in Belfast on 23 August 1842. His father was a mathematician who became a schoolteacher and then rector of the parish of Debach-with-Boulge, Suffolk (as were his grandfather and greatgrandfather before). Most of Reynold's early education was at Dedham Grammar School, where his father was a teacher. He left school at the age of 19 and entered an engineering workshop, where he applied his mathematical knowledge to further the understanding of the action and design of machines. He left these practical pursuits to study mathematics at Cambridge University. Like his father he attended Queen's College, from which he graduated in 1867 and was immediately awarded a Fellowship. Soon afterwards he went to work in London for John Lawson, a civil engineer.

In 1868 Reynolds was elected to the new Chair of Engineering at Owens College (now Manchester University). His course of lectures on civil and mechanical engineering included all the mechanical, structural and thermodynamic principles involved in the subjects and gave rise to a new generation of scientific engineers who were largely to take over from the older, purely practical men.

At the time academic engineering was not fully divorced from the pure sciences, and much of Reynold's early research into the behaviour of comets, electrical phenomena in the atmosphere and properties of materials would today be regarded as part of physics. His first real engineering research was concerned with the efficiency of screw propellers for ships, and with their stability. He used scale models, a technique which was to prove of value in his later work.

During the 1880s Reynolds made his famous contribution to hydrodynamics by studying the motion of water at various velocities in parallel channels. Poiseville and Darcy had already carried out research in this area but obtained conflicting results. Reynolds showed that for the flow of a liquid to be non-turbulent, it needed a high viscosity, low density, and an open surface. If these and other criteria were not met then the flow was turbulent - a phenomenon he often demonstrated using dyes. He formulated his results by demonstrating that the resistance to flow in a tube is proportional to $Vn/d3^{-n}$, where v is the velocity of the fluid and d the diameter of the tube. When the constant $n1$ the formula explains non-tubulent flow and Poiserville's results; when nz the flow is turbulent, corresponding to Darey's results. The two states, Reynolds found, are separated by a critical velocity, itself dependent on viscous forces (tending to produce stability) and inertial forces (tending to produce instability). The ratio of the two forces, which gives a measure for any given system, is now known as Reynolds' number (equal to $\rho vl/\mu$, where ρ is the density, v the velocity, l the radius of the tube and μ the velocity).

Reynolds applied much of what he had learned about turbulent flow to the behaviour of the water in river channels and estuaries. For one study he made an accurate model of the mouth of the River Mersey, and pioneered the use of such models in marine and civil engineering projects. His later studies led to discoveries about the forces involved in lubrication with oil and the design of an improved bearing that used this knowledge. He also worked on multi-stage steam turbines, but was disappointed by their low efficiency (not realizing that efficiency increases with size and that large efficient turbines are practicable). Using the experimental 100hp steam engine which he designed for his engineering department, he determined the mechanical equivalent of heat so accurately that it has remained one of the classical determinations of a physical constant.

Reynolds was elected a Fellow of the Royal Society in 1877, and during the following decade was honoured with many medals and honourary degrees. He was married twice, his first wife dying a year after the wedding.

Ricardo, Harry Ralph *(1885-1974)* was the English engineer who played a leading role in development of the internal combustion engine. His work was particularly significant during World War I and World War II, enabling the British forces to fight with the advantage of technically superior engines. His work on combustion and detonation led to the octane rating system for classifying fuels for petrol engines.

Born on 26 January in London, Ricardo was the eldest son of Halsey Ricardo, an architect, and Catherine Rendel, daughter of Alexander Rendel, a consultant civil engineer. He was educated at Rugby and designed and built a steam engine, putting it into production when he was 12.

Ricardo went up to Cambridge in 1903 where he designed and built a motor cycle, with its power unit. With it, he won a fuel economy competition and this success led directly to his concentration on internal combustion engine research.

In the summer of 1905 he designed and built a 2-cylinder, 2-stroke engine, called the *Dolphin*, for automotive applications but in the event, the first production power unit was a 4-cylinder version to power his uncle's large car. Ricardo qualified for association membership of the Institution of Civil Engineers and was given charge of a small mechanical engineering department to design site equipment for his grandfather's firm.

During World War I he worked on aircraft engines and designed the engine for the *Mk V* tank. In July 1917, Ricardo set up his research and consultancy company. Between the wars the company worked on engine development and categorization of fuels according to their ease of detonation. From 1932 until the outbreak of World War II, it was almost exclusively engaged in the design of light high-speed diesel engines.

When war broke out, Ricardo was living in Tottingon Manor, near Henfield. The house was requisitioned and the company was moved to a less vulnerable site in Oxford. After the war, it moved to Shoreham and Ricardo settled at Woodside, the family house at Graffham. It was here that he fell and broke his leg, resulting in his death six weeks later on 18 May 1974.

Ricardo was elected fellow of the Royal Society in 1929 and was president of the Institution of Mechanical Engineers for the 1944-1945 term. In 948 he was made Knight Batchelor and during his life received 12 medals from various learned bodies.

Ricardo is probably best known for his work on combustion and detonation in spark ignition engines. In 1912 it was believed widely that the ringing knock in engines with high compression ratios was due to pre-ignition - the firing of the charge in the cylinder before the correct time. Ricardo demonstrated in 1913 that the knock was due to the spontaneous combustion of a part of the charge.

One of the factors influencing the tendency for a fuel to ignite spontaneously was its stability, the paraffinic being the worst and the aromatic the best. An early contract won by Ricardo's embryonic company was one from Shell to investigate the behaviour of various fuels. The work led to the evolution of the Toluene Number System of categorizing fuels. This later became the octane rating.

Ricardo paid great attention to combustion chamber design and put his ideas into practice during a job to improve the performance of the popular, cheap, side-valve engine. In this he succeeded, so spectacularly, that the combustion chamber configuration was produced under licence, or pirated, throughout the world. This led to a patent infringement case, which Ricardo won in 1932.

One of the reasons for the success of the single sleeve valve engine was that the cylinder head, having no valve ports, could be made the best shape for correct combustion. The principle was used for aircraft engines, which were so successful that manufacturers adopted the Ricardo design. This type of engine became the last and best of the British piston engines, powering aircraft of World War II.

Zeppelins bombed Britain from heights of 4,877- 6,096 m (16-20,000ft) and out of reach of both aircraft and anti-aircraft guns. Ricardo's super-charged engine was re-designed in 1915 and 1916 to power an aircraft to tackle this menace. On its type test, the first engine developed 268.5kW (360hp) on supercharged air at ground level would have been able to intercept the *Zeppe-lins* with ease.

The first engine ran on the test bed in March 1917, exceeding its rated 111.9kW (150hp), developing 125.2kW (168hp) at 1,200rpm and just over 149.9kW (200hp) at 1,600rpm. The first *Mk V* tank ran in June 1917. When the weight armour and armaments on tanks was increased, Ricardo designed 167.9kW (225hp) and 223.7kW (300hp) units to provide the extra power.

Towards the end of World War II *Me 410s* (fast twin-engined fighter bombers) were making hit-and-run raids on British cities and were outdistancing British fighters. Ricardo proposed oxygen enrichment of the *Merlin* engine and after *Mosquitos* had been equipped, the losses of *Me 410s* increased dramatically and the raids came to an end.

When Ricardo began his work on internal combustion engine development, the techniques used were more akin to art than to science. He led the revolution in engine design, and his painstaking work laid a firm foundation for the meticulous programmes which have resulted in smaller engines producing more power on less fuel than ever before.

Roberts, Richard *(1789-1864)*, was a Welsh engineer who became one of the greatest mechanical inventors of the nineteenth century. His inventions included a screw-cutting lathe and a planing machine.

Roberts was born on 22 April 1789 at Carreghofa, Montgomeryshire, the son of a shoemaker. He had very little formal education and at an early age went to work on the newly opened Ellesmere Canal. From there he obtained work as a labourer in a lime-stone quarry. At 20 years of age he went to seek work in Liverpool and, later, Manchester - where he became a tool-maker.

To evade military service, Roberts moved to London where he worked as an apprentice to Henry Maudslay, one of the foremost engineers of the day. Roberts returned to Manchester, which was then the centre of the cotton industry, and in 1814 he set up in business for himself. In 1817 he designed a machine for planing metal - one of the first of the long series of inventions he made during his lifetime. In 1824, at the request of some manufacturers, he built a self-acting spinning mule which was a vast improvement on that devised by Samuel Crompton in 1779. He took only four months to complete the task.

In 1828 Roberts went into partnership with Thomas Sharpe to found the firm of Sharpe, Thomas and Company. Thomas was the director of the machine-making section. The firm manufactured machines to his design which he continued to improve. For example in 1832 he improved his mule by adding a radial arm for winding the yarn. When the Liverpool and Manchester Railway opened in 1830 the firm ventured into the business of building locomotives. Their products were bought by both British and Continental railway companies. In 1834 they produced a steam carriage with a differential drive to the back wheels. Thomas also designed a steam-brake and a system of standard gauges to which all his work was constructed.

The partnership ended when Sharpe died in 1842. The firm split up - the Sharpe family continued to control the manufacture of locomotives, while Roberts retained the remaining part of the company known as the Globe Works. In 1845 he invented an electromagnet - of which examples were placed in the Manchester museum at Peel Park and one was kept by the Scottish Society of Arts. In 1848 Roberts invented a machine for punching holes in steel plates. Incorporating the Jacquard method, he devised a machine for punching holes of any pitch or pattern in bridge plates and boiler plates. He later invented a machine for simultaneously shearing iron and punching both webs of angle iron to any pitch. As with his improvement to the self-acting mule a quarter of a century before, Roberts built his hole-punching machine in response to requests by company owners who this time found themselves faced with man-power difficulties as a result of the strike during the building of Thomas Telford's Conway suspension bridge.

At the Great Exhibition of 1851 Roberts received a medal for a turret clock he had made. Recognition of his contribution to engineering took other forms. He was elected member of the Institution of Civil Engineers in 1838 and was a founder member of the Mechanics Institute in 1824. But, despite his genius as an inventor, Roberts' financial position deteriorated almost to poverty and just before he died on 16 March 1864 a public subscription was being raised to support him.

Roe, Alliot Verdon *(1877-1958)*, was a British aircraft designer. The first Englishman to construct and fly an aeroplane, he also designed the famous Avro series of aircraft.

Roe was born on 26 April 1877 at Patricroft, near Manchester. He was educated at St Paul's School, London, but at the age of 14 he went to British Columbia. Returning from Canada a year later, he served a five-year apprenticeship at the Lancashire and Yorkshire Railway Company's locomotive sheds. He then spent two years at sea, after which he entered the motor industry. He became interested in aircraft design and, in 1908, flew a distance of 23m (75ft) in a biplane of his own design. This feat was accomplished nearly a year before the first officially recognized flight in England by John Moore-Brabazon (1884-1964).

In 1910, with his brother Humphrey, Roe founded the firm of A.V Roe and Company. It became one of the world's major aircraft companies and the builder of one of the most famous aircraft of its time - the Avro 504. In 1928, Roe severed all ties with the company and turned his attention to the design of flying-boats. He became associated with the firm of S.E. Saunders and founded Saunders-Roe Company at Cowes, Isle of Wight, and became its president. Roe was knighted in 1929, and became known as Sir (Edwin) Alliot Verdon-Roe. He died at his home near London on 4 January 1958.

The first aircraft from the Manchester works was the Avro 500, of historic importance because it was one of the first machines to be ordered for use by the British army. The order - for three two-seater biplanes fitted with 50hp Gnome engines - was placed by the Government in 1912. Before the Gnome engines appeared, Roe had completed a two-seater biplane powered by a 60hp ENV engine, and it was this aircraft that provided the basis for a succession of very successful planes.

The 500 was an equal-span, two-bay biplane of wooden construction. The undercarriage was of an original design, with wheels mounted on a transverse leaf-spring which attached to a central skid (there was no tail-skid). The machine rested its rear end on the base of a suitably re-inforced rudder; a modified rudder, still acting as a tail-skid, was fitted later.

The first of the 500s went into service on 12 May 1912, and two were used to form the strength of the Central Flying School of the Royal Flying Corps, which opened at Upavon on 7 August that year. Several of these aircraft were later used by the CFS and also by the naval and military wings of the RFC.

The orginal order was increased to 12 and this contract enabled the firm of A.V Roe to became solidly established. In 1913 the company produced its first sea-plane type. It was a large biplane originally known as the Avro 503.

The construction of the Avro 504, which followed the 503, began in April 1913. It made its debut in September of that year. The design, construction and performance were all considerably in advance of its contempories, and it was this aircraft which helped lay the foundations for decades of safe flying instruction. Adapted to a float-plane version in 1914, it is regarded as one of the first production machines. Although not basically a military aircraft, it was used extensively in World War I and took part in some famous actions - the attack on the Zeppelin sheds at Freidrichshaven being one. Further modification led to a long succession of successful aircraft, from the 504A through to the 504H, which was the first aircraft to be successfully launched by catapult.

Royce, Frederick Henry *(1863-1933)* was the British engineer who, in co-operation with Charles Rolls, produced the famous Rolls-Royce series of high-performance motor cars.

Royce was born on 27 March 1863 at Alwalton, Huntingdonshire (now Cambridgeshire). On leaving school he became an apprentice engineer with the Great Northern Railway. He later (1882-1883) worked on the pioneer scheme to light London's streets with electricity, and as chief electrical engineer on the project to light the streets of Liverpool. In 1884 he founded the firm of F.H. Royce and Co. Ltd, Mechanical Engineers of Manchester, and manufactured electric cranes and dynamos. In 1904 he built his first car and in 1907, with Rolls, he founded the firm of Rolls-Royce Ltd, motor car and aero-engine builders, of Trafford Park, Manchester (and later of Derby and London). Royce became the company's director and chief engineer.

By 1914, the firm had established a reputation for building 'the best cars in the world'. In 1920 an American factory was opened at Springfield, Massachusetts, and the Rolls Royce Ghost was made there until 1926. The Ghost was followed by the Phantom, manufactured from 1927 to 1931. In that year the company bought Bentley Motors and two years later the Bentley luxury model car, based on a Rolls-Royce three-litre engine, made its appearance. It maintained its reputation as a first class luxury limousine until 1950.

Royce was made a baronet in 1930. He was also awarded the OBE and was a member of the Institute of Mechanical Engineers, the Institute of Aeronautical Engineers and the Institute of Electrical Engineers. He died in Sussex on 22 April 1933.

Like all other industrialists at the turn of the century, Rolls at first knew nothing about motor cars and could only copy and improve on the good designs of others. In 1903 France led the world in automobile design. Taking a French car, the 10hp Decauville as his model, Royce used imported parts and set about improving the design. Because he was a craftsman-mechanic and possessed special skills, the cars he built were just that much better than the others being made at that time. They became noted for the extremely fine workmanship, which gave them exceptional running qualities.

The first Royce-built car appeared in 1904. It had mechanically operated overhead inlet valves - a great improvement on the Decauville's automatic inlets. Because it was so well made, the Royce car was also very much quieter and smoother-running. Three of these first models were built and, by chance, one of them was bought by a man called Edmunds who was a director of a car importing firm. Also working for the firm was Charles Rolls. Although he worked as a salesman, Rolls was rich, aristrocratic and well-known as a pioneer motoring and aviation enthusiast.

Rolls drove and tested the car and was so impressed by its performance that he undertook to sell Royce's entire output. The two men became friends, pooled their talents and started the world-famous partnership. The Rolls-Royce range was expanded to include three-litre, three-cylinder 'light' and 'heavy' versions of the four-cylinder Twenty and Six to sell at £900.

In 1906 a light Twenty, driven by Rolls, won the Tourist Trophy and also broke the Monte Carlo to London record. In that year, also, the partnership embarked upon its one-model policy based on a 40/50hp six-cylinder car which was later to win immortality as the Silver Ghost. The car's reputation was assured after a successful 24,000km (15,000-mile) RAC-observed trial in 1907, and it was in that year that the Rolls-Royce firm of car-makers officially came into existence. Over 6,000 of these cars were made at Manchester and later at the Derby works.

Rolls was killed in a flying accident in 1912, but the firm continued to prosper. An armoured version of the Ghost saw service both during and after World War I. Later, the firm was to win a reputation for its production of aero-engines as high as that for its motor cars.

Rühmkorff, Heinrich Daniel *(1803-1877)* was a German-born French instrument-maker, who invented the Rühmkorff induction coil, a type of transformer for direct durrent that outputs a high voltage from a low voltage input.

Rühmkorff was born in Hanover on 15 January 1803, but virtually nothing is known of his life before he went to Paris in 1819 and became a porter in the laboratory of the eminent French physicist Charles Chevalier (1804-1850). There Rühmkorff became interested in electrical equipment and soon began to manufacture scientific instruments. He opened his own workshop in 1840 but although he eventually became famous throughout Europe for his scientific apparatus, his factory remained small (after his death it was auctioned off for just £42).

Rühmkorff's first notable invention was a thermo-electric battery (1844). He then turned his attention to developing an induction coil, the principles of which had been worked out by Michael Faraday in 1831. After a long series of experiments, Rühmkorff eventually produced his induction coil in 1851. It consisted of a central cylinder of soft iron on which were wound two insulated coils - an inner primary coil comprising only a few turns of relatively thick copper wire, and an outer secondary coil with a large number of turns of thinner copper wire; an interrupter automatically makes and breaks the current in the primary coil, thereby inducing an intermittent high voltage in the secondary coil.

Rühmkorff demonstrated his invention at the 1855 Paris Exhibition, where it gained for him a decoration and a medal, and at the 1858 French Exhibition of Electrical Apparatus, where he was awarded the first prize of 50,000 francs. Later, however, the originality of his invention was contested by C G Page (1812-1868) who claimed to have invented a similar device some 20 years earlier in the United States.

The Rühmkorff induction coil played an important part in many later advances, including the development of gas discharge tubes and, indirectly, the discovery of cathode rays and X-rays. Today, coils working on the same principle are still used to provide the ignition spark in internal combustion engines.

Widely respected and a great philanthropist, Rühmkorff was made an Honorary Member of the French Physical Society - despite his lack of early education. He died in Paris on 19 December 1877.

S

Savery, Thomas *(c.1650-1715)*, was the British inventor and engineer who is generally credited with producing the world's first practical steam-driven water pump. It had only limited success and was not adopted widely, probably due to faulty materials and workmanship.

Much of Savery's life is unrecorded. He came from Devon stock and may have been born at Shilston near Modbury. He might have been a captain in the Military Engineers but it is more likely that he was 'captain' of a mine - a rank sometimes used in mining circles. The first definite record comes with the grant of a patent in 1696 for a machine for cutting, grinding and polishing mirror glass. His patent for a fire engine for raising water from mines, for which he is best known, was granted in July 1698. In 1705 he was appointed Treasurer for Sick and Wounded Seamen, a post he held until 1714. In 1706 he was elected Fellow of the Royal Society, and the same year he applied for a patent for a bellows for foundry work.

It is probable that he made a trip to Hanover in connection with his engine and on his return he applied, in 1710, for a patent for an improved oven. He also invented a mechanism for measuring the distance sailed by a ship. In 1714 Savery was appointed surveyor of the water works at Hampton Court and he designed a pumping system, driven by a water wheel, for supplying the fountains.

Obituaries place Savery's death in May 1715 and his will, dated 15 May, was proved on 19 May by his widow, Martha - his executrix and sole legatee. It is not known where he was buried.

For many years up to the first decades of the 18th century, pumping out British mines had been a major problem. Various suggestions had been made for using steam power but the Miners' Friend, as Savery's invention was called, showed most promise of significant advance.

His invention consisted of a boiler heated by an open fire, so it was technically an 'atmospheric engine' and not a 'steam engine' as we know it today. The engine was connected via a regulator and steam pipe to the top of a receiver the bottom of which was mounted on a hollow box or 'engine tree'. Also connected to the engine tree was the suction pipe, which extended into the mine, and a force (delivery) pipe. There were one-way valves (opening upwards) in the suction and force pipes.

To work the Miners' Friend, the operator opened the regulator, letting steam into the receiver, and driving air up the force pipe through the one-way valve. When the receiver was full of steam, the regulator was closed then doused with cold water to condense the steam it contained. Atmospheric pressure forced water up the suction pipe through the one-way valve into the receiver. The operator then opened the regulator, and the steam pressure forced the water up the force pipe. The steam in the receiver was again condensed, and the cycle repeated.

A contemporary writer described a basic engine built in 1711 or 1712 at Campden House, Kensington, which had a boiler holding 182l (40 gallons), a receiver of 59l (13 gallons), and 76.2mm (3 inch) wooden suction and delivery pipes, the former 4.88m (16ft) long and the latter 12.80m (42ft). It could pump 14183 litres (3120 gallons) per hour and cost £50.

A model exhibited to the Royal Society had two receivers working alternately to deliver water continuously and it was on this concept that Savery based his description of The Miners' Friend. He reckoned it could lift water 6.1-7.92m (20-26ft) and then force it to a height of 18.29-24.38m (60-

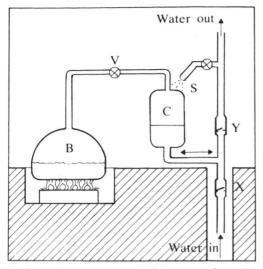

In Savery's steam pump (1696), steam from the boiler (B) entered a chamber (C) where, after the valve (V) was closed, a spray of water (S) condensed it. The vacuum created in the chamber lifted water into it past the one-way valve (X). Steam again admitted to C forced the water out past the second one-way valve (Y).

80ft). In deep mines two or more engines, one above the other, were to be used. Savery claimed that the draught to the furnace would help mine ventilation and that the water delivered above ground could be used to turn a water wheel.

There are no records, however, of any engines being installed in mines. A two-receiver engine built at York Buildings waterworks had continuous problems with blowing steam joints. Savery acquired facilities for production of his engines but it appears that poor workmanship and materials made them unworkable.

There is little doubt that Savery produced the world's first, practical, working steam engine. It was probably never used for the purpose for which it was intended and another Devonian, Thomas Newcomen, solved the problem in a different way. Savery's engine did work, however, and for this he deserves to take his place in history.

Shrapnel, Henry *(1761-1842)*, was a British artillery officer who invented the artillery shell which bears his name. He also invented the brass tangent slide and some types of fuses, compiled range tables, and improved the construction of mortars and howitzers.

Shrapnel was born at Bradford-on-Avon, Wiltshire, on 3 June 1761. He received a commission in the Royal Artillery in 1779, and in the following year he went to Newfoundland. In 1781 he

was promoted to First Lieutenant, and on returning to England two years later he commenced his investigations into the problems connected with hollow spherical projectiles filled with bullets and bursting charges and with their discharge from light and heavy ordnance. He was promoted Captain and served in the Duke of York's unsuccessful campaign against the French in 1793, being wounded in the siege of Dunkirk.

Promotions followed fairly regularly and by 1804 he was regimental Lieutenant-Colonel. In that year also, he was appointed inspector of artillery at the Royal Arsenal at Woolwich and, while he was there, succeeded in perfecting many of his inventions connected with ordnance. Further promotion followed and in 1814 he became regimental colonel. By this time, Shrapnel had spent more than 30 years and several thousand pounds of his own money in perfecting his inventions. The treasury granted him a pension of £1,200 a year for life, but he was disappointed not to receive a baronetcy. In 1819 he was promoted Major-General and, in 1837, Lieutenant-General. Shrapnel died at his home in Southampton on 13 March 1842.

When Shrapnel invented his new shell, he introduced a new name into artillery nomenclature. Although shells had been used for more than 400 years, Shrapnel's shell was different. It was fused and filled with musket balls - plus a small charge of black powder which was just sufficient to explode the container after a pre-determined period of time. When the fuse acted, the container - or shell-case - was blown open and the musket-balls it had contained scattered in all directions, causing great damage to anyone or anything with which they came into contact. The Duke of Wellington reported the success of Shrapnel's case-shot and wrote telling him of the performance of his invention against the enemy at Vimiera in 1808. Other generals, in other actions, also acclaimed the new weapon.

Although the first shells used as containers for the musket-balls (or schrapnel as they came to be known) were round, later they were of an elongated form with added velocity. Shrapnel's shells continued to be used and were very effective right up to World War I. They proved to be especially effective against large infantry units on open ground. They were less effective, however, against dispersed or protected personnel.

After World War I there came a period of rapid development and improvement in the design of artillery ammunition. Technological advances in metallurgy, chemistry and electronics led to the Shrapnel shell being replaced by more powerful projectiles containing bursting charges of TNT, Amatol, Explosive D and RDX. As a result it was no longer necessary to pack the shell with steel fragments - the disintegration of the shell case itself provided the same effect. Because the final effect was still achieved in the way Shrapnel had envisaged - by the blast of the explosion and the spraying of steel fragments - the term 'shrapnel' continued to be used, although erroneously, soperpetuating the association of Shrapnel's name.

Seguin, Marc *(1786-1875)*, was a French engineer who, in 1825, built the first successful suspension bridge in Europe using cables of iron wire. He also invented the tubular boiler.

Seguin was born in Annonay, France on 20 April 1786. He obtained his early education at a small boarding school in Paris, but was self-taught in engineering science. He had arrived in Paris at the age of 13 where his interest in engineering was stimulated by his close contact with Joseph Montgolfier, his grand-uncle. Shortly after Montgolfier's death in 1810, Seguin returned to Annonay.

In 1825, in association with Henri Dufour, using wire cables, Seguin erected the first suspension bridge of its kind in Europe. This bridge was built at Geneva and, over the next 20 years, Seguin and his brothers erected other cable suspension bridges in France - beginning with the one over the river Rhône at Tournon in 1827.

Seguin, again with his brothers, tried to establish a steam-boat service on the Rhône, and later turned his attention to railways. He was successful in establishing France's first modern railway between Lyon and St Étienne, completed in 1832. He discovered that the Stephenson steam engine then available was not capable of generating enough power for the high-speed operation he desired, so he invented a new type of boiler - the multi-tabular or fire-tube boiler.

By the time Seguin retired from active work in engineering in 1838, he had produced engineering projects which provided some of the earliest examples of large-scale civil engineering in France. In recognition of his services he was elected corresponding member of the Académie des Sciences in 1845.

Besides practical engineering, Seguin showed a great interest in the problems involved with heat and light. He published his first statements on the subject, made in 1824 and 1825, in a Scottish journal. He argued that matter consisted of small, dense molecules constantly on the move in miniature solar systems and he maintained that magnetic, electrical and thermal phenomena were the result of their particular velocities and particular orbits. He identified heat as molecular velocity and explained the conversion to a mechanical effect by stating that this occurs when the molecules transmit their velocities to external objects. In 1839 he published his *De l'influence des chemins de fer'* in which he rejected the calorific theory then dominant in France because it implied perpetual motion due to the supposed existence of heat as a fluid conserved in all processes. Seguin assumed that a certain amount of heat disappeared in the very act of the production of mechanical power and that the converse was equally true. He tried to determine the numerical relationship between heat and mechanical power and, in a table of results, he showed that the heat-loss as measured by a thermometer was not a true indication of the heat lost by the steam producing the power. However, he was unable to specify a relationship between temperature loss and loss of heat content. He could not, therefore, define a unit of heat or state its mechanical equivlent.

When James Joule succeeded in determining the mechanical equivalent of heat in 1847, Seguin supported his conclusions. Later Seguin attempted to claim priority over Joule, but it was decided that only in retrospect could the suggestions that Seguin made in 1839 be interpretated as a mechanical equivalent of heat. In 1853, Seguin published a weekly scientific magazine called *Cosmos*, and this became an important vehicle for the popularization of science in France. It also served as a forum for Seguin's theories including his particle theories for heat, light, electricity and magnetism.

Siemens, Ernst Werner von *(1816-1892)*, was the German electrical engineer who discovered the dynamo principle and who organized the construction the Indo-European telegraph system between London and Calcutta via Berlin, Odessa and Teheran.

Siemens was born on 13 December 1816 at Lenthe, near Hanover. In 1832 he entered the Gymnasium in Lubeck. Three years later he became an officer cadet at the artillery and engineering school in Berlin, and from 1835 to 1838 studied mathematics, physics and chemistry.

As a serving officer he continued his studies and, in his spare time, he made many practical scientific inventions. He invented a process for gold- and silver-plating and a method for providing the wire in a telegraph system with a seemless insulation using gutta-percha. Other inventions included the ozone tube, an alcohol meter, and an electric standard or resistance based on mercury.

In 1847, Siemens founded with Johan Halske, the firm of Siemens-Halske to manufacture and construct telegraph systems. The company was responsible for constructing extensive systems in Germany and Russia. In 1870, the firm laid the London-Calcutta telegraph line and later became involved in underwater cable telegraphy. In Britain, Siemens became scientific consultant to the British government and helped to design the first cable-laying ship, the *Faraday*.

Valuing the contribution science was already making to technological advancement, Siemens helped to establish scientific standards of measurement and was mainly responsible for establishing the Physickalische-Technische Reichsastalt in Berlin in 1887. He was also co-founder of the Physical Society. His contributions to science were rewarded with a honorary doctorate from the University of Berlin in 1860. He was elected member of the Berlin Academy of Science in 1873 and became a German nobleman in 1888. In 1889 Siemens retired from active involvement with his firm. He died on 6 December 1892 in Charlottenberg.

Siemens' genius for invention was developed on a very wide scale through the firm he established in Germany with Halske and also through the firm of Siemens Brothers which had been established in England. In 1846 he succeeded in improving the Wheatstone telegraph, making it self-acting by using 'make-and-break' contacts. He subsequently developed an entire telegraph system which included the seamless insulation of the wire. The firm obtained government contracts to provide extensive telegraph networks in Germany. But because of disagreements these Prussian contracts were cancelled in 1850, so Siemens went to Russia and established an extensive telegraph network there - one which included the line used during the Crimean War.

His greatest single achievement was the discovery of the dynamo principle. Siemens announced his discovery to the Berlin Academy of Science in 1867. He had already introduced the double-T aramature and had succeeded in connecting the armature, the electromagnetic field and the external load of an electric generator in a single current. This enabled manufacturers to dispense with the very costly permanent magnets previously used. Unlike other workers in the field, including Wheatstone and Varley, Siemens forsaw the use of his dynamo in machines involving heavy currents. This enabled his companies to become pioneers in the development of electric traction - including for street cars and mini-locomotives and -also in electricity generating stations.

Againunlike some inventor-engineers of his time, Siemens valued the contribution that science could make to practical engineering advancement. He advocated that technique should be based on scientific theory. He often published analyses of his telegraph and cable-laying technology in reports to the Berlin Academy of Science. He also maintained that a nation, in times of harsh international competition, would never maintain its status in the world if it did not base its technology on continuing research work.

Sikorsky, Igor *(1889-1972)*, was a Russian-born American aeronautical engineer, one of the great pioneers of aircraft design. He built the first multi-engined aeroplane, was the designer of a famous series of large passenger flying-boats, and built the first practical helicopter.

Sikorsky was born in Kiev, Russia on the 25 May 1889. His father was Professor of Psychology at Kiev University. He was brought up in a cultured family atmosphere and developed an interest in art and a particular fondness for the life and works of Leonardo da Vinci. During his studies of Leonardo he came across the well-known design for a helicopter. Early in his life he developed an interest in model aeroplanes, and when he was 12 he built a small rubber-powered helicopter which could actually fly. In 1903, at the age of 14, he entered the Russian Naval Academy for a career as an officer in the navy. Three years later he resigned because he wanted to devote his time to practical mechanical pursuits. He went first to Paris, where he studied briefly, and then entered the Kiev Polytechnic Institute. After only a year he left these studies because he wished to be a practical engineer, and he found the gap between the theoretical studies of physics and practical engineering too wide. His family was rich and he was not short of money; he equipped his own experimental workshop and attempted to develop his ideas.

In 1908 he spent the summer in France and came into contact with Wilbur Wright (1867-1912) and the new interest in aviation which his French trip had stimulated. He returned to Kiev, believing that he could build a helicopter with a horizontal rotor which would rise straight up into the air, and show that fixed wings were not necessary for flight. The following January he went to Paris to buy a suitable engine for his new machine, and in May 1909 he began to construct his first helicopter. Structural difficulties and the weight of the engine led him to begin work on a second, improved machine. This helicopter did not fly either, and he his attempts were abandoned until materials and engines were available which would make his designs practicable became available.

He decided to concentrate his efforts on fixed-wing aeroplanes and soon built his first biplane, the S1, with a 15hp engine. It was underpowered, but with a larger engine his S2 made a short flight. With these early designs he began the practice of taking the controls on the first flight, which he was to continue throughout his career as a designer and builder of aeroplanes. The same year, 1910, two more designs were built. In 1911 his S5 aeroplane with a 50hp engine flew for more than an hour and achieved altitudes of 450m (1,500ft). His cross-country flights enabled him to obtain an International Pilot's Licence (No. 64). By now he had achieved recognition and his next aeroplanes had military applications: the S6 was offered to the army. His famous aeroplanes *Le Grand* and the even larger *Ilia Mourometz* had four engines, upholstered seats, an enclosed cabin for crew and passengers and even a toilet. They became the basis for the four-engined bomber that Russia used during World War I.

After the War and the Russian Revolution, Sikorsky emigrated to the United States but found it difficult to gain a foothold in American aviation. After a number of years as a teacher and lecturer he founded the Sikorsky Aero Engineering Corporation on a farm on Long Island, and when this company showed promise it was taken over by the United Aircraft Corporation. This arrangement allowed Sikorsky a lot of freedom and gave him the money to build new aeroplanes. In 1929 he produced the twin-engined S38 *Amphibian*, and by 1931 the S40 *American Clipper* was in production. This large flying-boat allowed Pan American Airways to develop routes in the Carribean and South America. In 1937 the even larger S42 *Clipper III* was built. But with the coming of World War II and the demise of the flying-boat as the most popular method of passenger transport, Sikorsky again took up the idea of a helicopter.

1939 saw the construction of the VS300 helicopter. The new materials and expertise made his design practical, and on the 14 September 1939 Sikorsky piloted his helicopter a few feet into the air; the machine had a 4-cylinder 75hp air-cooled engine, driving a 8.2m (28ft) three-bladed rotor. In May 1941 an endurance record of more than 90 minutes was set by a Sikorsky helicopter, and in 1943 the R3, the world's first production helicopter, was flown. There quickly followed a whole series of production designs using one, then two, piston engines. With their usefulness for rescue and transport work in inaccessible or densely populated places helicopters came into their own and were designed for specific purposes. Later Sikorsky models had distinguished military service in Korea. During the late 1950s piston engines were replaced by the newly developed gas turbine engines as the source of power, and helicopters were built for even more rugged duties.

In 1957 Sikorsky retired as engineering manager from his company. During his lifetime he had received many honours. He married in 1924 and had been proud to become an American citizen in 1928. After a lifetime's devoted to aviation he died at Easton, Connecticut, on the 26 October 1972.

Singer, Isaac Merrit *(1811-1875)*, was an American inventor. His name will always be associated with the domestic sewing machine, which became such a feature of 'every good home' in the late 1800s.

Singer was born in Pittstown, New York, on 27 October 1811. He began his career simply enough as an apprentice machinist, and during his early working life patented a rock-drilling machine and, later, a metal- and wood-carving one. It was while he was employed in a machine shop in Boston that his main chance arrived. One day he was asked to carry out some repairs to a Lerow and Blodgett sewing machine. Singer not only did that, but at the same time decided he could add many improvements to the design. Eleven days later he produced a new model which he patented under his own name.

Litigation against his patent followed from Elias Howe, another maker, who claimed Singer had used his patented stitch method. Although Howe eventually won the case, Singer was already in production with his machine, having formed the I.M Singer Company in 1851 and, as a measure of his machine's success, his business went from strength to strength. Singer had formed a partnership with an Edward Clark in the June of 1851, and by 1860 the company was the largest sewing machine manufacturers in the world. In 1863 Singer and Clark formed the Singer Manufacturing Company and Singer retired to England where he settled in Torquay, Devon.

Sewing as a means of constructing clothes dates back to prehistoric times when bone needles were used to stitch skins together. From that, man progressed to using an awl with which to first make a hole, followed by a type of crochet needle for the stitch. The use of a steel sewing needle appears to have originated in the sixteenth century and hand sewing continued as the only method of stitching up to the end of the eighteenth century when inventive minds turned their attention to this domestic chore.

Barthelemy Thimonnier of France is credited with devising the first practical sewing machine as a means of speeding up the production of the Army's uniforms in 1841. By 1845, Elias Howe in the United States had designed his answer, the first lock-stitch machine, using a threaded needle and shuttle (bobbin). When Singer patented his improved machine in 1851, he used the best of Howe's design and altered some of the other features. The basic mechanism was the same, however: as the handle turned, the needle paused at a certain point in its stroke so that the shuttle could pass through the loop formed in the cotton. When the needle continued the threads were tightened, forming a secure stitch.

Singer's machines were very popular (and still are) and his marketing, aimed at the ordinary family - he introduced the first instalment plant payment system - was such a success that by 1869 more than 110,000 sewing machines had been produced for the American market alone.

Smeaton, John *(1724-1792)*, was a British civil engineer who rebuilt the Eddystone Lighthouse in 1759, but who was also greatly influential in directing the scientific research which was being carried out in the mid-eighteenth century. It was he who first adopted the term 'civil engineer' in contra-distinction to the fast-growing number of military engineers graduating from the Military Colleges.

Smeaton was born of Scottish ancestry in Austhorpe, near Leeds. He was encouraged to practise law, and after a good elementary education he served in his father's firm of solicitors. Later he went to London for further training in the Courts of Justice, but his natural inclination for mechanical science led him to leave law and become a maker of scientific instruments.

He soon introduced many technical innovations - one of which was a novel instrument with which he was able to measure and study the expansion characteristics of various materials. From 1756 to 1759 he was engaged in the rebuilding of the Eddystone Lighthouse. He was also a consultant in the field of structural engineering, and from 1757 onwards he was responsible for many engineering projects including bridges, power stations operated by water or wind, steam engines, and river and harbour facilities.

He was a charter member of the first professional engineering society founded in 1771, the Society of Civil Engineers which, after his death, became known as the Smeatonian Society. He was a Fellow of the Royal Society and, in 1759, received its Copley Medal. He died on 28 October 1792, at Austhorpe.

Although Smeaton's best known achievement was the rebuilding of Eddystone, his main contribution to engineering was his innovative ability to combine engineering with applied science. His work on waterwheels and windmills served to underline the importance of scientific research to practical engineering problems. It was his own research work that led him to question the relative efficiency of the, then, firmly-established undershot waterwheel (which operates through the action of the flow of water against blades in the wheel) and the overshot wheel (which is operated by water moving the wheel by the force of its weight).

Experimenting with models, Smeaton showed that overshot wheels were twice as efficient as undershot ones. He went further and speculated on the cause of this difference in efficiency. From his experiments, he concluded that the loss of 'mechanic power' in the undershot wheel was caused by turbulence, which he described as the loss of power by water and other non-elastic bodies in changing their 'figure' in consequence of their 'stroke'. Thus, only part of their original power is communicated when acting by impulse or collision.

In 1759 Smeaton presented his important paper to the Royal Society, 'An experimental enquiry concerning the natural power of water and wind to turn mills and other machines depending on a circular motion'. This paper was followed by two others, one on the necessary mechanical power to be employed in giving different degrees of velocity to heavy bodies from a state of rest, and the other on some 'fundamental experiments upon the collision of bodies'

Smeaton's work, with its emphasis on scientific investigation into practical engineering problems, provided one of the first examples of the interdependence of engineering and applied science. This led to other designers adopting his approach. (One early result of this was that the undershot waterwheel was abandoned as uneconomical.) It also lent a sense of urgency to the recurrent controversy raging at the time over the measure of force, in the discussions of which Smeaton's own research findings played a prominent role.

Later on in life Smeaton performed extensive tests on the experimental steam engine of Thomas Newcomen (1663-1729). These tests led to significant improvements in its design and efficiency.

Sperry, Elmer Ambrose *(1860-1930)* was the US inventor and engineer who exploited the technology of the gyroscope to develop the first commercially successful gyrostabilizer for ships, and the gryocompass and gyro-controlled autopilot for aircraft and ships. In doing this work he laid the foundations for modern control theory, cybernetics and automation.

Sperry was born on 21 October 1860, the son of Stephen Sperry, a farmer of Cortland county, New York, and Mary Burst from nearby Cincinatus who died soon after his birth. He attended the Cortland Normal School until January 1880 and then made informal arrangements to sit in on lectures at nearby Cornell and at the same time to develop his first invention (a generator with characteristics suited to arc lighting).

Sperry married Zula Goodman on 28 June 1887 and the following year set up his own research and development enterprise. He formed a mining machinery company and, moving to Cleveland, Ohio in 1893, developed and manufactured streetcars. He produced a superior storage battery, teaching himself chemistry in the process. He perfected a process for the production of caustic soda and was closely involved in a complicated process for the de-tinning of scrap from tin can manufacture.

The family moved to Brooklyn in 1907 and in the same year his interest in the gyroscope began to show itself, leading to the work for which he is best known. Sperry's gyroscope company, from a research and development concern, gradually evolved into a manufacturing organization and World War I brought a dramatic upsurge in foreign sales.

Sperry was also active in internal combustion engine research. He spent $1 million on a compounded diesel but the idea never came to fruition. He developed a track recorder car for detecting substandard railway track and went on to invent a device for revealing defective rails which were undetectable visually.

Sperry resigned as President of the Sperry Gyroscope Company in 1926 to become Chairman of the Board. During his lifetime he and his company filed about 360 patent applications which finally matured as patents. His wife died on 11 March 1930 and Sperry died in Brooklyn on 16 June the same year.

A gyroscope's major active component is a rapidly spinning wheel. This follows the natural laws of motion and inertia so that if its spindle is moved in one direction it will respond by forcing the spindle to move at right angles to the original direction of motion. This behaviour is called precession.

A considerable amount of work had already been done in Europe and the USA on gyrostabilization and in 1908 Sperry filed a massive patent application for a ship's gyroscope. It encapsulated the principle of an active system rather than the passive systems already used by Ernst Otto Schlick, a well-known naval engineer from Hamburg.

Sperry's scheme mounted the gyro with its axis vertical in the hold of the ship. The axis was free to move in a fore and aft direction, but not from side to side. He used an electric motor to precess the gyro (tilt its rotor) artificially just as the ship began to roll. The gyro responded by exerting a force to one side or the other. Since it was fixed rigidly to the ship in the plane, the ship's roll was largely counteracted.

In 1912 a full-sized prototype with two gyro wheels, each weighing 1814.4kg (4,000lb), was installed in the USS *Worden*, a 433-ton torpedo-boat destroyer. The installation cut a total roll of 30° to about 6°

A gyrocompass feels the force of gravity and precesses until the axis of rotation of the spinning wheel is parallel to the axis of rotation of the Earth. On a ship, however, the pendulous gyro will also sense the ship's motion so it precesses away from the meridian. Sperry solved this problem by incorporating a servomechanism and a mechanical analogue computer which together compensated for the unwanted inputs.

Dr Hermann Anschutz-Kaempfe (1872-1931) installed a system in the German fleet's flagship, *Deutschland*, in 1908. The prototype Sperry unit was fitted to the Dominion Line ship, *Princess Anne*, early in 1911 and the first production unit went into the USS *Utah* in November the same year.

The Sperry aircraft stabiliser had two components - one providing roll control and the other pitch control. Each unit opened compressed air valves, admitting air to slave cylinders. The pistons acted on the aircraft's controls to correct the error.

The roll component of the equipment was first flown in a Curtiss aircraft, with Curtiss himself at the controls, on Thanksgiving Day 1912. In the winter of 1913-1914 the Sperrys, father and son, designed and built an improved unit in which the four gyros were mounted together on a single stable platform. This arrangement has since become an essential component of guidance systems for missiles, aircraft and submarines.

The problems of blind-flying instruments proved to be extrememly tough and by the end of World War I virtually the only workable gyro instrument was for indicating rate of turn. The all-important gryocompass and artificial horizon eluded Sperry himself and his research teams due to the rapid accelerations of aircraft in bumpy air.

At the instigation of the US forces, Sperry designed the control equipment for a specially built Curtiss pilotless aircraft which was to deliver a 453.6kg (1,000lb) load of explosives to a target 80-160km (50-100 miles) away. This was officially called the 'flying bomb', thus anticipating the V-1s of World War II and the cruise missiles of the early 1980s.

After the War Sperry turned his attention to marine autopilots and a trial installation on an oil tanker performed well. Sales of the equipment increased until 1,000 merchant ships were so equipped by 1932.

Sperry introduced many of the concepts which are common in modern control theory. He did not use present-day jargon to describe his innovations but nevertheless he was one of the first in the fields of cybernetics and automation.

Stephenson, George *(1781-1848)*, was a British engineer who pioneered the building of the first railways in Britain and of steam locomotives to run on them.

Stephenson was born at Wylam, a village near Newcastle-upon-Tyne, the son of a fireman. He received no formal education and was employed when a boy to look after cattle. When he was 14 years old he became an assistant fireman to his father at Darley Colliery. He was illiterate until the age of 17 when, frustrated by his inability to follow the daily newspaper reports of the Napoleonic Wars, he attended evening classes and learned to read and write.

In 1808, at a time when his prospects seemed so bleak that he seriously thought of emigrating, Stephenson took a contract to work the engine of the Killingworth pit. While there he regularly took the steam pumping engine to pieces in order to understand its construction. The reward came with his success in modifying a Newcomen engine which was performing its pumping function inefficiently, when in 1812, he was appointed enginewright to the colliery at £100 a year.

Stephenson's first invention was a safety lamp for miners. This device avoided the dangers of combustion by allowing the air to enter along narrow tubes. He demonstrated the success of his discovery by entering gas-infested tunnels at the Killingworth pit with perfect safety. The simultaneous development of a safety lamp by Humphry Davy (1778-1829) produced fierce and sometimes acrimonius controversy as to who was the real inventor, before it was accepted that both men had reached the same goal independently and by different approaches.

In 1811 John Blenkinsop (1783-1831) constructed a steam locomotive for hauling coal wagons in a Yorkshire colliery but the machine, which used toothed wheels on a racked track, was ponderous and unwieldy. At Wylam colliery they were now anxious to introduce steam power on the horse tramways, and Stephenson produced a smooth-wheeled locomotive called The Blucher which, in 1814, successfully drew 30 tonnes (29 tons) of coal in eight wagons up an incline of 1 in 150 at 4mph (6.6km/h). Not satisfied, Stephenson introduced the 'steam blast' by which exhaust steam was redirected into the chimney through a blast pipe, bringing in air with it and increasing the draft through the fire. This further development made the locomotive truly practical.

Subsequently Stephenson started to make experiments with various gradients. He found that a slope of 1 in 200, common enough on roads, reduced the haulage power of a locomotive by 50 per cent (on a completely even surface, a tractive force of less than 5kg(10lb) would move a tonne or ton). Furthermore he discovered that friction

was virtually independent of speed. The obvious conclusion from such findings was that railway gradients should always be as low as possible. Cuttings, tunnels and embankments were therefore necessary. In 1819 the proprietors of Hetton Colliery, under Stephenson's direction, laid down a railway 11km (8 miles) long. It was opened in 1822, with traction provided partly by stationary engines and partly by locomotives.

In 1821 Stephenson succeeded in persuading Edward Pease, chief promotor of the scheme, that Stockton and Darlington could be better connected by steam locomotion than by the proposed horse traction. He was appointed engineer to the project and advocated the use of malleable iron rails instead of the cast iron which had been used hitherto. The gauge for the new railway was assessed by Stephenson at 1.4m (4ft 8in), a historic decision, since this has remained the 'standard gauge' for railways throughout the world.

Stephenson then induced Pease and Michael Longridge to support him and his son Robert in establishing locomotive works at Newcastle, where the engines were to be made for the Stockton and Darlington Railway. On 27 September 1825 the world's first public railway came into operation with the opening of the line. Stephenson's engine *Locomotion* took a party of passengers from Darlington at a top speed of 24km/h (15mph).

Before the Stockton and Darlington Railway was opened, Stephenson had been engaged to design a railway from Manchester to Liverpool, the trade between the towns having already grown too great to be accommodated on the existing canals. Surveyors for the projected railway met fierce opposition from the farmers and landowners through whose estates the railway was to run. A Bill to implement the scheme was thrown out by its opponents in Parliament, but a second Bill, introduced in 1826 (and showing an improved overall plan), was accepted. The greatest physical obstacle to Stephenson's plans was a large area of marshy ground known as Chat Moss. By distributing the load over a considerable surface of the bog Stephenson was able to take his line over the treacherous ground.

Having eventually convinced the railway directors that locomotives and not fixed engines should operate on the line, Stephenson took part in an open competition to discover the most efficient locomotive for the railway, the prize being £500. A mean speed of 16km/h (10mph) was to be attained and steam pressure was not to exceed 50psi ($3.3 \times 10^5 Nm^{-2}$).

Stephenson saw that if he was to succeed he had to find some means of increasing the heating surface of the boilers of his locomotives. He therefore adopted tubes passing through the cylindrical barrel and connecting the fire-box with the smoke-box. The engine Stephenson produced for the great trial, the *Rocket*, was built at the Newcastle works under the direct supervision of his son Robert, and after many failures the problem of securing the tubes to the tube-plates was overcome. The locomotive had a weight of 4.2 tonnes (4 tons) half the weight of *Locomotion*.

Three other engines were entered for the competition but basic inadequacy or ill-luck overtook them. On the testing day, the *Rocket*, the only engine ready on time, ran 19km (12 miles) in 53 minutes, and was duly awarded the prize. On 15 September 1830 the line was opened with great ceremony. If the Stockton and Darlington Railway announced the arrival of the steam locomotive, the Manchester and Liverpool Railway, providing the first regular passenger service, showed that it had come to stay. An unwelcome event on the opening day was the first railway accident in which William Huskisson, President of the Board of Trade, was killed. Ironically he had been Stephenson's most influential supporter in Parliament.

For the remainder of his life Stephenson worked as a consultant engineer to several newly emerging railway companies, all in the north of England or the Midlands. There was hardly a railway scheme in which he was not consulted or an important line constructed without his help and advice. The last great issue with which Stephenson was concerned arose in 1845, in the battle between the supporters of the locomotive and those who advocated the atmospheric railway system developed by Stephenson's great contemporary Isambard Brunel (1806-1859). The dispute arose in connection with the extension of the railway from Newcastle to Berwick. Although Brunel had many influential friends in the Board of Trade, Stephenson's supporters in Parliament were the more numerous and carried the day. This ended the last attempt to challenge the advent of the steam locomotive.

Stephenson, Robert *(1803-1859)*, the only son of George Stephenson (1781-1848), was an outstanding nineteenth-century British engineer and builder of many remarkable railway bridges.

Born at Willington Quay, near to Newcastle-upon-Tyne, Stephenson began his working life assisting his father in the survey of the Stockton and Darlington Railway in 1821. The following year he spent six months at Edinburgh University studying mathematics. He then returned to Newcastle to manage the locomotive factory which his father had established there. His health began to decline seriously, however, and seeking a warmer climate he accepted an offer to superintend some gold and silver mines in Columbia in South America. He was away three years, but difficulties in the management of the Newcastle locomotive factory led to a request for his return. He returned to England in 1827, when the controversy over the most suitable form of traction for the Liverpool and Manchester railway was at its height. The successful *Rocket* steam locomotive was eventually built under his personal direction, as were subsequent improvements to it.

In 1833 a scheme to construct a railway from Birmingham to London was introduced, and Stephenson became engineer for the line. The project was very important, being the first railway to be taken into the capital. Stephenson overcame with outstanding engineering skill many of the obstacles encountered, notably with the Blisworth cutting and the Kilsby tunnel. The railway was completed in 1838, and from then on he was engaged on railway work for the rest of his life.

Probably the most important and certainly the most conspicuous of Stephenson's achievements were the various railway bridges which he built in Britain and elsewhere. The High Level Bridge over the river Tyne in Newcastle and the Victoria Bridge over the river Tweed at Berwick are among his earliest and most striking achievements. The former, spanning the river between Gateshead and Newcastle, comprises six iron arches; James Nasmyth's newly invented steam hammer was used to drive in its foundations. In 1844 construction began, under Stephenson's supervision, of a railway line from Chester to Holyhead. He gave long and detailed thought to the best type of bridges for crossing the river Conway and the Menai Straits between the mainland and Anglesey. For the Menai Straits he designed a bridge in which the railway tracks were completely enclosed in parallel iron tubes. This proved so successful when put into service that the same plan was adopted for other bridges. One such, the Victoria Bridge over the St Lawrence at Montreal, was constructed by Stephenson between the years 1854 and 1859, and was for many years the longest bridge in the world.

Stirling, Robert *(1790-1878)*, was the Scottish minister of the Church of Scotland who is credited with the invention of a working hot-air engine. The principle has a large number of inherent advantages that could make it as important as the internal combustion engine, so intensive research is being carried out on the Stirling engine.

Stirling was born in Cloag, Scotland on 25 October 1790. He attended Glasgow and Edinburgh universities, studying advanced Latin and Greek, logic and mathematics, metaphysics and rhetoric. He was licensed to preach by the Presbytery of Dunbarton in 1815 and was ordained to the Ministry in 1816. In the same year he took out his patent on the air engine and heat regenerator. The patent was also signed by his younger brother, James, who was in fact a mechanical engineer. It seems probable, therefore, that Robert had the idea for the engine and James developed it.

Robert also designed and made scientific instruments and various other patents relating to air engines in the names of R and J Stirling were granted over the years, the last being in 1840.

In 1819 Robert Stirling married Jane, eldest daughter of William Rankine, a wine merchant at Galston, and 5 years later became minister of the church there. Early in 1840 St Andrew's University awarded him an honorary degree of Doctor of Divinity. He remained at Galston for the rest of his life, retiring in 1876 and dying two years later.

There were several patents for air engines before Stirling's first patent of 1816 but it is doubtful if any of them would have worked, with the probable exception of that of Sir George Cayley.

The Stirling cycle engine differs from the internal combustion engine in that the working fluid (in Stirling's case, air) remains in the working chambers. The heat is applied from an external source, so virtually any fuel, from wood to nuclear fuel, can be used. It also means that combustion can be made to take place under the best conditions, making the control of emissions (pollution) considerably easier. The burning of the fuel is continuous, not intermittent as in an internal combustion engine, so there is less noise and vibration.

Another advantage is the high theoretical thermal efficiency; in practice thermal efficiencies of Stirling engines of different designs are better than those of conventional diesel engines.

There are many arrangements for Stirling engines but the essential factor is that they use what is effectively 2 pistons to push the working fluid between 2 working spaces. One space is kept at a high temperature by the heat source and the other at a low temperature. Between these 2 spaces is a regenerator which alternately receives and gives up heat to the working fluid.

The pistons are connected to a mechanism which keeps them out of phase (usually by 90o). It is this differential motion which moves the working fluid from one space to the other. On its way to the hot space the fluid passes through the regenerator, gaining heat. In the hot space it gains more heat and expands, giving power. After the power stroke the fluid is pushed back through the regenerator, where it gives up its residual heat into the cold space and is ready to start the cycle again.

Stirling's first engine appeared in 1818. It had a vertical cylinder about 0.60 metres (10ft) in diameter. It produced about 1.49kW (2hp) pumping water from a quarry and ran for 2 years before the hot sections of the cylinder burnt out. This burning out is a problem which has plagued virtually every engine of the type ever since.

In 1824 the brothers started work on improved engines and in 1843 converted a steam engine at a Dundee factory to operate as a Stirling engine. It is said to have produced 27.6kW (37hp) and to have used less coal per unit of power than the steam design it replaced. In any event, the hot parts burned out continually after a few months, and after several replacements it was re-converted to steam.

The type lived on, however, until well into the next century and was used extensively for powering small pumps and similar domestic applications. Improved Otto cycle engines and the standardization and spread of electricity supplies helped to establish the small electric motor and led to the Stirling engine's eventual demise.

Steel was not to become common until after 1860 when Bessemer built his steelworks in Sheffield. Now even steel is not considered suitable for the high temperatures the engine requires for greatest efficiency.

The renaissance of the Stirling engine began in 1938 in the Philips laboratories in the Netherlands. In the early 1890s most effort was directed towards developing the principle for automotive applications. A joint Ford/Philips programme resulted in a Stirling-engined vehicle which was cleaner and had a fuel economy from 9 to 35 per cent better than the conventionally engined car.

The Stirling engine has yet to live up to its promise. Possibly the greatest hurdle is the huge investment already made in conventional internal combustion engines. For them to be deposed, the Stirling principle will have to show substantial advantages in most respects.

Sturgeon, William *(1783-1850)*, was a British physicist and inventor who made the first electromagnets.

Sturgeon was born on 22 May 1783, at Whittington, Lancashire, the son of a shoemaker. Sturgeon was himself apprenticed to a shoemaker in 1796, but in 1802 went into the army (militia) and two years later enlisted in the Royal Artillary. He studied natural sciences in the evenings, but in 1820 (at the age of 37) he again went back to shoemaking and set up a business in Woolwich. He became a member of the Woolwich Literary Society and in 1824 became lecturer in science and philosophy at the East India Royal Military College of Addiscombe. In 1832 he was appointed to the lecturing staff of the Adelaide Gallery of Practical Science, and in 1840 he moved to Manchester to become superintendent of the Royal Victoria Gallery of Practical Science. At this time, as an itinerant lecturer he was able to support his family from an income. He became a member of the Manchester Literary and Philosophical Society, and through the influence of the president of the society received a grant of £200 from Lord Russell. In 1849 he was granted an annuity of £50 to promote his work on electromagnetism, but he died in the following year on 4 December at Prestwick, Manchester.

Sturgeon was the founder of electromagnetism, and the first English-language journal to be devoted wholey to electricity was started by him. His scientific work only began in earnest when he returned to civilian life at the age of 37, although he had carried out occasional electrical experiments in Woolwich where he had developed various mechanical skills which were useful for making scientific apparatus, and was often in demand to lecture to schools and other groups.

In 1828 he put into practice the idea of a solenoid, first proposed by André Ampère (1775-1836), by wrapping about 18 turns of wire round an iron core so that they became magnetic when a current was passed through them. He found that each coil reinforced the next, since they effectively formed a set of parallel wires with the current moving in the same direction through all of them. He also noticed that the magnetic field seemed to be concentrated in the iron core and that it disappeared as soon as the current was switched off. He varnished the core to insulate it and keep it from short-circuiting the wires, and also tried using a core that was bent into a horse-shoe shape. (Joseph Henry (1797-1878) was later to insulate the wires themselves.) His device was capable of lifting 20 times its own weight.

He later invented an important new galvanometer. Sturgeon was one of a small group of lecturers and instrument makers who worked at demonstrating electrical science in new ways. In 1836 he established a monthly periodical *Annals of Electricity*, which ran into 10 volumes, ending in 1843. He then founded *Annals of Philosophical Discovery* and *Monthly Report of Progress of Science and Art* which terminated at the end of the same year. They were nevertheless landmarks, being the first electrical journals ever to be published in English.

Sutherland, Ivan Edward *(1938-   )*, is an American electronics engineer who pioneered the development of computer graphics, the method by which computers display pictorial (as opposed to alpha-numeric) information on a visual display unit (VDU).

Sutherland was born in Hastings, Nebraska, on 16 May 1938. His university education began at the Carnegie Institute of Technology, where he obtained a bachelor's degree in 1959, and continued at the Massachusetts Institute of Technology (MIT) where he obtained a master's degree in 1960 and a PhD in electrical engineering in 1963. He was then called into the US Army Signals Corps. In 1964 he became director of information processing techniques at the Advanced Research Projects Center of the Department of Defense. He stayed in this position until 1966 when he was appointed associate professor of electrical engineering at Harvard University. Two years later he moved to Salt Lake City, to a position as associate professor at the University of Utah, and there founded the Evans and Sutherland Computer Corporation. He became a full professor at Utah in 1972, but left in 1976 to become Fletcher Jones professor of computer science and head of department at the California Institute of Technology.

From 1960 to 1963 he worked in the Lincoln Laboratory at the MIT on the 'Sketchpad' project. This was the first system of computer graphics which could be altered by the operator in the course of its use for calculation and design. Sketchpad used complex arrangements of the data fed into the computer to produce representations of the objects in space as well as fine geometrical detail. Programs could be altered using light-pens, which touch the surface of the VDU.

While at Utah, Sutherland was engaged in the design of a colour graphics system able to represent fine distinctions of colour as well as accurate perspective. The image could be moved, rotated, expanded or made smaller to give a realistic image of the object, rendering the computer suitable for use in engineering and architectural design.

of displaying equipment, the arrangement of large integrated circuits, and the development of new high-performance computing machinery. He is particularly interested in the interaction between the computer and its operators, and in finding methods for the rapid solution of special problems.

Swan, Joseph Wilson *(1828-1914)*, was a British inventor and electrical engineer - trained originally as a chemist who invented an incandescent electric lamp. He also made major contributions to photographic processing, and lesser ones to electroplating methods, electrolytic cells, and the production of artificial fibres.

Swan was born on 31 October 1828 in

Sunderland. For a time during his childhood his parents allowed him to roam about Sunderland, where he became fascinated with the busy industries, towns and ports. Eventually he was sent to a 'dame school' run by three old ladies, and from there he went to a large school under the direction of Dr Wood, a Scottish minister. When he left school he became apprenticed to a Sunderland firm of retail chemists. Before his apprenticeship was finished both partners in the business died. Joseph then went to join his brother-in-law, John Mawson, in his chemical firm at Newcastle-upon-Tyne. During these times he was fascinated by scientific and engineering inventions, and he attended lectures and read books and journals which described them. It was then that he learned of the early interest in the electric lamp of J.W Starr and W.E Staite.

Swan quickly proved his worth and soon the firm was producing photographic chemicals. He developed a deep interest in the photographic process, making an experimental study of the various methods. One particular wet process for producing photographic prints, using a gelatine film impregnated with carbon or other pigment granules and photosensitized using potassium dichromate, was patented by Swan in 1864. This was known as the carbon or autotype process. A few years later, in 1879, he invented and patented a bromide printing paper, now a standard photographic medium.

Swan's interest in electric lighting is said to stem from a lecture given by Staite in Sunderland in 1845. From about 1848 he began making filaments by cutting strips of cardboard or paper and baking them at high temperatures to produce a carbon fibre. The recipes he used were often exotic, sometimes entailing cooking with syrup of tar. These filaments were made into coils or circles. In making the first lamps he connected the ends of a filament to wire (itself a difficult task), placed the filament in a glass bottle, and attempted to evacuate the air and seal the bottle with a cork. Usually the filament burned away very quickly in the remaining air, blackening the glass at the same time.

In 1865 the German chemist Hermann Sprengel (1834-1906) invented a mercury vacuum pump, which was used to evacuate the air from radiometer tubes produced by William Crookes (1832-1919). Swan read of Crookes' work and saw the pump as a means of producing an improved vacuum for his lamps. He came across Charles Stearn, who had become familiar with the technique of producing a vacuum using Sprengel's pump, when he read a newspaper advertisement. Swan them produced filaments for Stearn to use to make lamps using the Sprengel pump.

Although their first experiments were not very successful they found that, if after first producing the best possible vacuum a strong current was passed to make the filament burn brightly, and if the bulb was further evacuated (thus drawing out the products of the combustion of the carbon with the remnants of the air), then a fairly durable incandescent lamp was produced. Swan demonstrated his electric light and exhibited it throughout the north-east of England in 1878 and 1879, at the same time producing a new type of filament from cotton thread partly dissolved by sulphuric acid.

From the summer of 1880 onwards, Swan's electric lamps were manufactured. First they were made in a factory in Benwell, Newcastle-upon-Tyne, but soon a larger London company was formed. Thomas Edison (1847-1931), famous for his electrical inventions (including the phonograph), developed an electric light on a similar principle to Swan's. Edison was quick to take out patents while Swan hesitated. In 1882 he initiated litigation for patent infringement against Swan, but this was dismissed and the joint company Edison and Swan United Electric Light Company came into being in 1883.

In the 1880s electrical supply was in its infancy. there were few electric companies, and those which did exist distributed over very small areas; usually electricity users had their own generators. But the availability of the electric lamp had a great stimulus on the electricity industry, first in public buildings and the private residences of a few notables and then, within a few years, in shops, factories, offices and ships of the Merchant and Royal Navy. Also its potential for advertising was soon recognized.

Swan did not rest to merely reap the financial rewards of his invention. He made a miner's electric safety lamp which, although far too costly to be adopted at the time, was the ancestor of the modern miner's lamp. In the course of this invention he devised a new lead cell (battery) which would not spill acid. He had a life-long interest in electrical cells, and attempted to make an early type of fuel cell.

In the course of developing a method of producing uniform carbon filaments, Swan devised a process in which nitrocellulose (made by nitrating cotton) was dissolved in acetic acid and extruded through a fine die. This process had obvious advantages in producing lighting filaments, but it was also seen by Swan to be capable of producing an artificial silk. His wife and daughter crocheted some of the material and it was exhibited as 'artifical silk' at an exhibition in 1885, but Swan never considered commercial production.

Throughout his life Swan was an ardent and determined experimenter, with interests ranging from photography to electroplating. He carried out a very extensive study of the best conditions for the electro-deposition of copper and a number of other metals. Many of his discoveries were of practical use, and he took out more than 70 patents. He was elected a Fellow of the Royal Society in 1894, and 10 years later he was knighted. He held high offices in a number of professional societies and was in receipt of medals from both the Royal Society and the Royal Photographic Society. He died at home in Warlingham, Surrey, on 27 May 1914, aged 85.

Swinburne, James *(1858-1958)*, was one of the leading pioneers in electrical engineering and plastics.

Swinburne was born at Inverness, Scotland, on 28 February 1858. He was the third of six sons of a naval captain and spent most of his childhood on the lonely island of Eileen Shona, in Lock Mordart, where the common spoken language was Gaelic. Eventually he was sent to study at Clifton College, where the accent was on science subjects, a bias Swinburne's talents were quick to appreciate.

Swinburne began his career in engineering with an apprenticeship to a locomotive works in Manchester, after which he travelled to Tyneside and found employment with an engineering firm. It was during this time that his lifelong interest in electrical engineering developed, and in 1881 Sir Joseph Swan engaged him to take responsibility for setting up a new factory in Paris for the manufacture of Swan's electric lamps. Swinburne carried out the task so successfully that in the following year Swan sent him to the United States to set up a factory there. From 1885 Swinburne was employed as technical assistant to Rookes Crompton, at his Chelmsford factory. He worked on many aspects of electrical engineering and was particularly involved in the development of dynamos and the well-known 'hedgehog' transformer.

In 1894, Swinburne decided to set up his own laboratory and made himself available as a consultant. Some of the research carried out in his laboratory focussed on the reaction between phenol and formaldehyde and its commercial potential. Unfortunately when Swinburne came to patent the product in 1907 he was beaten to the idea by the Belgium chemist Leo Baekland (with his invention of Bakelite). Swinburne was able to obtain a patent on the production of a laquer, however, and set up his own manufacturing concern, Damard Laquer Company, in Birmingham. Baekland bought him out in the early 1920s and formed Bakelite Limited, Great Britain, of which Swinburne became the first chairman, a position he maintained until 1948. From then until his re-

tirement in 1951 he remained on its board of directors.

Swinburne lived to be 100 years old and was greatly respected by the scientific and industrial world, being affectionately known as 'The Father of British Plastics'

It was in the 1880s that the great march of electrical progress began to gather momentum. Swan and his filament lamp inspired the idea of using electicity for domestic purposes, and other great engineers concentrated on the development of heavier equipment such as dynamos and transformers. When Swinburne joined Crompton's team the impetus was reaching its peak, with many of the problems in electrical engineering being solved and with modifications being made to existing ideas.

Swinburne's own contributions were wide-ranging and included the invention of the watt-hour meter and the 'hedgehog' transformer for stepping up medium voltage alternating current to high voltages for long-distance power transmission. He was also responsible for numerous other smaller inventions and for work on the theory of dynamos. The words 'motor' and 'stator', thought to have been coined by him, are now in common use in electrical engineering.

T

Talbot, William Henry Fox *(1800-1877)* was the English classical scholar, mathematician and scientist who invented the calotype (or talbotype) photographic process. This was a negative-to-positive process on paper which laid the foundation for modern photography.

Talbot was born on 11 February 1800 at Melbury, Dorset, to William Davenport Talbot, an officer in the Dragoons, and Lady Elizabeth Fox Strangeways, daughter of the second Earl of Ilchester. He was educated at Harrow and Trinity College, Cambridge, and was elected Liberal Member of Parliament for Chippenham, taking his seat in 1833. During a trip to Italy he resolved to try to capture the images obtained in a camera obscura and by 1835 had succeeded in fixing outlines of objects laid on sensitized paper. Images of his home, Lacock Abbey, followed and Talbot then appeared to give up his experiments until the announcement of Daguerre's (1789-1851) success on 7 January 1839.

Talbot rushed into publication in case

Daguerre's process was the same as his own (there were similarities). He exhibited his work at the Royal Institution and again at the Royal Society on 31 January where he presented a hastily prepared paper. Some of the exhibits were positives and were probably taken between 1835 and 1839.

To publicize his process, Talbot set up a laboratory for printing calotypes in Reading. This produced *The Pencil of Nature*, the first book in the world to be illustrated by photographs. It came out irregularly in 6 parts, beginning 29 June 1844, each part containing from 3 to 7 photographs. Other books followed.

Talbot patented an enlarger in June 1843 and took the first successful photograph by electric light. This was also the first successful motion-freezing photograph taken by flash and it was demonstrated at the Royal Institution in 1851. He applied the principle of dichromate and gelatine to photoglyphic engraving and tried to lay claim to the collodion process. Squabbling over this claim culminated in a court case in which on 20 December 1854 it was found that collodion photography did not infringe calotype patents.

In parallel with his photographic work, Talbot was giving papers at Royal Society meetings, many of them on mathematical and scientific subjects. He published papers on archaeology and, with Sir Henry Rawlinson and Dr Edward Hincks, was one of the first to decipher the cuneiform inscriptions of Nineveh. He was also the author of *English Etymologies*. He died at Lacock Abbey on 17 September 1877.

Talbot's calotype process was patented on 8 February 1841. Good-quality writing paper was coated successively with solutions of silver nitrate and potassium iodide, forming silver iodide. The iodized paper was made more sensitive by brushing with solutions of gallic acid and silver nitrate, and then it was exposed (either moist or dry). The latent image was developed with an application of gallo-silver nitrate solution, and when the image became visible the paper was warmed for 1-2 minutes. It was fixed with a solution of potassium bromide (later replaced by sodium hyposulphite). Calotypes did not have the sharp definition of daguerreotypes and were generally considered inferior.

In the decade to 1851, Talbot took out 4 patents, many of which contained previously published claims. He stirred up considerable resentment by his activities, which are considered to have hindered the development of photography in England. However on 30 July 1852 he announced that he wished only to retain licensing on professional portraiture. This cleared the way for amateurs to use processes developed in other countries.

Telford, Thomas *(1757-1834)*, was a Scottish civil engineer, famous for building roads and bridges. He was also the first president the Institute of Civil Engineers.

Telford was born at Westerkirk, Dumfries, on 9 August 1757, the son of a shepherd. He began his career as a stonemason, but despite his humble origins he had strong ambition and educated himself in architecture in his spare time. In search of work he travelled to London and found employment building the additions to Somerset House in the Strand under the supervision of Sir William Chambers. Recognizing his talents, the rich and famous were soon consulting him about their own buildings and consequently he was launched upon a career which was to make him into one of the outstanding civil engineers of that time.

In 1786 Telford was appointed Official Surveyor to the county of Shropshire. This proved to be the start of 30 years' intense construction work for different organizations, dealing with anything and everything requiring his particular skills. He was responsible for reconstructing roads, building canals, aqueducts and harbours, erecting suspension bridges and surveying railway lines, but above all he will be remembered for the Menai Bridge which must remain his most famous achievement.

The state of the roads in Britain during the eighteenth century depended very much on the individual Turnpike Trust and whether it chose to pay for repairs. Telford and his contemporary, John McAdam, set about re-building the existing Roman routes, digging down to the foundations of these roads and levelling them to meet the need for faster travel. It was recorded that after such work had been carried out on a road, a mail coach could attain speeds on it up to 19km/h (12 mph) and could average at least 13km/h (8 mph).

In 1793 Telford was appointed engineer to the Ellesmere Canal Company, where he was responsible for the building of aqueducts over the Ceirog and Dee valleys in Wales, using a new method of construction consisting of troughs made from cast-iron plates and fixed in masonry. Ten years later he was asked to take charge of the Caledonian Canal project, an enormous conglomeration of plans which included not only the canal but harbour works at Aberdeen and Dundee and more than 1,450km (900 miles) of link roads with several bridges.

Throughout his entire career, bridges had formed an important part of his construction work. In his early days in Shropshire he had built three over the River Severn (at Montford, Buildwas and Dewdley) and later he tackled a complicated structure over the river Conway, but by far the most impressive was the Menai. Built as a suspension bridge over the Menai Straits to join Anglesey to the mainland of Wales, it took from 1819 to 1826 to erect and had a finished span of 176m (580 feet) with huge wrought-iron links supporting it.

Although Telford was well aware of the need for faster communications and improvements to the transport system, he chose to almost disregard the railways which were just beginning to be accepted as a means of transport, and concentrated entirely on roads and canals. Nevertheless, his contribution to the advance of civil engineering was considerable during the latter half of the eighteenth century and in the early part of the nineteenth, and it was only just that the Institute of Civil Engineers should reward him with the Presidency.

Thomas, Sidney Gilchrist *(1850-1885)*, was a British metallurgist and inventor who, with his cousin Percy Gilchrist, developed a process for removing phosphorus impurities from the iron melted during steel manufacture.

Thomas was born at Canonbury, London. His father died before he was 17, and the need for Thomas to earn a living became imperative. He spent a few months teaching and then in that same year, 1867, he obtained a post as a clerk at Marlborough Street Police Court. In the summer of 1868 he was transferred to a similar position at the Thames Court, Arbour Square, Stepney where, at a very modest salary, he was to remain until 1879.

His deep interest was in industrial chemistry, and he made his discoveries in his spare time. From about 1870 onwards one crucial problem in this field monopolized his attention - namely, the need to dephosphorize pig-iron when it was loaded into a Bessemer converter. Both the Bessemer and the Siemens-Martin processes (the most popular methods for converting pig-iron into steel) suffered from the serious drawback that in neither were phosphorus impurities removed. The steel produced from such phosphoric ores was brittle and of little use. Because only non-phosphoric ores could be used, the great mass of British, French, German and Belgian iron-ore was unusable for converting into steel. From 1860 onwards Henry Bessemer (1813-1898) and a great host of experimentalists unsuccessfully looked for the solution.

Thomas devoted the whole of his spare time to this question, experimenting systematically at home and attending the laboratories of various chemistry teachers. Towards the end of 1875 he arrived at a theoretic and provisional solution to the problem. The key was the chemical nature of the lining of the converter or furnace, which varied in composition but always contained silica. The phosphorus in the pig-iron was rapidly oxidized during the process to form phosphoric acid which, because of the silicous character of the slag was reduced back to phosphorus and re-entered the metal. The answer lay in providing a substance which would combine with the phosphoric acid and incorporate it into the slag. A long series of experiments had led Thomas to the conclusion that the material which could best withstand the intense heat of the furnace as well as providing durability which would make it economical to use was lime, or the chemically similar magnesia or magnesian limestone. Thomas foresaw that by using such a lining he was removing phosphorus from the pig-iron and also that phosphorus 'deposited' in the basic slag would itself prove to be of immense commercial use (as a fertilizer).

In establishing this theory, Percy Gilchrist (1851-1935), a cousin of the inventor and a chemist at a large ironworks in Blaenavon, proved to be of the greatest assistance to Thomas. In March 1878, at a meeting of the Iron and Steel Institute of Great Britain, Thomas announced that he had successfully dephosphorized iron in a Bessemer converter. This announcement was disregarded, but the complete specification of his patent was filed in May 1878, to be followed by successive patents over the next few years.

Two notable developments followed. One was that the high-phosphorus iron ore of Lorraine and other areas in Europe could now be used for steel-making. The other was that by lining furnaces with a lime or other alkaline material, the basic slag which formed could be an important by-product, with application, in the developing artificial fertilizer industry.

Thomas did not long enjoy the fruits of his discovery. Not until 1879 did he give up his clerkship, but he was already suffering from a lung infection. Following a cruise round the world he died in Paris in February 1885. After providing for his next of kin (he was unmarried), he left all his considerable fortune to charitable institutions.

Thomson, James *(1822-1894)*, was a British scientist and engineer who was responsible for important advances in the principle of water turbines.

Born in Belfast, Ireland on 16 February 1822, he and his brother William (who was to become Lord Kelvin) were sons of a Professor of Mathematics at Belfast University. They shared a common interest in the properties of water, but to James the subject was more than just an interest. He was constantly experimenting with the movement and power of water, and at the age of 16 he invented a device for feathering paddles.

In 1850, aged 28, he developed the 'vortex'

wheel and set up a workshop in Belfast to manufacture both this and a centrifugal pump he had designed. By 1857 he had been appointed Professor of Civil Engineering at Queen's College, Belfast; he remained there until 1872, when he took up a similar position at the University of Glasgow, replacing William Rankine (1820-1872).

Throughout the rest of his life Thomson remained intensely interested in the harnessing of water power, but he also devoted much of his time to the study of geology and meteorology, especially where these subjects had any bearing on the formation of ice and glacial movement. He died in Glasgow on 8 May 1892.

The idea of using water as a form of power was an old one. The ancient Chinese civilization knew its value, and in Roman times water wheels were used for grinding corn. The transition from water wheel to the concept of water turbine began in the 1750s with experiments by a Swiss mathematician, Leonhard Euler (1707-1783) and his son, Albert. In 1827 the French engineer Benoit Fourneyron (1802-1867), who had previously been a pupil of Claude Burdin, developed a basic turbine with an output of 6hp. There followed a succession of modifications and improvements, the most significant of these being the Francis turbine, invented in 1840 by James Francis (1815-1892), an American engineer. In this design the water was diverted inside the turbine, the division taking place at right-angles to the direction of entry, causing the 'runner' (turbine rotor) to spin round. In 1843 Jonval introduced an axial-flow turbine (in which the water passing through remained at about the same distance from the axis, so that the flow was unaffected by centrifugal force).

Thomson adapted Jonval's idea and incorporated it into his own inward-flow turbine, but in his design he used pivoted guide-vanes coupled together and controlled by a governor, so that there was no sudden enlargement in the guide-passage at any load. This modification increased the efficiency of the turbine at varying speeds.

Water turbines were an important feature of the Industrial Revolution and, in themselves, forerunners of the more sophisticated steam turbines of the late 1800s. Both these forms of power ultimately gave way to the gas turbine of the present age, but not before they had played a major part in the history of mechanical engineering, and water turbines have remained of key importance in generating of hydro-electricity.

Trésaguet, Pierre-Marie-Jérôme *(1716-1796)*, was a French civil engineer best known for his improved methods of road-building.

Trésaguet was born into a family that was connected with all aspects of engineering. He grew up absorbing the general principles of the subject, and spent many years working for the Corps des Ponts et Chaussées, where his learning was put to good use in civil engineering projects. At first he was a sub-inspector in Paris, then Chief Engineer in Limoges, before he finally became Inspector General.

In the seventeenth and eighteenth centuries most roads consisted of stretches of old Roman roads and rough tracks, well worn over the years by the passage of horses and farm carts. Pitted, pit-holed and often completely impassable for several months each winter because of mud, they presented an awesome prospect to anyone wishing to travel a long distance. Turnpike roads, with the levying of tolls to pay for maintenance, effected some improvements, although often the tolls were simply pocketed and the repairs left undone. Even for new roads, the emphasis was on providing a suitable surface. Trésaguet realized that the key to the problem was to provide a solid foundation, one which could withstand winter rains and frost, and the effects of traffic. He chose to dig out the road-bed to a depth of about 25cm (10in) and lay first a course of uniform flat stones, laid on edge to permit drainage. Well hammered in, they provided a solid base on top of which he spread a layer of much smaller stones for a smoother surface. His roads were built 5.4m (18ft) wide, with a crown which rose 15cm (6in) above the outside edge.

His method was first used for a major road that ran from Paris to the Spanish border, via Toulouse. It proved so successful that many other countries copied the idea, including Britain. The Scottish civil engineer Thomas Telford put the principle into practice when he was surveyor to the county of Shropshire.

Trevithick, Richard *(1771-1833)*, was a British engineer who constructed one of the first steam railway locomotives.

Trevithick was born on 13 April 1771, at Illogan, Cornwall, the son of a mine manager. As a boy he was fascinated by the mining machinery and the large stationary steam engines which worked the pumps. In 1797 he made a model of a steam road locomotive which he ran round a table in his home. He built various full-sized engines in the early 1800s and by 1808 he had built *Catch-me-who-can*, and ran it in London as a novelty for those willing to pay a shilling for a ride. Then in 1816 he left England for Peru. When he returned, after making and losing a fortune, he found that in his absence others had developed steam transport until it was a thriving concern, with the first railway being authorized to carry passengers by an

Act of Parliament in 1823. Trevithick was never able to resume his earlier position at the forefront of transport invention, and he died a poor man at Dartford, Kent on 22 April 1833.

The first steam-powered road vehicle was invented by the French army officer Nicolas Cugnot in 1769, for hauling cannon. It probably did not carry passengers, and credit for first doing this is usually given to Trevithick's *Puffing Devil* of 1801. It made its famous debut on Christmas Eve, but unfortunately burnt out while Trevithick and his friends were celebrating their success at a nearby inn. He then made a larger version which he drove from Cornwall to London in the following

Trevithick's locomotive of 1803, with a small condenser-less steam engine and smooth iron wheels that ran on iron rails, embodied most of the features that were to become standard on early steam locomotives.

year, at a top speed of 19km/h (12mph). The feasibility of a steam road vehicle was proven, but it was still unpopular. Passengers feared it might explode, and the weight of the vehicle damaged the road surface.

By 1804 Trevithick had produced his first railway locomotive, able to haul 10 tonnes and 70 men for 15km (9.5) miles on rails used by horse-trains at Penydarren Mines, near Merthyr Tydfil in Wales. A few years later he hired some land near Euston, London, where he set up his money-making novelty ride. He also applied his inventive genius to many other machines, including steamboats, river dredgers and threshing machines. But he will always be best remembered for his steam locomotives.

Tsiolkovskii, Konstantin *(1857-1935)*, was a Russian theoretician and one of the pioneers of space rocketry, hailed by his country as the 'Father of Soviet Cosmonautics'.

Tsiolkovskii was born on 17 September 1857 in the village of Izheskaye, in the Spassk District. His parents were peasants and he had very little formal education. Despite this disadvantage and despite being impeded by deafness, he showed a marked aptitude for scientific invention and from boyhood was particulary intrigued by anything connected with flight.

During the 1880s, Tsiolkovskii earned his living as a schoolteacher, but contined to work in his spare time on theoretical heavier-than-air flying machines and the possibility of flight into outer space. In 1883 he defined the 'Principle of Rocket Motion', which proved that it is feasible for a rocket propelled craft to travel through the vacuum of space. His brilliant conceptions on rocketry and space flight covered all aspects, including the use of 'high-energy' propellants. He never actually constructed a rocket, but his theories, sketches and designs were fundamental in helping to establish the reality of space flight as we know it today. He died on 19 September 1935, just at the time when Robert Goddard in the United States launched his first liquid-fuelled rocket.

When Tsiolkovskii began his theoretical research, early flight in the form of balloons, airships and fragile unmanned aircraft had already determined many things about the Earth's atmosphere and gravitation. He calculated that in order to achieve flight into space, speeds of 11.26km (7 miles per second) or 40,232km/h (25,000mph) would be needed - the so-called escape velocity for Earth. Known solid fuels were too heavy for such rocket propulsion, so Tsiolkovskii concentrated on potential liquid-fuels as propellants. In his notes he recorded, 'In a narrow part of the rocket tube the explosives mix, producing condensed and heated gases. At the other, wide end of the tube, the gases - rarefied and, consequently, cooled - escape through the nozzle with a very high relative velocity'. He also emphasized the value of what he called 'rocket trains' as a means of interplanetary travel. He suggested the 'piggyback' or step principle, with one rocket on top of another. When the lower one was expended, it could be jettisoned (reducing the weight) while the next one fired and took over.

Tsiolkovskii was one of three important pioneers working independently on the possibility of space flight. In the 1920s Hermann Oberth in Germany wrote a book about his ideas and stimulated much interest, while in the United States Goddard carried the work further by designing and actually constructing a liquid-fuelled rocket (in 1935). It attained a speed of more than 1,125km/h (700mph) and rose to a height of over 300m (1,000ft). How much of today's achievement in space travel can be attributed directly to the self-taught Russian genius is debatable, although Tsiolkovskii's work must at least have had a profound effect on thinking in his own country.

Tull, Jethro *(1674-1741)*, was an English lawyer and inventor of agricultural machinery, whose development of the seed-drill revolutionized farming methods and helped to initiate the agricultural revolution.

Tull was born at Basildon, Berkshire, but his education was anything but rural. He attended St John's College, Oxford, and later became a law student at Gray's Inn, London, where he was called to the Bar in May 1699. Ill-health, which had dogged him throughout much of his life, eventually forced him to return to the country where he began to look with new eyes at the long established methods of farming. He realized much could be done to improve the old system and his first invention, the seed drill of 1701, was an attempt to bring some order and economy into the process. Although local farmers were intrigued by his invention, they were reluctant to alter their ways until the advantages had been thoroughly proven. For the next 30 years, Tull was to struggle to bring his new ideas and inventions to agriculture, trying to change the system by simple reasoning and example. All of this he set down in his classic book on farming *The New Horse Houghing Husbandry*, which was published in 1733.

When Tull turned to farming at the beginning of the eighteenth century, the strip system was still generally practiced in most parts of Britain. Three common fields in a settlement were cultivated in rotation - two in use, one fallow. The fields were then divided up into approximately (about 1.25 hectare) half-acre strips, separated from the next by a grass balk or pathway, and each man had the right to a strip in all three common fields.

Tull's first invention was the seed-drill, designed to surmount the problems related to broadcast sowing which was the traditional method. It was a revolutionary piece of equipment, designed to incorporate three previously separate actions into one: drilling, sowing and covering the seeds. The drill consisted of a seed-box capable of delivering the seed in a regulated amount, a hopper mounted above it for holding the seed, and a plough and harrow for cutting the drill (groove in the soil) and turning over the soil to cover the sown seeds.

Tull then experimented with implements for ploughing, paying particular attention to the different requirements for different types of soil. He devised the 'common two-wheeled plough' or 'plow', as he called it, which could cut a furrow to a depth of about (17.5cm) 7 inches on the lighter lands of the Midlands and southern England. It had a single coulter for making the vertical cut and a share for the horizontal one. This type of plough was not suitable for the heavy clay lands of the eastern region, and for these he developed a more sturdy swing-plough with a longer horizontal beam and no wheels.

Although these ploughs proved successful to a certain extent, they did not solve one of the most difficult problems the farmer had to face: removing the top layer of grass and weeds. Often it was necessary to use a breast plough to cut through these before the main ploughing could take place. Tull solved this eventually by making a four coulter plough, with blades set in such as way that the grass and roots were pulled up and left on the surface to dry. This was the final stage in the development of the plough, and basically the design is much the same today.

Tull was perhaps the initiator of the farming revolution which during the next hundred years was to raise the productivity of the land beyond the requirements of the immediate village. He and such contempories as Charles Townsend (1674-1738), nicknamed 'Turnip Townsend' because he was responsible for the introduction of turnips as a field crop, for feeding livestock, enabling farmers to keep them alive through the winter, and Robert Bakewell of Leicestershire, who did much to improve animal breeding, the foundation of the new agriculturalism, by which enough food would be provided to feed the masses in the coming Industrial Revolution.

V

Vaucanson, Jacques de *(1709-1782)*, was a French inventor who pioneered the idea of making mechanisms automatic - particularly in textile machinery. It was an idea of Vaucanson's which Joseph Jacquard developed into punch-card controlled weaving.

Vaucanson was born in Grenoble in February 1709. He was educated at the local Jesuit College and even as a boy showed remarkable inclination for everything mechanical; he was particularly happy if left alone to invent his own toys.

In 1738 his inventions moved into the world of adult toys when he designed and made an automaton, a mechanical device which imitates a man or animal in a life-like way. His first, 'The Flute Player', was followed a year later by 'The Tambourine Man' and 'The Duck', the latter so well constructed that people marvelled at its ability to eat, drink and swallow!

Despite his apparent success in this field, he still found it necessary to a regular form of employment, and in 1741 he obtained a postion as an inspector at a silk factory. This was ultimately to lead him into abandoning his 'novelty' inventions in favour of more useful items for the silk industry. He solved many of the minor problems associated with weaving the delicate thread. In pursuit of one of his main objectives, the elimination of human error, he invented an automatic machine. This machine, although successful in principle, needed considerable development to make it commercially viable and it was not until after Vaucanson's death that its full potential was exploited.

During the later years of his life he devoted much of his energy to making a collection of inventions and machines designed by himself and other contemporary inventors. The result was the formation of what he called 'The Conservatory of Arts and Trades', which he opened to the public. In 1794 Jacques Jacquard visited the collection and was so impressed with Vaucanson's automatic loom that he took the design of the construction and improved it so that it became an important feature of the Industrial Revolution.

Prior to automation, the quality of a piece of woven fabric depended to a great extent upon the concentration of the weaver - one lapse and a length of silk could be flawed irretrievably. In 1725 Basil Bouchon had experimented with a simple design for an automatic machine, adding further improvements over the years, but it was left to Vaucanson to devise the first fully automatic loom, operated by a system of perforated cards. The cards acted rather like modern computer cards, controlling the action of the machine by the position of the perforations. Although Jacquard was responsible for perfecting Vaucanson's design and bringing it into use, the credit for the idea must surely rest with the original inventor.

Vernier, Pierre *(1584-1638)*, was a French engineer and instrument-maker who devised the precision measuring scale now named after him.

Vernier inherited an interest in scientific measuring instruments from his father, who was castellan of the château of Ornans, a lawyer by training and probably also an engineer. Vernier worked as a military engineer for the Spanish Hapsburgs, then the rulers of Franche-Conté, and he realized the need for a more accurate way of reading angles on the surveying instruments he used in map-making. He was aware of the work of the Portuguese mathematician and astronomer Filde Nanez Salaciense (Nonius) who, working on the same problem in about 1540, hit upon the idea of engraving on the face of an astrolabe a series of fixed scales laid out around concentric circles. On any one circle the scale was determined by dividing its circumference into an equal number of parts, one fewer than those dividing the next circle out but one more than those on the next circle in. Thus a line of sight (to, say, a star) would inevitably fall very close to a whole division on one of the scales. By calculation or by using tables it was possible accurately to determine the angle in degrees, minutes and seconds. But in practice it was extremely difficult to engrave with precision a different scale on each of the circles. As Tycho Brahe remarked, Nunez' method failed to live up to its promise.

Fifty years later Clavius (a former student of Nunez) found a way of engraving the scales, and his associate Jacobus Curtins further simplified the system so that angles could be read off directly (although 60 separate scales were required). The method was described in Clavius' *Gemetrica Practica* of 1604, which Vernier probably studied.

Vernier's solution to the problem was to use a single moveable scale, rather than a series of fixed ones, thus avoiding the difficulties of multiple engraving. The mobile scale was graduated with nine divisions equalling the space occupied by ten graduations on the main scale. In this way the accuracy of the reading was increased by a factor of ten. By this time (1630) he had acquired a reputation as an outstanding engineer and was appointed Conseiller et Général des Monnaies to the Count of Burgundy. He made a special journey to Brussels to present his invention to Isabelle-Clair-Eugénie, the Infanta of Spain and ruler of Franche-Comte, who told him to publish a description of it. After doing so in 1631 Vernier returned to Dôle where he designed and directed the building of fortifications. His other engineering projects included the design of a building for the harque busiers of Dôle, but in 1636 ill health forced him to give up engineering and he returned to Ornans, where he died a few years later.

Von Braun, Wernher *(1912-1977)* was a German-born American rocket engineer, who was instrumental in the design and development of German rocket weapons during World War II and who, after the war, was a prime mover in the early days of space rocketry in the United States.

Von Braun was born on 23 March 1912 in Wirsitz, Germany (now Poland), the son of a German baron. He was educated in Zurich and at Berlin University where he was awarded his PhD in 1934. In 1930 he had joined a group of scientists who were experimenting with rockets, and within four years they had developed a solid-fuelled rocket that reached an altitude of nearly 2.5km (about 1.5 miles).

In 1938 von Braun became Technical Director of a military rocket establishment at Peenemunde on the Baltic coast. In that year a rocket was produced which had a range of 17.5km (11 miles). In 1940 he joined the Nazi party, and two years later the first true missile - a liquid-fuelled rocket with an explosive warhead - was fired at Peenemünde. The next developments were the V1 (a flying bomb powered by a pulse-jet engine) and the V2 (a supersonic liquid-fuelled rocket), both of which were launched against England from sites on the western coast of the European mainland. Some 4,300 V2s were fired, 1,230 of which hit London. The rocket weapons came too late, however, to affect the outcome of the War.

In the last days of the War in 1945 von Braun and his staff, not wishing to be captured in the Russian-occupied part of Germany, travelled to the West to surrender to American forces. They went to the United States and soon afterwards von Braun began work at the US Army Ordiance Corps testing grounds at White Sands, New Mexico. In 1952 he moved to Huntsville, Alabama, as Technical Director of the US Army's ballistic missile programme.

In October 1957 the Soviet Union launched its first Sputnik satellite and American anxiety was not eased for several months until 31 January of the following year, when von Braun and his team sent up the first American artificial satellite Explorer I. Von Braun became a deputy associate administrator of the National Aeronautical and Space Administration (NASA) in March 1970, but two years later left the organization to become an executive in a private business. He died on 16 June 1977.

Von Kármán, Theodore *(1881-1963)*, was the Hungarian-born aerodynamicist who worked first in Germany and finally in the USA. He made a fundamental contribution to rocket research, enabling the USA to acquire a lead in this technology. He possessed remarkable teaching and organizational abilities, and co-ordinated many famous research institutions.

Von Kármán was born on 11 May 1881, in Budapest, Hungary, of intellectual parents. He would have been a mathematical prodigy if his father, Mōr (Maurice), a professor at Budapest University and an authority on education, had not guided him towards engineering. He completed his undergraduate studies at the Budapest Royal Polytechnic University in 1902 and the following year was appointed assistant professor there.

Three years later he accepted a 2-year fellowship at Gottingen to study for his doctorate. In 1908 he went to Paris and witnessed a flight by Farman, which inspired him to concentrate his efforts on aeronautical engineering. Returning to Gottingen he worked on a wind tunnel for airship research with Ludwig Prandetl (1875-1953) and

received his doctorate there in 1909.

Between 1913 and 1930, with the exception of the war years when he directed aeronautical research in the Austro-Hungarian Army, von Kármán built the newly founded Aachen Institute into a world-recognised research establishment. In 1926 he went to the USA and in 1928 decided to divide his time between the Aachen Institute and the Guggenheim Aeronautical Laboratory of the Califonia Institute of Technology (GALCIT).

As the political climate in Germany deteriorated, he became the first director of GALCIT, becoming professor emeritus at the California Institute of Technology. At the peak of his career, he became the leading figure in a number of international bodies, such as the International Union of Theoretical and Applied Mechanics, the Advisory Group for Aeronautical Research and Development, International council of Aeronautical Sciences, and International Academy of Astronautics.

Von Kármán never married and his sister, Pipö, first with the help of their mother, Helen (née Konn), managed his households in Aachen and in Pasadena. He received many honorary degrees and medals including the US Medal for merit (1946), the Franklin gold medal (1948) and the first National Medal for Science (1963). He died on 7 May at the Aachen home of his close firend, Bärbel Talbot, while on holiday. His body was flown by the US Air Force to California to be buried beside those of his mother and sister.

Von Kármán's work concerning the flow of fluids round a cylinder is among his best-known. He discovered that the wake separates into 2 rows of vortices which alternate like street lights. This phenomenon is called the Kármán vortex street (or Kármán vortices) and it can build up destructive vibrations. The spiral flutes on factory chimneys are there to prevent the vortices forming and the Tacoma Narrows suspension bridge was destroyed in 1940 by vortices which induced huge vibrations when the wind speed was exactly 67.6km/h (42mph).

In 1938 the US Army Air Corps asked the National Academy of Sciences to devise some means of helping heavily laden aircraft to take off. Von Kármán played a prominent part in the first work on jet assisted take-off (JATO) and in 1943, authored with H.S Tsien and F.J Molina, a memorandum which resulted in the first research and development programme on long-range rocket-propelled missiles. The programme called for the design and building of prototype test vehicles, basic research on propellants and construction materials, missile guidance systems and missile aerodynamics.

In aerodynamics and flight mechanics he developed a method of generating aerofoil profiles and produced papers on flight at high subsonic, transonic and supersonic speeds. He also worked on boundary layer and compressibility effects, stability and control at high speeds, propeller design, helicopters and gliders.

Von Kármán was one of the world's great theoretical aerodynamicists. He laid the foundations for the rocket and aircraft programmes which placed the USA in the lead in these fields. Many of the establishments he brought together, such as the famous Jet Propulsion Laboratory at Pasadena, show every sign of carrying on his work for an indefinite time.

Von Welsbach, Freiherr (Carl Auer) *(1858-1929)*, was an Austrian chemist and engineer who discovered two rare earth elements and invented the incandescent gas mantle.

Von Welsbach was born Carl Auer on 1 September 1858, in Vienna. He was the son of the Director of the Imperial Printing Press. He went to Heidelberg for his university training and studied under the German chemist Robert Bunsen, where he developed a strong interest in spectroscopy and lighting. He showed that didymium, previously thought to be an element, actually consisted of the two very similar but different elements praseodymium and neodymium. He also found that another rare earth element cerium, added as its nitrate salt to a cylindrical fabric impregnated with thorium nitrate, produced a fragile mantle that glowed with white incandescence when heated in a gas flame. The 'Welsbach mantle' was patented in 1885.

The major development in artificial lighting in the nineteenth century was the introduction of methods of generating and distributing coal gas in urban communities. The first successful experiments in this field are usually credited to Witham Murdoch, a Scotish engineer working in Cornwall who lit his own home by gas before being commissioned to instal gas lighting in London. For several decades the source of light was from the yellow gas flame itself, produced by a simple 'bat's-wing' burner. During the 1820s a new type of burner was introduced, in which a controlled amount of air was admitted to the gas current (as in a laboratory Bunsen burner): producing a high-temperature but non-luminous flame that heated a refractive material. At very high temperatures this material became the light source. But the method proved to be expensive and unreliable until the invention of the Welsbach mantle which, in its final form of a woven net (usually spherical or cylindrical) impregnated with the salts of thorium and cerium, could be made sufficiently strong and durable to be transported. (When a mantle was first used, the cotton burned away to leave a mesh of metal oxides which was fragile but continued to function as long as it was not roughly handled.)

Thomas Edison's electric lamp eventually replaced gas lamps for nearly all applications, although mantles are still used for kerosene lamps and for portable lamps powered by 'bottled' gas. More often than not, such lamps are lit using a cigarette lighter or automatic gas lighter which makes use of a 'flint', another of von Welsbach's discoveries. Most lighter flints consist of what he called Mitschmetal, a pyrophoric mixture containing about 50 per cent cerium, 25 per cent lanthanum, 15 per cent neodymium and 10 per cent other rare metals and iron. When it is struck or scraped it produces hot metal sparks. Mitschmetal is also used as a deoxidizer in vacuum tubes and as an alloying agent for magnesium.

When the Emperor of Austria conferred upon the title Freiherr von Welsbach, chose as his baronial motto 'More Light'. This has proven to be a prophetic choice, for both Von Welsbach's discoveries are still used in the production of light.

W

Wallis, Barnes Neville *(1887-1979)*, was a British aircraft designer who was responsible for devising the unique 'geodesic' construction of airframes. He also gained fame during World War II for his association with the development of a 'bouncing' bomb, used by the Allies to attack dams in Germany.

Wallis, later known as Barnes Wallis, was born in Derbyshire on 26 September 1887. He was educated at Christ's Hospital School and trained as a marine engineer at J.S White and Company, shipbuilders of Cowes, Isle of Wight. In early 1911 he joined the Vickers Company, and from 1913 to 1915 he worked in the design department of Vickers Aviation: During World War I he served briefly as a private in the Artist's Rifles, then returned to Vickers as chief designer in the airship department of their works at Barrow-in-Furness.

From 1916 to 1922 he was Chief Designer for the Airship Guarantee Company, a subsidiary of Vickers. From 1923 onwards he was Chief Designer of Structures at Vickers Weybridge works where he stayed as a designer until the end of World War II. In 1945 he became Chief of Aeronautical Research and Development at the British Aircraft Corporation Division at Weybridge - a post he held until his retirement in 1971.

Wallis was widely honoured by his fellow engineers and by a grateful government. He received the CBE in 1943 and was made a Fellow of the Royal Society in 1945; he held honorary degrees from London, Bristol, Oxford and Cambridge Universities. In 1965 he was made an honorary fellow of Churchill College, Cambridge, and in 1968 he was knighted. He died on 31 October 1979.

Towards the end of 1911 Wallis left shipbuilding to join H.B Pratt as an apprentice designer. (Pratt had been commissioned by Vickers to design a new rigid airship after the *Mayfly* debacle of 1911.) A series of successful designs followed, and in 1913 the British Government initiated the famous R series of airships - starting with the R26. Wallis himself designed the R80; and the performance of this machine was a significant advance on that of all the others.

In 1924 Wallis began designing the R100, and it was during this work that he got the initial ideas which he later incorporated in his geodetic structures for aircraft. Despite the success of the R100 and its proven structural strength, the disaster which befell the government-built (and differently designed) sister-ship, the R101, brought an end to rigid airship building in Britain.

Following the cessation of work on rigid airships, Wallis was transferred to the Vickers Weybridge works as Chief Structures Designer, and one of his first tasks was to design a lighter wing structure for the Vickers-built *Viastra 2*, which was being used commercially in Australia. The experience Wallis gained in this job - together with that gained in other structural research, particularly the design of the A1-30 torpedo-carrier and the 'wandering web' of the *Vivid* and *Valiant* - later enabled him to evolve the now-famous geodesic system for fixed-wing aircraft.

The breakaway from established structural design practice in airframes was made when a Wallis-designed fuselage was incorporated in the G4-31 biplane in 1932. In this design, Wallis sought to dispense with the primary and secondary members by substituting a lattice-work system of main members only - an idea he had originally derived from the wire-netting used to contain the gas-bags on the airship R100. An exploratory structure of this type had been used on the ill-fated M1-30 torpedo-carrier. The G4-31 structure represented a half-way stage between that and the full geodetic structure employed in the monoplane which was later to achieve world-wide fame as the *Wellesley* bomber.

A geodetic line is, by definition, the shortest distance between two points on the Earth - that is, on a sphere. Applied to airframes, the theory had many advantages, one being that the load transfer from member to member was by the shortest possible route. In the Wallis lattice pattern, if one series of members were in tension, the opposite members were in compression - thus the system was stress-balanced in all directions. The *Wellesley* was responsible for the great technical advance in design which took place in the mid-1930s and which eventually produced the *Wellington* bomber of World War II.

Critics of the geodetic form of construction condemned it on the grounds that, for quality production, it was impractical.

Wallis and his team at Weybridge rebutted this criticism by devising the necessary tools and methods: a complete *Wellington* airframe could be assembled in 24 hours. But the real proof of the essential simplicity of the *Wellington* structure came when nearly 9,000 airframes were produced for the War Effort at Blackpool and Chester using only a minimum of skilled personnel - much of the workforce was made up of semi-skilled workers new to aircraft production.

In all, 11,461 *Wellington* bombers were produced - the largest number of any British bomber. The *Wellington* served throughout World War II in almost every role possible for a twin-engined aircraft and in conditions as widely different as those in Iceland and the Middle East. Without it, the course of the War might well have taken a different course.

By harnessing his considerable knowledge of aerodynamic streamlining to ballistic problems, Wallis also devised new means of attacking the enemy by devising novel, but very effective, bombs. Among others, he designed the 544kg (1,200lb) *Tallboy* and the 10 tonne (10 ton) *Grandslam*. But his most notable invention in this field was the famous Wallis 'bouncing bomb'. The bomb itself was used to destroy vital and hitherto practically impregnable targets - the huge German dams. The dams were of paramount military importance to Germany because they fed the waterways essential for the production of war material.

To smash the dams, Wallis designed a cylindrical bomb to be hung crosswise in the bomb-bay of the aircraft. Each one, 1.5m (5ft) in length and almost the same in diameter, was designed so that if it was dropped at the correct height and speed, it would skim across the water enabling it to reach the target presented by the wall of the dam. To achieve this, 10 minutes before being dropped, the bomb was given a back-spin of 500 revolutions a minute by an auxiliary motor. Upon impact with the water, the backward spin caused the bomb to skim across the surface, bouncing along, in shorter and shorter leaps, until it hit the wall of the dam. Then instead of rebounding away from the wall, the back-spin caused a downwards 'crawl' to a depth of 9m (30ft), where a hydrostatic fuse caused it to explode. The raids on the dams were successfully carried out by *Lancaster* aircraft of RAF617 squadron.

Walschaerts, Egide *(1820-1901)*, was a Belgian railway engineer who invented a type of valve-gear for steam railway locomotives.

Walschaerts was born in Malines near Antwerp. He left school without any of the formal qualifications the bureaucratic administration preferred, but nevertheless began work as an apprenticed mechanic in the locomotive repair workshops of the Belgian State Railway in his home town. Promotion took a long time, but eventually in 1844 he was made a foreman at the Brussels-Midi locomotive works, a position he was to remain in for the rest of his working life. Even the success of his invention, which gained him the respect of railway engineers throughout the world, could not raise his prestige within the establishment of nineteenth century Belgium.

The valve-gear, an essential part of any steam locomotive, opens and closes the admission and exhaust parts of the cylinder(s) at the correct points in each cycle, allowing steam to enter behind the piston and leaving it free to exhaust in front of it. It is also desirable, for economy and efficiency, to cut off the steam supply just before the piston completes its stroke.

In the first half of the nineteenth-century, most locomotives used valve-gear invented by Robert Stephenson. Walschaerts completed his first design in 1844 but, because he was a mere mechanic, had to find a nominee who would lend his name to the patent application. A.F. Fischer obliged, and in some parts of the world the device is still referred to as Fischer's valve-gear. In 1848 Walschaerts modified and improved the design, but again he did not meet with the recognition he deserved. This time the patent was contested by Edmund Heusinger, a Prussian designer, who was Chief Engineer of the Taurus Railway. Walschaerts' and Heusinger's were both very similar, but after some dispute it was finally accepted that no copying had taken place and that they had been invented simultaneously. Both were great improvements on Stephenson's gear, being lighter, smaller and easier to maintain. Walschaerts was allowed to test his valve-gear on a locomotive at the Brussels-Midi depot. The trial was successful and the idea quickly taken up, although not initially for the state-owned locomotives (most of which were inside-cylinder types) but for the outside-cylinder kind used by some of the private Belgian companies. Walschaerts' valve-gear continued to be used throughout the age of steam railways, well into the twentieth-century.

Wankel, Felix *(1902-)*, is a German engineer who is known for his research into the development of the rotary engine which bears his name.

Wankel was born in Luhran on the 13 August 1902. He attended Vohlschule and Gymnasium before becoming employed by Druckerie-Verlay in Heidelberg in 1921. In 1927 he became a partner in an engineering works before opening his own research establishment, where he carried out work for Bayerisch Motorenwerke (BMW) in 1934. Later he carried out work for the German Air Ministry. At the end of World War II in 1945 he began to work for a number of German motor manufacturers at the Technische Entwicklungstelle in Lindon. In 1960 he was made Director of this institute.

During the 1930s Wankel carried out a systematic investigation of internal combustion engines. He became particularly interested in rotary engines and gradually began to make mechanical sense of the number of possible arrangements and engine cycles. Although many of his early ideas turned out to be only marginally successful, the German motor firm NSU sponsored the development of his engine with a view to its possible use in motorcycles. Eventually, after the War, and with the help of Froeda, he rearranged his early designs and produced a successful prototype of a practical engine in 1956.

The Wankel engine consists of one chamber of epitrochoidal shape (the path described by a point not on a circle rolling round another circle),

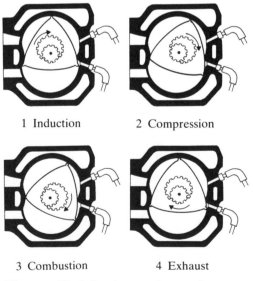

1 Induction   2 Compression

3 Combustion   4 Exhaust

The rotary Wankel engine uses the same four stages as the four-stroke Otto cycle: induction, compression, combustion and exhaust.

which looks like an elongated circle with two dents in it. Inside this chamber is a rotor in the shape of an equilateral triangle with rounded sides. In one revolution the rotor successively isolates various parts of the chamber, allowing for the intake of fuel and air, compression, ignition; expansion and exhaust to take place. While this driving cycle is taking place relative to one face of the rotor, two more are taking place relative to the other two faces; as a result the crankshaft rotates three times for every turn of the rotor. Thus the Wankel engine produces more power for its weight than the more conventional Otto and Diesel engines. There are no separate valves, because the induction and exhaust of vapours is controlled by the movement of the rotor. The great problem with the Wankel engine has been the effective and efficient sealing of the chamber into three parts by the rotor.

Wankel engines are easily connected together in pairs. There are very few moving parts compared with an ordinary motor car engine; there are no piston rods or camshafts. The saving in engine weight means that slightly less power is required from engines of this type when they are used in cars.

Over the years a number of motor companies have produced cars with this engine, including NSU in Germany and Toyo Kogyo of Japan. Other companies throughout the world have bought the rights to manufacture and use the Wankel engine. As yet it has not displaced the conventional engine, but this is mainly because of the difficulty of efficiently sealing the chambers for a long duration, and because of the now very stringent tests for pollution which any new engine has to undergo in many countries.

Watt, James *(1736-1819)*, was a Scottish mechanical engineer who is popularly credited with inventing the steam engine. In fact he modified the engine of Thomas Newcomen (1663-1729) to the extent that it became a practical, efficient machine capable of application to a variety of industrial tasks. In particular he devised the separate condenser and eventually made a double-acting machine which supplied power with both directions of the piston; this was a great help in developing rotary motion. He also invented devices associated with the steam engine, artistic instruments and a copying process, and devised the horsepower as a description of an engine's rate of working. The modern unit of power, the watt, is named after him.

Watt was born in Greenock on 19 January 1736, the son of a chandler and joiner. Throughout his life he suffered from serious attacks of migraine, and at school both his peers and his teachers took a poor view of this 'weakness'. His great delight was to work in his father's workshop, where a corner had been set aside for him with his own forge and workbench. Soon he developed great skill, and he wished to become an instrument maker. In his attempt to find an apprenticeship in this trade, he went first to Glasgow, where he worked with an optician and odd-job man for a year. Then, on advice from a friend, he went to London. Eventually, he secured a position with very unfavourable conditions. He did, however, learn the skills of instrument-making before illness forced him to return home to Greenock. After recovering, he set up in business as an instrument-maker in Glasgow and in 1757 obtained work from Glasgow University that allowed him to work in a room within its precincts, and he proudly described himself as 'Instrument Maker to Glasgow University'.

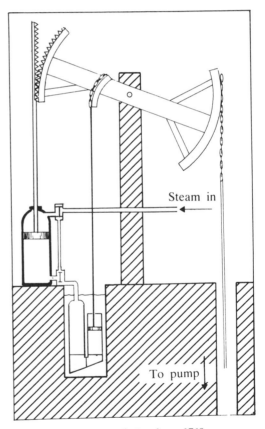

Watt's steam engines, dating from 1769, were an improvement on that of Thomas Newcomen in that they had a separate condenser (C) and permitted steam to be admitted alternately on both sides of the piston.

During this period he was asked to repair a small working model of Newcomen's steam engine. The machine proved to be temperamental and difficult to operate without air entering the cylinder and destroying the vacuum. He set about investigating the properties of steam and making measurements of boilers and pistons in the hope of improving Newcomen's machine which was, at best, slow, temperamental, inefficient and extremely costly to run in terms of the coal required to keep a sufficient head of steam in a practical engine. During a short period of inspiration, in the course of a Sunday afternoon walk, he had the idea of a separate condenser (separate from the piston). In Newcomen's engine, the steam in the cylinder was condensed by a jet of water, thus creating a vacuum which, in turn, was filled during the power stroke by the atmosphere pressing the piston to the bottom of the cylinder. On each stroke the cylinder was heated by the steam and cooled by the injected water, thus absorbing a tremendous amount of heat. With his separate cylinder, Watt could keep the cylinder hot, and the condenser fairly cold by lagging, thus improving the thermal efficiency of the machine and the economics of its operation. Watt's original engine of 1765 is now in the Science Museum, London. It was only a working model, and reveals the haste in which it was built.

As far as practical engines were concerned, Watt had a great deal of trouble in efficiently lagging the cylinder so that heat was retained and at the same time allowing the piston to move freely. He was helped with facilities and labour by John Roebuck of Kinneil, who eventually employed Watt's engine to pump water from his mines. In 1767 Watt again travelled to England, this time to patent his engine (patent granted in 1769). On his way back to Scotland he visited some friends of Roebuck in Birmingham and met Matthew Boulton. Boulton was a major manufacturer in Birmingham and had the finance to exploit Watt's engine. Because of the patent arrangements between Watt and Roebuck it was not until the latter got into severe financial difficulties that Boulton could buy him out and begin manufacturing the engine. In fact, between 1767 and 1774, Watt made his living as a canal surveyor. Although he was successful at this, his health was not up to an outside job in harsh weather and he suffered accordingly.

From 1775, financial difficulties being solved, Boulton and Watt went into partnership and manufactured Watt's engines at the famous Soho Foundry, near Birmingham. In 1782 Watt improved his machine by making it double-acting. By means of a mechanical linkage known as 'parallel motion' and an extra set of valves, the engine was made to drive on both the forward and backward strokes of the piston, and a 'sun-and-planet' gear (also devised by Watt) allowed rotatory motion to be produced. This new and highly adaptable engine was quickly adopted by cotton and woollen mills. A universally practical means of producing power for the evolving British industry was therefore at hand, with the consequent rapid rise in the adoption of larger machines.

During this same period, 1775 to 1790, Watt invented an automatic centrifugal governor, which cut off the steam when the engine began to work too quickly and turned it on again when it had slowed sufficiently. He also devised a steam engine indicator, which showed steam pressure and the degree of vacuum within the cylinder. Because of the secretarial duties connected with the business, Watt invented a way of copying letters and drawings; this was a chemical process and was displaced only with the advent of the typewriter and photocopier. Although his steam engines were usually built for specific purposes and individually priced, it was important to have a rational method upon which charges could be made. For this he considered the rate at which horses worked and, after many experiments, concluded that a 'horsepower' was 33,000lb (15,000kg) raised through 1ft (0.3m) each minute. He rated his engines in horsepower and in the English speaking world this method of describing the capability of an engine continued, until recent years.

In 1785 Watt was elected a Fellow of the Royal Society. During the last decade of the eighteenth century the active management of the Soho Works was taken over increasingly by Boulton and Watt's sons and in 1800, when the patent rights to the engine expired, Watt retired. He then kept an attic workshop and busied himself designing and constructing copying machines.

Watt died on the 25 August 1819 aged 83, leaving the legacy of high, useful machine power for the development and proliferation of industry. His name has become immortalized as the unit of power; a watt is one joule per second, and one horsepower is equivalent to about 746 watts.

Watson-Watt, Robert Alexander *(1892-1973)*, was a British physicist and engineer who was largely responsible for the early development of radar. He patented his first 'radiolocator' in 1919, and perfected his equipment and techniques from 1935 through the years of World War II. His radar was employed in the deployment of British fighter aircraft during the Battle of Britain.

Watson-Watt was born at Brechin, Angus, and educated at the University of St Andrews where he also taught from 1912 to 1921. His interest in the reflection of radio waves was first aroused during his time at the university and this subject became his life's work.

The first patent for a radar-like system had been granted in several countries to a German engineer, Christian Hulsmeyer, in 1904. Evolving from the search for a means of detecting radio waves from ships, his system worked, was demonstrated to the German Navy, but never accepted. The principles used in Hulsmeyer's system had been discovered much earlier through the experimental work of the British physicist Michael Faraday (1791-1867) and the mathematical investigations of the Scottish physicist James Clerk Maxwell (1831-1879), who predicted the existence of radio waves and formulated the electromagnetic theory of light. The German physicist Heinrich Hertz (1957-1894) tested Maxwell's theories experimentally, and in 1886 proved the existence of radio waves.

At its simplest, radar uses pulses of microwave radio waves which are transmitted by an aerial and any reflections, or echoes, received by the same aerial. The out-and-back time taken by the echoes can be used to calculate the range of the target.

When Watson-Watt started his work it was known that radio waves can be reflected, for it was their reflection from ionized layers in the upper atmosphere that made long-distance broadcasting possible. The reflection was sharper as wavelength decreased. The device which Watson-Watt patented in 1919 was concerned with radio-location by means of short-wave radio waves. It was based on quite simple principles. Radio waves travel at an accurately known velocity (the velocity of light) which for purposes of approximation may be taken as 300,000km/sec. When radio waves are radiated from a transmitting antenna and are interrupted by any object - such as a ship, plane or even a mountain - part of the energy is reflected back toward the receiver. The direction from which the echo is obtained is the direction of the obstacle.

Watson-Watt continued his experiments, and

by 1935 had patented improvements that made it possible to follow an aeroplane by the radiowave reflections it sent back. The system was called 'radio detection' and 'ranging' and from this comes the present abbreviation, 'radar'. Research and development was being conducted during the 1930s in Britain, France, Germany and the United States, although as the decade wore on only the British researched with any great energy. Watson-Watt's work was heavily subsidized by the British government, and was carried out in great secrecy. By 1938, when it was apparent that war was inevitable, radar stations were in operation, and during the Battle of Britain in 1940 radar made it possible for the British to detect incoming German aircraft as easily by night as by day, and in all weathers including fog. Early in 1943 microwave aircraft-interceptor radars were operational, ending night-bombing raids on Britain.

The first radar sets specifically designed for airborne surface-vessel detection had been flown early in 1943. Wartime pressures and the enthusiastic hard work of Watson-Watt had given Britain a clear lead in the field of radar, and before the entry of the United States into the War Watson-Watt visited the United State to advise on the setting up of American radar systems. In 1942 he was knighted.

Radar as a navigational aid, and for collision avoidance, has become a standard accessory on ships and aircraft. Harbour surveillance sets now guide ships when visibility is poor. Radar on planes detects storms and helps pilots to avoid bad weather and a phenomenon known as clear-air turbulence. A familiar police application is the use of radar to determine the speed of a car by the Doppler shift in frequency of the reflected signal. In weather forecasting the tracking of distant clouds and their development is accomplished by the use of radar, while in the military field it is used in the steering of guided missiles and in warning of their approach. The great radio telescope at Jodrell Bank, Cheshire, which has a bowl-shaped reflector 76.2m (250ft) across that can be pointed to any part of the sky, can be used as a radar set, the reflector being used to direct the pulses of microwaves in a narrow beam towards a chosen object. In this way echoes have been obtained from the Moon and the paths of satellites and spacecraft have been tracked.

Much research and development of computer-controlled and computer-linked radar continues. Development of higher power sources also continues and it is probable that further improvements in radar performance will be achieved by advances in receiving techniques. Here again, the computer will play an important role, storing information, separating signals from noise and in general increasing the sensitivity of the receiver. But however sophisticated, all uses of radar owe a debt to Watson-Watt's original invention.

Webb, Francis William *(1836-1906)*, was a British railway engineer and inventor who brought about several improvements in production methods using Bessemer steel.

Webb was born on the 21 May 1836 in the parsonage house at Tixall, Staffordshire, where his father was rector for 52 years. Little is known of Webb's early education, but a census of 1851 records him as being a 'Scholar-at-home', which suggests that he was most likely educated personally by his father. He soon began to show considerable mechanical aptitude, and at the age of 15 became an articled apprentice to Francis Trevithick, son of the well-known first superintendent of the London and North Western Railways' works at Crewe (a giant engineering plant which had been inaugurated eight years previously). He completed his apprenticeship in 1856 and, on reaching 23 years of age, was appointed Chief Draughtsman to the Company. During 1861 John Ramsbottom, who had become head of the locomotive department, appointed Webb to be Works Manager at Crewe. This rapid promotion at the age of only 25 confirms Webb's outstanding engineering ability.

During the five years 1866 to 1871 Webb also served as Managing Partner to the Bolton Iron and Steel Company in Lancashire. This company was responsible for the early development of Henry Bessemer's new steel which was patented in 1856, at that time the greatest advancement in the quality of steel production. Webb's experience in the Bolton company greatly influenced the making of Bessemer steel which was developed under his supervision at the Crewe works.

Webb's dominance at Crewe from 1871 onwards was greatly strengthened by the support he received from the Chairman of the Company, Sir Richard Moon. Webb's faith in the quality of the steel made at Crewe brought him further prominence, and it was generously acknowledged that this faith was fully justified. From the 1870s to the 1890s, including the 'Great Depression' period of 1873-1896, it demanded of Webb the greatest skill in directing the application of rational methods.

The introduction of 'double-engineering' as a system of adding power to long-distance running was an additional expense and could not be attributed to any official directive from Webb. Indeed, it was contrary to his systematic and economic legislation, and it can only be assumed that pressure was put on him from more powerful influences above. There was much arbitration, endless friction and even 'bad blood' over this running of the

LNWR's long-distance trains, but it has been duly substantiated that no charge could be laid against Webb on this matter.

Webb's creative ability is verified by the fact that more than 70 patents were taken out by him, either alone or in partnership with others in connection with the railways and in other metallurgical fields. His new steel sleeper was successfully adopted by the LNWR, as was the Clark and Webb chain-brake, although this was in some ways unsatisfactory. It must however be conceded that his tireless inventiveness did much towards developing effective and safe braking equipment, which undoubtedly brought British Railways to the forefront in safe travelling.

It says much for Webbs' splendid character and stable will power that although his life was overshadowed by what has been referred to as an 'hereditary mental complaint', he continued bravely to fill a number of civic positions with honour and esteem. It is known that he amassed a fortune through his inventiveness, but towards his decline he suffered severe delusions that he would end his days in ragged poverty.

Sadly, Webb was escorted for the last time from Crewe under the care of Dr James Atkinson to spend the period from 1903 until his death in 1906 in seclusion and under medical nursing at Red Lodge, Bournemouth. He left a fortune of £211,543, of which £96,000 went to various charities, including some religious bodies in Crewe, and to the upkeep of the Webb Orphanage.

Wedgwood, Josiah *(1730-1795)*, was a British pottery craftsman, one of the most celebrated and influential of all time.

Wedgwood was born in about June 1730 at Burslam, Staffordshire, the youngest son of Thomas Wedgwood, who was also a renowned potter. After his father's death in 1739 the young Josiah worked in the family business at Churchyard Works, Burslam, and in 1744 was apprenticed to his brother Thomas. At about this time he contracted smallpox, and he had to have his right leg amputated. During the period of forced inactivity he studied books about pottery and did much experimental work. He was refused a partnership with his brother in 1749, but shared one with John Harrison of Stoke-on-Trent, which lasted until 1753. A year later he joined Thomas Wheildon of Fenton Low, Staffordshire, who was also a leading potter of his day.

The partnership thrived, which enabled Wedgwood to become a master of the art and continue with what he termed his *Experimental Book*, which proved to be an invaluable source of information on the production of Staffordshire pottery. He also invented and produced his improved 'green glaze', which has remained popular until the present day.

Wedgwood then set up in business on his own at the Ivy House Factory in Burslam, and there he perfected cream-colonial earthenware, which became known as Queen's Ware because of the interest and patronage of Queen Charlotte in 1765. In 1768 he went into partnership with the Liverpool businessman Thomas Bentley and they expanded the company into the Brick House Bell Works Factory. They produce unglazed stoneware in various colours, formed and decorated in the popular Neo-Classical style. Wedgwood also continued with his black-basalts which, with added red acaustic painting, allowed him to imitate Greek red-figure vases and fine-grained Jaspar ware. He then built the Etruria Factory, using his engineering skills in the design of machinery and the high-temperature beehive-shaped kilns, which were more than 4m (12ft) wide. He named the factory after Etruria in northern Italy where coincidentally he died on 3 January 1795.

Wilkes, Maurice Vincent *(1913-   )*, is a British mathematician who led the team at Cambridge University which built the EDSAC (Electronic Delay Storage Automatic Calculator), one of the earliest of the British electronic computers. Since this project in the late 1940s, he has been deeply involved with the development of computers and is one of the world's leading authorities on the subject.

Wilkes was born on the 26 June 1913. He attended King Edward's School, Stourbridge, and then went on to St John's College, Cambridge. He graduated in mathematics and then carried out research in physics at the Cavendish Laboratories. After a short period as a university demonstrator, he became involved with war work in the development of radar and operational research. At the end of World War II he returned to Cambridge, first as a lecturer and Acting Director of the Mathematical Laboratory. The following year he was appointed Director of the Mathematical Laboratory and he has retained this position since then, although his official designation is now Head of the Computer Laboratory.

In the late 1940s Wilkes and his team began to build the EDSAC. At the time electronic computer developments were in their infancy, with only the American ENIAC having come into operation. There were many rival ideas concerning the principles on which a computer should be designed and how data should be stored. Of the rival serial and parallel systems, Wilkes chose the serial mode in which the information in the computer is processed in sequence (and not several parts at once, as in the parallel type). This choice of design involved the incorporation of mercury delay lines as the elements of the memory.

A means of delaying the passage of information was developed at the Radiation Laboratory at the Massachusetts Institute of Technology from an original idea of William Shockley (1910-   ) of Bell Telephones, who was later to share a Nobel Prize as one of the inventors of the transistor. It was originally intended that the device would be used in radar equipment. The delay lines were made up from tubes about 1.5m (5ft) long and filled with mercury. At each end of each tube was a suitably cut quartz crystal. By the piezoelectric effect, when alternating electric current met one of the crystals it altered its shape slightly; this sent a small ripple through the mercury, which in turn struck the other crystal and in disturbing it produced the current again. The time taken for the ripple to travel through the mercury was sufficient to store the signal, and the process could be repeated indefinitely provided suitable auxilliary amplification equipment was used.

At the time that EDSAC was being built there was considerable interest in this type of memory device, and a number of American computers were being built which incorporated them. It was by no means certain that either the delay line or the computer would work satisfactorily, but on 6 May 1949 it ran its first program and became the first delay-line computer in the world to come into operation. From early 1950 it offered a regular computing facility to the members of Cambridge University, the first service of its kind which involved a general-purpose computer. Much time was spent by the research group on the development of programming and in the compilation of a library of programs. The EDSAC was in operation until July 1958, although it had been modified during its period of operation. The expertise which Wilkes and his colleagues had gained was passed on to T.R Thompson and J.M.M Pinkerton who, with the Lyons Catering Company, developed the LEO (Lyons Electric Office) as a commercial computer.

In the mid 1950s EDSAC II was built, and it came into service in 1957. This, however, was a parallel machine and the delay line was abandoned in favour of the superior magnetic storage methods.

Maurice Wilkes has played a leading part in subsequent computer developments and has written many books and papers on the subject. In 1950 he was elected a Fellow of St John's College, Cambridge; he was elected a Fellow of the Royal Society in 1956, and in 1957 he became the first President of the British Computer Society.

Wenner-Gren, Axel Leonard *(1881-1961)*, was a

Swedish industrialist who developed a modern monorail system of transport.

Wenner-Gren was born on 5 June 1881 in Uddevalla. He was educated in Germany, and began his working career as a salesman for the Swedish Electric Lamp Company. Over a period of years he gradually gained promotion and eventually became a majority shareholder. In 1921 he founded the Electrolux Company to manufacture vacuum cleaners and, later, refrigerators. With the success of his first company well established, he widened his interests to include many aspects of Swedish industry, including the ownership of one of the country's largest wood pulp mills and of the Bofors munition works. From the profits, he donated a large sum of money for the foundation of an institute for the development of scientific research in Sweden, which became known as the Wenner-Gren Foundation for Nordic Co-operation and Research.

Engineers have been experimenting with monorails for more than 150 years but almost always their construction has proved to be more complicated than expected. The first monorail patent was taken out in 1821 by Henry Robinson Palmer, an engineer to the London Dock Company, who built a line that ran between the Royal Dock Victualling Yard and the River Thames. It consisted of an elevated rail made from wooden planks set on edge and capped by an iron bar to take the wear and tear of the horse-drawn 'car' wheels. The 'cars' were in two parts which hung down on each side of the rail like saddle-bags. Similar later designs were built by the Frenchman Lartigue and in 1869 in Syria, by J.L Hadden who built a steam-operated monorail). An electric version of the Lartigue line was operated in France in the late 1890s. Later systems used gyroscopes to stabilize the train.

Wenner-Gren's monorail, the Alweg line, consisted of a concrete beam carried on concrete supports. The cars straddled the beam on rubber-tyred wheels, and there were also horizontal wheels in two rows on each side of the beam. The system proved to be commercially successful, and it was used for the 13.3km (8.25 mile)· line in Japan from Tokyo to Haneda Airport.

Westinghouse, George *(1846-1914)*, was one of the foremost engineer-industrialists in the United States at a time of rapid commercial expansion. His early fame came from his invention of a safe and speedy braking system for railway trains, but later his ideas and influence spread to gas and electricity distribution systems, and to the electrical industry generally.

Westinghouse was born on 6 October 1846 at Central Bridge, New York. He was the eighth of ten children, and his father was a manufacturer of agricultural implements. When he was 15 he ran away from school to fight for the North in the American Civil War. His parents soon brought him home again, but a year-and-a-half later they allowed him to join the Union Army. In 1864 he joined the navy, but left the following year, having achieved the rank of acting third-assistant engineer. Westinghouse then spent a period of three months as a student at Union College, Schenectady, New York, after which he decided his place was in his father's workshop. In October of the same year (1865), he took out a patent for a railway steam locomotive - the first of his more than 400 patents. During the next four years he concentrated on inventing railway devices, the most important of which was his famous air brake system, patented in 1869.

Up to this time railway trains were slowed only by brakes on the locomotive, and then by manually applied brakes on each individual truck, or carriage, if necessary. Westinghouse's invention allowed the driver of the locomotive to apply the brakes on all the cars simultaneously - a so-called continuous braking system. This allowed the train to brake smoothly and rapidly, and consequently it was safe for them to travel at much higher speeds. In the same year Westinghouse formed the Westinghouse Air Brake Company.

The increased efficiency of the railways was quickly realized. Westinghouse further helped both himself and the nation with his pioneer efforts to standardize railway components and systems, including the development of a completely new signalling system. This needed electricity and electrical components, and he went on to invent and manufacture devices in this area. As his business grew he formed more home and foreign companies to manufacture his inventions.

Gas was then a source of power to industry and required efficient distribution; Westinghouse developed a system of gas mains whereby the gas was fed into the network at high pressure but was at the required pressure when it was received by the consumer. His initial high-pressure mains were narrow diameter pipes which fed into wider pipes (with a consequent drop in pressure), which in turn fed into even wider pipes until the gas was at the correct pressure in the right place.

During the 1880s electricity as well as gas was important, and Westinghouse built a single-phase alternating current distribution system in Pittsburg with French transformers and generators. He quickly realized its potential, and got his own engineers to design equipment suitable for a new high-tension (voltage) system. Westinghouse saw that high tension distribution avoided much of the loss through electrical resistance, which limited moderate voltage systems to a small distribution area, and enabled the building of large electrical networks. Alternating current (AC) was necessary because step-down transformers were needed to bring the voltage to a suitable level for use.

At about this time he secured the services of Nikola Tesla (1857-1943). He also bought the patents for the AC polyphase induction motor which made his AC system even more useful, because up to that time AC motors had to be started by rotating them at their running speed before the current was switched on. In 1893 the Westinghouse Electric Company lighted the world's first Columbia Exposition in Chicago. Two years later the same company harnessed the Niagra Falls to generate electricity for the lights and trams of the town of Buffalo, 35km (22 miles) away.

Many of the Westinghouse industries were based in Pittsburgh 'and nearby in Turtle Creek Valley, where in 1889 Westinghouse built a model town for his workmen. During the period 1907 to 1908 a series of financial crises and take-overs caused him to lose control of the Westinghouse Industries. He returned to active experimentation, designing a new steam turbine and reduction gear system and an air spring for use in motorcars. He also spent time reorganizing a large insurance society. From 1913 he suffered increasing ill health from heart disease, and he died in New York on the 12 March 1914.

Whitehead, Robert *(1823-1905)*, was a British engineer, best known for his invention of the self-propelled torpedo.

Whitehead was born on 3 January 1823 in Bolton, Lancashire, one of the 8 children of the owner of a cotton-bleaching business. He was educated at the local grammar school and at the age of 14 was apprenticed to a Manchester engineering company: Richard Ormond & Son. His uncle, William Smith, was the manager of the works, and Whitehead was thoroughly grounded in practical engineering. He also trained in draughtsmanship by studying at evening classes at the Mechanics Institute in Manchester. His uncle became manager of the works of Philip Taylor & Sons of Marseilles, and in 1844 Whitehead joined him there. Three years later he set up in business on his own in Milan, designing machinery.

Whitehead took out various patents under the Austrian Government, but these were annulled by the revolutionary government of 1848. He moved to Trieste and worked for the Austrian Lloyd Company for 2 years. From 1850 to 1856 he was manager there of the Studholt works, and then, at the neighbouring naval port of Fiume, he began working at the Stabilimento Tecnico Fiumano. It was there that in 1866 he invented the torpedo.

In 1872, with his son-in-law George Hoyos, Whitehead bought the Fiume establishment, devoting the works to the construction of torpedoes and accessory equipment. His son John became the third partner. In 1890 a branch was founded at Portland Harbour, England, under Captain Payne-Gallway and in 1898 the original works at Fiume were rebuilt on a larger scale.

Whitehead was presented with a diamond ring by the Austrian Empire for having designed and built the engines of the ironclad warship *Ferdinand Max* which rammed the *Re d'Italia* at the Battle of Lisa. In May 1868 he was decorated with the Austrian Order of Francis Joseph in recognition of the excellence of his engineering exhibits at the Paris Exhibition of 1867. He also received honours and awards from many other European countries. In his later years he formed a large estate at Worth, Sussex. He died on 14 November 1905 near Shriveham, Berkshire, and was buried at Worth.

While in business in Milan (1847) Whitehead designed pumps for draining part of the Lombardy marshes and made improvements to silk-weaving looms. From 1856, in Fiume, he built naval marine engines (for Austria) and in 1864 he was invited to co-operate in perfecting a 'fireship' or floating torpedo designed by Captain Lupins of the Australian Navy. But in secret, with his son John and a mechanic, he carried out a series of experiments which led in 1866 to the invention of the Whitehead torpedo. It travelled at 7 knots for up to 630 metres (689 yards), but had difficulty in maintaining a uniform depth. Within two years he had remedied this defect by an ingenious but simple device called a balance chamber, which for many years was guarded as the torpedo's 'secret'. A typical torpedo of this time was about 4 metres (*c*.4yd) long, weighed 150kg (330lb) (including a 9kg (20lb) dynamite warhead) and was powered by a compressed-air motor driving a simple propellor.

Non-exclusive manufacturing rights were bought by the Austrian government in 1870, by the British in 1871, the French in 1872 and by Germany and Italy in 1873; by 1900 the right to build the torpedoes had been purchased by almost every country in Europe, the United States, China, Japan and some of the South American republics.

In 1876 Whitehead developed a servo-motor, which controlled the steering gear and gave the torpedo a truer path through the water. Speed and range were gradually improved, so that by 1889 the weapons could maintain 29 knots for 900m (984yds). He devised methods of accurately firing torpedoes either above or below water from the fastest ships no matter what the speed or bearing of the target. The weapon was finally perfected in 1896 by the addition of a gyroscope, invented by an Austrian naval engineer, which was coupled to the servo and steering mechanism. Any doubts about the torpedo's usefulness were dispelled when, on 9 February 1904, outside Port Arthur, a few Japanese destroyers armed with torpedoes reduced the Russian battlefleet to impotence.

Whitney, Eli *(1765-1825)*, was an American lawyer who invented the cotton gin, a machine for plucking cotton fibres off the seeds on which they grow.

Whitney was born on 8 December 1765 at Westboro, Massachusetts the son of a farmer. His exceptional mechanical ability was evident at an early age, and when he was 15 he began manufacturing nails in a small metal-working shop on the family farm. Then in 1789 he went to Yale University to study law. After graduating three years later he moved to Savannah, Georgio, intending to become a tutor, but he continued to make various mechanical contrivances, for domestic use. He became acquainted with Mrs Nathaniel Green, the widow of the Revolutionary General, who pointed out to Whitney the local need for a machine for picking cotton. He devised such a machine, the cotton gin, and in May 1793 formed a partnership with Phineas Millar to manufacture the invention. The cotton gin was patented in March the following year. It was widely copied, and although the courts vindicated his patent rights in 1807, five years later Congress refused to extend the patent. Meanwhile, in January 1798, Whitney had secured a government order to make 10,000 guns. It took him eight years to complete the two-year contract, but even so he received a second order in 1812 and his manufacturing methods were later adopted by both the Federal armouries. Whitney died in New Haven, Connecticut, on 8 January 1825.

Even at Yale, Whitney earned pocket money by making and mending mechanical bits and pieces. In Georgia, Mrs Green introduced him to cotton growers, who realized that a mechanical picker could expand the cotton industry and bring wealth to the Southern States. Whitney's machine had metal 'fingers' that separated the cotton from the seeds, and he called it a cotton gin ('gin' being short for engine). It consisted of a wooden cylinder bearing rows of slender spikes set half an inch apart, which extended between the bars of a grid set so closely together that only the cotton lint (and not the seeds) could pass through. A revolving brush cleaned the cotton off the spikes and the seeds fell into another compartment. The machine was hand-cranked, and one gin could produce about 50lb (23kg) of cleaned cotton per day - a fifty-fold increase in a worker's output.

The introduction of a machine to clean cotton led to the expansion of the plantations and the demand for more labour, which in turn led to the increasing use of slaves - indeed the cotton gin has been cited as a contributory factor to the Amercian Civil War. Courts in South Carolina awarded Whitney and Millar a 50,000-dollar grant, with which they built a factory at New Haven, Connecticut. But the gin was so easy to copy and simple to manufacture that county blacksmiths constructed their own machines. Whitney spent so much of his money in legislation to defend his patent, that he eventually gave up the struggle and in 1798 turned to the manufacture of firearms.

In his arms factory, also in New Haven, Whitney used skilled craftsmen and machine tools to make arms with fully interchangeable parts. It is said that he once took a batch of unassembled rifles and threw then at a government official's feet, inviting him to pick out parts at random and build up a working firearm. This time Whitney made a fortune and kept it.

In 1818 he made a small milling machine, with a power-driven table that moved horizontally beneath and at right angles to a rotating cutter. This device is all that remains today of the machinery with which he launched what became known in Europe as the American system of manufacture. He also introduced division of labour in his musket factory, the beginnings of a production line and mass production.

Whittle, Frank *(1907-   )*, is a British engineer and inventor of the jet engine. The developments from his original designs were used first in the Gloster Meteor fighter at the end of World War II. Direct descendents of these engines are now the sources of power for all kinds of military and civil aircraft.

Whittle was born in Coventry on 1 June 1907. When he was ten the family moved to Leamington Spa where he attended secondary school. His aptitude and interest in engineering and invention was encouraged and often demanded by his father, who was himself a designer and craftsman of sufficient skill to run his own workshop. The workshop stimulated Whittle's interests further than his father's ideas. He became interested in aeronautics from a practical as well as a scientific point of view, and at about the same time he developed a preoccupation with the idea of finding a source of power superior to that of the piston engine. On leaving school he joined the Royal Air Force as an apprentice. His ability was such that he later entered the RAF College, Cranwell as a cadet, and trained as a fighter pilot. During the training, which included all aspects of the theory of flight and motive power for aircraft, he was able to further his ideas for an improved aero-engine and impress his instructors with the high standard of his flying.

In about 1928 the idea of using a jet of hot gas to cause motion according to Newton's Third Law (every action produces an equal and opposite reaction) seemed promising. He realized that a gas turbine could be incorporated to drive a compressor to compress the air entering an engine and the air would rapidly expand when fuel was ignited in it, causing a thrust of exhaust gases and hot air to push the aeroplane through the sky. The faster the turbine turned, the more the air was compressed and the greater the expansion and combustion, and thus increased thrust was obtained.

This idea was beautiful and simple; perhaps too simple since it took Whittle a long time, and considerable frustration, to convince the Air Ministry that the jet was a source of power with greater potential than the piston engines, which were still in the process of considerable development to new heights of performance. After initially being turned down, Whittle's idea sank into oblivion until about 1935 when, with some support, encouragement and financial backing, he formed the Power Jets Company. The RAF now gave him support and a partial release from his duties. In 1936 he began experiments with his engine at British Thomson-Houston, Rugby. His first engine looked like something between an ancient gramophone and an old vacuum cleaner, but soon his designs took a form that would be recognizable today as a jet engine. His intention was to create a power plant that would propel a small aeroplane at about 800km/h (500 mph). These early assemblies vibrated alarmingly and emitted a terrifying noise.

The prospect of war in 1939 finally prompted the Air Ministry to encourage Whittle's invention by giving Power Jets a contract to power an air frame designed and constructed by Gloster Aircraft. These developments culminated in the maiden flight of the experimental *Gloster E28/39* in May 1941. By the end of 1944 the twin-engined *Gloster Meteor*, the production model developed from the *E28/39*, was coming into service with the had produced the *Messerschmitt Me 262* slightly against the German VI flying bombs. Although it was the first Allied jet aeroplane, the Germans had produced the *Messerschmitt Me 262* slightly earlier.

In the years following the end of the War, the jet engine made possible the new generation of supersonic fighters and eventually the very high-speed civil air travel that is now commonplace.

The power and thrust of jets have increased by very large factors since Whittle's original designs, but his ideas, developments and innovations have influenced the invention's whole development to a degree which is very rare for original and early ideas.

For his inventions, Whittle received considerable financial compensation and a knighthood, but eventually Power Jets was removed from his grasp. In 1918 he retired from the RAF with the relatively senior rank of Air Commodore. He went to the United States, where he took up a university appointment. The famous prototype jet aeroplane, the *Gloster E28/39*, can still be seen hanging from the ceiling on the top floor of the Science Museum, London.

Whitworth, Joseph *(1803-1887)*, was a British engineer who established new standards of accuracy in the production of machine tools and precision measuring instruments. He devised standard gauges and screw threads, and introduced new methods of making gun barrels.

Whitworth was born in Stockport, Cheshire on 20 December 1803, the son of a schoolmaster. He was educated first at his father's school and then, after the age of 12, at Idle, near Leeds. When he was 14 he went to work in his uncle's cotton mill in Derbyshire. He was so fascinated by the mill machinery that, without permission, he left his uncle's employment and took a job as a mechanic with a firm that made machinery. When he was 22 (and newly married) he went to work for Henry Maudslay in his London workshops. In 1833 Whitworth moved to Manchester and set up in business as a toolmaker in a rented room which had access to power from a stationary steam engine. From this small beginning the large Whitworth works developed.

At that time it was the usual practice to build every machine and each machine part separately. Parts were not interchangeable and screw threads (particular-dimensions) were often used by only one firm or workshop. Whitworth, recognizing the advantages, brought standardization to his company and the engineering industry as a whole by developing means of measuring to tolerances never before possible so that shafts, bearings and gears could be interchanged. The well-known Whitworth standard for screw-threads was part of this process of modernization.

The Whitworth company produced many machines which were needed to work to his new standards and to cope with the new methods of production. There were machines for cutting, shaping and gearcutting, but of particular importance for the rapid production of high-quality goods was the planning machinery, which substantially reduced the time spent by skilled workmen on routine tasks. Whitworth also designed a knitting machine and a horse-drawn mechanical road-sweeper.

During the later part of the nineteenth century steel became available on a large scale from the Bessemer and Siemens open-hearth processes. At the Whitworth works, steel ingots of hexagonal cross-section were used to make gun barrels, axles, propellor-shafts and the like. Whitworth cast these under pressure applied by a hydraulic press so that imperfections caused by bubbles of air or variable cooling rates were minimized. Guns of all sizes were produced, and Whitworth supervised many experiments to investigate the forces acting on the breech and barrel of a gun and the amount of barrel wear (which affected the accuracy of the weapon). He also made advances in the design of rifling for the barrels of small-calibre weapons.

Whitworth was also concerned with the training, lives and leisure time of his workmen. He created 30 Whitworth scholarships for university engineering students. He donated large sums of money to the various Manchester colleges (now Manchester University) and other educational organizations. He received many honours, including a knighthood, Fellowship of the Royal Society, and admission to the Légion d'Honneur. Whitworth died after a long illness on 22 January 1887 while on holiday in Monte Carlo.

Wilcox, Stephen *(1830-1893)*, was an American inventor who, with Herman Babcock, designed a steam-tube boiler which was developed into one of the most efficient sources of high-pressure steam, remaining so from the latter part of the nineteenth century until the demise of steam engines in the present century.

Wilcox was born on 12 February 1830 in Westerley, Rhode Island, the son of a prosperous banker and anti-slavery campainer. He went to a local school and developed an interest in mechanisms in his spare time. After leaving school he went to work on improving old machines and inventing new ones - such as a hot-air engine for operating fog signals.

In about 1856, with his first partner D.M. Stillman, Wilcox patented a steam boiler in which slightly bent water tubes were set an an angle in the firebox. It was not entirely successful, largely because of difficulties in making joints that were water-and steam-tight at the high pressures involved. Ten years later, with a new partner and boyhood friend Herman Babcock, he designed an improved safety water-tube boiler.

The new boiler had straight tubes, although they were still inclined to the horizontal. Banks of tubes were connected together at their ends,

through which the hot water gradually rose by convention. The firebox surrounded the tubes to give rapid heating, and there was a reservoir of hot water above the firebox and tubes, with steam above the water. A patent was granted in 1867 and Babcock and Wilcox formed a company to manufacture the boiler. Their steam engines were used in the first American electricity generating stations and played an important part in the subsequent development of electric lighting.

Wilcox continued research into steam engines and boilers for the rest of his life. During his later years he worked on a marine version of the boiler with his assistant and nephew William Hoxie. Much of this work was carried out using his yacht Reverie for sea trials. Wilcox died in Brooklyn, New York, on 27 November 1893.

Throughout his inventing career Wilcox acquired nearly 50 patents and accrued a considerable fortune. He endowed a public library at Westerley and, after his death, his widow used the money to aid the building of parks and schools.

Williams, Frederick Calland *(1911-1977)*, was an electrical and electronics engineer with many accomplishments and inventions to his credit. He is particularly remembered for his pioneering work on electronic computers at the University of Manchester.

Williams was born on 26 June 1911, at Romiley near Stockport, Cheshire. After attending a private primary school near his home he went on to Stockport Grammar School, and in 1929 he was awarded an entrance scholarship to the University of Manchester. He studied engineering and graduated in 1932. The following year he carried out research and was awarded an MSc. After working for a short time with Metropolitan Vickers Electrical Company, he was awarded the Ferranti Scholarship of the Institution of Electical Engineers, which he took up at Oxford University by doing research on 'noise' in electronic circuits and valves. For this work he was awarded a doctorate in 1936. Also in that year he returned to Manchester as an assistant lecturer, where he stayed until the outbreak of World War II in 1939.

During the War Williams was involved in many applications of circuit design. He played a major part in the development of radar and allied devices, and in the design of the feedback systems known as servomechanisms, which had applications in aircraft controls and gunnery. In 1945, at the end of the War, he visited the Radiation Laboratory at the Massachusetts Institute of Technology where he worked on circuitry and also learned of attempts to use cathode-ray tubes to store information. On his return to Britain after his second visit to MIT in 1946 he began to develop cathode-ray tube storage devices, in which information was coded and stored as dots on the screen. The phosphor in the tubes allowed an image to persist for only a fraction of a second, and so the system needed considerable development. At first he transferred information to and from two tubes, but later he designed the appropriate circuitry to repeat the dots in one tube so that they would persist indefinitely.

In December 1946 Williams was appointed to the Chair of Electro-technics at Manchester University and he began to work with M.H.A Newman, who had a grant from the Royal Society for the development of computers. Their first machine began operation on 21 June 1948, the first stored-program computer to do so. The cathode-ray storage tubes allowed for immediate access to data. After modification, the machine went into production with Ferranti Limited, the first of several such computers. William's tubes, as they came to be known, were in great demand during the early 1950s because of their simplicity and cheapness. They were adopted in many computers in Britain and the United States; in particular they were a feature of the early 700 series of IBM.

Williams turned from computers when, because of their circuitry, they ceased to be a challenge to him and in the 1950s he began work on electrical machines, principally induction motors and induction-excited alternators. During his later years he worked on an automatic transmission for motor vehicles. He also played an increasingly large part in the administration of the University of Manchester. He received many awards, including election as a Fellow of the Royal Society in 1950 and knighthood in 1976. He died on 11 August 1977.

Wilkes, Maurice Vincent *(1913-   )*, is a British mathematician who led the team at Cambridge University which built the EDSAC (Electronic Delay Storage Automatic Calculator), one of the earliest of the British electronic computers. Since this project in the late 1940s, he has been deeply involved with the development of computers and is one of the world's leading authorities on the subject.

Wilkes was born on the 26 June 1913. He attended King Edward's School, Stourbridge, and then went on to St John's College, Cambridge. He graduated in mathematics and then carried out research in physics at the Cavendish Laboratories. After a short period as a university demonstrator, he became involved with war work in the development of radar and operational research. At the end of World War II he returned to Cambridge,

first as a lecturer and Acting Director of the Mathematical Laboratory. The following year he was appointed Director of the Mathematical Laboratory and he has retained this position since then, although his official designation is now Head of the Computer Laboratory.

In the late 1940s Wilkes and his team began to build the EDSAC. At the time electronic computer developments were in their infancy, with only the American ENIAC having come into operation. There were many rival ideas concerning the principles on which a computer should be designed and how data should be stored. Of the rival serial and parallel systems, Wilkes chose the serial mode in which the information in the computer is processed in sequence (and not several parts at once, as in the parallel type). This choice of design involved the incorporation of mercury delay lines as the elements of the memory.

A means of delaying the passage of information was developed at the Radiation Laboratory at the Massachusetts Institute of Technology from an original idea of William Shockley (1910-   ) of Bell Telephones, who was later to share a Nobel Prize as one of the inventors of the transistor. It was originally intended that the device would be used in radar equipment. The delay lines were made up from tubes about 1.5m (5ft) long and filled with mercury. At each end of each tube was a suitably cut quartz crystal. By the piezoelectric effect, when alternating electric current met one of the crystals it altered its shape slightly; this sent a small ripple through the mercury, which in turn struck the other crystal and in disturbing it produced the current again. The time taken for the ripple to travel through the mercury was sufficient to store the signal, and the process could be repeated indefinitely provided suitable auxilliary amplification equipment was used.

At the time that EDSAC was being built there was considerable interest in this type of memory device, and a number of American computers were being built which incorporated them. It was by no means certain that either the delay line or the computer would work satisfactorily, but on 6 May 1949 it ran its first program and became the first delay-line computer in the world to come into operation. From early 1950 it offered a regular computing facility to the members of Cambridge University, the first service of its kind which involved a general-purpose computer. Much time was spent by the research group on the development of programming and in the compilation of a library of programs. The EDSAC was in operation until July 1958, although it had been modified during its period of operation. The expertise which Wilkes and his colleagues had gained was passed on to T.R Thompson and

J.M.M Pinkerton who, with the Lyons Catering Company, developed the LEO (Lyons Electric Office) as a commercial computer.

In the mid 1950s EDSAC II was built, and it came into service in 1957. This, however, was a parallel machine and the delay line was abandoned in favour of the superior magnetic storage methods.

Maurice Wilkes has played a leading part in subsequent computer developments and has written many books and papers on the subject. In 1950 he was elected a Fellow of St John's College, Cambridge; he was elected a Fellow of the Royal Society in 1956, and in 1957 he became the first President of the British Computer Society.

Winsor, Frederick Albert *(1763-1830)*, was a German inventor one of the pioneers of gas lighting.

Winsor was born in Brunswick and educated in Hamburg, where he learned English. He went to Britain before 1799 and became interested in the technology and economics of fuels. In 1802 he went to Paris to investigate the 'thermo-lamp' which Philippe Lebon (1762-1804) had patented in 1799.

He returned to Britain at the end of 1803 and began a series of lectures at the Lyceum Theatre, London. A retired coach-maker named Kenzie lent him premises near Hyde Park to use as a gas works. In 1804 Winsor was granted a patent for 'an improved oven, stove or apparatus for extracting inflammable air, oil, pitch, tar and acid and reducing into coke and charcoal all kinds of fuel' (there was no specific mention of coal, although that was the 'fuel' mainly used).

In 1806 he moved to Pall Mall where, during the following year, he lit one side of the street with gas lamps. In that year he was also granted a second patent for a new gas furnace and purifier, followed in 1808 and 1809 by others for refining gas to reduce its smell. Another 1809 patent was for a 'fixed and moveable telegraph lighthouse for signals of intelligence in rain, storm and darkness'.

1809 also saw an application to Parliament for a charter for the Light and Heat Company. The Bill was thrown out but the Westminster Gas-Light and Coke Company was finally incorporated, with the blessing of Parliament, in June 1810, although this time Winsor was not involved. He went to Paris in 1815 and tried to form a similar company there. He made a point of mentioning that he had been one of the first to credit Lebon with the original invention of the gas oven (on his 1802 visit). In 1817 he lit up 'Passage des Panoramas' with gas, but his company made little progress and was liquidated in 1819.

Winsor died in Paris on 11 May 1830 and was buried in the cemetery of Pére la Chaise. A cenotaph was erected to his memory in Kensal Green Cemetery, London, with the inscription 'At evening time it shall be light' (Zach. XIV 7). He had a son, F.A. Winsor Junior (1797-1874), of Shooters Hill, London, born in Vienna and called to the bar in London in January 1840, who obtained a patent for the production of light as late as 1843.

In 1802, Winsor published *Description of the Thermo-lamp invented by Lebon of Paris* with remarks by himself. It was published in English, French and German and re-issued in English in 1804 as *An account of the most Ingenious and Important Discovery of some Ages*. There was also *Analogy between Animal and Vegetable Life, Demonstrating the Beneficial Application of the Patent light Stoves to all Green and Hot Houses* (1807), and others.

Winsor started his career as a company-promoting expert. At the time of his visit to Paris in 1802, William Murdock (1754-1839) had been working in Britain on lines similar to Winsor's and his experiments had first yielded gas as a practical illuminant between 1792 and 1798, when he built gasworks at the Soho factory of Boulton and Watt near Birmingham. There had been similar projects by Archibald Cochrane between 1782 and 1783, but apart from those of Murdock and Lebon experiments in gas-lighting had not progressed further than 'philosphical fireworks'. These were exhibited by a German named Diller (d. 1789) in London and Paris. Similar fireworks were shown by Edmund Cartwright (1743-1828) at the London Lyceum in May 1800, and the population was sceptical when Winsor advertised 'The superiority of the New Patent Coke over the use of coals in Family Concerns, displayed every evening at the Large Theatre, Lyceum, Strand, by the New Imperial Patent Light Stove Company'. He kept secret how he obtained and purified the gas, but he demonstrated how he carried it to the different rooms of a house. He showed a chandelier, in the form of a long flexible tube hanging from the ceiling, connected to a burner in the shape of a cupid grasping a torch with one hand and holding the tube with the other. He explained how the flame could be modified and showed how it did not go out in wind and rain, produced no smoke and did not scatter dangerous sparks. He was a man with plenty of perseverance but with less chemical knowledge and mechanical skill. He was undeterred by the fact that his gas was sneered at as offensive, dangerous, expensive and unmanageable. The distilling retort he used consisted of an iron pot with a fitted lid. The lid had a pipe in the centre leading to the conical condensing vessel, which was compartmented inside with perforated divisions to spread the gas to purify it of hydrogen sulphide and ammonia. The device was not very successful, and the gas being burnt was impure and emitted a pungent smell. He also tried lime as a purifier, with a little success.

When Winsor applied to Parliament for a charter he was opposed by Murdock and Watt, and Walter Scott wrote that he was a madman to propose to light London with smoke. The Corporation of the Westminster Gas-Light and Coke Company were from then on advised by Samuel Clegg, an old disciple of Murdock's, and not by Winsor.

Wright, Orville *(1871-1948)*, and **Wright, Wilbur** *(1867-1912)*, were two American aeronautical engineers famous for their achievement of the first controlled, powered flight in a heavier-than-air machine (an aeroplane) and for their design of the aircraft's control system.

Wilbur, the elder of the two brothers, was born in Millville, Indiana, on 16 April 1867 and Orville was born in Dayton, Ohio, on 19 August 1871. Their father was a bishop of the United Brethren Church. He brought up his sons to think for themselves, to have initiative and to have the enterprise to use their abilities and express themselves fully. They both went to the local high school in Dayton. During and after their school days they developed an interest in mechanical things. They taught themselves mathematics and read as much as they could about current developments in engineering. After some attempts at editing and printing small local newspapers, the two brothers formed the Wright Cycle Company in 1892. For the next 10 years they designed, built and sold bicycles.

Like any other serious innovative engineers, the Wright brothers must have considered the possibility of powered flight and how to achieve it, but the exploits of Otto Lilienthal, the German pioneer of gliders who was killed in 1896, brought home to them that much might be achieved in this direction with perseverance and daring.

Wilbur was convinced by Lilienthal's death that in order to avoid dangerous accidents it was important that they not only build successful aeroplanes but that they also learn to fly them correctly. Control of direction and stability were problems that occupied them for the next few years. in August 1899 they flew a kite with a wingspan of about 1.5m (5ft) with controls for warping the wings to achieve control of direction and stability. Their wing-warping method was the forerunner of the later idea of ailerons. They discovered that the kite would fly with the horizontal tailplane either forward or aft of the wings.

The following year, 1900, the Wrights built a larger kite of 5m (17ft) wingspan to carry a pilot.

After taking advice as to where to find steady winds together with suitable sandy banks, they decided on Kitty Hawk, North Carolina. The kite flew well and Wilbur achieved a few seconds of piloted flight. They also flew a glider with the tailplane in front of the wings. The following July they returned to Kitty Hawk and built a wooden sled at Kill Devil Hills, where there were large sand dunes. Their new machine was longer and had a different wing camber to the previous model; it also had a hand-operated elevator attached to the tail plane. Again they achieved encouraging results, particularly after further alterations to the wing camber. There were still however problems with stability and control.

During the following winter the Wrights built a small wind tunnel and tested various wing designs and cambers. In the course of these tests they compiled the first accurate tables of lift and drag, the important parameters that govern flight and stability. The new glider had 9.6m (32ft) wingspan and had, at first, a double vertical fin mounted behind the wings. Turning was still difficult, however, and this was converted to a single moveable rudder operated by the wing-warping controls. This configuration proved so successful that they decided to attempt powered flight the following summer. During the winter of 1902 they searched in vain for a suitable engine for their craft and for knowledge of propeller design. They eventually constructed their own 12hp motor and made their own very efficient propeller. After some initial trouble with the propeller shafts, the well-known Wright Biplane took to the air and made a successful flight on the 17 December 1903 at Kill Devil Hills near Kitty Hawk. The aeroplane had a wingspan of 12m (40ft) and weighed 340kg (750lb) with the pilot. The two brothers took it in turn to fly. Wilbur, in the last of the flights, stayed in the air for 59 seconds and travelled 255.5m (852ft) at a little under 16km/h (10mph) relative to the ground.

The following year the Wrights incorporated a 16hp engine and separated the wing-warping and rudder controls. They flew their new model at their home town of Dayton, learning to make longer flights and tighter turns.

In 1905 the Wrights were sufficiently confident of their design to offer it to the United States War Department. The following year they patented their control system of elevator, rudder and wing-warping. Although they spent time patenting and finding markets for their machines during the next few years, they did not feel sufficiently confident to exhibit them publicly until 1908. That year Wilbur flew in France and Orville in the United States. In 1909 Wilbur flew in Rome and Orville in Berlin. Their aeroplanes were now sufficiently well controlled and stable to allow Wilbur to make a flight of 32km (20 miles) in the United States.

During the next few years they and their Wright Company built aeroplanes, but by 1918 their competitors had gained ground and their patents were under pressure. During the ensuing litigation Wilbur caught typhoid fever and died at Dayton, Ohio, on the 30 May 1912.

Orville sold his interest in the Wright Company in 1915 and later pursued aviation research. He eventually became a member of the National Advisory Committee on Aeronautics. He died at Dayton on 30 January 1948 having received during his lifetime many awards and honours as tokens of the momentous achievement of the Wright brothers.

Wolff, Heinz Siegfried *(1928-   )*, is a biomedical engineer who works on high technology instruments and the application of technology to medicine.

Wolff was born on 29 April 1928. He worked in the physiological laboratory at Oxford University from 1946 to 1950 and then for a year in the Medical Research Unit in Glamorgan. He then went to University College, London University, to study physiology, and after graduating in 1954 he was employed in the Division of Human Physiology at the Medical Research Council's National Institute for Medical Research, where he specialized in the development of instrumentation suitable for field work. In 1965 he was appointed head of the institute's Division of Biomedical Engineering. He then became Director of the Biomedical Division of the MRCs Clinical Research Centre at Harrow, Middlesex.

Wolff's interests range from the invention of new high technology instruments to the widespread and sensible application of technology to the problems of the elderly and the disabled. He believes that small, specialized pieces of equipment that can be worked by doctors and nurses might be preferable to large centralized units which patients have to go to for tests or treatment. Machines should be simple to use and should show when they are not working properly and be capable of repair on the spot by the operator. The researcher should collaborate more with the manufacturer, and manufacturers should spend some resources on creating a market for the next generation of equipment as well as fulfilling existing market requirements. Technology should also be used to make the chronically ill more comfortable and to allow the partly disabled to remain in their own homes for as long as possible.

Z

Zeppelin, Ferdinand von *(1838-1917)*, was a German soldier and builder of airships.

Zeppelin was born in Constance, Baden, on 8 July 1838. He was educated in Stuttgart and trained to enter the army, which he did as an infantry officer in 1858. In the early 1860s he was appointed to Potamac's forces. This enabled him to join an expedition to explore the sources of the river Mississippi, and in 1870 at Fort Snelling, Minnesota, he made his first ascent in a (military) balloon. After returning home Zeppelin rose to the rank of Brigadier-General. He finally retired from the army in 1891 and turned his energies the design and construction of an airship.

After many setbacks, and helped by royal patronage and public subscriptions, he launched his first craft in July 1900. Eight years later he made a 12-hour flight to Lucerne, Switzerland. His exploits aroused the enthusiasm of the German people, who raised a national fund of more than 6 million Marks with which he founded the Zeppelin Institution. Many airships - now called Zeppelins - were built in the period leading up to World War I, which offered a chance to test their military potential. But enthusiasm for the machine rapidly waned in 1914, the first year of the war, when 13 Zeppelins were destroyed in action and many lives lost. Their chief targets - they were used as bombers - were in Belgium and England. Their vulnerability to anti-aircraft guns and the rapid development of faster and more manouevrable aeroplanes sealed the fate of the airship as an effective weapon of war. Zeppelin died before the end of the War, on 8 March 1917, at Charlottenburg near Berlin.

The early airships - the LZ5, for example - had chin-driven propellors and, in the stern, multiple rudders and elevators. The main principle of Zeppelin's invention was streamlining the all-over envelope, inside of which separate hydrogen-filled gasbags were raised inside a steel skeleton structure. In some craft, as in the design of the LZ1, a balancing rod ran the whole length of the ship below the envelope, and could be used for horizontal trimming. On the LZ18, German naval engineers incorporated several improvements by providing a covered-in passageway and fully-enclosed cars directly beneath the hull. The disastrous end to the *Hindenburg*, which burst into flames over Lakehurst on its momentous flight via

New York, effectively put an end to any airship being inflated with hydrogen. Since then the non-inflammable helium has almost always been used.

Zworykin, Vladimir Kosma *(1889-   )*, is a Russian-born American electronics engineer and inventor whose major inventions - the iconoscope television camera tube and the electron microscope - have had ramifications far outside the immediate field of electronics. Electronic television has become the major entertainments medium, and the electron microscope has proved to be a key tool in the development of molecular biology and microbiological research.

Zworykin was born in Murom, Russia, and received his higher education at the St Petersburg Institute of Technology, from which he graduated with a degree in electrical engineering in 1912. He then went to Paris to do X-ray research at the College of France, but at the outbreak of World War I in 1914 he returned to Russia, where he remained for the next 4 years working as a radio officer. When the War ended in 1918 he travelled widely throughout the world, before deciding to settle in the United States.

Having learnt to speak English, Zworykin joined the Westinghouse corporation in Pittsburgh, Pennsylvania, and in 1923 took out a patent for the iconoscope, followed a year later by the kinescope (a television receiver tube). In 1929 he demonstrated an improved electronic television system and was then offered the position of Director of Electronic Research for the Radio Corporation of America (RCA) at Camden, New Jersey. He subsequently moved to the nearby Princeton University to continue the development of television. He obtained his PhD degree from the University of Princeton in 1926.

In 1967 Zworykin was awarded the National Medal of Science by the National Academy of Sciences for his contributions to science, medicine and engineering and for the application of electronic engineering to medicine.

It is with this last aspect of his work that we are principally concerned here. Among the first of Zworykin's developments was an early form of an electric eye. Somewhat later, he invented an electronic image tube sensitive to infra-red light which was the basis for World War II inventions for seeing in the dark.

In 1957 Zworykin patented a device which uses ultraviolet light and television, thereby permitting a colour picture of living cells to be thrown upon a screen, which opened up new prospects for biological investigation. It is, however, the electron microscope, in the development of which Zworykin also contributed, that represents the greatest boon that physics has given to biology.

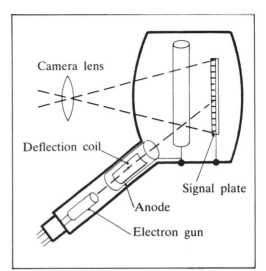

Zworykin's iconoscope television camera tube was an essential invention for the introduction of electronic television in the late 1930s. A charge pattern on the 'signal plate', corresponding to the pattern of light and dark in an image focussed onto it, was scanned by an electron beam and the resulting voltage variations amplified as the picture (video) signal.

Vastly extending the range of detail covered by an optical microscope, the electron microscope uses a beam of electrons to form a magnified image of a specimen. Useful magnifications of one million times can be obtained on the viewing screen of a powerful electron microscope, producing an amplification sufficiently large to disclose a disarranged cluster of atoms in the lattice of a crystal. (Optical microscopes have a useful magnification range of only several thousand times.)

The high degree of magnification of an electron microscope comes from its extremely low resolution. If, for example, a microscope has a resolution of a thousandth of a millimetre, it can reveal objects larger than that size. Smaller objects however appear blurred or distorted. The electron microscope image has a resolution several thousand times better than that achieved by the best optical microscope because the resolving power of the latter is limited by the wavelength of light, whereas the effective wavelength of an electron beam is several thousand times shorter.

Electron microscopes may be classified as either transmission or scanning instruments. With the former the image is usually produced by an electron beam which has passed through the specimen. In scanning instruments a finely focused electron beam sweeps through the specimen, and the image is formed by a process similar to that used in television.

Glossary

Words which appear in italic type are explained in the glossary.

absolute zero The lowest temperature possible in theory. In practice, it can never be attained. It is equal to about -273°C.

acceleration The rate of change of *velocity*. Typical units: metres per second squared (m/s2)

acceleration due to gravity The acceleration experienced by a body falling freely in a vacuum under the influence of *gravity* alone. For the earth, it has a value of approximately 9.81 metres per second squared.

accumulator A device for storing electrical *energy*. Usually, accumulators are in the form of *electrolytic cells* linked together. By connecting an accumulator up to an electric *current,* it is possible to charge up the cells by *electrolysis*. Once this process is complete, the accumulator can be connected to an *electric motor* to generate some action.

aerial A length of conducting material able to transmit and/or receive *electromagnetic waves,* such as *radio* waves or *microwaves*.

aerodynamics The study of the behaviour of bodies in air streams.

aeronautics Strictly, aeronautical engineering. The discipline concerned with the engineering design, testing, building and maintenance of aircraft systems.

aileron Flaps on the trailing edge of an aircraft wing which produce *roll* in the aircraft.

air pump A device used to pump air from one vessel to another, or to evacuate a vessel altogether to produce a *vacuum*.

alloy A material consisting of a mixture of two or more metals, for example steel, invar.

alternating current (AC) A flow of *electricity* that, on reaching a maximum value in one direction reverses, repeating the cycle continuously. In the UK, the domestic power supply is AC, with a change in direction 50 times a second, i.e. the supply *frequency* is 50 *hertz*.

amalgam Any *alloy* of mercury. Some amalgams are used in dentistry to fill cavities in teeth.

amatol A compound used in explosives, comprising four parts ammonium nitrate and one part *trinitrotoluene (TNT)*.

ammeter A device that measures *current* flowing in a circuit. A perfect ammeter has no electrical *resistance*.

ammonia A pungent *gas* obtained synthetically by the *Haber* process, consisting of three atoms of hydrogen to one of nitrogen. Extensively used in the production of fertilizers.

ampere The *SI* unit of electric *current,* defined by that current which, if flowing through two infinitely long *conductors* of negligible cross section separated by one metre, will produce within the two conductors a *force* of 2×10^{-7} *newtons* per metre of length.

amplification The boosting of the strength of a signal.

amplitude For any wave motion, the maximum deviation from equilibrium undergone during the motion; e.g. for a pendulum, half the length of the swing.

amplitude modulation A means of transmitting information by *radio* in which the *amplitude* of the *carrier wave* is *modulated* according to the *frequency* of the signal transmitted. AM is the most commonly used method of transmission by radio.

analog computer A *computer* that performs calculations by taking physical analogues of quantities involved, such as electric *current, fluid pressures* etc., the mathematical operations being performed by passing these analogues through suitable devices.

anemometer A device for measuring the *speed* of a moving *gas,* especially the wind.

anion See *ion*.

anode The positively charged *electrode* of a *battery; electrolytic cell* etc.

aqualung A device that enables air to be fed to a diver working independently, without restrictions of supply cables etc., and which can get rid of the carbon dioxide produced by respiration. See also *Scuba gear*

aqueduct A structure, usually in the form of a channel raised above the ground levels, for long distance supply of water.

arc The bright *discharge* produced when two *electrodes* are subjected to a large electric *current*. The effect, which produces *heat* of several thousands of degrees as well as light, is used in the *smelting* of metal, and also *welding*.

armature The rotating coils of wire in an *electric motor* or *dynamo*, or any electrically powered device where a *voltage* is induced by a *magnetic field*.

artillery Large-*calibre* guns used in warfare.

astrolabe A device for measuring the angular altitude of stars and planets above the horizon.

atmosphere A unit of pressure, defined as the pressure which will support a column of mercury 76cm in height. It is equivalent to 101 325 pascals, the *SI* unit of pressure.

atom The smallest part of an *element* capable of taking part in a chemical reaction. Atoms consist of a central *nucleus,* comprising *neutrons* and *protons,* and one or more orbiting *electrons*.

atomic number The number of *protons* in an atomic *nucleus*. Also equal to the number of orbiting *electrons*.

aurora A band or sheet of glowing, coloured light produced in the upper atmosphere by the interaction of particles from the sun with molecules of atmospheric gases.

autoclave A reactor vessel constructed to allow chemical reactions to take place at high temperature and pressure, e.g. the manufacture of chemicals, materials for the construction industry.

autogyro A **V/STOL** aircraft which uses horizontal rotor to achieve take-off and sustain height, and a forward propellor to provide forward motion through the air.

axle The structure connecting the wheels of a vehicle. It can either transmit driving *power* provided by a motor to each wheel, or simply connect the wheels together.

Bakelite Trade-name for a material used for insulating purposes, and in the manufacture of plastics, paints etc. Produced by condensing cresol or phenol with formaldehyde, the resin is brittle.

bandwidth The range of *frequencies* over which the capability of a receiver or other electric device does not differ from its peak by a given amount.

battery A set of *electrolytic cells* linked in parallel or series with each other to produce an *electromotive force (EMF)*.

ballistics The study of the trajectories and general behaviour of projectiles, such as bullets, artillery shells and missiles.

Bessemer process A method of producing *steels* from *cast iron,* using air blasted into the molten mixtures to remove carbon impurities, by *oxidation*. The molten *iron* is produced in a *blast furnace,* which delivers its charge to the Bessemer converter in which the steel is produced.

bi-metallic strip A length of two metals of different thermal *expansivities* welded together. When subjected to heat, the strip will deflect in a certain way, e.g. to complete an electric *circuit*.

bi-plane An aircraft with two parallel wings, set one above the other.

blast furnace A vessel for the *smelting* of iron from *iron* oxide ore, from which *steel* can be made. A mixture of the ore, coke and limestone is heated using a blast of hot air, and the consequent chemical reactions produce molten iron and slag, consisting of non-metallic impurities. This *pig-iron* is used to produce steel in the *Bessemer process*.

bobbin In weaving, the spool onto which *yarn* is wound.

boiling point The temperature at which the maximum *vapour pressure* of a liquid equals the external *pressure*.

Bourdon gauge A device for measuring a wide range of *pressures,* which exploits the change in cross section of a freely-hanging tube through which fluid at a certain pressure is passed. The tendency for the tube to straighten out is measured by a scale calibrated for pressure.

box girder A *girder* made from four lengths of metal sheet formed into a box cross section.

bridge A structure spanning a river, road etc., allowing transportation to take place. See *cantilever bridge, suspension bridge*.

bridge, cantilever See *cantilever bridge*

bridge, suspension, See *suspension bridge*

British Standard Whitworth thread See *Whitworth standard*.

broad gauge The rail track introduced by I.K Brunel, where the inside edges of the steel rails were separated by a distance of 7 feet (2.13m).

Bunsen burner A gas-powered burner fitted with a valve to allow different mixtures of air and gas to be burnt, and thus alter the temperature of the flame.

CAD See *computer aided design*

calibre The internal diameter of a bore or pipe.

caloric theory The theory that *heat* consists of a fluid called 'caloric' which flows from hotter to colder bodies. Abandoned by the mid 1800s.

calorimetry The measurement of the heat-related constants of material, e.g. thermal capacity, *latent heat* of vaporization.

calotype A photographic technique using silver iodide.

camber The curved surface of an *aerofoil,* road, etc.

camera obscura A darkened room in which images of objects outside are projected onto a screen using a long-focus *convex* lens.

cantilever bridge A *bridge* consisting of a long central span formed by the joining of two shorter self-supporting spans extending from piers.

carburettor The device in an *internal combustion engine* that mixes air with a jet of petrol to produce a combustible mixture, which, when ignited, produces driving *power* via *pistons* and *crankshaft*.

carrier wave A wave of *electromagnetic radiation* of constant *frequency* and *amplitude* used in *radio* communication. *Modulation* of the wave allows information to be carried by it.

cast iron A brittle, impure form of *iron*, containing a few per cent of carbon. Produced in a *blast furnace*, such material is turned into *steel* via a *Bessemmer converter*. Also known as pig-iron.

catalyst A substance that affects the rate of a chemical reaction without taking part in the reaction itself.

catenary The mathematical name given to the shape formed by a chain hanging from two points at equal height. It can be produced by using a simple function of the hyberbolic cosine (cosh x).

cathode The *electrode* towards which positively charged *ions* are attracted, i.e. the negatively charged electrode of an *electrolytic cell,* or of a *cathode ray tube.*

cathode ray The stream of *electrons* emitted from the negative *electrode (cathode)* on passing an *electric current* through a vacuum tube between the two electrodes at either end.

cation See *ion.*

cavitation The void left behind a body moving through a *fluid.*

Celluloid A *thermoplastic* that is strong, elastic and capable of being made into thin sheets. Used in early forms of photographic film.

centre of gravity the point within an object through which the resultant force of *gravity* always passes, for all orientations of the object.

centre of mass The point within an object at which all the object's *mass* may be taken as concentrated for dynamical purposes.

centrifugal force A *force* that must be invoked to satisfy Newton's third law of *motion* in rotating systems. It acts in a direction radially outward from the centre of the circular path, and opposite to the *centripetal force.*

centripetal force The *force* that constrains an object moving in a circular path to maintain the given path. It acts towards the centre of the circular path, and opposes the *centrifugal force. Gravity* is the centripetal force acting on an object in *orbit* about the earth, for example.

centrifugal governor A *governor* which controls the behaviour of an *engine* by a *feedback process* involving *centrifugal forces.* As the engine speed increases, the arms of the governor are lifted by the centrifugal force, the *power* supply to the engine is thereby reduced, cutting the *speed.*

charge, electric See *electric charge*

choke A valve in the *carburettor* of an *internal combustion engine* that can reduce the amount of air being mixed into the petrol jet.

circuit The total path travelled by an electric *current.*

civil engineering The discipline dealing with the design and construction of *bridges,* roads, tunnels, canals, dams and other large construction projects.

coal gas A fuel gas comprising mostly hydrogen and methane and carbon monoxide produced by processing coal.

coefficient of expansion A quanitity that describes the amount of expansion undergone by a material for a degree rise in temperature. It is expressed as the increase in length per unit length, per degree centigrade. For example, the metal with the lowest coefficient of expansion is *Invar,* at 2.3 x 10^{-6} metres of expansion for every metre in length, per degree centigrade rise in temperature.

coherent radiation A ray of radiation such as *light* in which all the radiation waves are in *phase* with each other.

collodion process A photographic technique that uses iodized cellulose tetranitrate to coat a plate after being sensitized to light using *silver nitrate* solution.

computer A device that can be programmed to carry out given logical processes on data, and give the results of the processing to an end user. There are two main types of computer: *analog computers* and *digital computers.*

computer aided design CAD; the use of a computer to design buildings, vehicles, etc., allowing prototypes to be checked and tested before proceeding further to model making.

computer, analog See *analog computer*

computer, digital, See *digital computer*

computerized axial tomography Technical name for the *EMI scanner,* which builds up a complete picture of a cross-section through the body using a narrow *X-ray* beam that scans through the patient.

conductor A material that supports the passage of an electric *current.*

concave An object, especially a lens, whose thickness is greater at its periphery than at its centre.

coil, electric A length of conducting wire which has been formed into a long series of loops. Used to form *transformers, electromagnets,* etc.

coke The solid, porous material produced from the carbonization of coal, all the volatile material having been driven off. Used in the production of *steel* etc.

colloid A solution consisting of particles of a material of sizes in the range of one ten-millionth to one billionth of a metre suspended in a solvent. The behaviour of the substance depends critically on the existence of these size particles.

conduction, electrical The ability of *electrons* to flow in a medium.

convection The transfer of *heat* through a *fluid* by motion of the fluid itself, as a result of the reduction in *density* produced by the higher temperature. See *thermal*.

convex An object, especially a lens, whose thickness is greatest at its centre than at its periphery.

cordite An explosive consisting of nitro-glycerine and cellulose nitrate.

coulomb The *SI* unit of electric *charge*, defined as the quantity of charge required to flow for one second to produce one *ampere* of electric *current*.

crankshaft The main shaft of an engine, by which *energy* produced in the *piston* cylinders is transmitted to the rotary *power* unit.

cresol Hydroxy toluene. An important constituent of explosives, plastics and dyestuff intermediates.

critical velocity The *velocity* above which the flow of a liquid ceases to be smooth following *streamlines,* and becomes *turbulent*.

crystal lattice The regular system of points in space (e.g. the corners of a cube) about which *atoms, molecules* or *ions* in *solids* vibrate.

cupola furnace A brick-lined *furnace* used in the conversion of pig iron into iron castings. Air is driven in underneath a charge of heated material; raising the temperature sufficiently to bring about the transformation.

current A flow of electrons in a conductor, measured in amperes.

current, alternating See *alternating current*

current, direct See direct current.

cybernetics The study of communication and control mechanisms in machines (including humans).

daguerreotype An early method of creating photographic images by exposing silver iodide coated plates to the light, and developing the image in mercury vapour.

Daniell cell An *electrolytic cell* consisting of a *cathode* of zinc, enclosed in a pot of dilute sulphuric acid, this pot in turn standing in cupric sulphate solution. It develops an *electromotive force* of about 1.1 volts.

density The mass of a substance per unit volume. Units: Kg/m^3.

diaphragm A thin membrane found in the human ear, and in telephone receivers and microphones onto which *sound* waves impinge, being converted into electrical impulses by a device which takes its input from the diaphragm movements.

Diesel egine An *internal combustion* engine that uses heavy (Diesel) oil as the fuel in the ignition and compression power cycle which produces motive *power*. Named after Rudolf Christian Karl Diesel (1858-1913).

differential drive See *differential gear*

differential gear A *gear* that allows two shafts to rotate at different rates. Such a system is used in cars to allow the wheels on the outside edge of a corner to rotate relative to those on the inside edge.

diffraction A phenomenon, resulting from the wave nature of *light*, which takes the form of patterns of light and dark bands on a screen produced when a beam of light from a narrow slit is allowed to fall onto it. A form of *interference*.

diffusion A phenomenon that is observed in *solids, liquids* and *gases* at temperatures above *absolute zero*, diffusion is the general mixing of molecules or *ions* of a substance through thermal agitation.

digital computer A computer that performs calculations on digits representing the quantities involved, converting these into a form that can be processed by electronic devices.

diode A *thermionic valve* used to *rectify* and de-*modulate* signals. It only allows the passage of current in one direction, and is so-called because it comprises simply an *anode* and *cathode*.

direct current A steady flow of *electrons* in one direction, such as that produced by an *electrolytic cell*.

discharge, electric A release of a stored electric *charge*.

ductility The ability of a substance to be drawn out into long wires. Gold is the most ductile metal, with 1 gram having been drawn out to a length of 2.4 kilometres.

dynamo A device which produces electrical *energy* from mechanical energy by causing a *current* to flow in a *conductor* which is made to move across a *magnetic field*. See *induction*.

dynamometer A device for measuring the *power* developed by a device.

earth pressure The *pressure exerted horizontally by earth behind a retaining wall*.

Edison effect Electrical *conduction* between a negatively charged filament, and a positively charged *electrode* kept together, though separated, in a vacuum chamber.

efficiency The ratio of the amount of *energy* obtained from a given energy input. This ratio can never be greater than unity.

efflux in *aerodynamics,* the combination of combustion products and air forming the propulsive medium of a *jet* or *rocket* engine.

elasticity That property of a material which allows it to regain its initial shape and dimensions on the removal of *forces* used to distort it.

electrical conduction See *combustion, electrical*

electrical energy The *energy* associated with moving electrical *charges*. A common unit of measurement in kilowatt-hours (KWhr), used in determining the size of domestic electricity bills.

electric charge That property of a substance that permits the substance to be influenced by the *electromagnetic force*. The smallest unit of charge is, for practical purposes, that on the *electron*, i.e. $1.6 \times 19^{-1}9$ *coulomb*.

electricity The general term applied to the phenomena caused by the effect of electric *charge,* whether static or flowing.

electric motor A device that converts electrical energy into mechanical energy, i.e. a dynamo in reverse. It works through the *force* exerted on a central *conductor* around which a *coil of current-carrying wire had been positioned.*

electrode The *conductor* which allows an electric *current* into, or out of, an *electrolytic cell, cathode ray tube* or *electric arc;* the positive electrode is the anode, the negative electrode is the *cathode.*

electrolysis The breaking down of substances *(electrolytes)* by the passing of an electric *current* through them.

electrolytic cell A device which produces an electric *current* through chemical action. More loosely, it is the container for *electrolytes* in the process of *electrolysis.*

electromagnet A device in which an electric *current* flows in a *coil* about a central core of *soft iron,* thus turning the soft iron into a temporary *magnet* whilst the current flows.

electromagnetic force One of the four *fundamental forces* of nature, the em force occurs between charged objects, such as the *electron* and the *proton.*

electromagnetic radiation *Radiation* produced by the *acceleration* of an electric *charge,* and consisting of waves of *electric* and *magnetic energy* at right angles to each other.

electromagnetic spectrum The band of *frequencies* (or, equivalently, *wavelengths*) over which *electomagnetic radiation* is propagated. The range runs from *radio* frequencies to those associated with *gamma radiation.*

electromagnetic wave A wave of *electromagnetic energy.* Such waves consist of separate waves of *electric* and *magnetic energy* at right angles to each other, and are *transverse.*

electromotive force EMF. The rate at which electrical *energy* is drawn from its source to flow into an external circuit, when unit *current* flows. It is essentially the driving *force* behind the *electrons* making up the current.

electron An *elementary particle* which carries the smallest unit of (negative) *charge,* and orbits the *nucleus* of an *atom.*

electronics The applied science concerned with the theory, design and use of *electron* control devices, such as *transistors.*

electron microscope A means of achieving very high magnification of objects. It uses high *energy electrons,* whose characteristic *wavelength* is much shorter than that of visible light used in ordinary microscopes. Its *resolving power* is thus far higher.

electroplating the use of *electrolysis* to coat a metal with another metal, for protection from corrosion, or decorative purposes. The metal to be coated is made the *cathode* of the *electrolytic cell,* which contains a solution of the coating metal as the *electrolyte.*

element A substance comprising entirely of *atoms* of the same *atomic number.*

elementary particle The basic constituents of all matter, for example *electrons, neutrons* and *protons.*

elevator A moveable part of a horizontal aerodynamic surface which changes the aircraft's *pitch.*

EMI scanner See *computerized axial tomography*

emulsion A light-sensitive material, such as a suspension of silver bromide in gelatin, used to record photographic images.

energy The capacity of a body to do *work.* It comes in various forms, which are interconvertible. For example, the *potential energy* lost by a falling body is converted into *kinetic energy* of motion.

energy, electrical See *electrical energy*
energy, kinetic See *kinetic energy*
energy, magnetic See *magnetic energy*
energy, potential See *potential energy*

engine A device for transforming one form of *energy* (e.g. electric) to another (e.g. *kinetic)*

engineering The study of the design, construction and operation of mechanical, electrical, hydraulic etc., devices.

entropy A quantity in theoretical thermodynamics that gives a measure of the amount of disorder in a system.

epitrochoid The *locus* of a point on a rolling circle moving round the circumference of another circle, that is not on the circumference of the rolling circle. Also known as the hypotrochoid, the locus is of importance in the *Wankel* engine.

equilibrium A state of balance between opposing effects or *forces.*

expansion coefficient See *coefficient of expansion.*

fatigue Failure of metals under cyclic applications of a *stress.*

feedback The coupling of the output of a system to the input. Negative feedback results in a decrease in the input *energy* if the output energy increases (e.g. a *centrifugal governor).* Positive feedback boosts the input energy, and is a source of *amplification.*

field The region in which an electrically charged, magnetized or massive body can exert an influence.

field strength See *magnetic field strength*

filament A thin wire, usually of tungsten, which is capable of acting as a light source when an electric *current* is passed through it.

fixation, of nitrogen. The conversion of free nitrogen in the atmosphere into nitrous compounds suitable for the manufacture of chemicals such as fertilizers, and explosives. See *Haber processes*.

fluid The generic term for *liquids* and *gases*.

flux density See *magnetic flux density*

flywheel A massive wheel fixed to a shaft, either to store rotational *energy* for propulsive purposes, or to smooth fluctuations in rotation rates.

force That which changes the state of rest, or of uniform motion in a straight line, of a material body. *Gravity* is an example of a force, the *SI* unit of which is the *newton*.

force, centrifugal See *centrifugal force*

force, centripetal See *centripetal force*

force, electromagnetic See *electromagnetic force*

force, electromotive See *electromotive force*

force, fundamental See *fundamental force*

formaldehyde A pungent *gas*, made by the oxidation of methanol, that is used as a disinfectant, and in the manufacture of *plastics* and dyes.

foundation The part of a structure which ensures stability by providing mechanical fixing with solid earth.

four-stroke engine An *internal combustion engine* employing the *Otto cycle*.

frequency The time required for one complete cycle of a wave or oscillatory motion. Measured in hertz (Hz), with one hertz being one cycle per second.

frequency modulation A means of *radio* transmission in which the *frequency* of the *carrier wave* is modulated, the *amplitude* remaining constant.

friction The *force* that resists the relative movement of two surfaces in contact with each other.

Froude brake A *dynamometer* which measures, *power* by determining *torques*.

fuel injection A system used in high-performance *internal combustion engines* whereby pure fuel is injected into the cylinder during the intake phase of the cycle. This eliminates the need for a *carburettor* and gives greater control over the burning mixtures.

fulcrum The point of support of a *lever*, about which the lever can pivot in lifting and lowering loads applied to it.

fundamental forces The basic *forces* which underlie all interactions in the universe. There are thought to be four such forces. *Gravity* and *electromagnetic force* are of particular importance to the macroscopic world whereas the so-called strong and weak interactions are of great importance in the atomic world. In strength, the forces can be ranked as strong, electromagnetic, weak and gravity, the latter being the weakest of all. Current physics suggest that the electromagnetic and weak forces are in fact manifestations of one single force.

furnace A device in which very high temperatures are produced to bring about chemical reactions.

fuse A device which prevents the passage of electric *current* above a pre-determined level in a *circuit*, by melting through the consequent temperature rise, and thus breaking the circuit.

gain The ratio of the output power of an electronic device, such as an amplifier, to the input power.

gallic acid Trihydroxybenzoic acid; a yellow crystalline substance used in making inks.

galvanometer A device that detects the presence, rather than measures in absolute units, of an electric *current*.

gamma radiation *Electromagnetic radiation* with a *wavelength* shorter than that of *X-rays*, at about a million-millionth of a metre. Such radiation is generated by the decay of the *nucleus* of an unstable *atom*.

gas A state of matter where the molecules of a substance move independently of each other.

gas mantle An illumination device made from impregnating a dome-shaped piece of rayon with compounds of thorium and cerium, which are decomposed by heat.

gas turbine An engine that uses *internal combustion* to convert the chemical *energy* locked up in a liquid fuel into mechanical energy. Mostly used in aircraft and trains.

gauge The distance between the inside edges of a railway for trains. Also, the diameter of wires, rods etc.

gear A system of moving parts that transmits motion of one part of a device to another. Gears typically take the form of notched wheels which interlink with each other.

gelatine A soluble protein-based substance with the ability to form a jelly on cooling. Used in photography, the making of glues, etc.

generator An electric *power* producer operating on the principle of the *dynamo*, i.e. by converting mechanical *energy* into electrical energy.

geodesic The shortest route between two points on any surface.

glycerine Glycerol A thick viscous substance obtained from fats, used in the manufacture of explosives, plastics and as an anti-freezing agent.

gondola The personnel-carrying car of an airship or balloon.

governor A device which regulates the *speed* of a motor or engine. See *centrifugal governor*.

gramophone A device for translating the variations in shape of grooves on a disk or cylinder into audio signals.

gravitation The attractive *force* that exists between all masses. Newton's law of gravitation states that the strength of this force varies directly as the product of the two masses, and inversely as the square of the distance between their centres of gravity.

gravity See *gravitation*

gravity, acceleration due to See *acceleration due to gravity*

gravity, centre of See *centre of gravity*

grid an *electrode* in the form of a mesh which, when placed between the *anode* and *cathode* of a *thermionic valve*, controls the flow of *electrons*.

Grid, National See *National Grid*

gunpowder A combination of sulphur, powdered charcoal and *saltpeter* which, when ignited, produces explosions within confined spaces.

gyroscope A rotating disk which is mounted in such a way that it is free to rotate about any axis. The ability of such a device to retain its axis of rotation regardless of the position of its mount, and to *precess*, make the gyroscope of great value in navigation aids.

Haber process A method for the *fixation* of nitrogen in the atmosphere, to produce industrial amounts of *ammonia*-based compounds. A mixture of nitrogen and hydrogen is passed under *pressure* and high temperature over a *catalyst*, the *gases* combining to form ammonia.

haematite Naturally occurring ferric oxide; an ore from which *iron* is extracted industrially.

hang glider An unpowered manned glider that achieves great manouverability through a basically triangular shaped expanse of fabric stretched over cross-struts.

head, of water The vertical distance between the top of a water stream and the point at which its *energy* is to be extracted.

heat the *energy* possessed by a substance by virtue of the *kinetic energy* of its constituents.

heat engine A device that converts *heat energy* into mechanical *energy*.

helical screw A *screw* whose thread is in the form of a *helix*.

helix A spiral, mathematically defined by a spiral curve which, when wound about a cylinder, crosses the axis of the cylinder at the same angle on each revolution about the cylinder.

hertz The unit of *frequency* of a wave, defined by one complete oscillation of a wave per second. For example, *alternating current* in the UK has a frequency of 50Hz.

heterodyne effect The superimposition of two waves of different *frequency* in a *radio* receiver, one of which is being received, the other transmitted within the device itself, producing an intermediate frequency which can be demodulated.

hodometer A device that enables the *acceleration* of an object moving with known *velocity* over a path to be determined.

hoist An *engine* used to *power* a wire-round drum, whose cable is used to lift heavy objects, usually using a *jib* and *pulleys*.

holography A means of creating permanent three dimensional images of objects using coherent light from *lasers*. The beam of *coherent radiation* from the laser is split into a reference beam (which falls directly onto the photographic plate), the other being *diffracted* by the object being photographed before falling onto the plate. The two beams interfere with each other on the plate, creating *interference* patterns that form the holographic, three-dimensional image.

horse-power British unit of *power,* equivalent to 745.7 *watts.*

hydraulic press A device which uses an *incompressible fluid,* such as water or oil, to transmit a small downward *force* applied to a piston of small area to a larger area *piston,* which then produces a proportionally larger upward force. Such a press is a demonstration of *Pascal's law of pressures.*

hydraulics The study of the theory and application of *fluid* flow to engineering problems, such as the design of *hydraulic presses.*

hydrodynamics The study of the *energy, forces* and *pressures* in *fluids* in motion.

hydroelectricity The generation of electric *energy* by the conversion of energy contained in a stream of water. The conversion is achieved using a *dynamo,* the mechanical driving *force* being provided by a water-driven *turbine.*

hydrography The *surveying* of oceans, lakes, rivers etc.

hypo See *sodium thiosulphate*

iconoscope A type of television camera where a beam of *electrons* scans a special mosaic, which can store an optical image electrically, and converts the image stored to electrical signals for transmission.

impulse the quantity used to measure the total change in *momentum* produced by a *force* acting on a body for a very short time. Given by the product of the force and the time interval for which it acts.

incandescence The emission of light caused by high temperatures. The hotter the temperature, the shorter the wavelength of the light; the relation is not, however, linear.

incoherent light Light which is not of a single *phase.* Daylight is an example.

incompressible fluid A *fluid* that resists changes in density, e.g. oil.

induction the production of an *electromotive force* by a change in the *magnetic flux* of a circuit. The effect is used in *dynamos* and other electrical devices.

induction motor A device which produces rotation by induction. An alternating current is fed to a winding of wires which thus induces electrical currents to flow in a second set of windings in a central rotor. Interaction between the two currents and the magnetic flux involved causes rotation.

inertia That property of all mass which measures its reluctance to be accelerated (or decelerated) by a *force.*

infra red radiation The region of the *electro-magnetic spectrum* with *wavelengths* between about 1mm and one millionth of a metre, i.e. between that of *microwaves* and visible light.

ingot A mould shape into which metal is poured in a molten state for further processing.

ingot iron *Iron* which has been produced in such a way as to reduce the amount of impurities within it, in the form of carbon manganese and silicon.

insulator a non-*conductor* of *heat* and/or *electricity*.

interference The combination of waves. This can be constructive, if the peak of one wave coincides with the peak of the other, or destructive, when the trough of one wave encounters the peak of another.

internal combustion The transformation of the chemical energy of a fuel into mechanical energy in controlled combustion in an enclosed cylinder sealed at one end by a piston.

internal combustion engine An engine that uses *internal combustion* to provide motive *power*, e.g. a petrol engine of a motor vehicle.

Invar An *alloy* of approximately 64 per cent *iron*, 36 per cent nickel and a small amount of carbon which possesses a very low *coefficient of expansion*. As a result, it is used in devices whose correct operation depend on maintaining constant length despite temperature changes, e.g. pendulums.

ion An electrically charged *atom*, or group of atoms. Cations have fewer *electrons* than the neutral atom from which they are formed, and thus have net positive *charge*, and are attracted to the cathode of an *electrolytic cell*. Anions have more electrons, and are thus attracted to the *anode*.

iron A white, metallic chemical *element* which, in the form of compounds such as *haematite* ore is used to make *steel* and other valuable alloys. See *cast iron, pig iron, wrought iron*.

Iron Lung A respirator which mechanically assists the breathing of those whose natural mechanism has ceased to function.

Jacquard system The use of punched cards to direct the operation of a *loom* in weaving patterns.

jet engine A *gas turbine* in which air taken in through the front is compressed, and then used to provide oxygen for the combustion of fuel. The consequent backward flow of heated, expanding gas provides propulsion, and also drives a turbine, which powers the compressor bringing the air into the combustion chamber.

jib the boom of a crane, made from a framework of girders in most cases. Half its length approximately defines the range of operation of the crane, the circle in which loads can be lifted and deposited.

joule The *SI* unit of *energy* and *work*, defined as the work done by a *force* is moving the point of application of the force through a distance of one metre.

kerosene A mixture of hydrocarbons produced by the distillation of petroleum, and used as a fuel in internal combustion engines.

kinematics A branch of *mechanics* that relates *accelerations* to the *velocities* and changes in distance they produce, without considering the forces that generate the accelerations involved. See also *dynamics*.

kinetic energy the *energy* possessed by a body by virtue of its motion. Can usually be taken at the product of half the mass of the body, with the square of its velocity.

knocking Premature explosion of the fuel-air mixture within the *piston* cylinder of an *internal combustion engine*, due to over compression of the mixture.

laser Light amplification by Stimulated Emission of Radiation. A device that consists of an optically transparent cylinder one end of which is reflecting, the other partially reflecting. The atoms of the cylinder (which can be a solid such as ruby, or a gas or liquid) are excited by exposing them to an *incoherent* source of *electromagnetic radiation*, with the result that the *atoms* are put into a higher *energy* state. When they return to the lower level again, they give out a pulse of highly *coherent* narrow beam radiation. Continuous emission using inert gases as the central medium is possible.

latent heat The amount of *heat* taken in or released when a substance changes its state (e.g. solid to liquid) without temperature change.

lathe A tool used to produce objects with cylindrical symmetry, such as bars, screws, barrels.

leading edge The edge of an *aerofoil* which first encounters the oncoming air stream.

Leclanche cell An *electrolytic cell* consisting of a carbon *anode,* surrounded by a mixture of powdered carbon and manganese dioxide in a porous pot, this in turn standing in a solution of ammonium chloride, in which is put the zinc *cathode*. An *electromotive force* of about 1.5 volts is developed.

lever A rigid beam provided with a *fulcrum* at some point along its length. This enables a *force* applied at one end to be transmitted to a point on the other side of the fulcrum. A lever in thus a very simple *machine*.

light *Electromagnetic radiation* visible to the naked eye, lying in the *wavelenth* range 4×10^{-7}m (violet) to 8×10^{-7}m (red).

light pen A device which, when pointed at a piece of data on a screen or paper can transmit the data to another device, e.g. a computer.

light, speed of A fundamental constant of nature,

the speed of light is the limiting *velocity* that any body can travel at. It is equal to 2.997925 x 10^8 metres per second, and is the same for all observers, no matter how fast they move themselves.

linear motor A device which uses *induction* to produce forward motion along a track.

liquid A state of matter intermediate between that of *solid* and *gas,* where the interatomic and molecular *forces* are greater than those in the gas state. Liquids are virtually *incompressible fluids.*

load Generally, the burden inflicted on a system. Thus, in *mechanics,* the load is the *weight* supported by a structure, whereas in electrical engineering it is the output of an electrical device such as a *transformer.*

lock A section of canal which separates two stretches of water at different heights. By using barriers with sluices at each end of the lock, a vessel can be transported from one level to another as the sluices transfer water from one stretch to another.

locomotive A source of *power* for transporting cargo on a railway.

locus the path described by a point whose position in space changes. Hence, an *orbit* is a locus; so is a *helix.*

longitudinal wave A wave in which the direction of vibration takes place in the same direction as that in which the wave is travelling. *Sound* waves are longitudinal. See also *transverse wave.*

loom A *machine* for weaving textiles.

lubrication The use of substances to reduce the frictional *forces* between two adjacent surfaces.

machine A device that enables *force* exerted at one point to be applied at another. A *lever* is a very simple example of such a device.

Mach number the ratio of the *speed* of a vehicle travelling in a medium to the *speed of sound* in the medium under the same conditions. Thus supersonic speeds are those with Mach numbers exceeding 1.

magnetic detector A device used in early *radio* systems, in which high-*frequency currents* were detected through their demagnetizing effect on a magnetized *iron* core surrounded by the wire-carrying currents.

magnetic energy Property of a *magnet* described by the multiplication of the *flux density* by the *field strength* on the *demagnetization curve* of a permanent *magnet.*

magnetic field The area surrounding a *magnet* in which an object could be affected by the *magnetism* of the central source.

magnetic field strength The property measured to define the strength of a *magnetic field.* The *SI* unit is the *ampere* per metre.

magnetic flux The flow of *magnetic energy* from the north pole of a *magnet* to the south pole. It is measured by the *SI* unit, the *weber.*

magnetic flux density The property of a region under the influence of a source of *magnetism,* given by the product of the *permeability* of the medium and the *field strength* . The *SI* unit is the *tesla.*

magnetism A property of certain materials to exert a magnetic *force* upon other materials, particularly iron-based substances. This ability is the result of imbalances of certain properties of *electrons* in the *atoms* of the substances concerned.

magnet, permanent See *permanent magnet*

make-and-break circuit A circuit which contains a device which, when *current* flows in one part of the circuit, causes the device to break that part of the circuit, and allow current to flow in another' part, and vice versa.

malleability The ability of a substance to be hammered into thin sheets. Gold has an extremely high malleability.

mandrel An accurately-turned cylinder onto which a bore-tube can be fitted for further turning, milling etc.

manometer A device for measuring the *pressure* exerted by a *gas.*

marine engineering The branch of *engineering* devoted to the design and production of propulsive devices and other mechanical devices for marine vessels such as ships and submarines.

mass The quanitity of material in a body; it may be regarded as the same as *inertia.*

mass, centre of See *centre of mass.*

mechanical advantage The ratio of the load lifted by a *machine* to the *force* required needed to maintain the machine at constant *speed.*

mechanical engineering The branch of *engineering* devoted to the study and production of devices capable of carrying out tasks, such as tools, vehicles etc.

mechanical equivalent of heat The constant by which the number of units of *heat* being converted completely into *work* must be multiplied to calculate the amount of work obtained. In *SI units,* both are measured in *joules,* so the constant is 1.

mechanics The study of the behaviour of bodies· under the action of *forces.*

metallurgy the study of the extraction, purification and properties of metals.

meteorology The study of the characteristics of the earth's atmosphere (such as pressure and temperature) in order to understand the weather, and predict conditions at a later date.

micrometer A device that can measure very small distances.

microphone A device that converts *sound energy* into electrical impulses suitable for transmission by electrical means.

microwaves Waves of *electromagnetic energy* with

wavelengths between about 1mm and 30cm, i.e. between those typical of *radio* and *infrared radiation*.

modulation The modification of a property of a wave (e.g. its *frequency*) in accordance with some characteristic of another wave.

moment of inertia A quantity for a body that represents the sum of the *mass* of each particle within it multiplied by the square of the particle's distance from a given axis. Of great importance in rotational *dynamics*.

momentum The quantity given by the *mass* of a body, multiplied by its *velocity*. It is used in *dynamics*, as the quantity is conserved under certain circumstances, and its rate of change gives the amount of *force* acting on the body. See *motion, laws of*.

monoplane An aircraft (powered or glider) which has only one *major aerofoil* structure providing lift.

monorail A means of transport whereby the vehicle is constrained to the path described by a single continuous, usually elevated, rail.

Morse code A communication system in which the letters of the alphabet are represented by strings of dots and dashes, the most commonly used letters (e.g. e,t,a) being simpler strings than those of the letters, j,z and q. Much used in simple *telegraphy*.

motion, laws of Devised by Sir Isaac Newton (1642-1727), these three laws are the foundation of classical dynamics and statics. The first law states that a body remains in its state of rest or of uniform motion in a straight line, unless acted upon by a force. The second states that the rate of change of momentum of a body is directly proportional to the force applied, and takes place in the direction of the force. For a body of constant mass, this statement implies that F=ma, where F is the size of the force producing an acceleration a in a mass m. The third law, that of action and reaction, states that to every action there is an equal and opposite reaction.

nacelle A streamlined housing on the fuselage of an aircraft, containing the engine intakes, radio antenna, etc.

negative feedback See *feedback*

National Grid The United Kingdom's system of high-tension cables distributing electric *power* from power stations to end-users.

neutron An *elementary particle* without electric *charge* that is found in the *nucleus* of all *atoms*, except that of hydrogen (which contains simply one *proton*).

newton The *SI* unit of *force*, defined as the force that, when applied to a mass of one kilogramme, produces in that mass an *acceleration* of one metre per second, per second.

nitrogen fixation, See *fixation, of nitrogen*

noise Spurious voltages occuring in a circuit as a result of random motions of electrons within it, or vibrations in the components of the circuit, etc.

nucleus The central part of an *atom*, comprising *neutrons* and *protons* held together by the 'strong' force. Most of the mass of an atom resides in this region.

octane rating A system of establishing the ability of a fuel to avoid *knocking* in an internal combustion engine. Based on the percentage volume of iso-octane in a mix of this with normal heptane that will give the same knocking characteristics as the fuel tested.

ohm The *SI* unit of electrical *resistance,* defined as the resistance which allows a *potential difference* of one *volt* produce a *current* of one *ampere* within a *conductor*.

ore A mineral containing a metal which is extracted from it. Haematite is an ore from which *iron* is obtained using a *blast furnace*.

open-hearth process Siemens-Martin process. A method of producing *steel* in which *pig-iron* and steel scrap or *iron* ore are heated together in measured amounts with *producer gas* on a hearth in a *furnace*.

orbit The path of an object under the influence of a radially-acting *force*.

Otto engine An *internal combustion engine* which produces *power* by four strokes: intake, compression, ignition and expansion, followed by exhaust and further intake. This involves two revolutions of the *crankshaft*.

optical fibre A thin thread of glass so constructed that it permits light to be transmitted down its length, even round corners, by *total internal reflection*.

oscilloscope A device which used a *cathode ray tube* to cause *electrons* to strike a screen enabling rapidly-changing *voltages* to be studied.

Otto cycle The cycle which powers the *internal combustion engine* intake of fuel-air mixture, compression explosion at constant volume, expansion and exhaust of gases, then back to intake stroke.

panchromatic film Photographic film which is reasonably sensitive to all *frequencies* within the visible *light spectrum*.

pascal The *SI* unit of *pressure,* defined as a *force* of one newton applied over an area of one square metre.

Pascal's pressure law *Pressure* applied within a *fluid* is transmitted equally in all directions, the *force* per unit area being everywhere the same.

patent A Government-endorsed document confering on its holder the sole right to proceeds from the manufacture, use or sale of the invention covered by the patent.

permanent magnet A *magnet* which retains its *magnetism* permanently, and not just when subject to some external *energy* source (as is the case with an *electromagnet).*

permeability the ratio of the *magnetic flux density* in a medium to the magnetizing force producing it.

perpetual motion The notion that a device can operate indefinitely, without using an external *power* source. One suggested example is the linking together of an *electric motor* and a *dynamo.* However, the impossibility of such everlasting motion is shown by the laws of *thermodynamics.*

persistence of vision The brief retention of the sensation of light by the brain, once the initial stimulus has been removed. Essential phenomenon for the success of televisual and cinematographic images.

phase The proportion of a cycle of a periodic motion completed by a given time, from a certain starting time. Often expressed in degrees.

phenol Carbolic acid, used in the manufacture of dyes and plastics, and as a disinfectant.

phonograph American name for the *gramophone.*

phosphor A chemical substance capable of storing *energy* received by it in the form of *electromagnetic radiation* (e.g. light), and re-emitting it. Used in fluorescent tubes.

photoelectric cell A device that produces an electrical output if exposed to light. *Selenium* is often used in such devices.

piezoelectric effect The property of some crystals to produce an electric *potential difference* across their faces when subjected to *pressure.*

photoelectricity The phenomenon whereby certain materials can produce electrical output if exposed to light; e.g. *selenium.*

photography The use of a system of lenses and emulsion to capture light images permanently.

pig iron Another name for *cast iron;* a brittle form of *iron* produced in *blast furnaces,* which contains a few per cent of carbon impurities.

piston A device which, when fitted into a chamber in which an explosion takes place, transmits the *force* of the explosion via its motion to a *crankshaft,* to provide motive *power.* Used in *internal combustion engines.*

pitch (aeronautics) Movement of the nose of an aircraft in the vertical plane.

pitch The distance between adjacent crests of a thread on a screw, measured parallel to the axis of the thread.

plastics Substances that are organic, and stable in shape within certain temperature ranges, but can be moulded, extruded etc., under certain conditions of temperature and pressure. Most plastics are *polymers.*

platinum resistance thermometer A thermometer which uses the change in the electrical *resistance* of a platinum coil with temperature to allow measurements over a very wide range (over 1300 degrees).

pneumatics The study and production of devices which rely on air *pressure* for their operation.

polymer A chain of *molecules* of chemical compounds.

porosity the percentage of empty space existing within a material.

Portland cement A widely-used building material comprising chalk or limestone mixed with clay or shale, burnt in a kiln after being finely broken up and mixed together.

positive feedback See *feedback* and *amplification*

potential difference the phenomenon which, when present in a *conductor,* allows an electric *current* to flow. Defined as the *work* done to pass unit positive electric *charge* from one point to another between which a potential difference exists. The unit of potential difference is the *volt.*

potential energy The *energy* possessed by a body by virtue of its location within a gravitational *field.* For a mass m, a height h above the surface of the earth, it may be taken as mgh, where g is the *acceleration due to gravity.*

power The rate of doing *work.* If a *force* acts over a certain distance over a certain time, then the power developed is the product the force and the rate of change of distance. The unit is the watt, equal to one joule per second.

precession The behaviour of a *gyroscope* when subjected to a *force* tending to alter the direction of its axis is to turn about an axis at right angles to that about which the force is applied. This is known as precession.

pressure *Force* per unit area. Expressed in *newtons* per square metre, otherwise known as *pascals.*

pressure, saturated vapour See *saturated vapour pressure*

pressure, vapour See *vapour pressure*

producer gas A gas used in *furnaces* and the generation of *power* formed by the partial combustion of coal, coke or anthracite in a blast of air and steam.

propulsion The source of motive *force* in a device.

proton An *elementary particle* found in the nucleus of an *atom,* and carrying one unit of positive electric charge, exactly equal and opposite to that on the *electron.*

prototype An experimental version of a system, where the initial design can be tested and improved upon in the light of tests carried out.

pulley A simple *machine,* which consists of a system of one or more grooved wheels which enable a *mechanical advantage* to be achieved, e.g. to lift heavy objects.

pyrometer A device for measuring very high temperatures, e.g. *platinum resistance thermometers.*

pyrophoric powders Finely powdered metals, or mixtures of metals and their oxides, which have a tendency to burst into flame, or oxidize when exposed to air.

radar Radio Detection And Ranging. The use of *microwaves* to locate such vehicles as ships, aircraft or missiles. Also used in navigation. The objects, on crossing the path of a radar beam, reflect the pulse of microwaves, the reflection being picked up by a suitable *antenna.*

radiation The emission of waves, rays or particles from a source.

radio The term generally applied to communication using *radio waves.*

radio waves Waves of *electromagnetic radiation* with *wavelengths* approximately in the range of tens of thousands of metres to a millimetre. Used in communication, such waves can be generated by the *acceleration* of *electrons* in electric circuits.

radiometer A device for the detection (and also measurement) of radiant *electromagnetic radiation.*

Rankine cycle A cycle used in steam *power* plants, where water is introduced under *pressure* into a boiler, evaporation taking place followed by expansion without loss of heat to end in condensation and a repeat of the cycle.

rare earths Lanthanides. A group of rare, metallic elements with similar properties, resembling those of aluminium.

ratchet wheel A wheel with inclined teeth on its rim, used in gearing systems.

reaction The equal, and oppositely directed, *force* which is generated by the application of force to a system, surface, etc.

reaper A device used to collect crops such as wheat, while it grows in the field.

reciprocator A device that uses a *piston* moving cyclically within a system to carry out some task, e.g. pumping water.

rectification The conversion of *alternating current* (AC) into *direct current* (DC).

rectifier A device that achieves *rectification* of *alternating current* into *direct current*, e.g a *diode.*

refraction The bending of light as it moves from one medium to another produced by the difference in the *speed of light* between the two substances, resulting from the *density* change.

refractive index The ratio of the *velocity* to that in a given substance.

refractive material Materials able to stand very high temperature, such as brick and concrete. Of special composition to withstand constant recycling.

refrigerator A device that uses an external *power* source to absorb heat at a low temperature, and reject it at a higher one. This is made possible through the evaporation of special *fluids* in the device's coils.

resistance The property of a device to restrict the flow of current. Measured in *ohms.*

resolving power The ability of an optical device to discern two closely spaced light sources as independent entities.

retaining wall A structure, usually of concrete, forming the wall of a structure sunk below the level of the ground, i.e. holding back the outer volume of earth surrounding the structure.

retort A glass vessel in the form of a glass bulb with an extended, fluted neck. Generally, any vessel in which a chemical reaction takes place.

revolver A pistol with a revolving magazine carrying the bullets and their charges, enabling five or six shots to be taken in succession before reloading.

Reynold's number A dimensionless number formed from certain quantities of a *liquid* whose size dictates whether the *velocity* of flow is fast enough to cause *turbulence* within the liquid column.

RDX Also known as cyclonite, and hexogen. A very powerful explosive compound.

rivet A fixing device which pins together two sheets of material, usually metal, by insertion through a hole through the sheets, and expansion of the heads by striking with a hammer or other tool.

rocket An engine which is powered by fuel and a supply of oxygen which it carries within itself. The hot, expanding, exhaust gases are expelled in one direction to provide motion in the other direction.

roll Movement of any aircraft about the axis running down the centre of the aircraft.

rotary engine Wankel engine, or epitrochoidal engine. A form of *internal combustion engine* in which an approximately triangular 'piston' is driven epicyclically in an elliptical combustion chamber containing the air-fuel mixture, ignited by a sparking plug.

rudder Part of the tailplane of an aircraft which moves about a vertical axis perpendicular to the wings, controlling the *yaw* motion.

saltpeter Potassium nitrate; A white crystalline substance which acts as a strong oxidizing *element* and is used in fertilizers and explosives. Also known as nitre.

saturated vapour pressure The *pressure* exerted by a *vapour* which exists in *equilibrium* with its *liquid.*

Schlieren photography A means of photographing turbulences in fast-moving *fluids,* through the change of *density* and *refractive index* that such turbulence produces.

screw A cylinder or cone onto which has been cut a helix thread.

scuba gear Self Contained Underwater Breathing Apparatus; See *aqualung*.

selenium A non-metallic *element* used in light-operated devices because of its ability to conduct *electricity* when exposed to *light*.

self induction *Current* carried in a wire produces a *magnetic field* which cuts the wire itself. Any change in the current produces a change in the magnetic field, which produces an emf by 'self-induction' which resists the change in current.

semiconductor A material, such as silicon, whose electrical *resistance* decreases in the presence of certain impurities, or in a rise of temperature. Such materials are used in *electronic* devices, such as the *transistor*.

servo mechanism A mechanism that uses relatively low *power* to control the behaviour of a much larger output device in a proportionate way.

shrapnel Strictly, an *artillery* shell filled with small spheres with an explosive charge gives rise to shrapnel. It now also covers general fragments of metal produced from an exploding device.

shuttle A device for carrying thread on a *loom*.

Siemens-Martin process See *open hearth process*

silver nitrate A white, crystalline substance used in chemical analysis and inks.

single phase Electrical *power* transmission involving a single sinusoidally-varying *potential difference*.

SI units Système International units. A system of units (often known as the metric system) which uses as its base units for length, mass and time, the metre, the kilgram and the second.

smelting The extraction of a metal from its *ore* by heat. The process usually involves a number of steps in order to refine the final product. See, e.g. *Open Hearth process, Bessemer process.*

sodium hyposulphite See *sodium thiosulphate*

sodium thiosulphate Correct chemical name for hypo and sodium hyposulphite, the substance used to fix photographic images after developing.

soft iron A form of *iron* with a low carbon content that does not retain *magnetism* once the current in a *coil* surrounding it has been removed.

soil mechanics A branch of civil engineering in which the properties (e.g *density, porosity* etc) of soil at a site is determined.

solder An *alloy* which is heated and used to join two metals together.

solenoid A length of wire wound about a cylindrical framework, whose length is long compared to the radius. Current passing in the wire produces a *magnetic field* within the centre of the cylinder, which can be used to magnetize *soft iron* objects placed within.

solid The state of matter where the strength of the intermolecular and atomic *forces* is such that there is no translational motion within the substance. The *molecules* do, however, vibrate about their average positions in the *crystal lattice*.

sound *Pressure* waves occuring in a medium such as air. Unlike *electromagnetism*, the waves are *longitudinal*, rather than *transverse*.

spar A beam running the length of a wing or tail-plane etc.

spectroscope A device which divides the light from an object into its characteristic *spectrum*.

spectroscopy The use of a *spectroscope* to study the composition of incandescent or illuminated objects.

spectrum The result of resolving *electromagnetic radiations* into their constituent *wavelengths*. The most common case is the splitting of white light into its components, stretching from ultraviolet to infrared wavelengths.

speed The rate of change of distance with time, expressed in units such as kilometres per hour, metres per second etc.

speed of light See *light, speed of*

standard gauge The distance between the steel rails on the majority of the world's railways; 4 feet 8 inches (1.435m).

statics The study of the *forces* which act on a system, when those forces are in *equilibrium*.

steam turbine A *turbine* that is powered by a jet of high-*pressure* steam.

steel *Iron* contining 0.1 per cent to 1.5 per cent of carbon impurities. Produced from iron *ore* using the *open hearth* and *Bessemer processes*.

stereoscopy A device that can produce the effect of three dimensional images using only two dimensional images, using the human brain to carry out the merging necessary.

STOL See *V/STOL*

strain The ratio of the size of the change caused in a given dimension of a material by a *stress* applied to it, divided by the original (unstressed) dimension.

stress A *force* applied over a given area that produces a *strain* within the material directly proportional to it (within certain ranges of stress). Stresses are usually measured in *newtons* per square metre *(pascals)*.

streamline A line in a *fluid* such that the *tangent* to it at every point gives the direction of flow, and its *speed*, at any instant.

supercharger In *internal combustion engines*, the use of a compressor to supply air or fuel/air mixtures at a high *pressure* to the *piston* cylinders; in aero engines, a device to maintain ground-level pressures in the engine inlet pipe when flying at high altitude.

supercharging Heating of a *liquid* above its boiling point.

supersonic *Velocities* greater than the *speed* of *sound* in the particular conditions prevailing, i.e. greater than *Mach* 1.

surveying The use of optical devices to determine the angular and spatial relationships of objects on the earth, enabling them to be accurately depicted on paper or other permanent media.

suspension bridge A bridge in which the main central span is suspended from two towers erected on either side of the space being bridged.

tangent A line which touches a curve at one point only, without cutting the curve.

telephony The conversion of audio signals into electrical impulses for transmission and subsequent reconversion back into sound.

tetrahedron A solid of four faces, each of which is a triangle.

telecommunication Communication between two places by electric or electromagnetic means.

telegraph A means of communication in which pulses of electric *current* are sent down wires connecting the transmitting and receiving stations. *Morse code* is often employed.

tesla The *SI* unit of *magnetic flux density*. It is defined as a magnetic flux density of one *weber* of *magnetic flux* per square metre.

theodolite A device used in *surveying* for measuring the relative angles and positions of objects, so that plans may be drawn up.

thermal A column of warm air, which is of a lower *density* than its surroundings, and contains rising currents of air.

thermionic valve A current-controlling device, consisting of a system of *electrodes* held within a vacuum container. The *cathode* is heated, emitting *electrons* to an *anode,* which collects the electrons. A grid between the two electrodes controls the flow of electrons.

thermocouple A device comprising two wires of different metals (e.g. copper and iron) joined, and with their other ends held at different temperatures. A small *current* is set up within the wire proportional to the size of the temperature difference between the two ends. This makes thermocouples useful in the determination of temperature.

thermodynamic equilibrium A system is said to be in thermal *equilibrium* if no *heat* flows between its component parts.

thermodynamics The branch of physics that studies the effects of changes of *heat* on systems.

thermodynamics, laws of The first law states that *energy* cannot be created or destroyed in a system of constant mass, only transformed. The second law states that *heat* cannot flow continuously and spontaneously from a colder to a hotter body. The

third law states that the *entropy* of a system approaches zero as the temperature of the system approaches *absolute zero.*

thermopile A device consisting of a number of *thermocouples;* it is used to detect and measure heat (infra-red) radiation.

thermoplastic A plastic that can be repeatedly remelted without losing its overall characteristics.

Thread, Whitworth See *Whitworth Standard*

three phase Electrical *power* transmission involving three cables, the alternating *potential differences* of which are at 120° relative *phase* to one to one

thrust The propulsive *pressure* exerted by, for example, a *jet* or *rocket* engine.

TNT Trinitrotoluene A pale yellow material, used as a high explosive.

tolerance The range in the physical dimensions of an object within which the true dimensions lie. Often expressed in the form of, for example ± 3mm for a length.

tomography See *computerized axial tomography*

torque A *force* which produces rotation

total internal reflection The phenomenon caused when a ray of light, in passing from a dense to a less dense medium (e.g glass to air) is bent sufficiently by *refraction* so as not to leave the denser medium. Occurs when the angle of incidence exceeds a certain critical angle.

transformer A device which uses *induction* to convert high voltage *alternating current* into low voltage, without change in *frequency,* and vice versa.

transistor A *semiconductor* capable of amplifying electric *currents.*

transverse wave A wave in which the vibrations take place in a plane at right angles to the direction of propagation, e.g. *electromagnetic waves.*

trim In *aerodynamics,* the slight actions on the controls needed to achieve stability in a particular mode of flight.

triode A *thermionic valve* consisting of an *anode,* a *cathode* and a *grid.*

triplane An aircraft that features three wings stacked vertically above each other.

turbine A system of a wheel with vanes on its rim, connected via a shaft to a device which either uses the *energy* developed by the turbine directly (see *jet engine*) or indirectly, through a *dynamo* for example. The turbine is powered by the *force* of water, steam etc., striking its vanes.

turbofan An aero engine in which part of the *power* produced by the gas turbine engine is used to drive an intake fan inside a duct.

turboprop An aircraft propulsion unit in which the *power* produced by burning gases is transmitted to a propellor via a *turbine* and *gear* system.

turbulent flow The flow in a column of *fluid* which does not follow *streamlines*. Such flow sets in at a *velocity* dependent on the *Reynold's number*.

turnpike A toll-gate across roads which taxes are charged of vehicles using the roads, for maintenance etc.

ultra violet radiation *Electromagnetic radiation* with a *wavelength* shorter than that of visible *light*, lying just beyond the violet part of the visible *spectrum* (hence its name). Typical wavelengths are of the order one hundred-millionth of a metre.

vacuum A region devoid of *atoms* of any substance. Hence, the *pressure* within a container enclosing a vacuum is zero.

valve, thermionic See *thermionic valve*

vanadium A very hard, white metal used in the making of tough *steel alloy*.

V.D.U Visual Display Unit; a television monitor that gives a visible display of the output of data from a computer.

vapour A substance in the gaseous state, which may be liquefied by raising the *pressure*, leaving that temperaure the same.

vapour pressure The *pressure* exerted by a *vapour* given off by a *solid* or *liquid* at a specific temperature. See *saturated vapour pressure*.

velocity of light See *light, speed of*

vernier A scale which, when used in conjuction with a scale measuring larger amounts of the property in question (e.g. length), allows subdivisions of the basic unit on the large scale to be read off accurately.

viscous force The drag which occurs on an object placed in a viscous medium. For example, air causes a viscous force on an aircraft travelling through it. For two parallel layers of *fluid* close to each other, the viscous force is proportional to the difference in velocity between the two layers.

viscosity A property of a *fluid* which causes it to resist motion within it. It determines other properties of the fluid, such as the *velocity* of flow at which *turbulence* sets in; see *Reynold's number*.

vision, persistence of See *persistence of vision*.

visual display unit See *VDU*

volt The *SI* unit of *potential difference*, defined as the potential difference which exists between two points of a *conductor* in which a *current* of one *ampere* flows, such that *energy* flow dissipated beteen the two points equals one *joule* per second, i.e. one *watt*.

V/STOL Vertical/Short take off and landing. The term applied to aircraft capable of taking off and landing without need for a runway.

vulcanization the hardening of rubber achieved by heating rubber with sulphur.

Wankel engine See *rotary engine*

warp Threads in weaving stretched lengthwise across the fabric. See *weft*.

water gas A mixture of carbon monoxide and hydrogen gas, produced by passing steam over hot coke.

watt The *SI* unit of *power*, equal to one *joule* of *energy* expended in one second.

wave, carrier See *carrier wave*

wave, electromagnetic See *electromagnetic wave*

wave, longitudinal See *longitudinal wave*

wave, transverse See *transverse wave*

wavefront The line of points in a wave motion which are all of equal *phase*.

wavelength the distance between successive crests (or troughs) of a wave.

weber the *SI* unit of *magnetic flux*, defined as the flux required to flow in a circuit such that, if it changes at a rate of one weber per second, will induce in the circuit an *electromotive force* of 1 volt.

weft the threads across the width of the material to be formed by weaving.

welding the use of heat to melt and fuse together two metal surfaces.

Wheatstone bridge A circuit which is divided into sections enabling the relative *resistances* or devices placed in the sections to be deduced.

Whitworth standard A standard of screw thread used before the advent of the metric standard, in which the pitch of the *helix* is standardized relative to the diameter of the bar on which the thread is cut.

wind tunnel An enclosure which contains a large *turbine* capable of sending air streams over any object (such as a model aircraft) whose *aerodynamic* performance is to be assessed.

wireless See *radio*

work The work done by a *force* is given by the product of the force and the distance moved by its point of application.

working fluid A *fluid* which is used in such a way that its internal *energy* is converted into external energy. One example is water in *hydroelectricty* generation.

wrought iron Iron from which essentially all carbon impurities have been eliminated.

X-ray *Electromagnetic radiation* with *wavelengths* shorter than those of *ultraviolet radiation,* but larger than those of *gamma rays*. Their ability to penetrate many materials make them very useful in insepection of products for cracks etc.

yarn Thread that has been spun.

Index

The entry in **bold** type will direct you to the main text entry in which the information you require is given